TENSIONS OF ORDER & FREEDOM

The Library of Conservative Thought
Russell Kirk, Series Editor

TENSIONS OF ORDER & FREEDOM

Catholic Political Thought, 1789-1848

Béla Menczer

With a new introduction by
Russell Kirk

Transaction Publishers
New Brunswick (U.S.A.) and London (U.K.)

Library of Congress Catalog Number: 93-21080
ISBN: 1-56000-133X
Printed in the United States of America

Library of Congress Cataloging-in-Publication Data

Menczer, Béla.
[Catholic political thought, 1789-1848)
Tensions of order and freedom: Catholic political thought, 1789-1848/Bela Menczer; with a new introduction by Russell Kirk.
    p.   cm.—(The Library of conservative thought)
Originally published: Catholic political thought, 1789-1848.
Includes bibiographical references.
ISBN 1-56000-133-X
1. Political science. 2. Church and social problems—Catholic Church. I. Title. II. Series.
JA36.M4   1993
320.5'5—dc20   93-21080
                                                        CIP

*Quia membra sumus corporis eius, de carne eius,
et de ossibus eius.*

TO MARJORIE

IN MEMORY OF ANOTHER DEDICATION

CONTENTS

INTRODUCTION TO THE
TRANSACTION EDITION

TO maintain a tolerable tension between the claims of order and the claims of freedom: that has been the primary problem of modern politics. Ever since the French Revolution and the regime of Napoleon, which overthrew all the old constitutions of Europe, society has been tormented by conflicts between the champions of order (sometimes a harsh order) and the champions of liberty (often an anarchic liberty). For the most part, Britain and the United States were spared such violent social hostilities during the nineteenth and twentieth centuries. But Latin America, from the beginning of the nineteenth century, has been afflicted by political ferocity, and during the twentieth century nearly all the countries of Asia and Africa have suffered hideously, their old political orders dissolved, but succeeded by new orders grimly tyrannical or by consuming disorders that illustrate Madame Roland's exclamation, "O Liberty, what crimes are committed in thy name!"

During the first half of the nineteenth century, a number of writers and public men, most of them Catholics, endeavored in Europe to keep the peace by finding a balance in thought and in institutions that might reconcile liberty with authority. Some of these were men endowed with strong powers of imagination. The source of any tolerable social arrangement, they argued, is religious truth. Their adversaries—whether liberals or radicals—held, to the contrary, that human societies create their own patterns, without transcendent origins.

Nowadays at the end of the twentieth century, the thought of such men of politics as Maistre, Bonald, Cheateaubriand, Balzac, Schlegel, Metternich, Donoso Cortés, Balmes, and Veuillot takes on a renewed significance. The collapse of the Soviet Union urgently raises again the question of how the claims of freedom may be reconciled with the claims of order, so to keep the peace. A virulent nationalism convulses Eastern Europe and the liberated fragments of the Russian imperial system; Africa and Asia have fallen under the misrule of squalid despots, in most countries; even in the United States, the roots of order seem

decayed, what with the delinquescence of family and local
community (a form of decadence predicted by Vicomte de
Bonald, whose book *On Divorce*, at last translated into English, is
now available in The Library of Conservative Thought).

The philosophers and statesmen succinctly and lucidly
described in this volume often have been labelled "reactionaries,"
and therefore ignored, on the assumption that they foolishly
resisted the March of Progress. But at the close of the twentieth
century it ought to be sufficiently obvious that the ideologues of
human perfectibility and the evangels of Progress have spread
ruin worldwide. The conservative Catholic leaders examined by
Menczer perceived the ineluctable truth of the dogma of
Original Sin: they knew, with Burke, that somewhere there must
exist a control upon will and appetite; and "the less of it there is
within, the more there must be without."

Fierce impulses toward violence and fraud are deeply
embedded in human nature; for the sake of true freedom, some
means of restraint upon these impulses is necessary; and
government exists to restrain those persons who cannot or will
not restrain themselves. In the year 1993, these "reactionary"
perceptions of the post-Napoleonic era are difficult to deny
convincingly. As the poet Roy Campbell put it, "A human body
that cannot react is a corpse." And so, Campbell went on, it is
with societies: those without power of reaction against challenges
to their existence must perish. Therefore "reactionary" ideas of
yesteryear become relevant to our present discontents.

A learned and courageous gentleman, the late Béla Menczer,
anthologist-editor of this volume, wrote interesting memoirs that
never have been published, entitling them *Bread Far from My
Cradle*. "In the history of my lifetime," he writes in the preface to
those memoirs, "the traditional political classes were finished, the
new ones had no real authority to express anything that the nations of Europe really wanted or cared for. In my youth I lit my
Diogenes lamp and until old age I have searched with it;
Diogenes was looking for Man, with a capital M. . . ." Menczer
lifelong, rather like Confucius in Lu, was looking for a
Statesman, with a capital S, whom he might beneficially
influence. He was helpful to the Emperor Haile Selassie, when
that African hero directed in London his government in exile; he
wrote memoranda and papers for General de Gaulle, Chatham
House, and "other institutions and government organs dealing
with Central European problems"; he published articles in many
serious weeklies and monthlies; yet he never found the great
Statesman whom he might have served by his high intelligence,

his knowledge of history and of the world, and his mastery of several languages.

Menczer was sixteen years old when the catastrophe of 1918 fell upon his native Hungary. In his youth he became a Socialist, despite his upper-class inheritance, but on reading Strindberg he "began to see that the true social problem is one of the rightful hierarchical values, and that it is not simply a problem of the rich and the poor. . . . Although I was a rebel and a Socialist, I had began to feel that all industrial society would be a Socialist state slavery and that the real problem concerns personal rights and human dignity."

Young Menczer was imprisoned during the Horthy regime, and on release, hastened to Vienna, where he joined Count Karolyi's circle of emigrés. (Later he reacted against Karolyi's friendliness toward the Soviet Union.) His descriptions of life in Paris, Berlin, and London in the 1920s are lively and valuable. In London he associated much with Wyckham Steed and his friends at Lansdowne House. In those years between the wars, he was acquainted with a great many of the notables in the realms of politics and of the intellect. As historian, literary critic, and commentator on European affairs, he earned the frugal bread of exile.

On the outbreak of World War II, Menczer endeavored to persuade influential friends to bring about the forming of a "European Army" composed of exiles, fugitives, and others from Italy, Germany, and the countries allied with Hitler and Mussolini. He did not succeed in this plan; it was Hitler, instead, who not much later organized his own "European Army" of non-German stock. In 1940, Menczer joined General de Gaulle's Forces Francaises Libres as a volunteer, and participated in the ill-fated descent upon Dakar by the expeditionary force of Free French and British.

Later he was active with Free French troops of equatorial Africa in their endeavor to link up with Allied forces in Libya. During this period he was baptized a Catholic in a congregation composed wholly of blacks; later he was confirmed at Brompton Oratory, in London. Malaria brought him low; returned to London, he left the French Army in 1946 and became a British subject in 1955.

Although unfortunate in much, Béla Menczer was most fortunate in his English wife, Marjorie. They kept a flat in St. John's Wood, London, to which resorted the exiles and refugees of many lands, in addition to British and American friends. Marjorie was the most charming of hostesses to frequent gatherings of twelve to fifteen such people for good conversation and re-freshments. "Nowhere else can I enjoy culture so inexpensively," said one guest.

When the Hungarian rising against the Communist regime and the Russian army of occupation occurred, Menczer, eager to join the patriotic "rebels," hurried so far as Switzerland, meaning to fight; but he was too old, and the rising soon was crushed.

During his declining years he and Marjorie took a house in Midhurst, Sussex. They made a trip to America, coming to stay with the Kirks at their old-fashioned house of Piety Hill, in the Michigan backwoods. There followed them the fiercest blizzard of many years, imprisoning them and their hosts for several days. Not at all disheartened, Béla sat content by the fireplace in the dining room, discoursing on Hungarian history and much else. If the bread he had found far from his cradle had been an austere diet—why, he had enjoyed much freedom, and had upheld a just political order.

"True life begins when earthly life comes to an end, and in the few things which in this life are done for the sake of the last-ing glory of God, I had my share," Menczer writes in the *envoi* of his memoirs. "A few stones in this terrestrial city I have recog-nized to be the stones of the City of God and I never refused to carry those stones on my shoulders, heavy as they may have been. I have known and seen two sorts of people: on the one hand those who were constructing the huge tower of Babel; on the other I have seen some people, few in number, who were building the city of God and who will inherit the earth."

A man at once of books and of action, Béla Menczer has left us the gift of this volume of political theory. The concepts he discusses may open some eyes to a view of society very different from the Marxist ideology that in 1848—the year with which this study concludes—began to ravage the world; very different, for that matter, from today's conventional liberalism.

Russell Kirk

INTRODUCTION

1. AUTHORITY AND LIBERTY IN THE WESTERN CONSCIENCE

OUR Faith is of the stuff of history. The Old Testament differs from all other sacred books venerated by the nations because it is history—an account of events full of mystical significance. Christian history differs from all other history because it comprises an era, because it is an account of a fundamental change in the order of the world, and the consequences of that change.

Man alone of all created beings has a history. Of all the records of human actions and events, the Old Testament is the first to be fully related to society, and to be in full relationship with the essential nature of man. Other civilisations have had their annals and chronicles, but these were never intended to reveal the essential. The names of Pharaohs have been recorded, and those of the rulers of China; their virtues were praised, and some of their actions made known and transmitted to posterity. Nearer to us in time, the historians of Greece and Rome—Herodotus, Tacitus—tell the story of events with a fuller and more personal characterisation of the actors; indeed they describe national characteristics with such penetrating observation that in the field of literature they remain unsurpassed. But what makes the Bible unique, and different in essence from all other venerated books of those distant centuries, is its focus. The biblical story moves visibly to a climax. Changes in institutions, the transition from the rule of prophets to that of kings, forced migrations, catastrophes and conquests, victories and defeats—all these occur because they have to occur. Nothing happens by mere chance. Everything has a discernible cause. Events have their context on a divine plane, the essentials of which are revealed. Reason and power were revealed in the act of Creation; love and sacrifice, as the essential relation of God to Man, were revealed on the Cross; justice and judgement are foretold for the end of the centuries.

Established on this threefold basis of will, sacrifice, and preparation for final judgement, life derives from Christianity a wholly new significance. Of all living things created, only man can voluntarily destroy himself; and only man can accept life voluntarily, in the full and certain knowledge of coming to a material end. Christ condemned self-destruction, and proclaimed the relativity of the material end, but by no means the insignificance of that end. He proclaimed its relation to the three fundamental bases of will, love and judgement, these three aspects of Divinity, faculties of supreme Reason.

Once the full truth has been revealed, a chosen people is no longer needed to serve as an example; mankind itself becomes the example. Survival after death, sensed in the cult of the Egyptians, stated in Buddhism, and pondered by the Greeks, is now demonstrated and defined. It is given a complete sense and a precise meaning, with no room left for either obscurity or indifference. Christ revealed the mystery. He conquered the world, and its conquest is final. History, the science of human actions, becomes the science of the definite, the science of accomplished finalities.

It was only a generation earlier that the poet Virgil, singing the glories of the age of Augustus, had foretold fulfilment, the coming fullness of time. Again, there is no place here for speculation or change. The meeting of Christ and Rome was a providential necessity; it was a message in action, a story with no episode of secondary importance. All is precision, like the Latin language itself, which as the common language of the Church was to unite the Christian peoples of the West.

Thenceforward they live in Time, the time between Creation and final Judgement. What is but a longing, a vague divination, in others, is for them a certainty; God conquers chaos and sets an aim to history. Before conquering space, European mankind recognised Time. It saw the dividing moment in Time, the presence of God on earth. Now that limits had been set to human time and history, it was to go out and conquer space. European mankind carried history into space by carrying Christ to distant peoples living in closed realms, who had never had any notion of time and whose history had therefore remained static. This achievement, which has altered the whole image of the world in such a tremendous way during the last few centuries, cannot be explained otherwise than by the fact that the European nations had a different notion of history— the Roman and Christian concept of history as a progress from

Creation, through Redemption, to Judgement. "Discovery" is a word peculiar to the vocabulary of a civilisation that is founded on Revelation. Other nations may conquer, but the Christian nations "discover": they open closed realms to the Light, and static realms to Time.

The evil inherent in the world becomes transitory. In the words of Tertullian, the Teacher of the Church who coined the expression *unum necessarium*: "God suffers, or the world breaks into pieces." God's suffering is not only a plausible explanation of the continued existence of the world, it is the only possible explanation: *Aut dissolvitur machina mundi, aut mundi creator patitur.* And St Augustine, otherwise so completely different from Tertullian in his appreciation of pre-Christian learning, says that this necessary belief is the necessary explanation of the unity of human history, and of the survival of an Empire in the throes of invasion and devastation.

To Christianity, and Christianity alone, we owe the historical conscience of Europe. And it is to Christianity alone that we owe the full meaning of both order and liberty.

The sense of order is an acceptance of Creation, the rational acceptance of necessity. Liberty is the moral acceptance of order, a voluntary action subject to final judgement. Liberty means choice: the choice of voluntary sacrifice, the means whereby a final and for ever undisturbed harmony of Order and Liberty can be established; it means the offering of a sacrifice made freely for the proclamation and explanation of the law of Order—the death on the Cross—and our personal participation in this supreme act of Liberty through the Mass. Christ has set us free for all time. Liberty is as final as the order of Creation: "The truth shall set you free."

The historical conscience which Christianity gave us is a recognition of the eternal in what is passing and ephemeral, a recognition of something which is not subject to change amidst the infinity of material changes. This principle of eternity is found in the very nature of an unchanging Creator. "All that He ever created," says St Augustine, the father of a Christian philosophy of history, "was in Him, in His unchanged fixed Will eternally one and the same."

Thus everything within Creation, within Order, appertains to the category of the necessary, and necessity is clearly defined and demonstrated. Yet Creation itself was a voluntary action, a gift, an effect of Liberty. Authority was established, not for the sake of the Creator, but for the sake of the creature: its establishment and acceptance should be equally final.

This divine finality in History, this acceptance of the final and definite in Revelation, of an authority freely given and accepted, became the quintessence of the Western Christian political doctrine. The elaboration and evolution of this doctrine was bound up with the fate of Charlemagne's Western Empire. Paris was the centre of the scholastic philosophy of Scotus Erigena; it saw within its walls St Albert the Great and St Thomas; there Duns Scotus taught, the Franciscan Doctor of the freedom of the will as the principal attribute of man, which had been created by the free sovereignty of the divine Will. Paris was also the capital of the monarchy of the heirs of Charlemagne, the capital of the kingdom of chivalry. All that survived the barbarian invasions of St Augustine's century in the south and east of the pagan Empire of Rome, survived because of its Christian baptism.

But this survival was not accomplished without pain and difficulty; it involved a temporary surrender of Caesarism to Christ, followed by attempts to create a Church subservient to Caesarism. It was in the West that the new Monarchy, entirely Christian in its origin, came into being, the monarchy of a Caesar who took the style and name of David, anointed by the Pope as David had been anointed by the high priest—the realm of voluntary obedience, sustained only by the tie of Faith, *Fides*, which is the derivation of the feudal idea.

" Frank," the name of the people who accepted authority in freedom, became synonymous in current language with sincerity and loyalty. Privilege, freedom and personal right was given the name " franchise "; the granting of freedom became known in Western languages as " affranchisement." From the time of the *Song of Roland*, the first epic poem of Christian Chivalry, through the Franciscan spirituality of the era of the Crusades and Duns Scotus's elaboration of the doctrine of voluntary creation, down to the very recent French spiritual revival on the eve of the First World War—to the poetry of Charles Péguy—we meet the same concept of free and voluntary sacrifice as the very essence of Christianity:

> *Comme j'ai créé l'homme à mon image et à ma ressemblance,*
> *Ainsi j'ai créé la liberté de l'homme à l'image et à la ressemblance*
> *De ma propre, de mon originelle liberté.*[1]

[1] *Prières*, Charles Péguy, Gallimard, Paris, 1934, p. 66.

2. THE RELIGIOUS CHARACTER OF THE FRENCH MONARCHY

THE Kingdom of the Franks, the Western Monarchy, was the first modern nation, just as St Augustine, the teacher of the West, was the first modern man. It was a nation with a history which was not simply recorded, but was above all related by all its laws, institutions and actions to the spiritual and moral focal point of History. This notion of the focal point in History replaced in the Western mind the idea of a geographical centre of the world. Since the time of St Augustine, who postulated the perfect unity of individual life with the universal and omnipresent life of the Divinity, the government of the World—of the City of God—had become known as " temporal," or " secular," adjectives which relate to Time and not to space; the Western Empire meant temporal power, secular government, related to the *saecula saeculorum* of the Western liturgy, a temporal power which was related to Eternity. Thus the people of the Western realm considered themselves to be the chosen people of the New Testament, whose actions were manifestations of the Divine—*gesta Dei per Francos*. Charlemagne's name became synonymous with a dignity, just as Caesar's had been in the Empire of antiquity, and the Slav and the Magyar titles for the new East European Royal dignity were taken from the name Charlemagne, or Karl—*Kralj, Kirdly*.[1]

Yet, at the same time that the Kingdom of the Franks was becoming the norm of Christian society the heritage of Charlemagne suffered a division, and the imperial heritage of Charlemagne ceased to be in the same hands as the royal sceptre of France. To tell the story of this division, and to relate all that followed upon it, would be nothing short of writing the European history of eight full centuries. We are not engaged here on such a tremendous task. Ours is infinitely more modest in scope; we are dealing with the historical background to the crisis of Authority and Liberty, which culminated in the French Revolutions of the eighteenth and nineteenth centuries, and the new direction of religious thought which originated in this crisis and transformed every concept of the " profane " order of Europe—we use the word in the sense underlined by Jacques

[1] Important new research material, and for the first time a full historical survey of the relations between the Kingdom of the Franks and East and Central Europe, is given in *The Making of Central and Eastern Europe*, by Fr. Francis Dvornik, Polish Research Centre, London, 1949.

Maritain in his *Humanisme intégral*, as a contrast to " sacred "—
the crisis of Authority and Liberty in France, which is not yet
at an end in Europe or the world today.

We can thus only touch slightly upon the centuries of struggle
between the two branches of Charlemagne's Monarchy and
the Papacy, and just mention in passing that there were conflicts between France and the Papacy in the reigns of Philippe-
Auguste and Louis XII, as well as conflicts between the Papacy
and the Empire. It must however be said that Charlemagne's
quality as defender of the Papal sovereignty, his title of " eldest
son of the Church " and of *Rex Christianissimus*—a title which
sovereigns imitated at the time of the great dynastic rivalries,
when the successors of Ferdinand of Aragon called themselves
Catholic Kings of Spain, and the successors of Maria-Theresa
called themselves Apostolic Kings of Hungary—gave the
French Monarchy a religious character of the first importance,
a claim of primacy over the secular rulers of Christendom, a
consciousness of that primacy which was sometimes questioned,
but which was the unalterable basis of French policy, and of
the whole political doctrine of the nation for centuries.

The unity of the Kingdom and the unity of Christendom
became, in a way which must be considered providential, one
and the same cause. The two greatest religious events of the
Latin West, the scholastic movement of the twelfth and
thirteenth centuries and the Counter-Reformation of the
seventeenth century, evolved in the context of French national
history. Neither of them was an exclusively French historical
phenomenon, and neither was restricted in scope to France
alone, but they were replies to heresies which threatened to
disrupt the unity of the French Crown, as well as the unity of
Christendom and the Church. They were replies to the
Albigensian and the Calvinist heresies and to the Jansenist
aberrations, the controversy in each case centring round the
freedom of the human will.

This is a paradox which needs emphasising in this century,
because it was often overlooked in the nineteenth century.
Modern historians, writing with a more or less conscious, or
even virulent, anti-Catholic bias and intention, have completely reversed this phenomenon and affirmed the exact opposite of the truth, by interpreting the various revolts in the
history of French Christianity as so many steps towards
" emancipation," an aim which was, according to them,
ultimately achieved with the triumph of the Great

Revolution, after several minor ones had proved abortive.[1]

This modern opinion, commonly held because it has been spread by historians, omitted to bear in mind the theological essence of the Albigensian, Calvinist and Jansenist movements, although the doctrinal documents are easily accessible, especially those concerning the two latter. They all challenged the authority of the Church, and at the same time, the doctrine of the freedom of the will; the relation between the two trends is obvious. The Crown and the Church recognised that they were a peril to moral responsibility, this indispensable basis of every legal and social order. To be free means to be responsible, and any doubt cast on this free, responsible and voluntary action is a danger to Church and State alike, whether it is a doctrine of predestination, or one which casts doubts on the sufficiency and efficacy of Grace.

The Revolution, which made Liberty the first of its catchwords, thus confessed its spiritual ancestry in all the negations of freedom.[2] The most memorable link in the chain from the

[1] The French Liberal historians, the grave and philosophical Guizot, the often attractive and epic Michelet, the frequently original and sometimes absurd Edgar Quinet and, somewhat platitudinous in their conclusions, but on account of the bulk of their researches and their output, the important Henri Martin and Ernest Lavisse, as well as Seignobos—more scientific in his method—have all attempted to show us that the movements which aimed at the disintegration of Christian unity were steps on the road of Progress, that these Western heresies were the precursors of the ideas of 1789. In the opinion of Jean Jaurès, the intellectual leader of French Socialism during the period when this movement had given up all idea of a new revolution, and postulated the thesis that all its aims had been realised with the "natural" development of the ideas of 1789, the unity of the Reformation and the Revolution was a foremost axiom of modern times. He devoted the thesis he wrote for the Sorbonne (one of the last ever to be written in Latin and almost certainly the only Latin contribution to the literature on Marx, his doctrine and his German precursors) to a demonstration of this unity. The postulate of a close Franco-German friendship, based on the affinity of the Reformation and the Revolution, became such a favourite rhetorical formula in Jaurès' public activities, that many of his followers left him on that account. This happened with the young Péguy—as we know from his own *Souvenirs* and from the books which some of Péguy's closest companions, such as Jean-Jérôme Tharaud and Henri Massis, devoted to his memory and the spiritual legacy he left behind. It also happened in the case of Charles Andler, Professor of German at the Collège de France, who took a less optimistic view of the "Germany of the Reformation" and its natural love for liberty and peace, which Jaurès saw in every historical phenomenon "emancipated" from Catholic authority.

[2] In the works of all its apologists, Michelet, Quinet and Jaurès. A possible exception is Alphonse Aulard, in whose analysis the Revolution is not so much the continuation of those older religious phenomena, but a new phenomenon, a rational, agnostic philosophy put into practice. But Aulard would admit that this theory only holds good in that aspect of the Revolution represented by Danton and Condorcet, and not in the one represented by Robespierre, who is the central figure of the revolutionary history—or shall we say apologetics?—of the late M. Albert Mathiez, Aulard's successor in the Chair of Revolutionary History at the Sorbonne.

Reformation to the Revolution was the thinker Jean-Jacques Rousseau, who relegated freedom and personal responsibility to the realm of his imaginary natural life, which was prior to a civilisation in which man's action was corrupted by social rules and regulations, his good intentions were frustrated by his surroundings, and by the institutions of society and the State. Inconsistent as it seems, the same determinist tendencies common, in various degrees, to the three great heretical movements which in three different centuries shook the Christian Monarchy in France to its foundations, proclaimed free and individual judgement as the only criterion in matters of Faith. Yet, this contradiction is more apparent than real: Christian ethical rule cannot be separated from Authority, a word which, in the vocabulary of the Christian, can only be derived from the *auctoritas* of God, manifested in Creation by His free and sovereign Will.

Any challenge to the notion of Authority must necessarily and logically lead to a denial, or at least to some major restriction, of the attributes which Man derives from Authority. Like everything, or almost everything in spiritual matters, this is largely a question of emphasis. We need not go so far as to accuse Calvinists and Jansenists of a flat denial of the free, voluntary action of God in Creation. This would assimilate them to a more remote heresy, that of the Manicheans, in whose theology God's own freedom becomes problematic, so that He acts in rivalry with an equally powerful force of evil, and acts by an inevitable necessity in an *undecided* struggle between Good and Evil. Yet by removing the Church, which is Authority incarnate, and the visible depositary of the divine guidance of men, as the link between God and Man, the relationship between them necessarily becomes more remote, so that Man is a less perfect being, enlightened only by his own intellect, and ultimately faced, as the Teachers of the Church are unanimous in underlining—St Augustine against the Manicheans, St Thomas against the Albigenses, the early Jesuits and Bossuet against the Reformation, and St Alphonsus Liguori against the Jansenists—by the alternative of despotism or anarchy. Nearer to our own day, the Spanish theologian Jaime Balmes shows, in the analysis of Protestantism which he makes from the point of view of historical progress and secular civilisation, that this alternative has been the hallmark of modern times since the sixteenth century.

3. THE CATHOLIC INTERPRETATION OF THE SECULAR ORDER: BOSSUET AND PASCAL

FRANCE is, on the historical plane, the centre of Western Christianity. The contribution which other countries have made is certainly not negligible; St Albert the Great, St Thomas, Duns Scotus and other masters of the scholastic era of Paris came from countries other than France. They came from Orders founded by St Dominic and St Francis outside France, although these Orders were largely founded to combat heresies which in France herself were the causes of real civil wars. From the extreme west of the Iberian Peninsula to the Sarmatian steppes of Poland and Russia, there were Christian Kingdoms and realms all over the European Continent. All were rivals for the common glory of Christendom.

Hegemony was a new term which grew out of the rivalry of the dynastic powers; thus in the political vocabulary of Europe, it is not older than the sixteenth century. There was no question in any modern sense of a French " hegemony " in the Middle Ages. France could however claim seniority through the succession of Charlemagne. Right up to the Revolution and the Restoration of the Bourbon dynasty in the early nineteenth century, we shall meet the argument—for the last time in Bonald's *Théorie de Pouvoir* and in his *Réflexions sur l'intérêt général de l'Europe* and in Joseph de Maistre's comments on topical events from St Petersburg—that the Empire east of the Rhine was a sort of political schism from the foundation of Charlemagne, just as the Church of Byzantium was a religious schism from Rome. The most monumental antagonist of this argument in the political literature of Europe was Dante, a keen enemy of the French kings and a supporter of the Imperial power. Yet it was only in the nineteenth century, when the Empire finally became Austrian and Danubian and withdrew from the West,[1] that the " seniority of Charlemagne's heritage " disappeared as a fundamental thesis of French policy.[2]

[1] A consequence and result of the Napoleonic wars, which the subsequent defeat of Napoleon (though largely due to Austrian participation in the " War of the Nations ") did not alter. Metternich preferred his monarchy to play the part of the centre of a " European " system, and wisely renounced all western claims (which in his position as one of the victors he could possibly have claimed from his allies).

[2] Bonald's comments on the Vienna Congress in *L'intérêt général de l'Europe* (like much of his philosophy) are a distant echo of Leibnitz' political theories, which aimed at a reconciliation between France and the Empire. They must be seen against the background of the time of Louis XIV in France and of Eugene of Savoy's liberation of the Christian Eastern Empire from Turkish rule and the re-integration of the latter into the Habsburg dominions.

This is but a part, although an indispensable part, of the central issue with which we deal in these pages, which is the evolution, from the Christian foundations of European politics and the European state-system, of the political conscience of the West. We have to bear in mind the primacy of France, in order to understand the central importance of the French Revolution for modern times, and the significant part it played in the dissolution of the European state-system. We cannot yet see the end of the crisis, although we can already discern—as even the best political intelligences of the generation of Bonald, de Maistre and Friedrich von Schlegel could not know—that in the twentieth century it means the growth and expansion of the deeper European problems to other civilisations and continents.

The ultimate meaning of this expansion of systems and institutions, which are themselves in a state of dissolution, may be, as we can already see, the implication of the whole world in concerns which are, for all those who are not satisfied with the most superficial appearances, the concerns of Christendom. A historical conjecture is that in a distant future the vocation of the Church may be the consecration and consolidation of a new world order and unity, which the European order failed to create, but which may slowly come into being through the spreading of a European chaos to distant parts of the globe.

We have previously indicated that each of the great steps taken to consolidate the Western Monarchy coincided—providentially—with the end of a great crisis in Christendom. The elevation of Clovis to the Kingdom of the Franks marked the end of the barbarian invasions of the West, and the triumphant emergence of Latin and Western Christianity, of the Catholicity of Rome, from the Manichean and Arian confusions of the East. The coronation of Charlemagne followed upon the first decisive victory of Christian Europe over Asia, although as far as the West was concerned, it was not a final victory. Its significance lay in the creation by the Papacy of a secular Christian order, or a monarchy which was spiritually dependent upon the prior existence of the Papacy, as David's monarchy was on Samuel's priesthood. French unity was achieved (apart from some conflicts over the frontiers of the north-east, which remained an open question until the wars of Louis XIV) by the victory over the Albigenses. The final consolidation and unity of the central monarchical power came about through the civil wars of the sixteenth century—in other words, the

Reformation was responsible for the unity of the French monarchy.

For many centuries, France enjoyed primacy, even in a more strictly geographical sense. The diplomatic thought, language and action which governed Europe for three centuries, and of which Metternich was the last classic master and depositary, used the expression " Central Europe " in the sense that the central powers in Europe were those which bordered the Rhine and the Alps, and were made the centre of Christendom by Charlemagne.

In the closing chapters of his *Lectures on the Philosophy of History*, Friedrich von Schlegel defined the key to German history as a strong German participation in the European system (an argument which was fairly general among the Austrian and Prussian-inspired publicists between Napoleon and Bismarck)[1] by pointing out that the German crises—the Lutheran Reformation and the Thirty Years' War—were bound to affect the whole of Europe, that order or chaos inside Germany were symptoms of the order or chaos of Europe; for Germany is, for good or ill, a sort of miniature Europe, with her naturally federal structure and local diversity, so that socially and historically, as well as geographically, she is the central nation.

France could also claim to be the " central nation " and that is one of the reasons why a Franco-German controversy has dominated the European scene for so long. The similarity between these claims hardly hides the differences between them, which make them ultimately irreconcilable. In France, the outcome of religious crises meant consolidation and unity, whereas in Germany similar crises led to disintegration, and an almost complete dissolution and absence of power in the seventeenth and eighteenth centuries; with the result that only Austria and Prussia, which were not purely Germanic powers, remained in the German East, and only Holland and Switzerland, which again were not purely Germanic societies, in the West.

One of the reasons for this evolution was certainly the sympathy France received from the Papacy, whose constant preoccupation was to keep the Emperor out of Italy. Richelieu

---

[1] This argument was taken up by F. W. Foerster in his analysis of the Germany between the two World Wars, *The German Question and Europe*, published in America, and also by the French scholar Edmond Vermeil, *Les doctrinaires de la Révolution Allemande*, 1938, and in *L'Allemagne : Une tentative d'explication*, 1940.

had the approval of Rome, not only because he safeguarded French unity by subduing the Huguenots at La Rochelle, but also because he opposed the Imperial power in the Thirty Years' War, an opposition which went to the extent of supporting Gustavus Adolphus and Protestant Sweden.

The preservation, restoration and the final triumph of French unity under Henry IV, Richelieu and Louis XIV, became one of the most significant events in Christendom, one of the greatest periods in the annals of European mankind. It was a secular event, but one which Bossuet—the mouthpiece of his century and nation, and by no means an isolated man of genius—interpreted as of the greatest religious significance. To him we owe the vision of History as the working-out of the designs of Providence. Bossuet had a mystical insight into History (as later on Joseph de Maistre was to have after the Revolution) and at the same time, in theology, he marked a return to St Augustine from the formal logic of medieval schoolmen, and a return to Revelation as a vision and a fact from a philosophy of the Absolute, which approached Revelation through syllogism. Bossuet's *Discours sur l'Histoire universelle* is an analogical synthesis. Religious and spiritual truth are seen here in the analogy between the Divine and the human. There are two histories for Bossuet: the universal history of immutable truth, foreshadowed in Eternity, and gradually and progressively revealed by action in time; and a history of " variations," a history of human errors and aberrations, of no final and definite significance, except that they prefigure what will be rejected on the day of final Judgement.

The importance of Bossuet in his own century, and in the whole of the intervening time between his day and ours, can hardly be over-estimated. For some people, his name may evoke the memory of stormy Gallican controversies which were intense in the seventeenth century, and still more so in the following one, not finally subsiding, indeed, till the Vatican Council of 1869.[1] How far Bossuet was the master-mind of the Gallican theories, which claimed special privileges for the French hierarchy and the French Crown—though neither he, nor any other thinker of his time, considered it as a purely secular government—and how far his theories encouraged the

[1] Heralded in the French Church by Louis Veuillot's lively "ultramontane" polemics against Mgr. Dupanloup and other " Gallicans " of the hierarchy, and against secular political leaders of the Liberal-Catholic variety such as Falloux and Montalembert.

Gallicans who favoured a restriction of direct Roman interference in the Church of France, could be made the subject
of a special study. The question has been examined by many
writers on Bossuet; it is of no great concern here. All that need
be said is that Bossuet's *Correspondance* and the published documents concerning his diocesan archives of Meaux, show him to
have been a bishop of moderately Gallican tendencies. Such
was the opinion of many of his contemporaries. But the
Gallican controversy is dead. It never contained any actual
threat of schism, still less of heresy. It was an ephemeral
political symptom, which disappeared, as such symptoms do,
with the transformation of the whole historical context—with
the Vatican Council of Pius IX and his Bull of Infallibility.

The Gallican controversy was not of primary importance in
Bossuet's achievement. To assert the contrary is to belittle this
monumental landmark which stands at the beginning of modern
French Christian thought.

In the spiritual history of Europe, the influence of Bossuet
can be discerned in the religious thought of Leibnitz. The
great German philosopher's plan for a reunion of Christendom
and for a European " Harmony " through restoration of peace
between France and the Empire—a more profound political
synthesis, and one that was more aware of historical reality
than Spinoza's abstract conception of an " equilibrium," or
balance of powers, to be established *more geometrico*—were
largely the fruits of Leibnitz's long and extensive exchange of
ideas with the Bishop of Meaux.

In theology, as we have already indicated, Bossuet signified
a great step forward from formal logic to historical understanding and—in a cultural sense, this was of equal importance—a step forward from the scholastic formula to that
perfect artistry of personal style, which is the main feature of
the French *grand siècle*. The *siglo de oro* in Spain saw God and
His work in the colours of passion and glory; the *grand siècle* in
France saw God and His work in the perfection of proportion
and form and language. It was the century of style—the style
of Boileau and La Fontaine, of Corneille, Racine and Molière,
of La Bruyère and Madame de Sévigné—which Bossuet
epitomised on the plane of divine knowledge. The French
style became the vehicle for all the dignified secular and
profane concerns of modern Europe; it occupied the third
place in Christendom, after the Greek of the Revelation which
united Jew and Gentile, and the Latin of the monastic rule,

of the liturgy and of the scholastics who spiritualised the Barbarian.

Bossuet made this triumph of style and artistic form a new triumph for the Church in the *grand siècle*. He was the foremost master of the unique and personal expression and the concise word, the power of which lay in allusion, in the concise manifestation of the deeper, hidden truth of the sign, the image and the symbol—in other words, the incarnation and fulfilment of the Word, *natum ante omnia saecula*, the fulfilment of that time which is contained within, and prefigured in, Eternity.

The French *grand siècle* changed the European vision by its idea of style, by the directness of its images, by its presentation of Truth, not in abstraction and reasoning, but in figure, image and word, which, in Bossuet's hands, became apologetic weapons wherewith to combat the heresy of a purely abstract, intellectual and rational Christianity, such as Calvin and his sect claimed to establish.

We are obliged to linger over Bossuet and his century, so important is he as a landmark in the spiritual progress of modern Europe. Indeed, without the *grand siècle* and Bossuet in particular, there would have been no Vico or Hegel to speculate on the unity of the spirit, as it is seen in its works and manifestations amidst the variety of the temporal and material order. A still greater loss, there would have been no Goethe, at any rate we should not have had the best of Goethe, who pushed rational effort to the extreme limit of the humanly possible, in order to recognise in the end the symbolic transcendence of all things created, *Alles Vergangliche ist nur ein Gleichniss*, the inexpressible which has been accomplished, *Das Unbeschreibliche, hier ist's getan*, and transcendent purity, *Das ewig weibliche. . . .*[1]

[1] Hardly anyone who has seriously attempted to understand Goethe could avoid quoting and analysing these lines. The latest comer is the French philosopher and poet Jean Guitton, in *La Pensée moderne et le Catholicisme*, in which he states that Goethe's concept of purity and his " eternal feminine " are expressions of a devotion, which is only a half conscious one, to the Blessed Virgin. Generally distrustful as we ought to be when well-meaning Catholic attempts are made to " annex " great thoughts from a strange or hostile camp to the Church—such attempts are dangerous because they minimise gigantic errors which we should face courageously—we feel that M. Guitton has probably said the last word on Goethe's Christianity, a controversial subject now fully resolved by a remarkable Catholic thinker of our own day.

An inevitable rapprochement of Goethe's *Alles Vergangliche* with the *Luce intellectual, pieno d'amore*, with the light of the " Paradiso," *ché transcende ogni dolciore* seems to contradict what we said above on the relation of Goethe to the French style of the seventeenth century and points to a still nobler origin of his transcendentalism. But between Dante and Goethe, there were the numerous attempts

The French *grand siècle* was misunderstood in the subsequent century, and has often been misunderstood since, as one which worshipped style and form, these two words being used in a pejorative sense to indicate an absence of " depth "; this was unfortunate, because it prevented any true appreciation, and even was an obstacle to any true understanding, of more recent French Catholic thought of the highest significance, the thought of Joseph de Maistre, Barbey d'Aurevilly, Ernest Hello and Léon Bloy, to which we shall come back later on in these pages.

It was not a century which worshipped style and form as an external ornament, but one in which the Faith acquired its modern style and expression. For Joseph de Maistre and the young Chateaubriand (of the *Génie du Christianisme* and the *Essai sur les Révolutions*) the Revolution meant a destruction of style, an interpretation which the former gave with irony and polemical wit, and the latter with melancholy. Chateaubriand, however, was perhaps the first French author to see style as a matter which only concerned aesthetics; unfortunately, this lowered the metaphysical, historical and religious level of his whole argument, so that the author of the *Génie du Christianisme* ranks below Joseph de Maistre or Bonald among the classics of modern apologetics. What de Maistre or Bonald considered to be an expression of Order, in accordance with the correct hierarchy of spiritual and social values which the Revolution had overthrown and cast into confusion, was for Chateaubriand an expression of subjective imagination and beauty. Therefore, what de Maistre saw as incredible human presumption, a substitution of human judgement and human creation for the divine, Chateaubriand was inclined to see as a mere rationalisation and levelling down of the poetic variety of imagination. In Barbey d'Aurevilly's view, the whole post-revolutionary period was marked by the 'decline of style, in a deeper sense

to separate the ideal *nomina* from created reality by abstractions which over-spiritualised and over-rationalised the former. This unity was restored by the French *grand siècle*, by " style," which, in other words, is unity in essence. It is a unity between the supernatural and the natural, visible in the harmony and the perfection of form and proportion. It was a unity that was restored above all by Bossuet, who as a theologian never ceased to be a historian, and as a master of prose never ceased to be a priest and bishop. The restoration of the unity between the supernatural and the natural by means of style followed upon the two parodies and caricatures of genius in France—that of the " purely natural " of Rabelais, and of the " purely spiritual " which Montaigne gave in his *Apologie de Raymond Sébond*—those parodies of genius which began the whole of modern French literature.

than was imagined by the English aesthetics of the nineteenth century (whom Barbey d'Aurevilly admired during his early days when he wrote his *Dandyisme* in the 1830's) from Byron to Wilde and from Carlyle to Ruskin, who considered theirs to be the century of utilitarian ugliness. Style declined during this time because human personality, of which it is the expression, was no longer a reflection of the personal reality of God in the current philosophies. It was a pantheist century, which believed in the difformity of the masses, and either praised difformity, or postulated uniformity under some future tyrant which Democracy would one day produce; the pantheism of Victor Hugo and of Michelet were the chief targets of Barbey d'Aurevilly's critical genius.

For Léon Bloy, "*les événements historiques sont le style de la Parole,*" the Word that was in the beginning and the full meaning of which has been gradually unfolded in the dimension of time throughout the centuries, the Word born *ante omnia saecula* and valid for Eternity. This philosophy, which underlies the whole of Léon Bloy's historical writing—his *Révélateur du Globe,* his *Byzance, Marie-Antoinette, L'Ame de Napoléon, Jeanne d'Arc*—gave him his whole vision of history: "*Il n'y a que les saints, ou les antagonistes des saints, capables de délimiter l'histoire.*"[1] Ernest Hello, that remarkable French mystic who was a monumental figure in modern Catholic thought between Barbey d'Aurevilly and Léon Bloy, and to whom some belated justice is rendered by admirers in our day,[2] thought that the century of style was Catholic and French in the truest sense: the Catholic Faith and French style have nothing in common with vagueness—Faith is affirmation and style is precision.[3] Essence and form cannot be separated; the appearance of Divinity in form was the Word humanly incarnate. God spoke when He made the Word incarnate. The vague, purely subjective value given to words is the great aberration of romantic sensitiveness, which characterised the century following Rousseau: "*Quand un homme s'égare, soyez sûr qu'il vient de se chercher.*"[4]

The commonplace in language is a fallen and debased fragment of the Word, with nothing left of its mystic origin, as the human beings who speak it are, so to say, fallen fragments of the Divine Person. Yet true style in poetry and prose

---

[1] *La Femme Pauvre,* Ch. XXII, p. 156 of the first edition. Paris. 1886.
[2] Stanilas Fumet: *Ernest Hello. Le drame de la lumière.* Paris. Egloff, 1946.
[3] Ernest Hello: *Le Style : Sa théorie et son histoire.* Paris. 1879.
[4] Ernest Hello: Ibid. p. 216.

can approach the divine and bring us back to the Word.[1]

We shall return later to this century of violent crises and national catastrophes. Meanwhile we must come back to the *grand siècle* of style, in order to consider it from another angle.

This is provided by someone who was perhaps as far removed from Bossuet as it was possible for a French thinker of the same century to be—by Pascal.

Pascal was the first lay apologist of the Church who developed a theological argument, not against the " Variations " of the heretical theologies, but against an enemy who never varies: Worldliness. Pascal refuted, and, in his own wisdom, surpassed worldly wisdom, even such wisdom " of this world " as can feel comfortable inside the Church and can conform perfectly to a secular order of Catholic inspiration. Pascal gave the full Christian answer to Montaigne and Descartes, and it is mainly for this reason that we are concerned with him here. His espousal of the Jansenist cause in *Lettres à un Provincial* remains a controversial subject. His attitude can be explained by his misunderstanding of the Jesuit case against the Jansenists, by his excessive austerity—perhaps even it was the result of insufficient knowledge concerning the Spanish Jesuit casuists, who were only known to him at second hand. As he himself admitted, they were read for him by Jansenist friends, who may well have been biassed. We may leave aside this, for some time the most widely discussed aspect of Pascal's work, as we left on one side the question of Bossuet's Gallicanism. Pascal's defence of Jansenism consisted of the argument that there was no such thing as " Jansenism," for the group who were known under that name did not accept the propositions which were condemned by the Sorbonne (and later by Pope Innocent X), as issuing from Jansenius's book on St Augustine, and that it was even doubtful if Jansenius, who died a Bishop of the Church, ever really meant to propose a doctrine on free will which was incompatible with that of the Church.

If Bossuet had only been a " Gallican," and Pascal only a " Jansenist," how would their reputation have survived? Who takes any interest today in the Abbé Noailles, who engaged

[1] Léon Bloy commented on these thoughts of Hello in his *Exégèse des lieux communs*. We may allude here to an important parallel: the critical approach to contemporary German writing of two German masters of aphorism, Theodor Haecker in *Satire und Polemik*, and Karl Kraus in the whole of his work.

We may also call attention here to Barbey d'Aurevilly's and Hello's analysis of the romantic subjectivism which began with Rousseau, reflected in the critical work of a later generation, in Pierre Laserre's *Les Romantiques* (1908) and in the various books of Ernest de Seillières.

in the Gallican controversy at the Sorbonne ? And who reads
Pascal's friends Arnauld or Nicole, except perhaps to find some
references to Pascal ?

Pascal, however, is one of the thinkers who did more perhaps
than anyone else to make his century great. He was, in his
various aspects, the highest expression of his time and of
religious thought.

He was, above all, in that broader and more complex sense
which we have explained, a master of style, and it was he who
defined style better than any other writer:

*Quand on voit le style naturel, on est tout étonné et ravi, car on
s'attendait de voir un auteur et on trouve un homme. . . . Ceux-là
honorent bien la nature, qui lui apprennent qu'elle parle de tout et même
de théologie.*[1]

*Un même sens change selon les paroles qui l'expriment. Les sens
reçoivent des paroles leur dignité, au lieu de la leur donner.*[2]

Eloquence qui persuade par douceur, non par empire, en tyran, non en roi.[3]

For Pascal, and for all those who have ever meditated like
him on this particular problem, the full religious truth is also
the full social truth. If not the first, Pascal is at any rate the
most powerful master of the religious argument in defence of
the social order. His unerring sense of precision, his geometrical
sense of perfect proportion, his mathematical experience of the
extreme limits of rational and intellectual truth, make him a
major figure in the history of modern apologetics. Right up to
the twentieth century, a great deal of French thought was to be
a comment and a gloss on those unique fragments, providentially left unfinished, which we know as the *Pensées*. As a
secular defender of the Faith, he is the spiritual ancestor of
Joseph de Maistre. His social doctrine on Order, which he
considers to be preserved by the sound sense of the common
people, who always instinctively prefer Order to anarchy, was
to be the social doctrine of Bonald. It was also to encounter the
criticism of Voltaire (for whom Pascal's relativism went too
far) and, more recently, that of Jacques Maritain, who, in his
attempt to define the Christian attitude to the *Things that are
not Caesar's*, and the Christian task in the *Rédemption du Temps*,
accuses Pascal of a " Christian cynicism " which, in his view,
the Angelic Doctor would never have approved. We shall
return to this debate.

---

[1] *Pensées:* Section I, 29, in the version edited by Léon Brunschvicg. Paris. 1904.
[2] Ibid. Section I, 225.   [3] Ibid. Section I, 130.

From the diametrically opposite philosophical camp, Henri Poincaré's *Science et Hypothèse* and Boutroux's whole system form something of a belated commentary on (and confirmation of) Pascal's fundamental thesis of the primacy of belief, which he preferred to that primacy of thought formulated by Descartes.

Cartesian philosophy attempted to jettison Aristotelian and medieval scholastics. In the end, it confronted man with the Absolute, in a world of pure syllogism and lofty abstraction. Pascal returned man to his natural level, he put human ethics back into the social and historical context, gave a more natural expression to notions of philosophy and gave Reason and Will back their natural direction: *La raison croit naturellement et la volonté aime naturellement* . . . a surprising and paradoxical statement at first sight, but it shows Pascal's wisdom at its deepest. It comprises his whole philosophy in one short formula, which can be meditated upon and commented on almost indefinitely. It gives us perhaps the final word in the controversy on the relation between Reason and Will, which has been familiar in the Church since the days of St Thomas and Duns Scotus. Pascal saw both Divinity and Humanity, the attributes of God and the faculties of Man, in the fullness of their nature. He fought two errors, two exaggerations: the Cartesian separation of the Absolute from the complex nature of Man, whose nature includes some of the attributes of the Creator, and at the same time, the exaggeration of Montaigne, who saw nothing but relativity, uncertainty and passing futility in the human world. Man is *ni ange, ni bête*, a warning against the exaggeration[1] of Descartes and against the sensualist dangers of Montaigne. These two dangers, in the following century—the fatal eighteenth, preceding the Revolution and the whole contemporary catharsis—marked the beginning, and were the cause, of all the aberrations of the French mind and of French-speaking Europe, since the *grand siècle*, the century of style, had made Europe French-speaking.

Yet before we attempt a survey of the eighteenth century, the period of the Revolution and the religious rejuvenation which followed it, let us hint at a few more aspects of the enormously extensive and rich inheritance which Pascal left us.

We often find an echo of Pascal in unexpected quarters. We

---

[1] Jacques Maritain in *Trois Réformateurs*—Luther, Descartes and Rousseau, Paris, 1929, gives perhaps the fullest analysis of this "*angelisme*" in Descartes' philosophy, the most systematic Catholic criticism of the postulate of knowledge separated from human nature and from society. Already in Barbey d'Aurevilly's *Les Prophètes du Passé*, we see this criticism of Descartes.

find one in Theodor Haecker's passionate polemics against the
" neo-Manichean "[1] tendencies of our time, present in all his
books, against the modern primacy of Liberty over Order
which the nineteenth century tried to establish and which
denied a divine quality to Order and to Power, thus decrying
Power as an evil which men, formed in this mental atmosphere—Communists, Nazis and Fascists—passionately embraced
as the means to achieve their evil ends. It was Pascal who
defined Power, and the right place of Power, and who thus
defined Tyranny as power used in the wrong place; Force,
which claims love and affection instead of obedience; beauty
and loveliness which claim not love, but obedience; eloquence
which tries to persuade not by strong and conclusive, but by
ingratiating argument; and above all, the human presumption
which assumes the force of absolute Justice, while the whole
condemned nature of Man can only hope to render that Power
and Force just, instead of transforming justice into Power—all
this signified for Pascal the various forms of tyranny. A contemporary of the English Revolution, Pascal had a foreboding of
the French Revolution and judged it one hundred and forty
years before it happened.

This is perhaps a somewhat neglected aspect of a much-
explored and much-commented-upon genius. There may even
be readers who are astonished to be told that Pascal was a
defender of Order. There are often indications to the contrary.
Many are inclined to see the author of the *Pensées* as the opposite
to Bossuet in every respect, and to class the latter as the spiritual
ancestor of more recent *bien-pensants*, of traditionalists, who
conform complacently; some of these—unfortunately the least
attractive makers and defenders of platitudes, such as a Henry
Bordeaux or a Ferdinand Brunetière—have often enough
attempted to cover their thin theories and thinner style with
Bossuet's great name and authority. In the face of all this,
does not Pascal represent a " revolutionary " sort of Catholicism, an unconventional style in defence of conservative values,
an unorthodox system of reasoning which concluded in orthodox
truth; is he not the spiritual ancestor of all great Catholic
writers who, in an unorthodox way, have defended orthodox
truth—Barbey d'Aurevilly and Hello, Bloy and Péguy, and

---

[1] " Neo-Manichean " is Theodor Haecker's own coinage. It originates in the
Manichean conclusion that the struggle between good and evil has no decisive
outcome, that God's power, not being the stronger of the two, does not give the
final word on the issue.

outside France, of Chesterton, and in a less direct and conscious line, even of Kierkegaard and Dostoievsky ?

We have made an effort in the preceding pages to elucidate the sense, and to ascertain the value of Bossuet's heritage, and we have taken up our position in a recurring controversy about classification. Bossuet and Pascal certainly form a contrast to each other. The author of the *Pensées* is undoubtedly also the spiritual ancestor of all those who defended orthodox truth in an unorthodox style, those whom we have already named and many more besides. Pascal's work is above all a demonstration. The mathematician which he always remained began his *Pensées* by distinguishing strictly between the *esprit de géometrie* and the *esprit de finesse*. His work is a demonstration, made with geometric precision, that Reason cannot exist without belief, the Will without Love, or human life without God. Pascal relegated all godless science to the chaos of the unthinkable, all godless ethics to the chaos of the unlivable; he it was who put Jacques Maritain on the right track when he coined the phrase *l'invivable athéisme*. The *Pensées*, despite its fragmentary character, is the first fully elaborated study of fallen nature, a study to which Pascal was after all brought by his opponents the Jesuits, casuists of the school of Escobar, and not by his Jansenist friends. It was the study which Balzac was to take up later in his novels, Léon Bloy in his volumes of spiritual autobiography—and far away from France and outside Catholicism—Dostoievsky and Kierkegaard. Pascal was the foremost teacher of a *vital* Christianity, of an " existentialist " Christianity, as it has lately been fashionable to say, although he would probably be the last to take part in any *querelle d'Allemands* on a possible separation of Essence and Existence, and fortunately the last author whose support can be claimed for any " ism."

Like most great spiritual figures, Pascal rejected worldliness and easy conformity. He rejected and condemned acceptance of the riches of this world by those who did so with an easy conscience. He even went further; he rejected that wisdom which, by serving the necessities of this world, or human concerns only, provides an easy moral satisfaction here below.

The primacy of Order over Liberty was Pascal's final conclusion. This primacy was manifest in the chronological sense in the Bible, it was obvious on the level of theology and clear in logic. It was a primacy established by a " revolutionary "—if we care to apply this term to any man who feels a passionate detachment from the world, which we do not dare to call holiness, but which we feel cannot be far removed from it—but a "revolutionary" who consciously judged in advance, and more sternly, all the revolutions which were to come than he judged the conventions and the platitudes of this world and of his century. Pascal realised this primacy of Order better than anyone else, better than those weaker minds and hearts who came after him, and attempted to challenge and destroy it by postulating an imaginary order which reflected Man's liberty and free will alone. That was why he loved Liberty, the Liberty of Man to know God and to love Him, the Liberty to follow the dictates of his heart and to act accordingly. *Dieu incline le coeur. . . .*

4. DECADENCE AND CRISIS: THE EIGHTEENTH AND NINETEENTH CENTURIES

For about a century, Europe spoke French. Her princes were brought up on Fénelon's *Télémaque*; the taste of the educated classes was formed on La Fontaine from their earliest years; La Bruyère and La Rochefoucauld were the masters of every conversation; passion spoke the language of Corneille, sentiment the language of Racine, good sense spoke the language of Molière and abstraction the language of Descartes. All cathedral pulpits echoed the eloquence of Bossuet and Bourdaloue, and few letters were written without a delicate and charming touch of Mme. de Sévigné. Italy stood for colour, rhyme and sound; Spain had once meant romance and imagination; now France epitomised thought, speech and style, and as infinitely more people speak and write in prose than in the language of colour, sound or image, France dominated more minds and assimilated an infinitely greater number of people, who, to think and write in French, needed not much more than a few brief stays in Paris. We must cast our imagination back to this French-speaking Europe, before we can understand why and how the French Revolution excited so many foreign passions, and why so many foreign thinkers produced their best work on French issues, without in the least feeling strangers to the quarrel—Burke and Horace Walpole in England, de Maistre in Italy, young Metternich and Friedrich von Gentz in Germany, Karl-Ludwig Haller and Johannes von Müller in Switzerland. There were great

French writers in the " French century of Europe " (which in the strict calendar sense began earlier than the eighteenth, and lasted on longer) who were leading men in their own countries: Joseph de Maistre, Ambassador and Minister of the Kingdom of Piedmont-Sardinia, and Prince de Ligne, Field-Marshal and Ambassador of Austria. They represented French thought, style and wit wherever they were, even when de Maistre was planning the downfall of Napoleon in St Petersburg, and even when de Ligne asked for a last opportunity to practise the principle of his life—*tonner et étonner*—at the head of an army composed of Walloons, Hungarians and Croats *pour décharlemagniser Bonaparte.* Right up to our own day, French has been the intellectual language of Egypt and of modern Greece, and hardly a generation has elapsed since José-Maria de Hérédia from Latin America and Jean Moréas from Greece were considered French, or at any rate, Parisian poets.

This is a unique case of the extension of a civilisation which is only equalled by the Hellenism of antiquity; never since the Oriental Philo and the Roman Marcus Aurelius wrote Greek has there been a case of a universal language being adopted voluntarily, for no other reason than love of style and intellectual delight. Yet this enormous and almost unprecedented peaceful conquest of a continent, based only on refinement of thought, taste and style, has not been altogether a blessing for France herself. The cause of the decay—the cause of all decay—is facility, the easily acquired technique of imitation and reproduction.[1] In the second part of his *Faust,* this is Goethe's vision of the Witches' Sabbath: an almost universal devaluation, through easy reproduction, of everything noble, even of everything sacred; the debasement of gold and of honour—of everything except the cross on the hilt of the Imperial sword, which pseudo-Field Marshals, as not truly consecrated men, were incapable of using. If we accept the proposed formula of facility as a warning of doom to come,[2] we cannot do otherwise than discern the signs of approaching catastrophe in the period of the French intellectual conquest

[1] Perhaps this one formula will dispense us from recapitulating the volumes of speculation on the decay of civilisations, which Vico, Hegel and Spengler, to mention only the dead, spent their whole lives in producing.

[2] This certainly offers us no happy augury for our own century of mechanical reproduction, although Catholics cannot fall into the aimless, unredeemed pessimism and confessed emptiness of the representative voices of the century, from the massive technician H. G. Wells to the refined intellectualist Paul Valéry, from the grave André Gide to the lucid cynic Jean-Paul Sartre.

of Europe. The Revolution itself, in all its consequences and
variations, the Revolution considered *en bloc*—as Georges
Clemenceau, a belated heir of Jacobinism, wanted to consider
it, that is, from 1789 to the Third Republic—must have appeared
to those who were still near enough to the old ideal of greatness
and of style as facile imitation run riot. The Revolution
invented its Deity and its cult, it re-enacted its own version of
Sparta, Athens and Rome—rather than an innovation, it was
a vast imitation of models. Almost a whole century of hybrid
facility preceded it and another century of regret followed. As
an anonymous and, for that reason, probably widespread
criticism of Voltaire put it—*il a fait de l'esprit pour ceux qui n'en
ont pas*. The whole century which followed him, and the
Revolution which quoted him so often, but which would
probably have guillotined him had he lived to see it, was one
of undoubted intellectual expansion, although it may be
doubted whether this expansion brought us any nearer to real
greatness—to the greatness of form and style of Bossuet. In
the seventeenth century, greatness was within the reach of a
man whose thought did not aim higher than La Fontaine's;
in the nineteenth century, the love of greatness, of form and
beauty, took the form of desperate protests against their time
on the part of Flaubert and Baudelaire in France, of Carlyle
and Ruskin in England, of Jacob Burckhardt and his pupil
Nietzsche in the German-speaking world; we leave aside for
the time being those who found in God and the Church a
remedy to this aesthetic despair, as we have dealt with them in
another context, and shall have to return to them.

Decadence, a decay of greatness in style, began what has
grown into one of the greatest and most significant spiritual
and moral crises of modern mankind. Just as, in the mechanical sphere, most mortal accidents occur because machines get
out of control, so in the sphere of human history and the history
of human thought all catastrophes can be traced back to words
and values which have lost their original meaning, and have
passed beyond the control of those minds which once fully
possessed their original sense. Three figures divided the intellectual atmosphere of the *grand siècle* from the Revolution and
from the whole trend which began with the principles of 1789,
that crucial trend which is not yet at an end. They are
Voltaire, Montesquieu and Rousseau.

The change was gradual with Voltaire; it was hardly
noticeable at the beginning of his literary output and only

became final when, at a mature age and with a considerable achievement behind him, he made a prolonged stay in England, and received the influence of English thought and literature. This was the only foreign thought which came to full maturity later than the French, for the golden age of Dante and Petrarch, Tasso and Ariosto, the *siglo de oro* of Cervantes and of the great spiritual teachers of Spain preceded the full maturity of French thought and expression. Voltaire interpreted, in a language which the whole of intellectual Europe spoke and read, English thought from Hobbes to Locke. Even before *Candide*, which was a challenge to the French-inspired European thought of Leibnitz, political and social "Voltairianism" hardly existed.

Voltaire had style, and according to the lights of his century (the taste of which was largely formed by him) even poetry. But unlike Corneille and Racine, in whom poetry and style were the natural accompaniment to dramatic action, style in Voltaire became merely decorative and moralising was the chief aim of poetry.[1] But rhyme and drama were accidental forms of Voltaire's philosophy and do not concern us here. We are not writing a French, or even a West European literary history, but an analysis of the evolution of the theme of Authority and Liberty in the Western, and above all in the French mind, since the religious and moral crisis arising from these two notions first broke over France, and by French intellect was propagated throughout the world.

To decry Voltaire as an " atheist " is a simplification. Some of his contemporaries applied this term to him: with a true woman's instinct, Maria-Theresa detested him and his whole sect of " philosophers," and Mozart frankly rejoiced at the end of this " hideous atheist " whose dry reasoning was in such contrast to his own simplicity and angelic purity as a musician.[2] Since his own time, Voltaire has found a champion, surprisingly enough, in Jacques Maritain, who, in his *Humanisme Intégral*, is

[1] A similar evolution of English literary style, a transformation of poetry and style under the influence of the English philosophical movement of the eighteenth century, which was the decisive influence on Voltaire's mind, is described in *The Life of Reason—Hobbes, Locke and Bolingbroke* by D. G. James. London. Longmans, Green & Co., 1949.

[2] For the influence which conflicting opinions on Voltaire played on the politics of the eighteenth century, it is useful to read Capefigue's *Marie-Thérèse et Frédéric II* and his *Madame Pompadour*, although prudence and caution must be exercised before accepting the views of this very enjoyable, but strongly anti-revolutionary historian, who judged Voltaire and the Revolution from the perspective of Louis-Philippe's time and from his own loyalist feelings.

" grateful to him for his idea of civic tolerance," and in the English Catholic poet Alfred Noyes, who (censored, it is true, in Rome for so doing) saw in Voltaire a critic of the Church who was imbued with a truly Catholic spirituality, and was thus superior to all Protestant heresiarchs.

Voltaire is a very complex case indeed. He did not simply open up a wrong path, as many others did, but he summed up (so to speak) aberrations from the right path of Faith and Reason: he *epitomised* the aberrations of all those who had stopped half way before him on some wrong path. He was a " Gallican " with Bossuet in his *Siècle de Louis XIV*, and in the *Essai sur les moeurs* he was far more Jansenist than Pascal.[1] A believer in God, this champion of logic denied most of the logical implications of Divine omnipotence, such as the possibility of miracles and revelation.

Human wisdom was the only authority he accepted, yet—like Berkeley, Hume, and Kant after him—he denied that the human mind could ever know final certainty. That his passion for justice was genuine and that he attacked real abuses and scandals of his time, we do not want to deny. There was compassion and even charity in Voltaire; but a total lack of humility spoiled even this, the highest of his gifts. Indignant over the abuse of power, he proposed (again illogically enough for a champion of Reason) that philosopher princes should enjoy absolute power; yet, at the same time, this keen moralist, in his *Lettres sur l'Angleterre*, was ready to pay the heavy price of oligarchical and aristocratic corruption, for the sake of " Liberty." To sum up his importance in the field which is our present concern, Voltaire secularised both Authority and Liberty, not admitting that either had any other foundation than human reason and human need. In this sense alone, he is the father of Revolutions, yet no writer, thinker, or critic of public affairs was more at home in a Catholic, monarchical and aristocratic society. And nobody has felt more uprooted in a secularist and democratic Republic than belated Voltairians such as Charles Maurras and Anatole France. The first made a desperate attempt, in the early part of our century, to reconstruct mentally a monarchical and aristocratic society without a religion, but founded on merely pragmatic necessities, recognised by Reason; he even tried to construct a Church which

[1] When it suited his purpose: when he wanted to argue the immediate presence of divinity in the soul, which does not therefore need the mediation of Church or priesthood.

would teach doctrines that were admittedly problematic in the light of Reason, but which were needed for the social discipline of the masses. The second belated Voltairian clung desperately, under cover of a self-imposed and permanent ironical smile, to what remained of monarchical, clerical and aristocratic France, to all the red robes of Cardinals, gala swords of Academicians and tiaras of great ladies that survived in the drawing-rooms of the Faubourg St Germain, until the eve of the twentieth century and the First World War.

Opportet ut fiant scandala. . . . Voltaire was the scandal of a narrow world which was disguised in the solemn robes of Authority; but it sinned in its Liberty, for the substance of Authority, the primacy of Order, was no longer present in its mind and heart. He was the minor, very minor, scandal of a world which had lost every Cartesian perspective of the Absolute, every Pascalian sense of the Infinite, every sense of the unity of essence taught by Bossuet, and thus even of every measure of true human greatness. Even when this world, a little more than a century after Voltaire had shaken it with laughter rather than indignation, took " lessons in energy " from Maurice Barrès, or listened to the pious, complacent reassurances of Paul Bourget, it will not deceive us. This was just " the world," the one rejected by Pascal. The greatest glory and the culminating point of French letters, as we said before, came when Pascal, a man not of the Church but of the world, rejected worldly wisdom, and at the same time made it quite clear that the primacy of Order was the first principle on which society was based, and when human society, a unit in the natural order, received from a thinker in its own ranks a declaration of its own supernatural nature. As the Abbé Brémond[1] said, the true history of literature, like the true history of a nation, is the religious history of the people, and this is more so in the case of France than of any other nation.

The Gospel tells us to judge people by their fruits. We may weigh the fruits of Voltaire, Charles Maurras and Anatole France, and we may taste them. They are not very substantial or very sweet. The first of them adopted the pose of intransigent affirmation and of strict doctrine: he assumed the attitude of the depositary of a great classic, monarchical

---

[1] Henri Brémond: *Histoire du sentiment religieux dans la littérature française depuis le XVIIe siècle jusqu'à nos jours:* a work whose chief trend may be described as religious and Catholic romanticism, a religious history based on the study of profane texts.

doctrine, dignified by the scarlet robe of Richelieu; yet he was
nothing more than the teacher of rabid semi-literates, worthy
of the black shirt rather than of the scarlet robe. Maurras,
recognising a fellow-Voltairian in Anatole France, singled him
out as the great writer of his generation, despite the revolutionary sympathies of this latter, arguing that his aesthetic
preference for every sort of intransigence was more favourable
to the anarchist worker than to the moderate bourgeois of the
Third Republic. The fact is that Anatole France's whole
message and style died with the moderate bourgeois of the
Third Republic, and in any case were no more worthy of
survival than this era itself. The said bourgeois felt that Balzac,
the " reactionary," execrated them; felt offended by the
impotent ill-humour of Flaubert; was shocked, not by the
opium-smoking of Baudelaire, or the absinthe-drinking of
Verlaine, but by the final conversion of both *poètes maudits*. He
was delighted and pleased, on the other hand, by Anatole
France, the " revolutionary " sophist; flattered rather than
disquietened by Maurras, the " monarchical " sophist, who
offered him plenty of justification for a comfortable social
immorality, and a comfortable escape from serious affirmation
into an easy and pleasant position of prolonged and unperturbed scepticism—a position which was compatible with the
external cult of those ancestors of the *bourgeoisie*, the Athenians
(much beloved by both Maurras and Anatole France) who put
Socrates to death.

A fruit of Voltaire, outside France, was Heinrich Heine.
Many critics on both sides of the Rhine have dwelt on the
Plutarchian parallel between this German who served the
French king, and Voltaire who served the King of Prussia.
The parallel goes further than that; but, unfortunately for
Voltaire, what was really noble in Heine was not his wit or
his persiflage, still less his grim and presumptuous laughter and
his facile sentiment, but the infinite regret, behind all this, at
the slow approach of a terrible end, the tragic collapse under
what he felt to be the double curse of Germany and Juda, his
break with atheism " not only out of disgust," but through " a
fear " which he admitted—the fear of a sensitive artist in the
face of Revolutions that were yet to come in an apostate
Germany, and a faithless modern Israel which had denied
Jehovah.

Perhaps the best spiritual descendant of Voltaire was
Stendhal. Practically ignored during his life-time, he was the

last writer to belong to the eighteenth century, although he wrote exclusively in the nineteenth.[1] Stendhal was undoubtedly of the family of Voltaire. In him there was no melancholy regret, none of the nostalgia for a more beautiful past, which began with Chateaubriand, the German romantics, young Victor Hugo and Walter Scott, and continued throughout the whole of the nineteenth century. This melancholy and nostalgia sounded a more sincere note than all the artificial paroxysms concerning the " future," all the semi-scientific, optimistic philosophies which, in most cases, were nothing but retrospective Utopias, transferred to the future from some imaginary past. Stendhal, like Voltaire and the eighteenth century as a whole, believed in the power of the senses, and in almost nothing else. Curiosity concerning the sensual nature of man comprised almost his only philosophy. His was an exceptional case of a narrow and insufficient philosophy which did not spoil the greatness of his art. He was fortunate in that he inherited sensualism, rather than dry rationalism, from Voltaire; and he nourished it with Italian impressions and ample subjects for meditation drawn from history and politics, especially in the *Chartreuse de Parme*. But Balzac, Stendhal's pupil, who was greater than his master and who virtually discovered him, saw in the author of the *Chartreuse de Parme* more of Machiavelli than of Voltaire. He recognised in Stendhal's *Conte Mosca* a portrait of his much-admired Metternich, a homage to superior statesman-like principles and intelligence, and he deplored the fact that only some fifteen hundred men who formed the brain of Europe would be able to understand Stendhal and the book which a nineteenth-century Machiavelli would have written.[2]

Voltaire's heirs did not therefore always choose the side of Liberty in the great debate between Authority and Liberty, despite the blessing their master gave to Benjamin Franklin's grandson in the name of " God and Liberty." We have already pointed out that it would be very difficult indeed to make a modern democrat out of the very loyal chronicler of *Le siècle de Louis XIV* and *Le siècle de Louis XV*, the man who at one moment sought and obtained the favours of Madame de Pompadour and her circle, and who, before his disgrace at Potsdam, was

[1] Just as Chateaubriand was the first writer of the nineteenth century, although his early period belonged to the eighteenth.

[2] *Etude sur M. Beyle*, par Honoré de Balzac. Epilogue to an 1846 Paris edition of *La Chartreuse de Parme*, p. 484 sq.

at any rate a devoted friend of the King of Prussia. He admired tyranny in Peter the Great, he admired the absolute philosophy of China, he reproved Leibnitz for not making the new Alexander, Charles XII of Sweden, his pupil, as Aristotle made Alexander of Macedon his pupil. But when it comes to Charles XII sending the royal boots to preside over the Stockholm Senate, Voltaire expressed little democratic objection, just as his much praised humanitarian tolerance did not go so far as to make him a friend of the Jews—as Bonald remarked in *La Question Juive*[1] (1806).

The secularisation of Liberty by Voltaire, which we have analysed above, required a full and complete Catholic answer, which he did not live to receive, and which could not perhaps even have been given without the practical experience of an integral Voltairianism which mankind received with the French Revolution. This answer was given by Joseph de Maistre. It cannot be repeated too often that Christian thought has always triumphed when it possessed the knowledge and the spiritual weapons of its opponent. The Redeemer and His Apostles knew the Scriptures better than did the Synagogue; St Augustine knew Greek thought better than any of the pagan philosophers, and the force of evil better than the Manicheans; St Thomas was more unprejudiced and tolerant towards the thought of those who did not possess the full measure of Christian grace than any of the Albigenses; St Ignatius was superior both in independence of mind and self-discipline to any Protestant; St Alphonsus Liguori was stricter and more austere in his submission to Authority than any Jansenist, who rejected it for allegedly purer forms of Liberty and austerity. Pascal was superior to Montaigne in *esprit de finesse* and to Descartes in *esprit de géométrie*.[2] Joseph de Maistre had a finer

---

[1] *Oeuvres complètes de M. le Vicomte de Bonald, Pair de France.* Paris, 1859. Vol. 2, p. 934:

"*Quand je dis que les Juifs sont objet de la bienveillance des philosophes, il faut en excepter le chef de l'école philosophique Voltaire, qui toute sa vie a montré une aversion decidée contre ce peuple infortuné.*

"*Il est probable que cet homme célèbre ne haïssait dans les Juifs que les dépositaires et les témoins de la vérité et de la révélation qu'il a juré d'anéantir.*"

Thus Bonald discerned in Voltaire the beginnings of a more recent anti-Christianism, disguised as hatred of the Jews, that anti-Semitism which moved Léon Bloy to write *Le salut par les Juifs*.

[2] We mean naturally *esprit de géométrie* in philosophical thought and style. The respective greatness of Pascal and Descartes in geometry and mathematics proper is not our province, although creditable sources inform us that no scientific authority questions that Pascal is entitled to the very highest rank. We have done our best to study his scientific work as far as it is relevant for his philosophy and theology.

love of history than Voltaire and did not mind appearing, when the necessity of the argument required, even pedantic. He was fully prepared to appear as a " philosopher " in order to refute the bad, eighteenth-century meaning of the word, which no longer bore any relationship to the *philosophia perennis*, but followed Descartes in purely individual reasoning, or Berkeley, Hume and Kant in considering the consciously and confessedly doubtful individual judgement as the final authority. When he had to play this rôle, it was in order to establish a common ground for discussion; then, after demolishing his opponent's arguments, he appeared in his true colours as a man of the *philosophia perennis*, as a Christian whose concern it was to believe, rather than to be omniscient, for—this is the noblest aspect of de Maistre's thought—he admitted fully that it is more difficult to believe than to know, but he insisted that the effort to believe, and the sacrifice which acceptance of belief entails, is in itself heroic, and an act of moral greatness.

The primacy of morals is the subject of Joseph de Maistre's great dialogues called *Les Soirées de St Pétersbourg*. Taking part in these conversations, in the first year of the century, were an Imperial Russian Senator, a young French *émigré* nobleman in the Czar's service, and de Maistre himself. He waited almost twenty years before he wrote them down. The argument in the dialogues, however, is not addressed to the elderly Russian and the young Frenchman, but to the whole of the eighteenth century, in which Joseph de Maistre spent the greater part of his life, forty-seven out of his sixty-eight years. Voltaire separated morals from faith and dogma and put the accent on morality. When Voltaire challenged Pascal by coining aphorisms in opposition to the *Pensées*, he challenged him on moral and intellectual sidelines, not indeed on real fundamentals: belief in God and in Christ. Joseph de Maistre replied to Voltaire. Voltaire said in essence that he was not concerned with a man's beliefs, as long as his actions were moral. De Maistre replied that, as a rational sceptic, he was unable to trust anybody's morals, unless they were prepared for the first and most difficult sacrifice of all, the effort to believe. Voltaire and his whole century dismissed the Catholic position by saying that it was easy to believe, that any child could do so, whereas to know demanded a serious and manly effort. Joseph de Maistre replied that it was quite easy to know, but that it was a gift and a grace to believe; that it required a heroic effort on the part of all the human faculties, purity, imagination and emotion.[1] And he illustrated his point with his habitual sense of paradox: it was easy enough, he said, to know the Theses of Wittenberg, the Thirty-nine Articles of the Church of England, the Confession of Augsburg, or the Helvetic Confession, whereas a man needed rhythm, musical sense and deep emotions to sing the Nicene Creed.

Joseph de Maistre created new matter and a new style for apologetics, although there is no doubt that he owed much to Pascal and to Bossuet.

He was indebted to Pascal for his sense of paradox and for his wit, which defeated Voltaire and disconcerted the Voltairians for ever. Wit, satire, jokes, these terrible arms which Voltaire used against the Church, were mastered in the *Soirées*, and turned against him. Only a few Voltairians in later years dared to try to use them again after de Maistre: Paul-Louis Courier, in whose hands the Voltairian weapons became either vulgar or heavy and pedantic, like his German-inspired Hellenic science, and Victor Hugo, when he wrote *Les Châtiments*. Yet ever since Péguy's brilliant exposure and unmasking of Hugo's pseudo-democracy and pseudo-pacifism,[2] we can never again believe, to Hugo's credit, that this grandiose bard of military glories, this rhetorical but genuine mystic, was ever a Voltairian. After all it was not the Church, but the Liberal bourgeoisie, who rallied round the flag of conformity waved by Napoleon III, which was the target of *Les Châtiments*; and we must not forget that, as we are told in the *Memoirs of Granier de Cassagnac*, Hugo wished his disciples *de dire franchement que Voltaire est bête*, many years before committing the blasphemy in *Actes et Paroles* of comparing the tears of Jesus with the smile of Voltaire, as the two most powerful weapons against the evils of this world. Anatole France tried to make Voltairian jokes; he was at best an unconscious humorist when he created

---

[1] We may quote here a few echoes, only partly conscious and direct ones, of Joseph de Maistre and the *Soirées*: When Balzac declared so emphatically in the Preface to the *Comédie Humaine* that he was on the same side as Bossuet and Bonald, he certainly echoed de Maistre; also when he said that human society did not need masters to teach it how to doubt, but masters who knew how to affirm and how to believe, i.e. Authority, which, in the thought of this great inventor of an imaginary society, was the keystone of social justice and happiness. Chesterton found truth in the irresistible paradoxes of the Faith, and not in logical but unimaginative reasoning. The whole life-work of Kierkegaard was an auto-biographical comment on the moral value of the effort to believe. For Romano Guardini, real knowledge begins " beyond the self-evident," in the mystical sphere which can only be entered at the cost of sacrifice.

[2] In *Notre Jeunesse et Victor-Marie, comte Hugo*.

Professor Bergeret, and only succeeded in making us smile happily in small masterpieces like *Le Jongleur de Notre Dame*, at stories of child-like devotion. Joseph de Maistre banished the enemies of the Church into that " Sorbonne-esque " and pedantic gravity which they assumed in the nineteenth and early twentieth centuries, amidst the scorn and the laughter— and what laughter!—of Veuillot, Barbey d'Aurevilly, Charles Péguy, Chesterton, and Theodor Haecker. He laughs longest who laughs last, and thanks to Joseph de Maistre, the Church laughed last on all the topics raised by the eighteenth and early nineteenth centuries. But let us rather quote de Maistre, the superior protagonist of paradox, before we show him as the spiritual son of Bossuet in his graver, but not necessarily more mystical or greater moments:

Rien n'égale la patience de ce peuple qui se dit libre. En cinq ans on lui a fait accepter trois constitutions et le gouvernement révolutionnaire. Les tyrans se succèdent et toujours le peuple obéit. Jamais on n'a vu réussir un seul pour se tirer de la nullité. Ses maîtres ont réussi à le foudroyer en se moquant de lui. Ils lui ont dit: Vous croyez ne pas vouloir cette loi, mais soyez sûrs que vous la voulez. Si vous osez la refuser, nous tirerons sur vous pour vous punir de ne pas vouloir ce que vous voulez.[1]

He could show the party who believed in the primacy of Liberty, fellow-exiles of his in Lausanne before his St. Petersburg period—Mme. de Staël and Benjamin Constant—those who were later to be answered more fully by Bonald than de Maistre ever cared to do, that he, the Piedmontese whose mother-tongue was French, knew his Europe, and did not suffer from any sort of French " provincialism," which Mme. de Staël tried to overcome by recommending English politics to France in her political writing, German learning and sentiment in *De l'Allemagne*, and Italian emotions in *Corinne*. Not only did he know his Machiavelli to such a degree that he could be fair and just to this ardent republican, from whom he took most striking arguments against attempts made to replace with paper constitutions the natural conditions consecrated by history and experience; but he knew his Kant and Lutheran Germany, whose intellectual influence he saw spreading to schismatic Russia, where the secular authority confined itself to resisting the true authority of the unbroken tradition of

[1] *Considérations sur la France.* Lausanne. 1797. Ch. VIII.

Rome, instead of resisting the intrusion of wild intellectual liberties from heretical Germany.[1] He knew English philosophy and the English language well enough to conclude his famous polemics against Locke with the half-serious, half-comic lament: " *L'esprit européen est emprisonné.* . . . It is locked in."

When she was in Lausanne, Mme. de Staël delighted in the frankness and naturalness of great military style, personified in Prince de Ligne, for the publication of whose aphorisms and recollections she was responsible.[2] We share in this delight, and are almost inclined to like Mme. de Staël better because of it. But only Joseph de Maistre could show in *Les Soirées de St Pétersbourg* the essence of military style and morals, in a way which established a relationship between all dedicated lives, and showed that all manifestations of purity come from a sense of dedication and sacrament:

Le spectacle épouvantable du carnage n'endurcit pas le véritable guerrier. Au milieu du sang qu'il fait couler, il est humain comme l'épouse est chaste dans les transports de l'amour.

And only he could explain so pleasantly, a little further on in the *Soirées*, that it is love of liberty and love of humanity that may make a man reject popular revolutions and pacifist utopias, which are inhuman and only possible at the price of tyranny, and more cruel " wars to end war."

It is rather an echo of Bossuet that we hear in the early de Maistre of the *Considérations sur la France*. It is the belief in the providential mission of Charlemagne's monarchy. For de Maistre, it was the hand of Providence which had prevented the destruction of France, the country which had been given the mission of unifying Europe, not under a sceptre or a sword, but in Christian civilisation and liberty. This devotion to France—Joseph de Maistre was Piedmontese by citizenship, and if he had a second country it was Russia—this devotion was such

[1] Joseph de Maistre: *Quatre chapitres inédits sur la Russie.* Paris, 1859. The volume was edited by Admiral Count Robert de Maistre, who during his father's term of office at St Petersburg served as an officer under Czar Alexander I, and who, with his uncle General Xavier de Maistre, the author of *Voyage autour de ma chambre, La jeune Sibérienne,* etc., had an immense and intimate knowledge of the Empire of the Czars.

[2] Cf. M. Louis Witmer's most interesting study of the anti-revolutionary and anti-Napoleonic party in Europe: *Le Prince de Ligne, Frédéric de Gentz et Jean de Müller. Leur correspondance inédite.* Paris, 1925.

a constant factor in everything that he wrote,[1] from the *Considérations* in 1797 to *Du Pape*, composed at the time of the fall of Napoleon, that it is understandable that Friedrich von Schlegel, or Joseph Görres, reproached him for misunderstanding the Germanic *sacrum Imperium*, concerning which de Maistre was hardly less critical than Voltaire, and never far removed from the views of the author of *Essai sur les mœurs*, who sided with the traditional French concept of European primacy, but without the religious content and the significance of this concept.

Joseph de Maistre is the great lay Doctor of Christian Authority. He gave the various enemies of the Church a nostalgia for a supreme religious authority. From the queer sect of Saint-Simon, to the still queerer philosophical school of Auguste Comte, called " positivist," from Mazzini and his Young Europe down to Charles Maurras and his sect, this nostalgia for a spiritual authority, for a social theology without the Church, was to appear on every page, and in almost every manifestation of the coming century of secular sects. This applies even to the most highly organised and the most powerful of these sects, the only one among them to achieve material power, the Communist International of Moscow. Theoretically it even denies what the earlier sects had still affirmed—the primacy of the spiritual—and replaces it by a crude and rough materialism, apparently daring and intransigent, but in reality

[1] Much of de Maistre's work remained in fragments during his life-time, and the final picture of his intellectual evolution and a final analysis of his work in the light of his biography is a fairly recent achievement. The best contributions have been made by the Savoyard historian F. Vermale, who reconstructed his youth and early life in Chambéry and Turin; Georges Goyau: *La pensée religieuse de Joseph de Maistre*, Paris, 1921, whose study was based on material which had remained unpublished for a hundred years. For de Maistre's influence on German romantic thought, we are indebted to Hermann von Grauert's *Görres und de Maistre*, in the *Jahrbücher der Görres-Gesellschaft*, Köln, 1922; and Richard von Kralik's *Das Neunzehnte Jahrhundert*, in *Zeitgemässe Broschuren*, Frankfurt, 1905; and in the same author's analysis of the romantic period *Oesterreichische Geschichte*, Wien, 1913, p. 320 sq. On de Maistre's action in Russia, see the biography of Madame de Swetchine by Alfred de Falloux, 1860. C. Ostrogorsky: *Joseph de Maistre und seine Lehre von der höchsten Macht*, Helsinki, 1932; M. Jugie: *Joseph de Maistre et ·l'église greco-russe*, 1922, and the publications—in Russian—by M. Makoshin and M. Stepanov, under the auspices of the Russian Cultural Centre in Paris, 1937. See also Frederic Holdsworth: *Joseph de Maistre et l'Angleterre*, Paris, 1935. The most intuitive critical survey on de Maistre is to be found in Barbey d'Aurevilly's *Les Prophètes du Passé*, 1850. Among the serious and appreciative, although hostile, students of de Maistre's thought, the first place goes to Sainte-Beuve. Among the most recent studies, we may mention an analytical anthology with comments: *La politique expérimentale de Joseph de Maistre*, by M. Bernard de Vaulx, Paris, Fayard, 1940.

shameful and cowardly, calling itself " dialectical " to imply the independence of the spiritual element, which it otherwise denies. This usurpation of authority does not hesitate to condemn miscreants, brands " deviations " from the doctrine without ever stating what it is that sets that doctrine above the human level, and by what means that doctrine has been authentically transmitted or can possibly be proved.

We have already shown that, challenged by Voltaire's laughter, Joseph de Maistre drove the enemies of the Church into an attitude of ridiculous gravity and imitation. He it was whom even intelligent opponents like Sainte-Beuve tried to decry as a mind preoccupied with praise of the past, who made the clearest guess as to the future; we can be more sure of this than even Barbey d'Aurevilly was in 1850, when he first called him a prophet. His central thesis was that Man is essentially unfit to " create " anything, so that the attempt to create " new worlds," instead of accepting the order of Creation, can only lead to vast, grotesque and sanguinary scenes in future history. With a genuine love of Russia, and a long personal devotion to Alexander I, which was only too ready to overlook the well-known weaknesses of this sovereign, and his tendency to strange " illuminist " mysticism, de Maistre was perhaps the first man to foretell prophetically the dangers which might one day threaten Europe from this remote Empire of the North and the East. His correspondence with Russian friends, and his *Quatre chapitres inédits sur la Russie* show that he was full of these anxieties. It was not the simple political anxiety, inspired in Horace Walpole, in Joseph II and Kaunitz, by the size and resources of Russia, her expansive ambition and the dynastic instabilities which had often brought unscrupulous men and women to posts of command in St Petersburg; neither was it the anxiety which filled Metternich at the Vienna Congress, and again during the Greek War of Independence and during the various Polish crises, to combat which he tried, in the months preceding the *Cent Jours*, and often afterwards, to make Austria as much an ally of the West as of Russia, in order to be able to play the mediating—or the decisive—part one day in a conflict between East and West. Joseph de Maistre recognised in the penetration of Western ideas to Russia, and in the uncritical spirit in which Russia was ready to accept ideas from the West, a perspective which was frightening for discerning eyes:

Tout me porte à croire que la Russie n'est pas susceptible d'un gouvernement organisé comme les nôtres; et . . . si la nation, venant à comprendre nos perfides nouveautés, si le peuple était ébranlé et commençait, au lieu d'expéditions asiatiques, une révolution à l'européenne, je n'ai point expression à dire ce qu'on pourrait craindre:

Bella, horrida bella!

Et multo Nevam spumantem sanguine cerno.[1]

Within less than ten years after de Maistre's departure from Russia,[2] and only four years after his death, the " December conspiracy " disclosed to an astonished world the widespread presence in Russia of " our perfidious novelties "; young noblemen and Imperial officers who had won their promotion during the campaigns in Germany and France, in the last phase of the Napoleonic Wars, had dreamed in their secret societies of a future United States of all the Slavs, had taken the Pan-Slav oath[3] and sworn on their daggers, to the glory of the " Goddess of Reason," to build ports from Dalmatia to the Arctic Sea, and to unite and " liberate " all Slav peoples in Bohemia, Hungary and Transylvania, Moldavia, Wallachia and Servia! Metternich's nightmare, that German philosophy and Western modernism should prevail in Russia, rather than the conservative and Christian concept of Monarchy, which Russia held in common with Europe, was based on close knowledge of tendencies of this kind which were inherent in Russia's political system and in the whole trend of the Czarist tradition established by Peter the Great.[4]

One of the claims of Joseph de Maistre to the admiration of posterity is this: he was the first European who, more than half a century before Dostoievsky, visualised the prospect of a Godless Russia, and urged on the schismatic Empire the alternative which may yet come in the future—integration into the spiritual unity and authority of Christendom, instead of the degradation and catastrophe of Godlessness.

[1] Op. cit. (*Quatre chapitres*, etc.), p. 218.

[2] He left Russia in 1816, and after meeting Vicomte de Bonald for the first time in his life in Paris, returned to a post of no great importance, although it was of Cabinet rank, in Turin. His last years in St Petersburg were embittered by the conflict between Alexander I and the Holy See over the Church in Poland and the Jesuit province in the Russian Empire. This cooled his relations with the Czar. See Georges Goyau, *op. cit.*

[3] *La conspiration de Russie. Rapport de la Commission d'Enquête de St Pétersbourg à S. M. Nicholas I, Empereur de Russie*, Paris, 1826, p. 70. The general conclusion (p. 10) was that German ideas and German secret student societies had acted ever since 1813 on the minds of young Russian officers.

[4] In addition to the many references in Metternich's posthumous *Mémoires et Documents* (1880), see *Correspondance de Lebzeltern* (Austrian Ambassador in St Petersburg under Alexander I) published by the Imperial Russian Academy, St Petersburg, 1913.

5. THE PRIMACY OF POLITICS: FROM MONTESQUIEU TO BONALD

THE second most important thinker in the eighteenth century was, without any doubt, Montesquieu. The quintessence of Voltaire lay in the independence of morals from belief; Montesquieu's message was the primacy of politics over religious concerns. The author of *L'Esprit des Lois* was infinitely less hostile to Christianity than was Voltaire, he was even perhaps the most positive Christian amongst the outstanding writers of his century. He stated several times, in all sincerity, we feel, and not out of mere opportunism, that he preferred his own Catholic religion and that of his King to all others; he went so far as to engage in lengthy polemics with Pierre Beyle, the ex-Huguenot leader of a "natural" religion, which claimed that a perfect Christianity was incompatible with civic virtues and the interest of the State. In contrast to the witticisms of Voltaire, Montesquieu's humour and wit was never malicious, or inspired by hatred or bitterness; his aphoristic style is kindly and full of polish; the irony of the *Lettres Persanes* was not directed against sacred feelings.

Yet perhaps by reason of his greater moral seriousness and his more unselfish literary purpose—he was more concerned with objective truth than Voltaire ever was—the harm Montesquieu did was perhaps even greater than the harm Voltaire intended to do, and in fact accomplished.

Montesquieu saw the co-existence of various forms of religion in history. Some of them were more suitable in a Monarchy, others in a Republic. Social forms were largely a question of natural surroundings and climate. Even the desert could have a religion which was politically and socially suitable—for example, Islam. Political truth is relative; so, implicitly, is religious. The best form Liberty can take is one in which the three powers of the State, the executive, the judicial and the legislative, enjoy the greatest independence one from the other. Here again, more implicitly than explicitly, Montesquieu denied the unity of purpose in a governing power, the essential unity in diversity of social forms, the central significance of any revealed law or Scripture, the primacy of any Order over Liberty. The eighteenth century, still so near to Bossuet, interpreted the thesis of *L'Esprit des Lois* as a negation of that of the *Discours sur l'histoire universelle*.

L'Esprit des Lois was, of course, the great book of 1789 and of almost the whole Liberal school of the nineteenth century. The separation and the balance of the three powers within the State has been the profession of Faith of all moderate revolutionaries, from Madame de Staël and Benjamin Constant, via Guizot and Thiers, down to the recent constitution-makers of the Fourth Republic in France. Precisely because Montesquieu was sincere, and expressed in moderate terms his preference for Christian Monarchy, his theory was taken up even by the post-revolutionary and post-Napoleonic movements of Catholic revival—Lord Acton in England and Montalembert in France were both influenced by the ideal of a political and social " equilibrium." We can recognise fragments of Montesquieu's thought in the liberal-democratic half-truths of recent decades. In the name of a political theory of equilibrium, some people characterised Nazism as an " anti-progressive " reaction and Bolshevism as " dictatorship "—terms as politically adequate as would be the medical description of cancer as " indigestion," and tuberculosis as a " spring-cold "—and they postulated compromise between parties as the supreme political ideal. This supreme ideal of an " equilibrium " is, they say, only possible in a " Democracy," a vague term for a form of government which does not even claim to be right by any absolute standards, but only to be " tolerant " out of consideration for the counter-balance of an opposition party, possessing likewise a half-truth.

One may easily argue of course that Montesquieu was superior to the many belated and sometimes only half-conscious imitators of his thought. Texts to this effect could certainly be found in abundance, but this is not our concern here, and in any case such a defence of Montesquieu would not differ from any defence put forward by disciples of Machiavelli or Hegel, for example, in justification of the original thought of their master, which was in most cases superior to any latter-day interpretation of it. It is enough if we sum up Montesquieu as the thinker who taught the primacy of political expediency over absolute religious truth on society, who for the first time envisaged religious truth as subordinate to the pragmatic moral aims of government and society, and who judged governments and social systems according to an outward criterion of the formal legitimacy, intactness and inviolability of the respective sphere of each power.[1] Only much later, when Equality

---

[1] The best recent study of the intellectual and political atmosphere of Montesquieu's time and doctrine is *La crise de la conscience européenne au XVIIIe siècle* by Paul Hazard, professeur au Collège de France. Paris, 1930.

became a new idol, one which was unforeseen by Montesquieu
—to whom aristocratic, senatorial and parliamentarian governments were more familiar than real democracies—was this
" inviolability of the spheres of power " combined with the
" people's will " as the criterion of formal legitimacy; this
caused no little surprise and considerable embarrassment to
those followers of Montesquieu who belonged mostly to the
privileged political and social classes, and who were unaware
that there was anything in the traditions of their master's
thought which justified such doctrines.

In the great debate concerning Authority and Liberty which
we have followed throughout the ages, until it reached its most
acute stage in the eighteenth and nineteenth centuries,
Vicomte de Bonald[1] was the counterpart of Montesquieu.

Bonald had more of a systematic, and even scholastic, mind
than Joseph de Maistre. Writing in a style which was not less
elegant than the latter's, he resisted all temptation to take his
opponent by surprise and deal the last stroke with some brilliant
paradox, which, final as it might be, would be questioned on
second thoughts by the defeated enemy. The author of the
Soirées de St Pétersbourg preferred the liveliness of the Platonic
form, being a master of dialogue. The author of the *Théorie du
pouvoir*[2] was more of a pure Aristotelian. De Maistre gave the
impression that he greatly enjoyed scoring over an opponent.
Bonald hits out almost accidentally, although he did it
frequently enough, at the anglophile school of Benjamin
Constant and Mme. de Staël, at Voltaire, Rousseau and
Montesquieu, at Locke and Kant, *si tristement célèbre*. Writing
in exile at Heidelberg, or in his provincial retreat during the
time of Napoleon (who would have much preferred to see this
Doctor of Authority serve him, " the restorer of Order and
Religion," instead of persevering in a discreet but indomitable
opposition), his starting point was naturally enough the

[1] We use his name thus, as he expressly disapproved, in *Considérations sur la
noblesse* and in *La théorie du pouvoir*, of the habit of putting Christian names instead
of titles before the family names of French noblemen, and because Joseph de
Maistre, himself less of a purist, in deference to his friend's insistence on this point,
requested a correspondent of his to write " Vicomte de Bonald," " M. de Bonald,"
or simply " Bonald," but never " de Bonald." The usual reference to the author
of the *Soirées de St Pétersbourg* as " Joseph de Maistre " and not " Comte de
Maistre " is to be explained by the fact that the title belonged also to his brother
Xavier de Maistre, who was hardly less known in the literature of his time.

[2] Practically speaking, he wrote one book only. The *Essai analytique sur les lois
naturelles* ; the *Intérêt général de l'Europe, Du divorce au XIXe siècle* and his countless
shorter essays, maxims, aphorisms and fragments are mere extensions and applica-
tions of, or additions to, his *Théorie du pouvoir*.

contemporary French and European scene. Yet, going far beyond the historical context of his time and country, he aimed at stating absolute truth in theology and philosophy, at making definitions which would hold good for all time.

Bonald gave a complete and full reply to almost every proposition which was part of the intellectual currency of the eighteenth century. The sensualist psychology of Condillac, the " natural man " of Rousseau, Locke's and Diderot's theory of knowledge which comes through the experience of the senses, were all answered by his monumental theory concerning language. He said that human language is unable to express, and is not meant to express, anything that is not either an image or an idea. The first proof of religious truth is the existence of the idea, that is of the word " God " in every human language. History is the evolution from the image to the idea, a transition of mankind from childhood to maturity:

Un enfant a des images avant d'avoir des idées; ainsi un peuple cultive son imagination avant de développer sa raison. Ainsi dans l'univers même, la société des images ou des figures, le judaisme, a précédé la société des idées, ou le christianisme, qui adore l'Être suprême en esprit et en vérité.[1]

Instead of Montesquieu's theory of equilibrium through the separation of powers, Bonald propounded the unity of power, the unity of purpose seen in nature, because *one* mind has created nature and established its laws, which are gradually and progressively revealed to Man. We see a constantly recurring motive in all the political theorising of Bonald, a three-fold division, as in Montesquieu, but formulated differently and re-stated in order to establish a different conclusion. According to him, there is a singleness of purpose in society: Power is given for the preservation of religion and morals and of the natural law, i.e. for the preservation of identity to which every species in Nature tends. Judicial and executive power provide the means for this preservation, and fight the internal and the external enemy, which are obstacles to preservation. Thus, kings rule with the help of two classes, both of which are symbolised by the Sword—the Sword of Justice and the Sword of defence—although usually they are referred to as the *noblesse de robe* and the *noblesse d'épée*. In the spiritual society, the Church, power is transmitted to a spiritual successor. In the natural society, the State, power is transmitted in natural succession from father to son. The social unit is the family, not

[1] *Essai analytique sur les lois naturelles*, p. 221 in the first edition of 1800.

the individual. The liberties people really care about are not such things as the liberty of the Press, or the liberty of a jury, for few people publish anything, and few ever have to appear before a jury; but the liberty to preserve, in the form of safe property, the fruit of a family achievement, the liberty of a family to rise to a higher status, and the liberty to preserve this status for future generations.

It is fairly usual to identify Revolution with optimism, and post-revolutionary tendencies—the romantic period—as the reaction of pessimism, although they still professed a " religious attachment to Liberty."[1]   The Italian historian Guglielmo Ferrero did much to spread this judgement in his numerous essays on the post-revolutionary era; he later revised it in his book *Bonaparte in Italy*, in which he classified the European parties into " groups of violence " and " groups of fear."

Reading Bonald's *Essai analytique*, we see that progressive optimism was not in the least absent from the anti-revolutionary party. He greets the new century with great hope, as one in which as much progress in the knowledge of the laws governing society will be made as the eighteenth century made in the knowledge of the laws governing nature. The law of society, he declares, is still in its infancy, just as religion was in the early centuries which saw the conversion of the Barbarian. The appeal for the unity of Europe is made by the anti-revolutionary party, not only in the writings of Bonald and Joseph de Maistre (in his *Essai sur le principe générateur des institutions humaines*, 1814) but also in the whole of the literature which prepared the way for, or commented upon, the Vienna Congress—Friedrich von Gentz, Adam Müller, Johannes von Müller, Friedrich von Schlegel, Novalis—all of whom, in their respective countries, looked for some principle to replace Spinoza's and Montesquieu's theories concerning the " balance " and the " equilibrium " of power; a principle which it was impossible to maintain in Schlegel's view[2] on account of the British possessions in Asia, and the extent of the Russian Empire the very vastness of which precludes any possibility of balance.

But we have to note a more radical change in European political thought, which was due mainly to Bonald—the revaluation of history as the science of social law and as the principal weapon in apologetics and religious controversy.

[1] Benedetto Croce: *Storia de l'Europa nel decimonono secolo*, Bari, 1932. See especially the introductory chapter.
[2] See his *Lectures on the Philosophy of History*, which we have already mentioned.

The immense change in the European outlook and in the
modern historical sense, which pervades the artistic imagination with Chateaubriand, Walter Scott, the young Victor Hugo,
Schiller, the German romantics, and Manzoni in Italy, is connected with the religious thought of the post-revolutionary era
as exemplified in Bonald. Others had defended the religion of
man: he would defend the religion of society; they had
proved religion by religion, but he intends to prove it by
history. Metaphysics is a science of *realities*; *et si certains
écrivains qui ont traité de l'être sont vagues et obscurs . . . c'est qu'ils
ont voulu expliquer l'être pensant par l'être pensant, au lieu de l'expliquer
par l'être parlant, qui est son expression et son image.*

Bonald was the reply to Montesquieu as was de Maistre to
Voltaire. As we have already pointed out, Montesquieu was
the man whose intellectual influence was the least intentionally
hostile to the Church in the eighteenth century. We find both
religious and spiritual truth in him, disguised as irony, or even
cynicism. When Montesquieu permitted himself such jokes as
a defence of monogamy on sensual grounds, saying that the
recollection of the by-gone youthful charm of women always
acted as an attraction for husbands, he was still defending—in
a curious manner—religious and social truth in the institution
of marriage. When he justified slavery on the ground that the
Africans are so stupid as to prefer shining glass to shining
diamonds, *puis, ils ont le nez tellement écrasé qu'il est presque impossible de les plaindre*, he was stating the truth which Pascal never
tired of demonstrating by all possible means: the truth concerning the extreme relativity and unreliability of every merely
human judgement, one which Pascal himself had to wrap up
in some cynical disguise. Bonald has much of Montesquieu's
manner; we cannot help thinking of Montesquieu when we
read Bonald's explanation of the English habit of eating raw
meat, and the English legal institution of divorce, as the two
signs of the raw and barbaric origin of this island people. But
how much more deeply he goes into any subject proposed by
Montesquieu for meditation, and how sternly he refuses to stop
at any half-truth! Yet it was only a part of Bonald's achievement to reply to Montesquieu; of greater importance in his
century was his discovery of a new field of historical and social
theology. This historical argument in theology received its full
elaboration in the work of Cardinal Newman, and still dominates a new Catholic spirituality, with Chesterton, Hilaire
Belloc and Christopher Dawson in England, Theodor Haecker

in Germany, Jacques Maritain and Étienne Gilson and Jean Guitton in France.[1]

Bonald stands for the transition from the *individualist* thought of the eighteenth century to the *social* thought of the nineteenth. It is sufficient to recall our last textual quotation from his *Théorie du pouvoir* to show how conscious he was of a *transition* period in human thought, the transition from individual to social religion, from rational to historical theology. We may also recall Metternich's frequent characterisation of his time as a " transition " period, Metternich who was almost the only statesman who understood Bonald's philosophy (and almost the only statesman of his time worthy of the name, in the opinion of Bonald's enthusiastic pupil, Honoré de Balzac). Metternich stood consciously at the close of an epoch, and was heroically determined to face the end of his world. In his view, the Primacy of Order was going to prevail[2] after the chaos which would separate the Old Europe from the New, and he wished he could have been born round about 1900 or later, so that he could have helped the new Europe come into being, instead of burying the old one.

Just as the Roman Emperor Marcus Aurelius, who wrote Greek in the same city of Vienna, was the last word of Classic Hellenism, the Imperial Chancellor of Austria, who wrote mostly in French, was the last great word of baroque, French-speaking, monarchical Europe. But as the ancient Greek wisdom expressed itself in melancholy, as befitted wise men, and was conquered by Christian hope, the last great word of monarchical Europe, Bonald or Metternich, gave a message not of melancholy, but of a transition towards an ultimate hope. We enter this period of transition from a rational to a historical and social theology, as we said, in the nineteenth century. Prophets in the Old Testament were men who announced a

---

[1] We allude here more particularly to Theodor Haecker's epilogue to a German translation of Cardinal Newman's *The Grammar of Assent*, written in 1921, to the *Rédemption du Temps* of Jacques Maritain and to Jean Guitton's comments on Newman's historical theology in *La justification du temps*.

[2] In his political testament (*Mémoires et Documents*, Vol. VII, p. 640) he writes —in French, which we prefer to keep, because it is Metternich's grand style—*Le mot de liberté n'a pas pour moi la valeur d'un point de départ, mais celle d'un point d'arrivée réel. C'est le mot d'ordre qui désigne le point de départ. Ce n'est que sur l'idée d'ordre que peut reposer l'idée de liberté* (sic!). *Sans la base de l'ordre, l'aspiration à la liberté n'est que l'effort d'un parti quelconque dans le but qu'il poursuit.*

Dans l'application à la vie positive, cette aspiration se traduira inévitablement par la tyrannie. À toutes les époques, dans toutes les situations, j'ai été un homme d'ordre, et j'ai toujours visé à l'établissement de la liberté véritable et non d'une liberté mensongère. La tyrannie, quelle qu'elle soit, a toujours été pour moi synonyme de la folie pure.

transition in time; transition always moves towards a new aspect of man's knowledge of God.

What was Bonald's concept of " Society " ? What does his repeated emphasis on the " social " and " historical " truth really mean ? He most certainly does not mean by " social law " the primacy of material concerns, as our time understands the term, led astray by a century of " material " Socialism, which even some emotional Catholic, or at any rate, Christian thought is ready to endorse and accept, confusing it with the primacy of charity. Neither does he mean by his notion of " historical situation " the distorted materialist sophistry of a variable relativity, determined by the temporary context of " economic conditions." He means the primacy of Order, such as we have tried to define it in these pages; the framework of real Liberty, that stability of consecrated Order, which for him was the only safeguard against the tyranny which the rule of individual judgement inevitably entails, for individual judgement is the *least* safe of foundations, and can only maintain its rule by violent means.

Society in Bonald's thought means first and foremost the family, " domestic society," of which God Himself was the legislator. The nations are extended domestic societies, i.e. they are " public societies." The international and European order is, or should be, a Society of Nations. The fundamental principle of association in all these phases is the social law, the law of God for the family, for the Church and for the nation.

History for Bonald is the science of the varying forms of an unalterable essence. His study of History is a prophetic one, a study of the transition from one stage of our knowledge of God to the next one, this new stage always being in his view a higher stage. There is a Progress. The word belongs to our vocabulary, therefore only Christians can understand the true meaning of the word. Only Christian society has known progress; non-Christian empires, at any rate before their contact with Christendom, only knew stability, so that the Muslim East presents a picture of arrested progress to all European observers.

With this summary of Bonald's thought, our earlier analysis of Joseph de Maistre, and the above—to our mind almost inevitable—comment on progress, we hope we have made it clear that such common-place descriptions as " reaction," " traditionalism," etc., are quite out of place in any characterisation of Bonald and Joseph de Maistre, who was fully aware of the truth that *si la Providence efface, c'est pour écrire*. Even a truly great mystic mind such as Léon Bloy could be so mistaken as to see " mere " traditionalism, unaware of God's plan to change the face of the world,[1] in the *Soirées de St Pétersbourg*, and in both de Maistre and Bonald to hear only *l'oraison funèbre de l'Europe civilisée*.[2]

Events inside the Church, however, were responsible for this widespread misunderstanding of the two foremost thinkers of the era of the French Revolution, which only a very close study of both Bonald and Joseph de Maistre can dispel. When on the death of Pope Gregory XVI in 1846, Cardinal Mastai Ferretti succeeded to the Papal throne under the style of Pope Pius IX, it seemed that the Catholic-Liberal school of thought would come into the forefront of Catholic action all over Europe.[3] These Catholic Liberals in France were, roughly speaking, the new variation of Gallicanism, as is shown by the support given them by members of the hierarchy known to have Gallican leanings—Mgr. Sibour, for instance, and Mgr. Dupanloup. Gallicanism had its counterpart in Germany under Joseph II, and derived new strength in the Napoleonic period under the régime of the Confederation of the Rhine and its Chancellor, Archbishop Dalberg. It also had its counterpart in England in the circle of Lord Acton—a nephew of Mgr. Dalberg, which is a biographical detail worth noting.

Did Pope Pius IX disapprove of the intransigent views expressed in Joseph de Maistre's *Du Pape* ? Did he ever disapprove of the same author's sharp criticisms (and Bonald's also) of individual judgement as the basis of modern political institutions ? There is not the slightest hint to this effect in any of his pronouncements. What he tried to achieve by the " Liberal " initiatives of his early years was the greater independence of the Papal See from European Powers, and what he achieved in his later period by the Bull of Infallibility (opposed by the same groups in 1869 who had hailed the new policy in 1846—by Montalembert and his friends) was a

---

[1] Léon Bloy: *Le Désespéré*. Ch. XLV.

[2] Léon Bloy: *Les dernières colonnes de l'Eglise* (essays, or rather polemics, against K. J. Huysmans, F. Brunetière, Paul Bourget, etc.).

[3] It had previously been discredited by the apostasy of Lamennais, though it was later strengthened by the prestige of the Dominican Fr. Lacordaire (a priest of holy zeal and ascetic spirituality, but at the same time a surprisingly conciliatory defender of the Faith), by the attractive oratory of Montalembert, and by the appearance in his circle of such a pure and zealous lay apostle as Frédéric Ozanam, the Catholic scholar and philosopher of the Romantic movement.

strengthening of the central power of the Papacy over the Universal Church. A monarch whose means of government were essentially spiritual, Pius IX was satisfied by the definition of this central power, and showed wise restraint and moderation in the exercise of it, as his successors have done ever since.

A whole generation after Napoleon's fall believed in the imminent conflict between the two victorious powers, both of whom were partly extra-European: Russia and Britain. Metternich's personal prestige in St Petersburg was one of the few obstacles to Russia's westward drive; Prussia's and Austria's reluctance to help Russia in any conflict (except in simple police operations against revolutionary upheavals, where the monarchical principle was at stake) was pointed out by Frederick von Gentz[1] as the chief factor delaying a conflict between East and West. Such a conflict Fichte had already foretold in 1814,[2] and its possibility was largely responsible for the desire of Emperor Francis I and Metternich to strengthen the Kingdom of Hungary by modernising reforms. With Metternich an old man, and the romantic-theocratic atmosphere which prevailed in Berlin since the accession in 1840 of Frederick-William IV (whom Europe believed to be a simple satellite of his brother-in-law Nicholas I of Russia), the conflict between East and West was more in the air than ever. Not wishing to be involved by Austrian protection of Italy on the side of schismatic and Muscovite concept of Imperial theocracy, not wishing either to rely on the protection of Protestant England and its Liberal and Radical admirers in Italy, the Papacy took the lead in the action to achieve Italian unity and independence. Two contemporary authors explain the full European background to this Papal policy, both of them Spaniards, Jaime Balmes and Donoso Cortés. Both were more inclined towards a pro-French, than to the pro-British tendency which prevailed over their country; for ever since the help given to Spain by Wellington against Napoleon, various British Foreign Ministers, and especially Lord Palmerston, had tried to bring that nation into the British orbit, through the influence of the *Exaltados* of the constitutional party. Both Balmes and Donoso believed in the concept of a great continental system of alliance to counterbalance the might both

---

[1] *Aus dem Nachlasse von F. v. Gentz.* Edited by General Count Prokesch-Osten. Wien, Leipzig, 1867. Vol. I, p. 206 seq.

[2] In his *Vermichtniss.*

of Britain and Russia,[1] and young as they were, they already had some experience of the minor revolutions which the *Exaltados'* admiration for British institutions and the British party-system had brought to Spain ever since the Cadiz constitution of 1812.[2]

With Balmes and Donoso, the leadership of Catholic thought might have passed from France to Spain, the country which had once led the way, before the *grand siècle*. A sign of the times, the stronger and the more original though not the more systematic of the two thinkers of the early years of Pius IX's reign was not the priest and theologian Balmes, but the secular historian and political philosopher, Donoso Cortés; this was the century of secular thinkers and of the secular concerns of the Church.

This promising new Spanish period of European Catholic thought had no time to mature. Balmes died at the early age of thirty-eight during the first phase of the European Revolution of 1848; Donoso lived only to his forty-fourth year, the last five years of his life being spent watching the European Revolution and its consequences from his diplomatic posts in Berlin and Paris. He lived to see that Revolution which was French no longer, but European in extent, and which we can now see was the first step towards the World Revolution which began with the 1914-1918 war, and in which we live today. He lived to regret much of his own earlier writing, and to hear Louis Veuillot refer to him as the future head of a new European party, as the new leader of secular spirituality. He also lived to suffer from the attacks of the neo-Gallican, Liberal-Catholic tendencies represented by Mgr. Dupanloup and a few members of the French hierarchy, but not long enough to see Rome set her final approval to his thought, or to hear Barbey d'Aurevilly call him " the third lay father of the Church "—Joseph de Maistre and Bonald being the first and second. Donoso's speeches and his thought provided melancholy consolation for Metternich after his fall.[3]

[1] A concept that was much discussed, and which owed its influence (in the opinion of many observers) to the personal rapprochement between Metternich and the French Prime Minister Guizot. Marx and Engels commented on it in the *Communist Manifesto* as the New Holy Alliance between the Pope, Metternich and Guizot against Communism, the mutual enemy.

[2] That ideological banner of Spanish military revolts, and even of the revolutionary movement in Italy, which began in Naples in 1820, where Spanish influence was still uppermost.

[3] See the present writer's *Metternich and Donoso Cortés—Christian and Conservative Thought in the European Revolution, Dublin Review,* No. 444, 1948, and *A Prophet of Europe's Disasters—Juan Donoso Cortés, The Month,* May 1947.

A deeper mystical, more passionate and dramatic version of Joseph de Maistre's and Bonald's thought began in France with Donoso Cortés, on the morrow of the European Revolution. Donoso sensed what Bonald and de Maistre had not yet sensed: the profound and universal cultural crisis of Europe—the great theme which Burckhardt and Nietzsche took up a little later—that deepening crisis which was promoted (so to say) by natural progress, the natural progress of mass movements of religious aberration. This, in Donoso's vision, could ultimately be arrested only by the triumph of supernatural over natural force; for the essence of history, according to him, is not the natural triumph of evil over good, but the supernatural triumph of good over evil.

6. THE PRIMACY OF IMAGINATION: FROM DIDEROT TO BARBEY D'AUREVILLY — THE PRIMACY OF EMOTION: FROM ROUSSEAU TO BLOY AND PÉGUY

FRANCE was still the foremost theatre of the European Revolution in the sense that here the social conflict predominated, whereas in other countries the principal element of the Revolution seemed to lie in the various national aspirations. The primacy of politics and of moral liberties, both of which were proposed by Montesquieu and Voltaire, seemed to come to an end. The dominating problem was henceforth to be the individual and society. Bonald and de Maistre saw a world which reasoned ill, erring in matters of religion, and removing itself from truth and law. Veuillot now saw a world which was ugly and decrepit in its self-sufficiency, and its vanity; his biting, satirical pages in *Les Odeurs de Paris* make Flaubert's aching sensitiveness, offended by bourgeois taste, and Baudelaire's despair at the decomposition of every beauty in modern life, appear as almost tame reactions to the social reality.

Bonald and Joseph de Maistre defended the Papacy and the Monarchy against the " party of the philosophers," and against the new institutions which Catholic Liberals tried to baptise from inside, but at the risk of some compromise with their non-Catholic theoretical and philosophical foundations. Barbey d'Aurevilly saw the Revolution when it had advanced a stage further; his main concern—and the concern of Bloy and Péguy

after him—was the defence, not of old and consecrated institutions against new and man-made ones, lacking any authority
for their basis or support, but the defence of spiritual truth and
spiritual beauty against the materialistic ugliness of the masses,
which was promoted by intellectual conceit and intellectual
demagogy. Not that either Veuillot or Barbey d'Aurevilly, any
more than Bloy or Péguy after them, would ever have been
hostile to the " masses," or insensitive to the suffering of the
poor. There are plenty of signs to the contrary. Nobody in the
nineteenth century exalted the ideal of simplicity, or the virtue
of humble work, higher than did Louis Veuillot in *Les Libres-
Penseurs*; nobody imposed on himself the duty of active service
in the cause of the poor more rigorously than Veuillot's
master, Donoso Cortés.

Not in the sharpest polemical prose of Barbey d'Aurevilly
was charity ever absent, even towards opponents; and with
this went humanity and compassion for the multitude. Léon
Bloy had no aristocratic contempt for the weak and the poor;
on the contrary, his contempt was reserved wholly for the rich,
and he never tired of prophesying the victory of the poor,
although there was all the difference in the world in his eyes
between the victory of the poor and the " suppression of
poverty," which is the Socialist ideal—this debasement of man
to an artificial, inhuman and impersonal life. If Léon Bloy
disliked the Republic, it was because the republics of antiquity
were founded by slave-owners, while the " Kingdom " was the
promise given to the poor; because the poor delighted in
Christ the King, who stood above mankind and did not govern
a republic of equals. Finally, more than any other French or
even European poet, Péguy has the child-like simplicity and
sincerity of the hard-working and patient people.

There is a world of difference between the people and the
" masses," and souls devoted to the people are all united, however much they differ in other things, in their disgust at the
" masses," an ugly word for an uglier thing. The people are
composed of men and women who have souls, of children who
have hearts, the masses are a dead weight driven on by traffickers
in murdered souls:

*Ils ont voulu bannir Dieu et ressusciter César. C'est à quoi ils travail-
lent et ils sont en train de réussir. Déjà ils ne disent plus: Gloire à
Dieu, et déjà il n'y a plus de paix. Ils ont diminué le nombre des
hommes de bonne volonté, la bonne volonté a diminué avec l'intelligence
de la vérité parmi ceux qui ont encore la vérité, et il n'y a plus de gloire*

ni de paix pour personne. Par un enchaînement formidable de bassesse et d'erreur, les peuples méprisent, haïssent et obéissent, formant mille désirs sauvages de briser le joug et de se venger. Ils se vengeront, mais ils ne briseront pas le joug, et plus ils le secoueront, plus il sera ignoble et dur.[1]

Louis Veuillot commented in these terms on the third revolution he had seen, that of the Paris Commune of 1871; this picture largely summarises the attitude of the great Catholic polemical writers who bring the last century to an end and usher in the present one.

We have seen the reply which Catholic thought gave to Voltaire's paradoxical moralism in Joseph de Maistre. We have seen also the full Catholic social and political theory which Bonald stated in reply to Montesquieu. Now we come to the third part of the dialogue between the eighteenth and the nineteenth centuries, that dialogue between Authority and Liberty which ever since the Middle Ages has been present in the Western conscience. This third and final part extends from the European Revolution to the First World War, which in turn began the World Revolution. The subject of the debate is now the individual and the world. Diderot gave his opinion on this subject as a neo-stoic, and worked out his argument in particular in a memorable discussion with a neo-cynic, *Le neveu de Rameau*, Goethe's favourite French masterpiece. It is exactly the same topic on which the stoics and the cynics of antiquity argued. The world, they said, makes all true sensibilities suffer. Diderot advised that moral principles should be elevated to a level higher than the world, he wanted us to give a fine example of principles, of a higher taste, of a sterner criticism of the profane world, and in this way he inaugurated a criticism of art and literature which was in itself literature, an art which was sometimes higher and more inventive than imaginative art—an art of which there have been many masters since Diderot, Sainte-Beuve being the foremost. In other words, Diderot postulated the stoic ideal of what we might call intellectual aristocracy, an ideal which greatly appealed to Goethe and attached him to Diderot more than to any of the other French authors of his youth. The " three Musketeers " were, as we know, four, and so were the three " masters of the European mind " in the eighteenth century. Diderot has a shadowy existence compared with the trio Voltaire, Montesquieu and Rousseau, and on account of his haughty artistic and

[1] Louis Veuillot: *Paris pendant les deux sièges en 1870-1871*. Vol. II, ch. xcviii, p. 23.

scientific pedantry, was less popular in his sensual age than
Voltaire with his superficial brilliance, Montesquieu with his
irony and Rousseau with his sentimental emotion.

In reply to Diderot, and his aesthetic descendants—Sainte-
Beuve, Flaubert, the brothers Goncourt and others—Barbey
d'Aurevilly made havoc of the aesthetic ideals of pedants. He
showed that Judgement in the name of eternal law, rather than
an endless comparison of relativities, is the key to true art;
that true art, like true History above all, was a social responsibility. It is not an individual fantasy, or a pastime for the
bored, or an emotional consolation for the over-sensitive. It
is a task for the manly and the brave, and for them alone. It is
a defence of Order for the sake of true Liberty. True art is
Justice, which despite the frequent verbal violences and the
unrestrained personal aversions, was the essence of Barbey
d'Aurevilly's immense critical work, collected in over thirty
volumes, *Les oeuvres et les hommes*. True art and true history mean
judgement in the light of Eternity, and only one light has ever
been cast on Eternity which was visible to human eyes. Barbey
d'Aurevilly called himself the *sagittaire* of his century, and still
near the preceding one in time, he replied to the eighteenth
century by shooting his arrows at it:

*Ce temps d'anarchie si universelle que le désordre passait dans la
physiologie, faisant de Gustave III de Suède homme-femme et de
Catherine femme-homme.*[1]

Style is judgement, art is justice, history is a manifestation of
public conscience. This theme of Barbey d'Aurevilly was to be
elaborated and summed up in a very concise version in Ernest
Hello's truly monumental study on *Le Style*.

While Barbey d'Aurevilly demolished affectation and
pedantry, Louis Veuillot in the same generation was making
havoc of the solemn pose of " stoic virtue," of the rhetorics of
the politicians (" moderate," " understanding," " modern-
minded," Catholics not excepted!), and of the learned common-
places of all parties. Less of an artist than either Barbey d'Aurevilly or Léon Bloy, he was not less vigorous as a fighter. Vain
are all the virtues, he showed, in which humility plays no part,
and vain is all the learning that has any other motive than the
charitable desire to teach those who have no knowledge.
Between them, Barbey d'Aurevilly and Veuillot defeated
presumption and pedantry.

But the virtuous neo-cynicism of emotional romance was to

[1] *Les oeuvres et les hommes. De l'histoire*, p. 333 of the first edition (1875).

be defeated by the poets, and by them alone. The isolation, the suffering which the hardness of this world inflicts upon the sensitive man, the suffering which comes from the violence of the senses, the hell-on-earth of poverty and loneliness—all these things Rousseau showed in a self-indulgent and a self-pitying way, to prove that man is intrinsically better than the society which surrounds him. At first hearing, nothing seems to be wrong with the proposition. Man has a soul, society has not. The incorruptible, divine substance of the soul was given to Man, the image of God, and not to society, to which only the Law was given. A whole life, noted down day by day, with humility, with humour, with outbursts of savage indignation and then again with overwhelming love—Léon Bloy's life—was needed to show not the abstract and the rational, but the vital and existential proof of the falsity of a proposition which had at first sounded plausible and seductive, and which has in fact seduced the world.

The immortal soul belongs to Man alone. But Man has a Creator, who gave him liberty within His order, and within His order alone. He suffers because God, in His moment of human Liberty, chose to suffer on the Cross, and because—and this is a thought so difficult to understand that it has separated the Muslim world from Christendom, probably until the end of History—He participates fully in human suffering. Léon Bloy interpreted his sufferings as a call from God to him to "conquer the world," to defeat worldliness. His Catholic spirituality was of the militant sort. This volunteer of 1870 never ceased to have a warrior's soul. Nothing is further removed from him than a Catholic spirituality of submission to an unpleasant world, as taught by Claudel or Mauriac, and while his polemics were direct and personal (and often coarse, absurd or unjust, the very opposite of what Barbey d'Aurevilly always strove to be) he was in the last resort infinitely more charitable in his indignations than writers who are satisfied with the mild observation of meanness and egotism, and the bestowing of Catholic consolation on weak souls. In spiritual as in physical suffering, the knife is often better than doubtful pills, coated with chocolate. Perhaps Léon Bloy dismissed too summarily the psychological approach to full and ultimate spiritual truth seen in Henri Bergson; perhaps, after helping Jacques Maritain towards conversion,[1] he was too impatient to

[1] See Madame Raissa Maritain's *Les Grandes amitiés*, 1946; Jacques Maritain: *Léon Bloy*, 1927; and the full and detailed biographical notes of M. Joseph Bollery in the first analytical edition of Léon Bloy's *Oeuvres complètes*, 1948-49.

see all " Bergsonians " travel along the same road—and as we now know, he did not guess what the final great gesture of Bergson's thought and life was to be. He ought perhaps to have shown more patience and humility towards a noble and generous Christian like Albert de Mun, who with the Austrians Vogel-sang and Prince Aloys Liechtenstein began the Christian Social movement in the 1890's. He should have made a better attempt to understand the thought of Pope Leo XIII and *Rerum Novarum*, and he should perhaps have foreseen the high spirituality of Don Luigi Sturzo, Canon Cardijn and so many others, out of which would grow, like a new triumph of Christ, the social apostolate of the Church in an industrial society; perhaps he should have done all this instead of persevering in his endless mourning for the Salic Monarchy, destroyed, as he never ceased to reiterate, by God's wrath at the sins of kings. It may be that this hagiographer of the highest grace dwelt too long on the literary vanities of a world of mediocrity, and wasted time which he might otherwise have spent saying things that only he could say, on the saints of his own time in France—St Jean-Baptiste Vianney, the Curé d'Ars, on Chaminade and the *Société de Marie*, on Blessed Joseph Liebermann and his aposto-late of the Holy Ghost in Africa, on the life of Père Foucauld and the White Fathers of the Desert.

The gravest and most frequent of his errors might have been that he altogether misunderstood the essence of religious peace in the secular order (as it is best defined by Friedrich von Schlegel) and this arch-enemy of modern Democracy com-pletely failed to see how much nearer religious peace—counting mankind as spiritual units rather than as isolated individuals—was to perfect social wisdom, than was the individualistic, soul-less and numerical " representation," which, as we have since seen in Germany and elsewhere, can only promote the domina-tion of those units which are numerically and materially the strongest. Differing from Joseph de Maistre and Bonald, Balzac and Barbey d'Aurevilly, who were concerned to save society, since the individual was condemned by fallen human nature, he perhaps abandoned hope for society altogether, and was concerned only for the salvation of the individual soul, a path which once misled many into Protestantism or Jansenism.

Still, if we feel bound to register all these possible exceptions, without examining them in detail, we are happy to record the fact that chosen souls and hearts in our own days begin to understand Léon Bloy; they quite rightly prefer to be overwhelmed and over-awed by him, rather than to approach him by critical analysis, adequate enough for the spiritual artistry of Mauriac or Claudel, and perhaps the right approach to the passionate emotionalism of Georges Bernanos, but not the means of grasping the essence of Léon Bloy. The *Thankless Beggar* never wrote to please, to convince, or even to act. He wrote in tears, to move others to tears, and he still moves us.

We may dismiss the absurdities of his imagination, when they occurred in the wrong place; we may miss the humble sense of justice which we find in Barbey d'Aurevilly, or the immaculate elegance and the clear intelligence which reached out to the supernatural in Joseph de Maistre, Bonald and Donoso Cortés; yet it is in Léon Bloy that we find the prophetic thunder of Judgement Day. Living in a conceited and prosperous world, he saw this world on the eve of the Apocalypse. In a world of psychological curiosities, he could find the answer only in eschatology. With the great geologist Pierre Termier, he saw the full discovery of the physics and geography of the earth as the approaching fullness of time, with its urgent alternative of Grace or Doom, unknown to the ages of indifference. The Dreyfus affair was all that was needed to make him predict the devastating hatred and persecution which would be the lot of those Gentiles who were united in soul to the celestial Jerusalem, following upon the hatred and persecution which had fallen upon the Jews, the seed of Abraham. Of all those who, during a hundred years of " emancipated " Jewry, spoke and wrote on this question, Léon Bloy (and young Charles Péguy, as he then was at the time of the Dreyfus case) knew full well what was at stake in this controversy. For seven generations the sins of the fathers will be visited upon the heads of the sons, and for a thousand generations true love of God will be rewarded, as we know from Genesis. The spectacle of the material prosperity and the success of an apostate Jewry is hateful enough to God. But infinitely more hateful to Him is the envy of that success felt by Christians who desecrate the name they bear, and in their hatred for Abraham's seed deny the spirit transmitted through the seed of Abraham. The rest is clamour: the clamour of Lenin and Trotsky in 1917, the clamour of Hitler in 1933. A deafening, horrid, poisonous, unspeakable clamour, from which our generation seeks refuge in the spirituality of Max Picard's *Welt des Schweigens*. The clamour of horrid strident voices and desecrated words, which still rages despite the silence which follows upon massacres and exhausting famines.

The prophetic word on the eve of all this horror was said by Léon Bloy, Charles Péguy, and by at least two Germans who probably never knew either and were certainly unknown to them: Theodor Haecker and the Austrian Karl Kraus. Sovereign emotion, this poetic religion set up by the late eighteenth and early nineteenth century, came to its plenitude with these two Frenchmen and the two Germans, with a recall to God, the Word that was in the beginning. All that followers of the old sovereign emotion could describe after the First World War was a confession of failure, movingly told by André Gide, and differently by Paul Claudel—by him in avowed submission and with the right conclusion, although still with a remnant of vanity, and regret for out-moded forms.

Bloy, Péguy, Haecker, Kraus—these names mean the effort to create new forms in the two principal peoples of the Continent. It is the effort of a language unalterably personal, radically untranslatable and not for one moment utilitarian, once it is spoken in the personally-felt presence of God. The association of thought and word leads to such a complete expression of the thought, that nothing is left unsaid and nothing is left unexplored. They thirst for the spirit in its entirety. Total are the means of possessing the earth, total the means of destruction, and only the total Spirit can save the world and even the human person. It is from this perspective of the total dangers and the total hopes of consolation, that we survey the great debate between Authority and Liberty, between the individual and society, which is as old as the world.

To put the truth concerning this great debate into writing, God gave the written Law on Mount Sinai, and His prophets showed the writing on the wall. To demonstrate it fully, God gave His only Son. The long and laborious effort of the men of the West to understand it received its Crown, the Crown of the Christian Monarchy of Order and Liberty placed on the head of Charlemagne. Century followed century, until the immense temple of the West was built up, with stone laid correctly on stone, until the great age was reached when, with a perfect economy of words, passion spoke in the right place with Corneille, emotion with Racine, reason with Molière, divine truth and glory with Bossuet in the pulpit, while the congregation answered *de profundis* with the words of Pascal.

Then came the time of weakness and of collapse. This or

that stone of the Temple was removed, and faithless men transformed passion and emotion, reason and humour, into thrones from which to preside as lawgivers. The temple was slowly reduced to fragments and ruins—and around it we heard the lament and the tears of the prophets, of the children of the desolate city. But the sacred stones of Charlemagne reached far away lands of the earth. Even now the construction of a greater temple has probably begun, and the foundation has been laid by invisible workers, who have nothing but scorn and laughter for those who try to build the Tower of Babylon once more, instead of their own new Temple of the World Jerusalem. The scorn from above answers the tumult of Babel, a tumult which will die down as others did before it. On high no struggle rages between diversity and unity, between quality and equality. The voice of prayer alone is heard there from the altar of the Temple:

Et in personis proprietas, et in essentia unitas, et in maiestate adoretur aequalitas.

Burke's central theme, that constitutions are the slow, invisible work of history and are never made by individuals assembled in parliaments and conventions, which, at their very best, can only make administrative regulations, and approve or disapprove the way public money is spent, de Maistre goes a step further than Burke and asks the questions: Whose will is the Law ? and Who moves History ? Burke was certainly no agnostic; he was probably the first Anglican who, when discussing French events, dared to defend the Catholic Church, without fearing to be denounced by his fellow-countrymen as a " papist." But de Maistre openly calls for a return to the great tradition of the theologians, who see the problem of human government as one entirely subordinated to the will of God, politics as a branch of theology, and Providence as the only acceptable explanation of history.

In 1799 Joseph de Maistre was sent to St Petersburg as the plenipotentiary Minister of his King, who soon afterwards lost his kingdom of Piedmont and was confined to the island of Sardinia. Even before the accession of General Bonaparte to power, the unfortunate King Victor Amadeus had felt compelled to adapt himself to a policy of submission to French interests. Joseph de Maistre was in these circumstances unwelcome at home, as a letter captured by the French Republican army in Italy revealed that the Comte de Provence—later King Louis XVIII—showed a great personal interest in the author of the *Considérations*.

In the years that followed, Joseph de Maistre exerted a considerable personal influence in St Petersburg, somewhat out of keeping with his modest position as the Minister of a practically powerless King. Czar Alexander I was interested in his thought, which was considered not without misgivings and suspicion by Orthodox and Pravoslav circles, who had little or no objection to the spread of " free " thought from the Protestant Universities of Germany, propagated by the numerous German professors employed in Russia, but who did their best to prevent the penetration of " Jesuitism."

The sixteen years which Joseph de Maistre spent in St Petersburg bore considerable fruit. Here he wrote his various fragments on Russia, Orthodoxy and Protestantism, his comments on the philosophy of Bacon, his *Essai sur le principe générateur des institutions humaines* and, finally, the *Soirées de St Pétersbourg*, his greatest book, publication of which he never lived to see. De Maistre left St Petersburg after the fall of Napoleon, not without some bitter disappointment over the anti-Jesuit decrees of Alexander I, which temporarily put an end to the Society's activities in Russia; but he had the joy of seeing some excellent converts from Orthodoxy, amongst whom was Prince Dmitri Galitzin, S.J.

The main subject of the *Soirées* is the working of Providence in human institutions and in history. It is perhaps the best philosophy written in dialogue form since Plato; the persons taking part in the conversations are a Russian, a member of the Imperial Senate, a young French Royalist *émigré* and the " Comte," i.e. de Maistre himself. Almost every subject is touched upon in these dialogues: justice, human and divine, war and peace, social order and personal liberty, but first and foremost—for de Maistre was a true philosopher, though academic pedants deny him this title and treat him as a " mere writer," on account of the brilliant wit of his style—the ultimate sense and meaning of all words, which relate to the one " Word Incarnate." To quote Léon Bloy:

" Joseph de Maistre said, almost a century ago, that man is too wicked to deserve to be free.

" This seer was a contemporary of the Revolution; he meditated like a prophet on the grandiose horror it inspired, and confronted it face to face.

" He died, appalled at what he saw and full of contempt, pronouncing the funeral oration over civilised Europe."

1. HUMAN AND DIVINE NOMENCLATURE[1]

ONE of the great errors of a century which professed all possible errors, was to think that a political constitution could be written down and created *à priori*, when both reason and experience affirm that a constitution is a divine creation, and that precisely what is most fundamental and most essentially constitutional in the laws of a nation cannot be written down.

. . . The essence of a fundamental law is that nobody has the right to suppress it: now how can it be above *everybody*, if *somebody* made it ? The consent of the people is an impossible foundation for it; and even if it were otherwise, agreement by consent in no way constitutes a law, and constrains nobody, unless it is safeguarded by a higher authority. Locke attempted to define the nature of law as an expression of united wills; a fortunate man, who can thus discover the nature of law in something which, on the contrary, excludes the very idea of *law*. Indeed, united wills make a *ruling*, not a *law*, which latter necessarily and manifestly pre-supposes the existence of a higher will, strong enough to command obedience. " According to Hobbes's system "—the same one which has had so great a success in our century in the works of Locke—" the validity of

[1] Extract from *Essai sur le Principe Générateur des Constitutions Politiques.* H. Goemacre. Brussels. 1852.

the civil laws depends only on the consent of the people; but if no natural law exists which ordains the promulgation of the laws that have been made, of what use are they? Promises, contracts, oaths, are only vain words: it is as easy to break this frivolous link as it is to form it. Without the dogma of God the Lawgiver, all moral obligations are merely an illusion. Strength on the one hand and weakness on the other, that is all that binds human societies together."[1]

The words of this wise and profound theologian on the subject of moral obligation can be applied with equal truth to a political or civic obligation. Law is only really *law*, possessing a real sanction, when it is presumed to emanate from a higher will; with the result that its essential characteristic is *that it is not the expression of the general will*. Otherwise laws are *mere rulings*, as we have just said, and as the author whom we have quoted above goes on to say: " those who have been able freely to enter into these agreements, did not debar themselves from the right to revoke them; and their descendants, who took no part in them, are even less bound to honour them."[2] From whence it follows that primeval good sense, happily in existence before the birth of sophistry, sought on all sides a sanction for laws in an authority superior to man, whether such an authority acknowledged that sovereignty comes from God, or whether it venerated certain unwritten laws, as coming from Him.

The men who drafted the Roman laws discreetly interposed a very remarkable piece of Greek jurisprudence in the first chapter of their collection. " Amongst the laws which govern us," says this passage, " some are written down, others are not." Nothing could be simpler and yet more profound. Does anyone know of a Turkish law which expressly allows the sovereign to send a man to his death, without a court of law having first pronounced sentence? Does anyone know of any *written* law, even a religious one, which forbids the Christian sovereigns of Europe to do the same thing?[3] Yet the Turk is no more surprised at seeing his master order the immediate death of a man, than he is at seeing him go to the mosque. With the whole of

---

[1] Bergier: *Historical and Dogmatic Treatise on Religion*. Vol. III, ch. iv, para. 12, pp. 330, 331. (Following Tertullian, *Apologia*, 45.)

[2] Ibid.

[3] " The Church forbids her children, even more formally than the civil laws, to take justice into their own hands; and it is in this spirit that Christian kings abstain from doing so, even in crimes of high treason, and hand over the criminals to judges, so that they can be punished according to the laws and within the framework of justice." (Pascal, *Provincial Letters*, XIV.)

This passage is very important, and ought to be better known.

Asia, and indeed with the whole of antiquity, he believes that it is a legitimate prerogative of the sovereign to exercise an immediate power over life and death. But our princes trembled at the very idea of condemning a man to death; for according to our way of seeing things, this condemnation would be an atrocious murder; yet I doubt if it would be possible to forbid them to do it on the strength of a fundamental written law, without causing far greater evils than those it was intended to prevent.

Look at Roman history to see precisely in what the power of the Senate consisted; it throws no light on the matter, at least as regards the precise limits of this authority. It is generally speaking true that the authority of the people and that of the Senate counter-balanced each other, and were consistently hostile one to the other. It is easy to see that these dangerous struggles were always brought to an end either by patriotism or by lassitude, by weakness or by violence, but *we* know no more than that.[1] When we contemplate these great events of history, we are sometimes tempted to think that events would have turned out much better if there had been precise laws to circumscribe authority. This however would be a great error: such laws, perpetually compromised by unexpected happenings and by out of the way exceptions to the rule, would not have lasted six months, or they would have meant the overthrow of the republic.

The English constitution provides an example nearer home, and is therefore a more striking one to take. When we examine it carefully, we see *that it only works because it is unworkable* (if I may be allowed this play on words). It derives its stability from the exceptions to the rule, rather than from the rule itself. The *habeas corpus*, for example, has been suspended so often and for such long periods, that one wondered if the exception had not become the rule. Supposing for a moment that the authors of this famous Act had had the presumption to state cases in which it could be suspended, they would thereby have destroyed it.

The theory of names is a very important question. Names

---

[1] I have often meditated on this passage of Cicero (*De Leg.* II, 6): *Leges Liviae praesertim uno versiculo senatus puncto temporis sublatae sunt.* By what right did the Senate assume this liberty? And how did the people allow them to do so? It is certainly not an easy question to answer, but why need we be astonished at this, since after all that has been written on Roman history and Roman remains, men still have to write theses to show how the members of the Senate were recruited?

are in no wise arbitrary affairs, as so many men have affirmed *who had lost their names*. God says of Himself: *I am*; and all creatures say of themselves: *My name is This or That*. The name of a spiritual being relates necessarily to the action he performs, which is his distinctive quality; whence it follows that among the ancients, the greatest honour possible to a divinity was *polyonymy*, or *plurality of names*, which proclaimed the number of his functions or the extent of his power. Ancient mythology shows us Diana, when still a child, asking Jupiter to grant her this honour; and in the verses attributed to Orpheus, compliments are addressed to her under the title of *polyonymous spirit* (or spirit bearing many names). Which means, after all, that God alone has the right to give a *name*. Indeed, He has *named* everything, since He created everything.

It is the same with nations as with individuals: some there are *who have no name*. Herodotus observes that the Thracians would be the most powerful people in the world if they were united. " *But*," he adds, " *this union is impossible, for they all have a different name*." This is an excellent remark. There are also modern peoples *who have no name*, and there are others who have several; but *polyonymy* is as disastrous for nations as it has been thought honourable for spirits.

Since names have nothing arbitrary about them, and since, like all things, they derive their origin more or less directly from God, we must not think that a man has the unrestricted right to name even those beings of whose existence he has some right to consider himself the author, and to impose on them names according to his own ideas. God has reserved for Himself in this matter a sort of immediate jurisdiction, which it is impossible not to recognise. " *Oh, my dear Hermogenus! the imposition of names is a very important matter and one which cannot be the prerogative of a bad or even of a vulgar man. . . . This right only belongs to a creator of names (onomaturgos); that is, apparently, only to the legislator; but of all human creatures, the rarest is a legislator*."

Man however likes nothing better than to give names to things. He does this, for example, when he applies significant epithets to words; a talent which is a distinctive mark of a great writer and especially of a great poet. The felicitous choice of an epithet enhances a noun, which becomes distinguished under this new sign. Examples can be found in every language; but to confine ourselves to the language of the nation which itself bears so great a name, since it gave its name to *frankness*, or else *frankness* received its name from the nation: what cultured man is not familiar with *miserly* Acheron, *careful* steeds, *shameless* bed, *timid* supplications, *silvery* rustling, *rapid* destroyer, *pale* sycophants, etc.? Never will man forget his primitive rights; we can even say in a certain sense, that he will always exercise them, but how curtailed have they become because of his degradation! Here is a true law, such as God made it: *Man is forbidden to give grand names to things of his own making, and which he thinks important; but if he has acted in a legitimate fashion, the commonplace name of the object will be ennobled by the object itself, and will achieve greatness.*

What is the real origin of this word *Tuileries*, which is so famous?[1] Nothing is more commonplace; but the ashes of dead heroes, mingling with the soil, had consecrated it and the soil consecrated the name. It is somewhat curious that at such a great distance in time and space, this same word TUILERIES, famous in olden days as the name of a tomb, should acquire new lustre as the name of a palace. The authority which came to dwell in the *Tuileries* did not think of giving it a more imposing name, which might have been more fitting. If it had committed this mistake, there would have been no reason why, on the following day, the place should not have been inhabited by pickpockets and street girls.

. . . There are therefore two infallible rules by which we may judge all human creations of whatever kind: their *basis* and their *name*, and these two rules of course are free from any pejorative interpretation. If the basis is purely human, the construction cannot last; and the more men there are who have been concerned in it, the more deliberation, science and *especially writing*, in a word, the more human the means of every kind that have been employed, the more fragile the institution will be. It is chiefly by applying this rule that we must judge all the enterprises of sovereigns or of assemblies of men in the cause of civilisation, and in the establishment or the regeneration of peoples.

. . . The second rule concerning names is, I think, neither less clear nor less decisive than the first. If the name has been imposed by an assembly; if it has been established by discussion before the object itself was created, so that the name precedes the object; if the name is pompous,[2] if it has a grammatical

---

[1] Tuileries, broadly interpreted, retains some connection with pottery.

[2] Thus, for example, if a man other than a sovereign confers upon himself the title of legislator, it is a sure sign that he is not one at all; and if an assembly has the temerity to call itself " legislative," not only is it a sure sign that it is nothing of the sort, but a sign that it has gone mad and will soon be the laughing stock of the whole world.

relation to the object it represents; finally, if it has been taken from a foreign language, especially from a dead language, all the characteristics of nonentity are there, and we can be sure that the name and the object will disappear in no time. The contrary assumptions proclaim the principle of legitimacy, consequently that the institution will last. We must take care not to pass over this subject lightly. A true philosopher ought never to lose sight of the language as a real barometer, the variations in which are an infallible guide to *good and bad weather*. To confine myself to the subject in hand, it is certain that the disproportionate introduction of foreign words, applied in particular to national institutions of every kind, are one of the most infallible signs of the decadence of a people.

If the formation of every empire, the march of civilisation and the unanimous verdict of all history and all tradition were not enough to convince us, the destruction of empires would complete the demonstration begun by their origin. Just as the religious principle created everything, so the absence of this same principle has destroyed everything. The sect of Epicurus, which might be called the scepticism of antiquity, first degraded, then destroyed every government which had the misfortune to give it protection. Everywhere, Lucretius proclaimed the coming of Caesar.

2. WAR, PEACE, AND SOCIAL ORDER[1]

THE fearful sight of carnage does not harden the true soldier's heart. Amidst the blood he sheds, he remains as human as a wife is chaste in the ecstasy of love. Once he has sheathed his sword, sacred humanity comes into its own again, and it is probably true to say that the most exalted and the most generous sentiments of all are felt by the soldier. Cast your mind back, Sir, to the *grand siècle* in France. The harmony which existed in that century between religion, military courage and science, is responsible for the noble character which all nations have hailed with universal acclamation as the pattern of the European man. Take the first element away from it, and the unity, or in other words, the whole beauty of it, disappears. Men do not realise how necessary this element

[1] Extract from the 7th Dialogue of the *Soirées de St Pétersbourg*. H. Goemacre. Brussels. 1852.

is in all things, nor the part it plays in matters in which it might seem irrelevant to superficial observers. The divine spirit, which has singled out Europe as its dwelling-place, even mitigated the scourges of eternal justice and the *type* of war waged in Europe will always be outstanding in the annals of the universe. Men killed each other of course, burned and ravaged and committed thousands of useless crimes, I admit, yet they began their war in May and stopped in December; they slept under canvas; the fighting was confined to soldiers. Never were nations as such at war with each other, and weakness was held to be sacred in the lamentable series of devastations which this scourge brought in its train.

It was moreover a magnificent sight to see all the sovereigns of Europe, restrained by a mysterious and irrepressible urge towards moderation, refuse ever to demand the utmost, even in moments of great peril, that their people could give them; they used men gently, and all of them, guided by an invisible inspiration, avoided dealing any of those blows to the sovereignty of the enemy *which could rebound on them*: glory, honour and eternal praise to the law of love which was unceasingly proclaimed at the heart of Europe! No one nation triumphed over the other; the wars of antiquity were forgotten, except in books, or amongst people *seated in the shadow of death*; fierce wars were brought to an end when a province, or a town or even in many cases a few villages, changed hands. Mutual consideration and the most delicate courtesy could be found amidst the clash of arms. Bombs were never directed at the palaces of kings; balls and displays on more than one occasion interrupted the course of battle. The enemy officer, who was invited to these celebrations, would come in order to joke about the battle to be fought on the morrow; amidst all the horror of the most sanguinary engagement, the dying man could still hear the voice of compassion and words of courtesy. The first shots were no sooner exchanged, than huge hospitals sprang up everywhere: doctors, surgeons, chemists flocked to offer their skill; from their ranks would arise the presiding genius of St John of God, or of St Vincent de Paul, greater and stronger than ordinary men, constant as faith itself, as active as hope, and as skilful as love. Every victim of the battle who still breathed was picked up, received treatment and was given consolation: every wound was touched by the hand of science and of charity!

Gentlemen, the functions of a soldier are terrible, but they surely derive from a major law of the spiritual world, and we must not be surprised that all nations agree in seeing something more particularly divine in this scourge than in the others. Believe me, it is for a great and fundamental reason that the title *GOD OF HOSTS* illumines every page of Scripture. . . .

War is divine then of its very nature, because it is a law of the world.

War is divine in its consequences, both general and particular, which are of a supernatural order; consequences which are little known because few people care for them, but which are none the less beyond all question. Who could doubt that death on the battlefield entails great privileges ? Who could think that the victims of this fearful judgement shed their blood in vain ? Yet the time is not propitious for insisting on these subjects; our century is not prepared yet to think about them. Let us leave natural philosophy to this world and keep our own eyes ever fixed on the invisible world, which will give us the answer to everything.

War is divine in the protection granted to the great leaders, even to the most daring, who seldom fall in battle, and then only when their fame can reach no further heights and their mission is fulfilled.

War is divine in the manner in which it is declared. I have no desire to exonerate any man inopportunely, but how obvious it is, that those men whom we consider to be the immediate authors of wars are themselves swept along by circumstances! At the exact moment prepared by men and prescribed by justice, God intervenes to avenge the iniquity which the inhabitants of the earth have committed against Him. . . .

War is divine in its results, over which human reason speculates in vain: for they can be totally different in two nations, although both were equally affected by the war. Some wars debase nations and debase them for centuries; others exalt them, perfect them in every way, and within a short space of time, even repair momentary losses with a visible increase in population, which is very extraordinary. History often presents us with the picture of a population which remains rich and goes on increasing while the most desperate battles are being fought. But some wars are vicious and accursed, which our conscience, rather than our reason, recognises to be so: nations receive their death-blow in these wars, both as regards their power and their character. Thus even the conqueror seems degraded and impoverished, and although he is crowned with laurels, he is left sad and lamenting, while in the vanquished country there is soon not a workshop or a plough which is not working to capacity.

3. ON SOPHISTRY AND TYRANNY[1]

THINK of him, if you will, as possessing a fine talent; it is none the less true that when we praise Voltaire, we ought to do so with certain reservations, I nearly said with reluctance. The unbridled admiration lavished on him by too many people is an infallible sign of a corrupted soul. Let us be under no illusion: if a man runs his eye over his book-shelves and feels attracted to the *Works of Ferney*, God does not love him. People have often laughed at ecclesiastical authority for condemning books *in odium auctoris*; in reality, nothing was more just; *Refuse honours due to genius to the man who abuses his gifts.* If this law were severely applied, we should soon see poisonous books disappear; but since we are not responsible for promulgating it, at least let us beware of going to the extreme (far more reprehensible than we think) of praising guilty writers to the skies. Voltaire above all. He pronounced a terrible judgement against himself without realising it, for it was he who said, " A corrupt mind never reached sublime heights."

Nothing is more true, and that is why Voltaire, for all his hundred books, is never more than *attractive*. I make an exception of his tragedies, in which the nature of the medium obliged him to express noble sentiments which were alien to his character; yet even in his dramatic work, in which he triumphed, he does not deceive the experienced eye. In his best plays he resembles his two great rivals as the most cunning hypocrite resembles a saint. I do not intend in any case to question his merits as a dramatist, but maintain what I said in the beginning: that as soon as Voltaire speaks in his own name, he is nothing more than *attractive*; nothing can arouse his enthusiasm, not even the battle of Fontenoy. *He is charming,* people say; I agree, but I use the word in criticism of him. Moreover, I cannot endure the exaggeration which makes him

---

[1] Extract from the 4th Dialogue of *Soirées de St Pétersbourg.*

universal. To tell the truth, I see certain exceptions to this universality. He is a complete failure in the ode: and no wonder. His deliberate impiety had killed the divine flame of enthusiasm in him. He is also a complete failure, even a ridiculous failure, in lyrical drama, his ear being as completely deaf to the beauties of harmony, as his eye was blind to the beauties of art. In the genres which best suited his talent, he is dull: he is mediocre, cold and often (who would credit it ?) heavy and coarse in comedy; for the evil man is never comic. For the same reason, he was unable to coin an epigram, the smallest outpouring of his venom needing at least a hundred lines. If he tries his hand at satire, he borders on scurrility; he is unbearable when he writes history, despite his art and the elegance and grace of his style; no quality in him can replace those he lacks, namely a feeling for the life of history, a serious purpose, good faith and dignity. As for his *epic* poem, I am not qualified to speak on it: for we have to read a book before we judge it, and we must be wide awake before we can read it.

A monotonous torpor hangs over most of his writings, which consist of two subjects only, the Bible and his enemies: he is either blasphemous or insulting. His jokes, which receive so much praise, are however far from being beyond reproach: the laughter they arouse is not real laughter; it is a grimace. Have you ever noticed that the divine anathema was written large on his face ? After the lapse of so many years, there is still time to prove it for yourself. Go and gaze at his face in the *Hermitage* Palace; never do I look at it without congratulating myself that it has not been handed down to us by some sculptor, who took his inspiration from the Greeks, and who would perhaps have idealised it. Everything is as nature made it in this portrait. There is as much truth in this head as there would be if a death mask had been taken of him. Observe the abject brow, which never blushed for shame, the eyes like two extinct craters, in which lust and hatred still seem to be seething. That mouth—perhaps I should not say so, but I cannot help myself—that frightful *grin* stretching from ear to ear, like a spring ready to open and release a blasphemy or a piece of sarcasm, when his cruel malice demands it.

Do not talk to me of this man, I cannot endure the thought of him. Oh, what harm he has done us! Like the insect which is the scourge of our gardens, because it attacks the roots of our most precious plants, Voltaire unceasingly pricks with his *goad* at the two roots of society, women and young men; they imbibe his poisons, which he is thus able to transmit from generation to generation. It is in vain that, in order to cover up his unspeakable outrages, his stupid admirers deafen us by quoting the sonorous tirades in which he spoke of the most venerated objects in a masterly fashion. These people, who are wilfully blind, do not see that they are putting the final touch to the condemnation of this guilty writer. If Fénelon had written *The Prince* in the same style in which he painted the joys of Elysium, he would be a thousand times more vile and more guilty than Machiavelli. Voltaire's great crime is the abuse of a talent, and the deliberate prostitution of a mind created to sing the praises of God and of virtue. He cannot allege in excuse, as so many other men can, his youth, thoughtlessness, the allurements of passion, or, finally, the melancholy weakness of our nature. Nothing can absolve him: his corruption is in a class by itself; it takes root in the deepest fibres of his heart, and is fortified by all the powers of his understanding. Always closely linked with sacrilege, it defies God by leading men astray. With a fury which is unequalled in this world, this insolent blasphemer goes to the length of declaring himself the personal enemy of the Saviour of mankind; from the depths of his nothingness, he dares to give Him a ridiculous name, and the adorable law which the God-Man brought on earth he calls INFAMOUS. Abandoned by God, who punishes by withdrawing Himself, he throws off all restraint. Other cynics have startled virtue, Voltaire startles vice. He plunges into the mud, rolls himself in it, slakes his thirst with it; he delivers his imagination up to the enthusiasm of Hell, which lends him all its strength to drag him to the extreme limits of evil. He invents wonders, monsters which make us grow pale. Paris crowned him, but Sodom would have banished him. Shameless desecrator of the universal language, and of her greatest names, the very last of men, after those who love him! How can I express the feelings he arouses in me ? When I see what he was capable of doing, and what he in fact did, his inimitable talents inspire nothing less in me than a kind of sacred rage, which has no name. Divided between admiration and horror, I sometimes feel I would like to have a statue erected to him . . . by the hand of the common hangman.

. . . There is moreover a certain *rational anger* which goes very well with wisdom; the Holy Ghost Himself has expressly stated that it is free from sin.

4. RUSSIA AND THE CHRISTIAN WEST[1]

" HUMAN nature was created for the benefit of the few."

This maxim, expressed in natural terms, shocks us no doubt by its Machiavellian turn of phrase, but from another point of view it is well said. Everywhere the mass of the people is led by the few; for without a reasonably strong aristocracy, the public authority is weak.

There were far fewer free men in antiquity than there were slaves. Athens had forty thousand slaves and twenty thousand citizens. Rome, towards the end of the Republic, had about twelve hundred thousand inhabitants, of whom barely two thousand were landowners; which by itself proves the enormous number of slaves that there were. One man sometimes had several thousands of slaves in his service. Once four hundred slaves were executed in a single house, by virtue of the terrible law which pronounced that all the slaves who lived under the same roof should perish when a Roman citizen was killed in his own home.

. . . Then the divine law appeared on earth. It immediately took possession of the hearts of men and changed them in a way which arouses the eternal admiration of any sincere observer. Above all, religion began to work unremittingly for the abolition of slavery, a project which no other religion, no other legislator or philosopher had ever dared to undertake, let alone conceive. . . .

Generally speaking, human nature is only fit to receive civic liberty in proportion as it is penetrated and led by Christian principles.

Wherever any religion other than Christianity is practised, slavery exists as of right, and wherever religion grows weak, the political power becomes proportionately more dominant and the nation is less fit to enjoy general liberty.

This paramount truth has just been demonstrated before our very eyes in the most illuminating and terrible way. For an entire century, Christianity suffered continuous attack by an abominable sect. Those princes who were perverted by their doctrine allowed them to pursue their work, and on more than one deplorable occasion even helped on their ill-intentioned endeavours, undermining, with the very hands that were created to preserve, the pillars of the temple that later crashed around them. What was the result ? There was finally too

---

[1] Extract from *Quatre Chapitres inédits sur la Russie*, ch. i. Paris. Aug. Vaton. 1859.

much liberty in the world. The depraved will of men, having cast off all restraint, gave itself up completely to pride and corruption. The mass of emancipated men attacked the first institution in the land that had the greatest influence over all the others. In less than twenty years, the European edifice crumbled, and the principle of sovereignty still struggles to survive amidst the ruins, compromised perhaps for ever.

In our day, the two anchors of society, religion and slavery, have been lost, so that the vessel of State has been cast adrift and shattered by the storm.

These truths are so obvious that it is impossible to question them. It is now an easy matter to apply our conclusions to Russia.

If we ask why serfdom is still the common lot of the Russian masses today, the answer is self-evident. *Serfdom is present in Russia because it is a necessity and the Emperor cannot rule without it.*

The primordial antipathy between Rome and Constantinople; the crimes and the orgies of the Byzantine Empire; the extraordinary paroxysm which overwhelmed the West round about the tenth century; the ill-chosen and consequently the vicious Popes who were created at the time by petty, semibarbaric princes and even by base women who had seized power; the Tartar invasion; the previous invasion by a power of another kind, which had entered Russia as a liquid flows into an empty vessel; finally the disastrous dividing wall which had been deliberately erected during the eleventh and twelfth centuries; all these causes, I repeat, removed Russia perforce from the general stream of civilisation and emancipation which came from Rome.

. . . In the West, the civil authority did not abandon slaves to their own devices when it freed them; they lived under the protection of the priests, and in any case, life at that time was very simple. Science had not yet kindled the pride which, like a devouring flame, has already destroyed a part of the world and will destroy the whole of it, if it is allowed to continue.

Circumstances in Russia are very different. Every lord, or rather every noble, is a real magistrate, a kind of civil governor who is responsible for the policing of his estate, and who is endowed with the necessary authority to repress, at least to a large extent, the reckless impulses of individual wills.

If this magistrature should ever be suppressed, what authority could the sovereign put in its place to maintain order? The laws, you will say; but the laws are precisely the weakest part of this great empire. The tribunals all have more duties to perform than authority to wield; they complain of public opinion, which in turn is dissatisfied with the tribunals; these grievances are one of the things that strike foreigners especially the most forcibly. As a crowning danger, Russia, alone amongst nations, ancient or modern, refuses to exercise the death penalty in the public interest; a circumstance which must be borne in mind.

. . . Now the great conservative and preservative force of loyalty to the throne does not exist in Russia. Religion has a certain influence on the human mind, but none at all on the heart, the seat of all desires and all crimes. A peasant would probably rather risk his life than eat meat on one of the forbidden days; but if the problem is to prevent an outburst of passion, the outcome is uncertain. Christianity does not consist of words only, it is a concrete thing; if it no longer possesses its strength, its penetrating influence, its primeval simplicity and a powerful priesthood, it is not *itself* any more, it is no longer what it was when it made a general liberation of slaves possible. Let the Russian Government beware: its clergy do not even possess a voice in the State, they dare not speak and are only consulted when it cannot be avoided; a foreigner by no means says: *It is unfortunate*; he simply says: *It is a fact*.

. . . The danger of rebellion, following upon an emancipation of the serfs, would be indescribably great on account of the peculiar character of this nation, which is the most excitable, impetuous and enterprising in the whole world. The writer has sometimes said (and I hope the joke is not entirely without foundation) " that if the longing in a Russian heart could be imprisoned in a citadel, it would blow it to pieces." No man *longs* for something as ardently as the Russian does.

Watch how he spends his money, and how he pursues all his pleasures as the fancy takes him; you will see how he wants things. Watch him as he engages in trade, even amongst the poorer classes, and see how intelligent and alive he is to his own interests; watch him as he fulfils his most hazardous enterprises, watch him finally on the battlefield, and you will see the full extent of his daring.

If we imagine liberty being given to thirty-six millions of men, more or less of this calibre—never can it be repeated too often—we should immediately see the outbreak of a conflagration which would destroy Russia.

. . . Russia does not possess any powerful reinforcements to authority (such as Turkey possesses in the Koran, or China in the maxims and laws of Confucius); consequently she ought to beware of giving full reign to too many individual wills. Moreover, her legislators ought never to lose sight of a fact of the greatest importance: Russian civilisation coincided with the period of the greatest corruption the mind of man has ever known; and that a series of circumstances which we cannot examine here put the Russian nature into contact with, and amalgamated it, so to speak, with the nation which has been at one and the same time the most terrible instrument and the most pitiable victim of this corruption.

Such a thing has never been seen before. Priests and oracles have always presided over the infancy of nations; here we have the opposite. The germs of Russian civilisation were fermented and developed in the corruption of the Regency period in France. The dreadful literature of the eighteenth century arrived in Russia suddenly and without any preparation; the first French lessons which this people received consisted of blasphemies.

This fatal disadvantage which Russia possesses over other nations ought to make her rulers take special precautions when it comes to the point of giving liberty to the immense mass of the nation which still does not enjoy it. As these serfs receive their liberty, they will find that they are placed between teachers who are more than suspect, and priests who are weak and enjoy no special consideration. Exposed in this unprepared fashion, they will infallibly and abruptly pass from superstition to atheism and from passive obedience to unbridled activity. Liberty will have the same effect on these temperaments as a heady wine on a man who is not used to it. The mere sight of liberty given to others will intoxicate those who still do not share it. With men's minds prepared in this way, any University Pugatscheff[1] has only to appear (they can be manufactured easily enough, as all the factories are open) and if we add indifference, incapacity, the ambition of a few nobles, foreign bad faith, the intrigues of a detestable sect which never rests, etc., etc., the State, according to all the rules of probability, will literally *burst asunder*, like an over-long beam which only holds firm at the two extremities. *Elsewhere there is only one danger to fear; here there are two.*

If an emancipation of the serfs is to take place in Russia, it

[1] Pugatscheff: Leader of a peasant revolt in the reign of Catherine II, whom his followers proclaimed to be the murdered Czar, Peter III. Executed 1775.

will come about in the course of nature. Quite unforeseen circumstances will make it generally desirable. The whole
process will take place quietly and will be carried through without a hitch (like all great enterprises). If the sovereign gives
his blessing to this national movement, it will be his right and
his duty to do so; but God forbid that he should ever stimulate
it of his own accord!

II. VICOMTE DE BONALD

1754 - 1840

Louis-Gabriel-Ambroise, Vicomte de Bonald, came from an ancient noble family of Provence, was educated at the Oratorian College at Juilly, and after serving with the Artillery he held a post in the local administration of his native province. Elected to the States General of 1789 as a deputy for Aveyron, he strongly opposed the new legislation on the civil status of the clergy and emigrated in 1791, as many Royalists did, to Germany, when Louis XVI, a virtual prisoner of the Revolution, lost all control over the situation. After serving for a few years in the Royalist army of Prince Condé, Bonald retired to Heidelberg when the Condé army was disbanded. In 1797 he published his *Théorie du pouvoir politique et religieux dans la société civile démontrée par le raisonnement et l'histoire* in Constance, which was banned by the *Directoire* in France. Although he returned to France later, Bonald remained faithful to the Bourbon dynasty and declined every offer of public service under Napoleon. With his *Essai analytique sur les lois naturelles* (1800), *Du Divorce* (1801), *La Législation primitive* (1802), *Recherches philosophiques sur les premier objets des connaissances morales* (1818) and with the hundreds of shorter essays and newspaper articles on topical subjects which he wrote, Bonald became for a generation the leading theorist of Legitimism. He was also an active exponent of this principle in the Peerage, in the French Academy, in the Royal Council of the Universities, to which Louis XVIII appointed him, and at the head of the Ministry of Education under this same King. In 1830 Bonald retired from politics and adopted an attitude of passive opposition towards King Louis Philippe and the Orleanist monarchy.

Bonald is a foremost apologist of Catholic political and social doctrine, combating the various schools of romantic political thought and of English utilitarianism. His importance lies in the fact that he was a most penetrating critic of the ethics of Kant, of Rousseau's notion of the " general will " and of Montesquieu's " division of powers." To Kant's individual judgement Bonald opposes dogma and authority; against Rousseau he establishes the primacy of thought over will in his analysis of primitive legislation and of the origin of human language; in place of Montesquieu's " division of powers," he demonstrates his brilliant historical and theological theory of the " unity of power," given by God for a unique and undivided purpose. According to Bonald, the safeguard against the misuse of power does not lie in institutions to curb power, as the Liberal school thought, but in the ethical limitations of power set by the religious conscience.

Bonald distinguishes between the " social " and the " political " sphere, the first comprising all legitimate private concerns and activities, and the second providing force in the service of justice. The foundation of the Christian State is in Bonald's view justice. The sword against the internal and the external enemy—the sword of justice and the sword of defence—are one and the same and are carried by the same monarch, in whose service there are two kinds of nobility, the *noblesse de robe* and the *noblesse d'épée*. The foundation of both society and State is the family, marriage being " eventual society," which becomes " actual " with the birth of children. The sacred character of family life safeguards it against interference by the State in the social sphere. All ethical principles governing State and society are derived from the family and thus Bonald wishes to see at the head of the State, not a " first citizen," but a " first family," and the political and public services assured, not by individuals, but by such families who are ready to renounce otherwise legitimate and lucrative private activities for political honours and distinctions.

Bonald preached the essential unity of Europe as a society of Christian public law, and he may be quoted as the classic opponent of modern tendencies of nationalism, which he showed are of revolutionary origin.

Among the great Catholic writers of the post-Revolutionary era, Bonald occupies a first and unique place. Less of an elegant paradoxical wit than Joseph de Maistre, with whose apologetic thought he concurred in many essential points, he is a more systematic thinker, whose achievement shows a rare consistency and unity in thought, an unusual purity of style and an unmatched conformity of life to the principles he constantly defended.

The light and the truth of the Christian heritage, reached by men like Donoso Cortés, Louis Veuillot or Barbey d'Aurevilly after hard struggles against the intellectual trends of their time, Bonald inherited safely; he was never misled by the aberrations of his century and transmitted it safely to future generations. In the history of French philosophy, he will be mainly remembered for his theory of the origin of human language. Bonald concluded from the fact that the name of God exists in every language, that it expresses a correct and *plausible* idea, and sees in this the proof of God's existence: man, in his view, is only capable of imagining what exists in reality. While Descartes, and the whole school of thought which followed his method, took individual thought and reasoning as their point of departure, the existence of society is for Bonald the first and foremost problem. Society exists, in his view, for a Thought conceived, human association being the means employed to achieve this end. The expression of this Thought is the *Word* and the Word became incarnate in Christ.

Thus Bonald's reasoning leads to a perfect harmony and perfect faith, and he is perhaps the first modern philosopher to rejoin the great medieval tradition of Christian philosophy.

The first part of the following extracts was written by Bonald in 1799, the second in 1819. The two essays from which they are taken both relate to the same subject, the pacification of Europe after the wars of the Revolution. In the *Analytical Essay on the Law of Nature* we follow Bonald's thought during the period of consolidation after the fall of Robespierre, and which soon afterwards took a more definite shape in the Consulate of Bonaparte, proclaimed on the 18th Brumaire of the Year VIII (November 9th, 1799). The *Essay on the General Interest of Europe* (1814) was meant as a piece of advice to the Congress of Vienna, and as a comment on the basic principle of this Congress, which Metternich proclaimed to be the restoration of " the public law of Europe, as it can be seen in facts incontestably established by history." Bonald takes the principle formulated in Vienna as his point of departure and also as a method of approach. He underlines very emphatically the central importance of the Church in the making of Europe, and at the same time he directs his polemics by implication against the political theories of non-Catholic philosophical schools: Spinoza's theory of the geometrical equilibrium in the division of powers, and Kant's theoretically Republican " Eternal Peace," which neglect to define, or relegate to the second plane the first principle of Power (a human part of the divine attribute of the Almighty) and the principle of facts and rights clearly established by history.

1. THE UNITY OF EUROPE

I

THERE has arisen in our time, in the midst of Christian Europe and at the very heart of civilisation, an independent State which has made atheism its religion and anarchy its system of government. Although it was at war with society, this monstrous State has yet shown all the marks of a society; its sovereign was a stupendous spirit of error and of lies; its basic law, a hatred of all order; its subjects were men tormented by the passions of covetousness and greed; its instruments of authority and its ministers were men who were either thoroughly corrupt, or had been wretchedly seduced from their duty, men who, bearing titles and names which will remain for ever celebrated, united by the same oaths, united more closely still by the same crimes, led this terrible *action* with all the devices of genius and carried it out with the blind devotion of fanatics.

Scarcely had this sinister society been formed and so to say constituted, than the *inevitable* and metaphysical distinction between truth and error, and good and evil, which began with man himself and will last as long as he lives, became a physical reality. Then France, where this infernal State materialised for a time, intoxicated with *the wine of prostitution*, and as if carried away by a superhuman frenzy, despatched her principles, her soldiers and the memory of her famous men to extinguish all truth, to overthrow every semblance of order, and threatened the whole world with a return to savagery.

Anarchy has been dethroned and the armies of atheism are defeated; but the precedent lives on after these successes and the principles survive the precedent. A generation has grown up which hates authority and is ignorant of its duties, and which will transmit to succeeding generations the fatal tradition of so many accepted errors and the noxious memory of so many crimes which remain unpunished. The causes of disorder, which always subsist at the heart of society, will sooner or later reproduce their terrible effects, unless the authority vested in the different societies substitutes its unlimited powers of preservation for this thorough system of destruction; unless our rulers return to the natural constitution of societies, in order to make their social action completely effective; unless finally they bring the whole might of public institutions into play, to fight and call a halt to the deadly consequences of occult institutions.

In France especially, it is both possible and necessary to relate the question of authority, and those who administer it, back to their natural origin; that is to say, to form a society. France has always served as a model to other nations, in good things as well as in bad; and alone perhaps in Europe, she is in just the requisite position to establish a society in a final and complete form, because she is, I think, the only nation which has reached the limits set to her territory by nature. A nation which has reached this stage ought not, and even cannot, have any other ambition than to maintain her position, to arm herself only against the enemy from without, and still more against the enemy from within: that spirit of pride and revolt which, curbed but never destroyed, and ever present in society because it is always alive in man, will wage an internecine and stubborn war until the end, in the bosom of society as well as in the heart of man. For let us make no mistake: society itself is a real state of warfare, in which virtue combats error, and good combats evil, while nature, which desires that all men should combine in a society, wars against man, who tends to isolate himself from society, or rather to create a society all by himself; the name of the *Lord of Hosts*, which is assumed by the creator and preserver of human nature, means first and foremost the God of societies.

We are approaching a great phase in the social development of the world. The Revolution, which, like all revolutions, was both religious and political, was the result of the general laws governing the preservation of societies, and is to be compared to a terrible and salutary crisis, by means of which nature roots out from the social body those vicious principles which the weakness of authority had allowed to creep in, and restores to it its health and pristine vigour.

Hence the Revolution will restore to the principle of authority in France the requisite strength which will enable it to preserve society, that same strength which it had lost in proportion as it repudiated the real bases of authority and in some cases over-estimated its scope. " Upheavals have always strengthened the hand of authority," says Montesquieu, who observes the fact without referring back to the principle. Hence the Revolution will restore religious and political *unity* to Europe, that natural constitution based on the authority of religion and the authority of the State, from which she was separated by the Treaty of Westphalia. It was, as a matter of fact, in this treaty, famous for all time, that the *atheistic* dogma of the religious and political sovereignty of man was first propounded and in a sense consecrated, that principle of every revolution and the germ of all the evils which afflict society, the *abomination of desolation in high places*, in other words, in a society which is subject to the sovereignty of God. Then it was that the leaders of the nations, united in the most solemn act that has been performed since the foundation of Christian society, recognised the public and social existence of political democracy, in the illusory independence of Switzerland and the United Provinces, and of religious democracy, in the public establishment of the reformed religion and the evangelical body of German princes, thus legalising in Europe usurpations of religious and political authority, which had hitherto only received a provisional and precarious recognition in imperfect States.

The treaties which sooner or later will bring the present war to an end will be based on contradictory principles, irrespective of the period in which they are signed. They will propose the abolition of all government by the mob, the organisation of Europe into great States, and perhaps even the overthrow of that dividing wall which, thanks to a policy torn by party hatreds, has separated certain peoples from the ancient faith of Christian Europe. Already we see the opposition to religious unity weakening in England, as, on account of the accession of Ireland and other events which are perhaps already in preparation, she becomes more firmly attached to the principle of monarchy. Russia, weary of the despotism which, as Montesquieu says, "is more burdensome to her than to her peoples themselves," is progressing towards a *unified* and natural organisation of political authority, through the law of succession which she has recently promulgated; at the same time, we can discern unequivocal signs in her government that she is trying to return to religious unity and that she will perhaps be able to bring the Orient back into that unity. Finally, in France herself, pseudo-authority is refraining from persecuting pseudo-religion, until such time as authority can lend religion its support. Every event of this ever-memorable era brings nearer to us the universal revelation of this fundamental truth of the science of society: that *outside religious and political unity, man can find no truth and society no salvation.*

The greatest genius the world has perhaps ever seen, Leibnitz,[1] who lived at the beginning of this century, and who, placed historically as he was between the reverses which afflicted the old age of Louis XIV and the upheavals which were inevitable during the minority of his successor, dared, at the time of France's greatest weakness, to foretell her future greatness, and to write these remarkable words to his friend Ludolphus: "Would you like me to tell you my fears more explicitly? It is that France, bringing the whole of the Rhine under her domination, will, with a stroke of the pen, reduce the College of Electors by one half, so that the foundations of the Empire being already destroyed, the structure itself will fall

---

[1] See Note 3, p. 94.

into ruin." Leibnitz wrote in his *Further Essays on Human Understanding* lines which are no less prophetic: " Those who imagine that they have broken free from the inconvenient fear of a watchful Providence and a threatening future, give their brute passions full rein and apply their minds towards seducing and corrupting others. If they are ambitious and *somewhat hard men*, they are capable of *setting the four corners of the earth ablaze* for their own pleasure or advancement, and some I have known of this metal. . . . I have even come to the conclusion that similar opinions, which gradually insinuate themselves into the minds of those great men who control other men and are responsible for government, and which slip into fashionable books, prepare the way for *the general revolution which threatens Europe. . . .* If we still have the strength to cure ourselves of the spiritual infection, the bad effects of which now begin to be visible, the evils can perhaps be averted; *but if it spreads, Providence will punish the faults of men by that very revolution to which it will give birth:* for whatever happens, *everything will in general and in the long run happen for the best. . . ."* In other words, all things will tend towards the improvement of mankind or of society, an opinion which is in conformity with this great man's system, a religious and philosophical optimism which was misunderstood and ridiculed by Voltaire,[1] and to which so many other men have subscribed, without fully understanding it.

Therein, and therein only, lies that *social perfectibility* which is promised us by men who do not understand the term, and whose opinions, at least in their consequences, drag down society to a state of ignorance and barbarity. Writers who attempt to hasten the progress of society reject it without examination, when they defend the principles of morality, reason and good taste against the encroachment of barbarians; a remarkable contradiction in terms, which proves that truth and error are often but the same things, seen from two different angles. Indeed, the opponents of *perfectibility* can be excused for failing to recognise it, when it is offered to them by men who, in morality, politics and literature, mistake the unnatural and the *extraordinary* for a novelty, who think that they are progressive, when they are only caught in a circle of errors and follies taken over from the Greeks in a new form, and when they see happiness for the peoples of the world only in riches, and progress for society only in the arts.

[1] See Note 4, p. 95.

II

Until the sixteenth century the life of Europe had been based on the two principles of monarchy and the Christian religion. Peace had been disturbed from time to time by wars between neighbours. Yet these wars, in which hatred was unknown, these passing disputes between peoples who were united in political and religious doctrine, merely provided a means of testing the strength of States, without there being any danger to their power or their independence; furthermore, they had often yielded to the intervention of the head of the Church, the common father of all Christian peoples and the universal link between members of the great family.

A great schism in religion occurred in the sixteenth century and a great cleavage in politics was the inevitable result.

A new system of religion, which was soon extended to politics, the presbyterian and popular system, hostile to the idea of monarchy, was born in Europe. Principles so diametrically opposed to each other were bound to come into conflict. So the struggle began in Europe, and will never perhaps be concluded.

The two great parties had resort to pen and arms alike; controversy divided intellects and war disturbed States. Each party endeavoured to retain power, or if it was not in power to seize it; and when they were exhausted by this bitter struggle, they drew breath under cover of treaties which were broken as soon as they were signed, so that for a while they were evenly matched. Then it was that Europe had its first glimpse of the idea of political equilibrium, which the publicists of the Northern countries[1] adopted enthusiastically, hoping thereby to tilt the balance in their own favour.

It might be interesting to examine this notion of political equilibrium, at a time when it appeared to be as *weighted* and steady as was possible. " After the peace of Aix-la-Chapelle," says Voltaire, " Christian Europe was divided into two great parties, who treated each other with consideration, maintaining in their own fashion the balance of power, *this pretext for so many wars*, which was supposed to guarantee eternal peace. One of these great factions consisted of the States of the Queen-Empress of Hungary,[2] a part of Germany, Russia, England, Holland and Sardinia; the other comprised France, Spain, the

Two Sicilies, Prussia and Sweden. Each power remained *under arms*. It was hoped that a lasting truce would result from the fear that each half of Europe inspired in the other. They flattered themselves for a long time that no aggressor could arise, because each State was armed in self-defence. Vain hope. A trifling quarrel between France and England over some native territory in Canada led all the sovereigns of Europe to formulate a new policy." Such was, and always will be, the strength and the extent of this system of the balance of power, *in which each power remains under arms*. It is an exact parallel to the principle of mechanical equilibrium, which only consists of a pause of a second between the two swings of the pendulum.

In vain can weights be changed, or the two halves which should counter-balance each other be combined in different ways: only war will result. The reason is that according to this system *each power remains under arms*, and it is only by putting their swords into the balance that they can achieve a moment's equilibrium: a situation more dangerous than ever today, when third-rate powers produce, or hold in reserve, a military strength which is quite disproportionate to the size of the population. Moreover, when we balance interests, or even military strength, is it possible for us also to put into the balance the moral strength of nations and the passions and talents of those who govern them ?

It was on less unsure foundations than this, that one of the greatest kings of modern times, and one of the greatest minds of all time, endeavoured to build order and peace in Europe. Both of them set at the head of Christendom, as arbiter and moderating influence, the common father of Christians. Although this plan for a Christian republic would have been difficult, not to say impossible, to realise, and although today we could not persuade that part of Europe which has rejected his spiritual supremacy to appreciate the political pre-eminence of the head of the Church, we must be careful not to reject contemptuously a plan which seemed practicable to Henry IV and Leibnitz.[1]

These two excellent minds understood to the full that Christendom is a great family, composed of young and old, a society in which there are strong and weak, great powers and small ones. The whole of Christendom was subject to the law common to families and States alike, which are not governed by a system of balances, but by various authorities.

[1] See Note 3, p. 94.

Dare we hope that in the facts we are about to present, and the opinion we are going to give, reason and experience will triumph over national prejudices ?

Since the time of Charlemagne, there has always been an authority in Europe which was respected, even by its rivals, and recognised, even by its enemies: the preponderance of France. It was not a preponderance based on force, for French politics have always been more successful than her arms, but it was based on the dignity, respect, influence and good counsel which her age and her memories brought her. There was also such consistency in the counsel she gave, her progress was so felicitous, in spite of mistakes in administration and military reverses, that a great Pope was moved to say that " France was a kingdom governed by Providence." France was the eldest of all these European societies. While the peoples of Great Britain and the Germanic lands were still living in their forests and marshes, Gaul, cultured through her study of Greek and Latin literature, strong in the Roman discipline, educated in the school of these masters of the World, refined by their arts and their urbanity, which had even in the end been driven into exile from Rome and had taken refuge within the confines of the Empire; Gaul, like a well-prepared soil, received all the advantages of Christian civilisation. Soon she became a monarchy; the antiquity of the noble line of her kings, itself older than any other royal line, the excellence of her constitution, the virtues and the intelligence of her clergy, the dignity of her magistrature, the fame of her chivalry, the learning of her Universities, the wisdom of her laws, her gracious way of living, the character of her inhabitants, rather than the strength of her arms, which were always evenly matched and often unfortunate—above all, the genius of Charlemagne, had raised her to a position in Europe which none contested. No great political act was ever performed without France; she was the trustee of every tradition of the great family, and the repository of all the *State secrets* of Christendom. I dare to say that no great act will ever be performed without her, and what assures her of this pre-eminence for all time, and in a measure sets the final seal on it, is the universality of her language, which has been adopted by Cabinets and Courts, and is consequently the language of politics: the mildest and at the same time the strongest domination which one people can exercise over another, since by imposing its language on others, a people bestows at the same time a measure of its character, its spirit and its thought, which is faithfully reflected in its language.

Hence France has always exercised a sort of authority over Christendom. She was always destined to teach Europe, sometimes by the example of her virtues, sometimes by the lesson to be drawn from her misfortunes. If we can trace great motives which led to great events, every nation is guilty and every nation has been punished; and France, the guiltiest nation of all, because she had received the most, has found a frightful retribution in the terrible revenge which made her its instrument.

The most striking tribute however to the importance of France in the social field, and to the political *need* for her existence, comes from the prodigious events we have just witnessed. I dare to say that no other society could excite the same interest, or call forth the same effort. The peoples of the North and East have had to join forces in order to restore to France that legitimate authority over herself which she had lost, when all they thought they were engaging in, and all they perhaps had desired to do, was to escape from her tyranny. All the noble scions of Christendom have had to bring back the first-born of this illustrious family with their own hands, to the house of his fathers. The elements themselves collaborated with mankind in this great undertaking; and when the head of the family crossed the threshold of France, this superhuman authority, the most formidable that the world has ever seen, and *before whom the earth was silent,* vanished like a dream, with all its fortresses, its treasure and its armies. This mighty storm grew calm in an instant and the last roar of gunfire seemed to be the signal for the piping days of peace.

Let nobody place on France the entire responsibility for the madness into which she fell, and for the unparalleled misfortunes she brought on Europe; the foreign doctrines brought into France over a period of years, and propagated by our writers with such lamentable success, have had only too great an effect on our destinies. It was easy to see through the foreign intrigues, even in the very early days of our troubles. The inconceivable tyranny beneath which in the end the whole of Europe groaned was connived at and supported by people outside France; she can say with a clear conscience to other governments: Let him who is without sin amongst you cast the first stone.

It would be a big mistake at the present time, and a great danger for the future, if political action, which is responsible for the wellbeing of Europe, were consciously to be motivated by memories of the past, instead of by a vision of the future.

This line of policy has been in the position of misleading Europe for a long time. With her eyes turned towards the past, she does not take the future sufficiently into account; in her desire to be forearmed against any imaginary peril, she exposes herself in her defenceless position to real dangers.

Because the House of Austria united for one historical moment the most splendid parts of the Old and the New World under her domination, France, who had no real reason to fear her, always imagined that Austria was anxious to swallow her up; their mutual hostility, under Charles V and Francis I, brought about the ruin of Europe, since it gave Lutheranism the opportunity to spread its influence. Richelieu reduced the nobles to the status of courtiers and paid officials, because he still feared the shadow of the great landed aristocracy which had long since been broken. Coming to our own days, France was only able to win such sweeping victories because the great powers of the North could not forget that they were age-old enemies and spent their strength in jealous rivalry.

There is no doubt that France has shown extraordinary might and caused Europe infinite misfortunes; yet it was the might that fever brings in its train, nay, a real frenzy. The revolution, like some supernatural engine which had been applied to a powerful nation, transformed her suddenly, and by means of terror, into a blind and dumb instrument whose only action was destruction and whose only movement was a flight towards ruin. This incredible combination of events, inconceivable until our own day, cannot happen again. To take precautions against such an unlikely event at the expense of France would be like conjuring up phantoms merely for the pleasure of fighting them. It is not the revolutionary armies of France which other States have to fear now, but rather the principles of licence and insubordination which she has sown in Europe, and which probably have more supporters outside France than in France herself.

We must not therefore reproach each other with our mistakes and errors, but must guard against the only danger which peoples who have reached a high level of civilisation and know-ledge need fear, the danger of false doctrines which impercep-tibly undermine laws, morals and institutions. When Europe emerges from this violent crisis, she cannot perish except by wasting away. The day when the atheistic dogma of the sovereignty of the people replaces in politics the sacred dogma of the sovereignty of God; the day when Europe ceases to be Christian and monarchical, she will perish, and the sceptre of the world will pass to other hands.

* * *

As we have said before, Bonald defines the unity of Christendom as a " Society of States," the State as a " public society " and the family as a " domestic society." The family is therefore, in his view, the first social unit, and the principle of the family is the basis of every other larger association. In his *Theory of Power,* Bonald expounds the idea that in the analysis of any phenomenon, three problems have to be faced and defined by every philosophy worthy of the name: the Cause, the Effect and the Means employed to achieve the Effect. In the social order, this means power (or authority, or will), ministry (or the service of power), and in the religious society spiritual wellbeing, or in the political society the security and the liberty of the subject. In the religious society, the Power (or Authority, or Will) is God; the ministry is the clergy; the effect aimed at is the salvation of the community. In the State, the Power is represented by the principle of Sovereignty; in its service, " ministry " is exercised by all those who administer the law and defend the territory (i.e. all those who " combat the obstacles to integral sovereignty," " the internal and the external enemy "); the effect to be desired is the security and the liberty of the subject to fulfil the natural purpose of Man, which is the procreation and preservation of the divine substance through the medium of the family. Within the family, the Power belongs to the man, whose " ministry " is exercised by the woman, and the effect desired is the child, i.e. the preservation of the divine and human substance in a new generation.

It follows from these fundamental notions of Bonald's system of philosophy, that in the political controversies of his time he considered the defence of marriage to be a foremost task. The following extract is taken from *Divorce in the Nineteenth Century,* a pamphlet published in 1802 and intended as a piece of advice to the Committee presided over by the First Consul Bonaparte, which was to codify the civil and penal laws of France. This was one of the rare writings of Bonald which achieved an immediate and practical result: Bonaparte read it, and under the influence of Bonald's arguments, he took the initiative of withdrawing the original draft authorising divorce.

2. ON DOMESTIC SOCIETY

THE authors of the draft Bill on the statute book, after having informed us " that until today, the nature of marriage has been misunderstood, and that it is only in recent times that people have had clear ideas on marriage . . . are convinced that marriage, which existed before the establishment of Christianity, which preceded all positive law, and which derives from the very composition of our being, is neither a civil nor a religious act, but a natural one, which attracted the attention of legislators and which has been sanctified by religion." (Introduction, on the draft Bill of the statute book.)

It is well worth while to discuss the principles set forth in the passage which we have just quoted, since they form the basis of all the draft bills on the possibility of divorce, from the first bill in which it was proposed to grant divorce, to the final one which received the sanction of the legislature.

How has it been possible to maintain in France, after fifteen centuries of the public profession of Christianity, that is, of everything that was most perfect in public morality and in the principles underlying the laws, according to all men in the most enlightened nations who are versed in the knowledge of civil and religious legislation, " that until today people have misunderstood the nature of marriage," this element which is present in all societies, this *contract* which really is *social*, the act by which a family is founded, the laws governing which are at the basis of all political legislation ? How has it been possible to suggest " that it is only in recent times that people have had clear ideas on marriage " ? And to which period do " *recent times* " refer ? Are they referring to the time of Luther, who allowed the dissolution of marriage, or to the period of modern philosophy, which, not content with allowing the greatest possible facility in the dissolution of the conjugal tie, has justified concubinage and extended its indulgence as far as adultery ? And are they not already biased in favour of the usefulness of divorce, when they state in the preamble of the Bill which authorises it, " *that only in recent times has marriage been understood* " ?

" Marriage, which existed before the establishment of Christianity, which preceded all positive law, and which derives from the very composition of our being, is neither a civil nor a religious act, but a natural one, which attracted the attention of the legislator and was sanctified by religion." *Marriage existed before Christianity and preceded all positive laws;* but did it precede the natural relationships between men in society, the most perfect evolution of which is seen in the Christian religion, and to which all religions and civil laws give expression and bear witness ?

The sentence we have just quoted deceives the mind, and the differing meanings which it seems to suggest will not bear examination.

Marriage is a civil affair from the point of view of the interests at stake; it is religious, spiritually speaking; it is *animal* and physical from the point of view of the body; and as the family has never at any time been able to subsist without the social proprieties, and as man has always embarked on marriage in possession of all his moral and physical faculties, it is true to say that the nature of marriage has always fundamentally been a simultaneous civil, religious and physical act. It was not a civil affair in the earliest times, in the sense that the interests of the family were protected by public authority and regulated according to public laws, which comprise what we call our civil status. But they were protected by domestic authority, which is an element of the public authority, and regulated by domestic customs and laws, which are themselves the germs of the public laws, just as the domestic society, or the family, is itself the element and the germ of public society. Marriage was not religious in the sense that it was divine, and that the Creator had said of the woman: " She shall leave her father and her mother and cleave unto her husband," and of husband and wife: " They shall be two in one flesh." It is because marriage was, in the earliest times, and before the establishment of public, political and religious societies, a divine and at the same time a human act (I mean by human: moral and physical), just as it has been a civil and religious act since the foundation of public societies; I say it is because it derives from the very composition of our being and of our nature, that it is a *natural* act. For the real nature of man, and the true composition of his being, consist in a natural relationship with the author of his being, and in his natural as well as his moral and physical relationship with his fellow-men. It is entirely because marriage was a divine and a human institution, in the sense in which I understand it, that it *attracted the attention* of civil legislators, and that it was sanctified by religion. For if the orator, whose reasoning I question, because he makes a distinction between the *natural* and the civil or religious state, as if what is civil and religious is not also natural, understands by nature the animal instincts of man, he is falling into the same error as the senator who submitted the government draft of this Bill, when he says: " Philosophers are only concerned with the physical side of marriage." They are certainly curious philosophers, be it said in passing; apparently only anatomists are allowed to consider the union of man and woman in this light.

Natural marriage, which is neither *civil* nor *religious*, gives birth to the *natural* man of J. J. Rousseau, who is likewise neither *civil* nor *religious*; and to say that marriage *is neither a civil nor a religious act, but a natural act*, is to suggest that the civil and religious state is not within the nature of man. It is to descend to the level of the doctrine of the writer whom we have just quoted, when he says " that society is not natural to mankind," and elsewhere that " everything that is not contained in nature has certain disadvantages, civil society having more than all the rest put together."

Let us say then that marriage is simultaneously a social, domestic, civil and religious act; the act by which domestic society is founded, the interests of which are bound to be safe-guarded by the civil authority as it comes to the aid of domestic harmony, and in which religious authority introduces the divine element in an external and sensible manner, in order to consecrate the union of two hearts and purify the union of two bodies.

No problem could be clearer in its principles, or more fruitful in its consequences, than the question of divorce, since by its nature it brings into play all those problems of *authority* and our *duties*, which are fundamental to society. I do not hesitate to affirm, and I hope even to prove, that on the dissolution or the indissolubility of the conjugal tie depends the fate of the family, of religion and of the State, in France and in the whole world.

Divorce was made legal in 1792, to the surprise of nobody, since it was the inevitable *consequence*, long foreseen, of that system of destruction which was pursued with such enthusiasm at that time. But today, when we want to reconstruct, divorce appears to be almost a *principle* at the base of the social edifice, and those who are destined to inhabit it ought to tremble.

I will go further. Divorce was in harmony with that brand of democracy which has held sway for too long in France, under different names and in different forms. We have seen domestic and public authority delivered up on all sides to the passions of *subjects*; it brought about disorder in the family and disorder in the State: there was an analogy between the disorganisation in both of them. There is indeed, if one may say so, even some semblance of order, when everything is confused in the same style, and for the same reason. Furthermore, divorce is in direct contradiction with the spirit and the principles of hereditary or indissoluble monarchy. We have, then, order in the State and disorder in the family, indissolubility of the one and dissolution of the other, with a subsequent lack of harmony, so that the situation is such that the family will finally disorganise the State or the State will have to govern the family. Nay, more. In a democracy, the people have the privilege of making the laws, or abolishing them, according to their fancy. Since the magistrates they elect only hold office for a short time, it rarely happens that individual men are powerful enough to make the laws serve their passions, whereas in a monarchy, where men hold eminent positions, which can be hereditary, or else are conferred for life, and derive from them a great reputation and a great fortune, it can happen that laws are not made by influential men, but are interpreted in their favour. What judgements could be solicited with greater passion than those concerning divorce, and what laws lend themselves to arbitrary interpretation to a greater degree than those which limit or extend facilities for divorce ? Now where great men have trod, the crowd treads in its turn. What was once difficult becomes easy; what was once rare becomes a frequent occurrence; what was forbidden is now permitted; the exception acquires all the force of law; the law is soon nothing but the exception and the time comes when there is no other alternative to disorder than extreme disorder or revolution.

*   *   *

Note 1: " publicists of the Northern countries."

Bonald mainly refers to the seventeenth-century Swedish statesman of German birth, Puffendorff, whose *States of Europe* was for a century or more considered to be the classic handbook of diplomacy. He may, however, equally have in mind Spinoza's *Tractatus theologico-politicus*, another classic (and more metaphysical) summary of the theory of the balance of power, the perfect balance being the result of politics conceived *more geometrico*, like an architectural construction.

This idea of Spinoza was very popular among English Whig publicists of the early eighteenth century. Dean Swift however thought that the diplomatic balance of the European house might become so perfect that any sparrow which settled down on the roof would upset it!

Note 2: " Queen-Empress of Hungary."

Maria-Theresa, Archduchess of Austria, daughter of Emperor Charles VI, b. 1717, d. 1780. By the Act of Pragmatic Sanction of her father, promulgated at the Hungarian Diet in 1723, she succeeded to the Crown of Hungary in 1740. As this Act was also endorsed by the Imperial Diet, the hereditary " Kingdoms and Provinces " of the House of Habsburg (Bohemia, Moravia, Silesia, Upper and Lower Austria, Tyrol, Vorarlberg, etc.) belonging to the Holy Roman Empire were to remain " undivided and inseparable " under her rule, although on account of her sex she could not succeed to the Empire, which fell in 1740 to the Prince-Elector of Bavaria, who ruled as Charles VII until 1747, and to which Prince Francis of Lorraine, Grand Duke of Tuscany, Maria-Theresa's husband, was afterwards elected (d. 1765 and succeeded by his son Joseph II, who, on his mother's death in 1780, also became King of Hungary and ruler of the hereditary States). Thus, in the diplomacy of her time, Maria-Theresa, ruling Queen in Hungary and Empress-Consort, later Empress-Mother, was referred to as " Queen of Hungary," or more ceremoniously as " Her Apostolic Majesty," a title which referred exclusively to the Papal privileges of St. Stephen of Hungary, and not to her other dominions.

The European situation here described by Voltaire underwent changes, by reason of the fact that Britain and France could never be on the same side during the great eighteenth-century rivalry. During the War of the Austrian Succession, which ended with the Peace of Aix-la-Chapelle in 1748, Britain supported Maria-Theresa against France and Prussia. Subsequently the Austrian Chancellor, Prince Kaunitz, conceived the plan of a great continental alliance between France, Austria and Russia, mainly in order to moderate growing Russian aims in the East by having greater security on the Western flank of the Austrian power. As a reply, Walpole and the Whig party sided with Prussia, against both France and Austria. The European situation which Voltaire summarises here and Bonald quotes, prevailed between the end of the War of the Austrian Succession (1748) and the Seven Years' War (1756-1763).

Note 3: " Leibnitz."

Gottfried Wilhelm Leibnitz, 1646-1716, a German philosopher writing mostly in Latin and French, a mathematician and scientist, also an author on politics and international law, one of the most versatile intellects of modern Europe. The fundamental notion of his philosophical system is the " pre-established " or " pre-existing " harmony between spiritual and material reality. Each species (" Monadology ") follows its own intrinsic law and naturally tends towards its reproduction for the sake of the perfect preservation of its internal value.

Bonald's *Theory of Power* which considers " preservation " as the aim of the power established in religious and political societies, and " perfectibility " (i.e. the capacity to realise the " best possible " order), the principle of which is the " pre-established harmony of

Creation," is very largely an application of the methods and principles of Leibnitz in politics and society.

Leibnitz was the first Protestant thinker to advocate the reunion of the Protestant communities with the Church: a leading idea in his correspondence with Bossuet, Bishop of Meaux, which extends over a period of years.

Note 4: " ridiculed by Voltaire."

Bonald alludes here to Voltaire's *Candide*, the grotesque and fantastic story of an unfortunate young man educated in Leibnitz's doctrine that the world lives under " the best possible order." The aversion of Voltaire and of many other writers of the eighteenth century to Leibnitz is to be explained by the fact that (unlike other thinkers of the great European philosophical movement which followed the religious wars and which relegated the theological issue to a secondary plane), Leibnitz aimed at a definition of the metaphysical world order, and not only at a method of individual reasoning (like Descartes), at experimental science (like Bacon or Locke), or an analysis of the critical mind (like Kant). In other words, Leibnitz was the philosophical opposite, for the eighteenth century, of rationalistic and ethical individualism.

At the same time, Leibnitz is still nearer to the Realism of St Thomas than either Descartes or Bacon and he emphatically recognises the primacy of belief and the conformity of rational knowledge with the truth of Revelation.

III. FRANÇOIS RENÉ DE CHATEAUBRIAND

1768 - 1848

CHATEAUBRIAND's place in a chronological survey of Catholic thought since the French Revolution comes immediately after Joseph de Maistre and Vicomte de Bonald. The *Considérations sur la France* of the first writer, the *Théorie du Pouvoir* of the second and Chateaubriand's *Essai sur les Révolutions* were the three great commentaries published on the events of 1789-93. All three were written abroad and were influenced by, and to a great extent inspired by an English book, Burke's *Reflections on the French Revolution*.

Bonald's book was the final expression and the systematic summary of the thought of an author in his forties; everything else he wrote in his life was but an addition or glossary to it. Joseph de Maistre, about the same age as Bonald, wrote his principal book—the *Soirées de Saint Pétersbourg*—a quarter of a century later; his *Considérations sur la France* and even *Du Pape* were but prefaces to his final thought. In Chateaubriand's case, however, his comment on the Revolution was not so much as a preface even to the ultimate summary of his thought and it merely marked one step towards the final pinnacle of his style. The subject, however, was of immense importance in his life. Like Joseph de Maistre and Bonald, Chateaubriand, half a generation younger than they, became a writer because of the French Revolution; a principal feature in his work is the new historical and political approach to theology, which resulted from the context of the Revolution. Yet, he is, above all, one of the masters, perhaps the foremost one, of a new concept of literature. He is a master among the new post-Revolutionary secular religious writers. He is the first of those modern poets who are not craftsmen of rhyme and stage technique—there were many such during the eighteenth century—and he it was who gave to the word " poet " that larger, more universal meaning which it still keeps in German. According to this new concept, the poet is a writer, often a prose-writer (Chateaubriand himself wrote almost entirely in prose, for his attempts at verse and at poetic tragedy were a failure), who must be judged above all by standards of personal feeling and temperament. In other words, Chateaubriand was the father of Romanticism. In aesthetics he saved that part of Rousseau's message which was valid truth, and the rest of which was otherwise so disastrous in politics.

A recapitulation of Chateaubriand's life and work is hardly necessary here; he is a writer whom few read today, but who is nevertheless known to all. This has happened because, as Oscar Wilde said of himself, he gave to his books his talent only, while he gave to his life his genius. Chateaubriand created at least one work of genius, which was the story of his life, the *Mémoires d'outre-tombe.* The conclusion of these Memoirs tell what was the central inspiration of his life and his work.

This inspiration was already clear in *Le Génie du Christianisme* and in *Les Martyrs.* In his early sensualist outlook he was still a son of the eighteenth century, of Condillac and especially of Rousseau. His return to the old religious foundations of France was only partly political and social in origin; it was to a large extent visual and aesthetic. He rediscovered Gothic architecture at a moment when medieval art found no defenders and when the Greek colonnade, with its more geometrical form, was the fashionable ideal of the day. He introduced into the art of epic prose imaginative detail, colourful landscape, historical atmosphere and spectacular costume—all visual elements—and so he became the master of Sir Walter Scott and the historical novel. Chateaubriand revolutionised European taste and European art almost more than any other writer contemporary with the Revolution. He discovered the East and the Holy Land for many of his contemporaries; he was perhaps the first French author fully to understand Shakespeare; the first modern writer who interpreted the saints, the Fathers and the early teachers of the Church as thinkers and mystical poets, rather than as theologians and authorities on the liturgy—a new approach at the end of the eighteenth century and an unusual and a new angle for scholarship and letters, which before Chateaubriand had kept secular humanism and theology apart.

There are, of course, as we have already pointed out in the Introduction, obvious limitations and shortcomings in this artistic and aesthetic religiosity. They were already present in Chateaubriand's work; they led to worse aberrations in his followers and imitators: to a superficial pose of melancholy over a lost tradition and to the *culte du moi* of Maurice Barrès, for example. Chateaubriand had neither the grave objectivity of Bonald, nor the penetrating, critical wit of Joseph de Maistre, so that ultimately little survives which is of any objective value in his religious, political and philosophical thought.

As to his career as a statesman, he was Plenipotentiary Minister of the First Consul Bonaparte to the Vatican, Ambassador in London and Berlin and once more at the Vatican, and Minister of Foreign Affairs for a short while under the Restoration; he was the author of pamphlets such as *De Buonaparte*[1] *et des Bourbons* (1814)

---

[1] By insisting on the Italian spelling of the name which the family abandoned when they left Corsica for France during the Revolution, Chateaubriand wished to emphasise the fact that he considered Napoleon to be a usurper.

and *La Monarchie selon la Charte* (1816), great political events at the time. Yet he left behind him only the memory of a temperamental opposition, first to Napoleon, then even to the Bourbons, whose cause he had promoted, and finally a long voluntary exile from the political scene in Paris, at the memorable salon of Madame Récamier, during which he foresaw the future triumph of Democracy over Louis Philippe's imitation-Monarchy and over the bourgeoisie, the "*monarchie de la boutique*," and during which he once more espoused the lost cause of the elder branch of the Bourbons.

He ended his long career with this melancholy love for a cause he believed to be lost, dying at the age of eighty on July 4th, 1848. Mental decay preceding his physical end, during the last year of his life he was hardly conscious of the new Revolution and of the fighting at the barricades in June 1848, which absorbed the general attention, while Chateaubriand, the great personal link between the eighteenth and the nineteenth centuries in France, was on his deathbed.

His life exhausted all the possibilities of an age. He saw America during the life-time of Washington, Europe under Napoleon; he knew the destitution and solitude of an exile in London during the Revolution; he enjoyed the adventures of a soldier in the Royalist cause and the flamboyant but hollow splendours of the victorious diplomacy of the era of the Congresses. And to this life he gave an imperishable monument, the great story of an indefatigable sensibility, of the emotions of a long and varied life, of a personality which was too exuberant to create a consistent system of thought. Chateaubriand's greatness lies in his imagination, his sensibility and emotion.

Any account of Chateaubriand's life is bound to centre round the problem of " pose," so that both his critics and admirers must devote a fundamental study to the question of sincerity and ostentation. Chateaubriand, no doubt, liked ostentation. Yet there is hardly a more insincere book in existence that Sainte-Beuve's attack on Chateaubriand's sincerity. Sainte-Beuve, the least sincere of the Romantic generation, the least loyal character among men of talent, if anything a Jansenist in religion (not on account of a misguided religious passion, but out of spite for the spiritual gifts of others and out of spite for the Church), Sainte-Beuve was a bad judge of Chateaubriand's sincerity in religion, and was not even the best qualified judge of his genius. Sainte-Beuve's talent grew in the service of those greater than he; Chateaubriand, even at his worst, was a sovereign temperament. The proud ostentation of honour is to be preferred to that of informed pedantry; the pose of a hopeless love for lost causes is preferable to the critical pose of a bitter and pedantic talent, who, after all, placed himself voluntarily in Chateaubriand's shadow for over twenty years before he discovered any blot on his sun. As the deliberate distortions and, we may say, the bad faith of Sainte-Beuve's *Chateaubriand et son groupe littéraire* has been exposed by two Catholic literary scholars of incontestable probity, this debate may be considered closed.[1]

There is ostentation in Chateaubriand, but no morbid self-seeking, no indecent and effeminate exhibitionism, nothing approaching decadence. His place in the history of secular spirituality is best defined by himself in the conclusion to *Mémoires d'outre-tombe* which follows here.

PROGRESS[2]

DURING the eight centuries of our monarchy, France was the centre of the intelligence, the continuity and the peace of Europe; no sooner had that monarchy been lost than Europe tended in the direction of democracy. The human race, for good or for ill, is now its own master; princes once had the keeping of it; having attained their majority, the nations now claim that they have no further need of tutelage. From the time of David down to modern days, kings have always been called; now the vocation of the peoples begins. Apart from the short-lived and minor exceptions of the Greek, the Carthaginian and the Roman republics, with their slaves, the monarchical form of government was normal throughout the entire world. Modern society in its entirety has forsaken the monarchy since the flag of the kings of France no longer flies. In order to hasten the degradation of royal power, God has in various countries delivered up the sceptre to usurper kings, to young girls who are either still in the nursery, or are just of marriageable age; it is lions such as these, without any jaws, lionesses without any claws and baby girls suckling at the breasts, or giving their hand in marriage, whom the men born of this believing age must follow.

The wildest principles are proclaimed under the very noses of monarchs who imagine that they are safeguarding themselves behind the triple hedge of a doubtful protection. Democracy is overtaking them; stage by stage, they are retreating from the ground floor of their palaces to the topmost part, so

[1] L'Abbé G. Bertrin: *La sincérité religieuse de Chateaubriand.* 1893. Edmond Biré: *Chateaubriand, Victor Hugo, Balzac.* 1897.

[2] Taken from the epilogue to *Mémoires d'outre-tombe.* Written in November 1841, this epilogue was first published in *La Presse,* edited by Emile de Girardin, in October 1850.

that finally they will cast themselves upon the waters from the attic windows.

Furthermore, consider a phenomenal contradiction: material conditions are improving and education is spreading, yet instead of this being a boon to the nations their stature is diminishing—from whence comes this contradiction?

The explanation lies in this: that we have deteriorated in the moral order. Crimes have always been committed, but they were not committed in cold blood, as they are today, because we have lost all feeling for religion. They no longer fill us with revulsion today, they seem only to be a consequence of the march of time; if they were judged differently in former times, it was because, as they dare to assert, our knowledge of human nature was not advanced enough. Nowadays crimes are analysed; they are passed through a crucible in order that we may discover any useful lesson accruing from them, as chemistry discovers constituents in garbage. Corruption of the mind, far more destructive than corruption of the senses, is accepted as a necessary result; it is not only to be found now in a few perverted individuals; it has become universal.

Men of this type would feel humiliated if it were proved to them that they had a soul and that after this life they will discover the existence of another one; they would think themselves devoid of all steadfastness, strength and intelligence if they did not rise above the pusillanimity of our fathers; they accept nothingness, or if you prefer it, doubt, as an unpleasant fact perhaps, but nevertheless as an incontestable truth. How admirable is our fatuous pride!

The decay of society then and the increasing importance of the individual can be accounted for in this manner. If the moral sense developed logically from the increase in intelligence, we should have a counterweight and humanity would increase in stature without any danger, but the exact opposite happens; our apprehension of good and evil grows dim as our intelligence becomes more enlightened; our conscience contracts as our ideas broaden. Yes, society will certainly perish; liberty, which might have saved the world, will not work, because it has cut itself off from religion; order, which could have ensured continuity, cannot be firmly established because the present anarchy of ideas prevents it. The purple, which once denoted power, will henceforth serve only to cradle disaster; no man will be saved unless he was born, like Christ, on straw. When the monarchs were disinterred at St. Denis, as the revolutionary tocsin rang out; when, dragged from their crumbling tombs, they were awaiting plebeian burial, rag merchants came upon this scene of the last judgement of the centuries; holding high their lanterns, they gazed into the eternal night; they rummaged amongst the remains which had escaped the original pillage. The kings were no longer there, but royalty was still there; they tore it out of the entrails of time and cast it on the rubbish heap.

So much for ancient Europe: it will never live again. Does the young Europe offer us any higher hopes ? The world of today, lacking any consecrated authority, seems faced with two impossibilities: it is impossible to return to the past or to go forward into the future. Do not run away with the idea, as some people do, that if we are in a bad pass today, good will be reborn out of evil; human nature, when it is out of order at its very source, does not function so smoothly. The excesses of liberty, for example, lead to despotism, but the excesses of tyranny lead only to tyranny; tyranny, by degrading us, makes us incapable of independence; Tiberius did not have the effect of making Rome return to the republican form of government, he merely left Caligula behind to succeed him.

Not desiring to find the true explanation of our present situation, men are content to say that a political constitution which we cannot as yet discern may possibly be hidden in the bosom of time. Did the whole of antiquity, including the most splendid of its geniuses, understand that a society could exist without slaves ? Yet we know that it can. People say—I have said it myself—that mankind will increase in stature in this new civilisation which is to come: yet is it not to be feared that the individual man will decrease in stature ? We can well be busy bees, engaged in making our own honey together. In the *material* world, men group themselves together for the purpose of work, because many people working together find what they want quicker and by devious means; individuals working in the mass can build pyramids; these individuals, studying each in his own way, can make scientific discoveries and explore all the corners of the physical creation. But do things work out in this wise in the *moral* order ? A thousand brains can collaborate in vain: they can never compose the masterpiece which comes out of the head of a Homer.

It has been said that a city, all the inhabitants of which have an equal share of wealth and education, will be a more pleasing sight in the eyes of Divinity than was the city of our fathers.

The folly of the age is to achieve the unity of the peoples, while turning the whole species into a single unit—granted; but while we are acquiring these general faculties, is not a whole chain of private feelings in danger of perishing ? Farewell to the sweetness of home; farewell to the delights of family life; amongst all these white men, yellow men and black men, reputedly your brothers, you will not find one whom you can embrace as a brother. Was there nothing then in your former life, nothing in that restricted piece of space which you could see from your ivy-mantled window ? Beyond your immediate horizon, you conjectured the existence of unknown countries from the presence of the birds of passage, the only travellers that you saw in the autumn days. Happiness lay in knowing that the surrounding hills would always be there; that they would be the scene of your friendships and your loves; that the sighing of the night wind around your retreat would be the only sound to lull you to sleep; that the peace of your soul would never be disturbed and that the familiar thoughts would always be waiting for you to commune with them. You knew where you had been born, you knew where your tomb would lie; as you penetrated deeper into the forest you could say:

> *Beautiful trees that saw my birth,*
> *Soon you will see me die.*

Man has no need to travel to become more powerful; he carries immensity within him. The impulses of your heart cannot be measured, they find an echo in thousands of other hearts; he who has nothing of this harmony in his innermost being will implore the universe to give it to him in vain. Sit on a fallen tree-trunk deep in the woods: if in these moments of complete self-forgetfulness, in your immobility and silence, you do not find the infinite, it is of no avail to wander along the banks of the Ganges.

What sort of a universal society would it be which possessed no individual country, which would be neither French nor English, nor German, nor Spanish, nor Portuguese, nor Italian, nor Russian, nor Tartar, nor Turkish, nor Persian, nor Indian, nor Chinese, nor American, or rather, what would all these societies be like if they were rolled into one ? What would the effect be on the way of life, on the sciences, the arts and the poetry of a universal society ? What expression could be given to passions felt at the same time by different peoples under different climates ? How would this medley of needs and images which the sun produces in divers lands, and which light up the youth, the maturity and the old age of men, enter into the language ? And what language would it be ? Will a universal idiom be born out of the fusion of societies, or will there be a business dialect for everyday purposes, whilst each nation retains its own language, or, on the other hand, will all the divers languages be understood by all ? Under what sort of rule and under what sort of universal law would this society live ? How should we find a place on an earth which has been extended by the·power of ubiquity and shrunk by the small proportions of a globe which is everywhere dishonoured ? It only remains to ask science to show us how we can go and live on another planet.

Let us suppose that you have had enough of private property and that you propose to turn the government into a universal landlord, who is to distribute to the destitute community that share which each individual deserves. Who is to be the judge of individual merits ? Who will have the strength and the authority to carry out your decrees? Who is to be responsible for and assess the capital value of this human property ? What is to be the contribution of the weak, the sick and the stupid in a community burdened by their unfitness ?

There is another suggestion: instead of working for a salary, men could form limited companies, or limited partnerships between manufacturers and workers, between intelligence and matter, whereby some would contribute ideas and others their industry and their work; profits would be shared in common. It is an excellent thing thus to acknowledge complete perfection in mankind: excellent, if quarrels, avarice or envy are unknown: but once an associate registers a grievance, the whole edifice crumbles; dissension and lawsuits will henceforth be the order of the day. This method, which is slightly more plausible than the others in theory, is as impossible in practice.

Would you prefer to follow a moderate line and build a city in which each man has a roof, fuel, clothing and adequate food ? You will no sooner have presented each citizen with these things, than individual qualities and defects will either upset your system of distribution, or will make it unjust: one man needs much more food than the other; this man cannot work as hard as that one can; men who are frugal and work hard will become rich, those who are extravagant or idle will

relapse into poverty; for you cannot bestow the same temperament on all: an innate inequality is bound to reappear in spite
of all your efforts.

Do not be under any illusion that we are going to allow ourselves to be caught up in all the legal processes which have
been invented for the protection of the family, for inherited
rights, the guardianship of children, claims to property, etc.;
marriage is notoriously an absurd oppression: we shall abolish
all that. If a son kills his father, it is not the son, as we can
very well prove, who is guilty of patricide, it is the father, who,
by the very act of living, sacrifices the son's chances. Do not
let us trouble our heads then with the labyrinths of an organisation which we intend to raze to the ground; it is a waste of
time to linger over the obsolete nonsense of our grandfathers.

Notwithstanding this, some of our sectarian modernists,
having an inkling of the impractibility of their doctrines, introduce certain phrases concerning morality and religion, in an
attempt to make them more palatable; they imagine that all
they can realise at the moment is to bring us into line with the
American ideal of mediocrity, ignoring in their blindness the
fact that the Americans are not only landowners, but very
enthusiastic ones, which makes all the difference.

Others, who are of a kindlier disposition still, and who are not
hostile to the polish which a civilisation can confer on men,
would be satisfied if they could transform us into *constitutional*
Chinamen, atheist to all practical purposes, enlightened and
free old gentlemen, sitting for centuries amongst our flower-
beds in our yellow robes, whiling away our days in a wellbeing
which has spread to the masses, having invented all things and
discovered all things, peacefully vegetating amidst all the
progress which has been accomplished, carried in the train like
a parcel merely to go from Canton to the Great Wall to discuss
with another business man of the Celestial Empire a piece of
marshland which has to be drained, or a canal which is to be
cut. In either hypothesis, American or Chinese, I should be
thankful to have departed this world before such felicity befell
me.

There is one final suggestion: it could happen that, as a
result of the total deterioration of the human character, the
peoples of the world would be content to make do with what
they have got: love of gold would take the place of a love of
their independence, while kings would barter their love of
power for love of the civil list. A compromise would thus be

reached between monarchs and their subjects, who would be delighted to fawn upon them without let or hindrance in a bastard political order; all men would display their infirmities in front of each other, as they used to do in the old lazar houses, or as sick people do today, when they take mudbaths as a cure for their ailments; mankind would flounder in unmitigated mud after the fashion of a peaceable reptile.

It is, nevertheless, a mere waste of time at the present stage of our development to desire to replace intellectual pleasures by the delights of physical nature. These latter, as we can well imagine, filled the lives of the aristocratic peoples of antiquity; masters of the world, they possessed palaces and vast numbers of slaves; their estates comprised whole regions of Africa. But under which porticoes can you wander now, in your rare moments of leisure ? In which huge and ornate baths can you find nowadays the perfumes and flowers, the flute-players and courtesans of Ionia ? You cannot be Heliogabulus[1] for the asking. Where would you lay hands on the necessary treasure for these material delights ? The spirit is frugal, but the body is extravagant.

And now, to be more serious, a few words on the question of absolute equality: such an equality would mean a return not only to bodily slavery, but to spiritual slavery; for it would mean nothing less than the destruction of the moral and physical inequality of the individual. Our wills, controlled and supervised by all, would witness the atrophy of our faculties. The infinite, for example, is part of our very nature; if you forbid our intelligence, or even our passions, to dream of unbounded prosperity, you reduce a man to the level of a snail and you metamorphose him into a machine. For make no mistake, if we cannot hope to penetrate the ultimate, if we do not believe in eternal life, there is annihilation everywhere; no man is free if he does not possess any property of his own; a man who has no property cannot be independent, he becomes a member of the proletariat or he works for a wage, whether he live within our present system of private property, or in a future one of communal property. Property held in common would mean that our society would be like one of those monasteries which used to distribute bread to the needy at the gates. Property which we hold inviolate from our fathers is our means of personal defence; property really means the same thing as

---

[1] Roman Emperor, b. 204 A.D. Reigned from 218-222. The prototype of dissolute and pleasure-loving youth.

liberty. Absolute equality, which presupposes *complete submission* to this *equality*, would make us revert to the most wretched servitude; it would make of individual man a beast of burden, submitting to his bonds and obliged to walk endlessly along the same path.

. . . Enlightened people cannot understand why a Catholic such as I should so obstinately take my stand in the shadow of what they think are ruins; according to them, it is bravado on my part, or prejudice. But for pity's sake, tell me where I could find a family or a God in the individualistic and philosophical society which you propose for my acceptance ? Tell me, and I will follow you; if you cannot, do not take it amiss if I lay myself down in the tomb of Christ, the only refuge you left me when you abandoned me.

No, it is not out of bravado: I am sincere; my conclusion is this: that out of all the plans and studies I have made, and after all my experiences, there only remains a complete disillusionment with all the preoccupations of this world. As my religious convictions developed, they absorbed all my other convictions; no man here on earth is a more faithful Christian, or more sceptical in the things of this world, than I. Far from being exhausted, the religion of the Liberator is just entering its third phase, the political phase of *liberty, equality* and *fraternity*. The Gospel—that verdict of acquittal—has not yet been proclaimed to all men; we have progressed no further than the maledictions pronounced by Christ: Woe to you who weigh men down with burdens too heavy to be borne, and who would not touch them with the tips of your fingers!

The Christian religion, stable in its dogmas, is yet mobile in its inspiration; as it develops, it transforms the whole world. When it has reached its highest point, darkness will finally be made light; liberty, crucified on Calvary with the Messiah, will descend from the Cross with Him; it will put back into the hands of the nations that New Testament which was written for their benefit, and the message of which has hitherto been fettered. Governments will pass, moral evil will pass and the renewal will announce the consummation of the centuries of death and oppression which started with the Fall.

When will this longed for day dawn ? When will society be reorganised according to the secret ways of the principle of generation ? No man can tell; the resistance which human passions will offer cannot be measured.

Death will more than once engulf the peoples in torpor and

will enshroud events in silence, as the snow fallen in the night deadens the noise of the wagon. Nations do not develop as rapidly as the individuals who comprise them, and do not disappear so quickly. How long it takes to find out the meaning of a certain event! The Byzantine Empire believed that its agony would be prolonged for ever; the Christian era, already so long drawn out, has still not seen the abolition of slavery. Such considerations do not, I am aware, suit the French temperament; we have never admitted the element of time in our revolutions: that is why we have always been dumbfounded at the results, which were the opposite of what we so impatiently desired. Young men hurl themselves into the fray, animated by generous courage; with their eyes on the ground, they climb towards the heights which they can dimly see and which they struggle to attain: nothing is more admirable; but they will waste their lives in these attempts and when they have reached the allotted span and piled error upon error, they will impose on succeeding generations by bestowing the burden of their disillusionment upon them, which they in turn will carry to neighbouring graves; and so on. The times of the desert have returned; Christianity starts afresh in the sterility of the Thebaid, amidst a formidable idolatry, the idolatry of man for himself.

History has two sequels, one which is both immediate and instantly recognised, the other which is more distant and not immediately perceived. They are often mutually contradictory, for one derives from our brief human wisdom and the other from the eternal wisdom. The providential event appears after the human event. God is seen to have worked through the actions of men. Deny as much as you please the supreme purpose, refuse to acknowledge its action, quarrel over words, name what the vulgar call Providence the force of circumstances, or reason—observe what the result of a certain course of action was and you will see that the opposite of what was intended invariably came to pass, if it was not primarily based on standards of morality and justice.

If Heaven has not pronounced its final decree; if a future is to come into being which will be both strong and free, this future is still very distant, far beyond our present horizon; we can only attain it with the help of that Christian hope whose wings extend ever wider, as all things appear to betray it, a hope which is more lasting than time itself and stronger than disaster.

IV. HONORÉ DE BALZAC

1799 - 1850

An account of Balzac's life and even a short appreciation of his immense achievement would be out of place here. Studies of the great novelist's art abound in every language, as do anecdotes on the great eccentric. He has even sometimes been introduced as a moralist and author of aphorisms.

None the less, Balzac is little known as a defender of the Faith. Despite the Preface to his *Human Comedy*, in which he describes himself as an author " definitely on the side of Bossuet and the Vicomte de Bonald," and in which he expressly states that he wrote on human society " in the light of the spiritual truth of the Church and the social truth of the Monarchy "; despite his declarations of faithful attachment to the elder branch of the Bourbons under Louis Philippe and the Second Republic, not a few critics have tried to prove that various contrary philosophies can just as well be derived from the *Human Comedy*—a utilitarian Liberalism, which encourages unlimited speculation for material gain, or a Socialism or a Communism, which unmasks the corruption and the inner rottenness of the rich ruling classes. Sometimes even Catholic critics—Ferdinand Brunetière, for example, whom some people considered to be the official Catholic voice in literary criticism round about 1900, and whom few care to read today—advanced the opinion that the often-quoted appraisal of " the two great truths, the Church and the Monarchy " is more vocal in the Preface to the *Human Comedy* than it is borne out in the novels, in which the reader may easily find a lesson of immorality.

Again, Balzac has often been claimed as a master and precursor by schools far removed from Catholic spirituality: by Flaubert and the Brothers Goncourt, as a master of minute observation and description; by the numerous commentators and critics of Sainte-Beuve's school, as the prophet of scepticism, and able exposer of " conventional values "; even by Zola and the " Naturalists," as the precursor of the " photographic " novel, which largely owes its success to the needless accumulation of unsuppressed filth. The most combative and fearless Catholic critics of Balzac's period and of French society as a whole did not altogether accept the author of the *Human Comedy* as one of their own. In his *Literary Confessions*, Louis Veuillot is not too favourable to Balzac. He places him above his imitators, but is hardly prepared to exonerate him from the suspicion of being a literary exploiter of the commercial possibilities of a well-described social corruption, and he praises him mainly for stopping short at mere discreet allusion, where Eugène Sue would have given a prolonged exhibition of bad taste and cynicism.

Still, the whole case of Balzac is perhaps wrongly placed on this plane of good taste and decency, to which a great part of contemporary criticism reduced it. Balzac is somewhat outside this central concern of aesthetics, just as the moral lesson of his world is outside the classic concern of ethics. This most strange and curious world of his imagination has few, perhaps no characters which are symbolic of moral virtues. Indeed, he would have been the last to defend his invented world on moral grounds, and the last to claim to be a teacher of good ways by inventing good examples, or by a consoling and redeeming and extenuated representation of historical and social reality. Balzac did not compose a world of essentially good men, accidentally corrupted by society, such as the fictitious Citizen of Jean-Jacques Rousseau. He did not plead the mysterious and unexplored laws of pathological heredity as an explanation of vice, and an excuse for it, like Zola. His most monumental convict, Vautrin, is not a half-innocent victim like Victor Hugo's Jean Valjean. He is a hardened criminal, capable of one virtue only, a frank and cynical appreciation of the ambition of others, and of one sacrifice, to support the ambition of those men whose minds and will he is prepared to recognise as superior to his own.

For it is this very harshness, this lack of any emotional element or sentimentality, that brought Balzac close to the Church. He had shown a world which was without hope—except for the Redemption. A society which was lost—except for the infinite wisdom of the first Principle ruling it. A contemporary society which was rotten, composed of men who were capable of doing anything— except to strive after the ultimate social truth, which an infinite and almighty wisdom had placed beyond their devilish and devastating power, by sending them, not apostles and priests, whom they would once more have scorned and in the end martyred, but bad priests, who, in the shape of the unholy trio, Talleyrand, Fouché and Siéyès, saved France from the French, their hidden theological intelligence giving them the gift of statesmanship, although their sinful hearts refused the milder gifts of Christ. (*Une Ténébreuse Affaire*.) The ambition of a Napoleon and the intelligence of the three bad priests saved France from the dissolution and anarchy which was produced by the complacent sentimentality of Rousseau's followers. Balzac was ultimately on the side of a God who saves men, not because of their merits, but because He is infinitely more wise and generous than men are. If Balzac sometimes failed to be touched by the compassion of the Son, he did not fail to pay trembling respect to the Father, nor to proclaim in humble admiration the wisdom and the firmness of the Holy Ghost as man's surest guide.

The redeeming feature in Balzac's mankind is its Secret, a word used with a capital letter in Balzac's sense. The uncommon man differs from the rabble because he has a Secret: the secret knowledge of the law governing the world. Balzac saw the Church as the depositary of wisdom. Wickedness is stupid, although he thought—and this may be a dangerous doctrine indeed—that wisdom itself has no choice but to fight wickedness by evil means. Christ never appeared to Balzac otherwise than as the Judge of the Last Day, of iron firmness, like the vigorous, bare-armed figure painted by Michelangelo on the wall of the Sistine Chapel. Perhaps because he saw the shrewdness of the serpent too clearly and praised it too often, Balzac was too inclined to forget the gentleness of the dove, which should always take precedence over the serpent for those who follow the evangelical precept. But if there are dangerous precepts which could be derived from the philosophy underlying Balzac's art, let us not have the slightest doubt on his firm and unmistakable adherence to the Catholic order of values and Catholic reasoning. He often described moral and even physical filth at great length, just like Zola and the naturalists who came after him. But he put it into its right sphere, into the sphere of the grotesque and the comic (*Les Contes drôlatiques*, or the description of the boarding-house in the Rue Neuve Ste. Geneviève in *Père Goriot*). He was not the father of Zola, but the son of Rabelais. Not the finest spiritual ancestry, to be sure, and no guarantee against grossness and even a streak of vulgarity.

We need not idealise either Balzac or Rabelais. Rabelais was a scandalous friar, who ran away from his monastery, which would have been wiser to chase him away in time, and what he wrote was of course not intended to be an auxiliary of the Daily Missal, or a companion-book for readers of the *Imitation*. An avowed spiritual descent from Rabelais does not put Balzac necessarily among the guides to good religion and good morals. Yet, may we not argue that a *healthy* faith is better than " good religion," for the very reason that it is a more definite and precise term? " Religion " may be vague, may stand in danger of being " a " religion, or even of degenerating into " some sort of religion," " the religious need of mankind," and like things that we hear from doubtful quarters today. Faith, however, does not tolerate misunderstanding. A man believes, and then he is ready to sacrifice intellect to belief, or the belief is missing, and the lack of it deprives a man of all the gifts of the intellect. Balzac believed in the primacy of the gifts conferred by Faith. Much as he thought intellect to be a supreme agent in history and in human action, his search was for the Absolute, not for " lost time," not for subtle observation and not for good social guidance, as did his decadent imitators of later generations. Faith stood in the same relation for him to the intellect, as Charity stood to Faith for St. Paul.

SOCIETY AND THE INDIVIDUAL

I[1]

Man is neither good nor bad. He is born with certain instincts and aptitudes. Society, far from corrupting him, as Rousseau says, perfects him. But self-interest brings out his evil propensities also, and Catholicism is the *only* complete system which represses the vicious tendencies in man. Hence it is the greatest element in social order.

Every thinking man must march under the banner of Christ! He alone consecrated the triumph of spirit over matter; He alone revealed in practical terms the intermediate world which separates us from God.

Christianity created the nations of the modern world; it will preserve them.

Nations can only achieve long life by husbanding their vitality. In this the life of society resembles the life of a man. Education, or rather up-bringing, by the religious bodies is therefore the great principle on which the existence of nations depends.

Crimes which are of a purely moral order and escape human justice are the vilest and the most hateful of all. . . . God often punishes them on earth. Herein lies the explanation of those dreadful misfortunes which seem incomprehensible to us.

Any moral regeneration which does not spring from a deep religious feeling, and which is not pursued within the bosom of the Church, rests on foundations of sand. All the practices prescribed in such detail by Catholicism, and which meet with so little comprehension, are so many breakwaters indispensable to withstand the storms of the Evil One.

[1] Extracts from Balzac's *Maximes et Pensées*, collected and edited by Barbey d'Aurevilly.

The cult of a religion lies in its form, and societies only exist by their form: the national colours and the Cross.

Have you noticed the deep sense of security in the true priest, when he has given himself to God, listens to His voice and strives to be a submissive instrument in the hands of Providence ? . . . There is neither vanity nor pride left in him, nor anything which, to those in the world, is a continual source of offence. His tranquillity is as complete as that of the fatalist and his resignation helps him to endure all things.

All the religious who were forced to leave their monasteries by the Revolution and who engaged in politics have proved, by the coolness of their demeanour and their reserve, the superiority which ecclesiastical discipline confers on all the children of the Church, even on those who desert her.

Patriotism only inspires transitory sentiments. Religion gives them a permanent character. Patriotism is a momentary forgetfulness of self-interest, whilst Christianity is a complete system of opposition to the corrupt tendencies in man.

Christianity is a perfect system which combats the corrupt tendencies in man and absolutism is a complete system which controls the divergent interests of society. Each one is necessary to the other. Without Catholicism the law has no sword to defend it, and we see the result of this today.

Protestants have done as much harm to art as they have done to the political body.

That man amongst us who makes the most fun of his religion in Paris would not abjure it in Constantinople.

The Virgin Mary (even if we only consider her as a symbol) eclipses in her greatness all Hindoo, Egyptian or Greek prototypes. Virginity, the mother of great things, *magna rerum parens*, holds the key to higher worlds in her fair white hands. In short, this grandiose and terrible exception deserves all the honours which the Catholic Church bestows upon her.

In the Protestant faith, there is nothing woman can do after her fault, whilst in the Catholic Church, the hope of forgiveness makes her sublime.

Suicide ought to be the final word of unbelieving societies.

When it beheaded Louis XVI, the Revolution beheaded in his person all fathers of families. The family no longer exists today; there are only individuals. When they wanted to become a nation, Frenchmen gave up the idea of being an empire. By proclaiming the equal division of the father's property, they killed the family spirit and created the tax-gatherer mentality! On the other hand they paved the way for the weakening of the better elements, and the blind impulses of the masses, the extinction of the arts, the reign of self-interest, and opened up the path to conquest.

The family! I repudiate the family in a society which, on the death of the father or mother, divides up the property and tells each member to go his own way. The family is a temporary and fortuitous association, which is dissolved immediately by death. Our laws have broken up our homes, our inheritance, and the perennial value of example and tradition. I see only ruins around us.

The march of civilisation and the wellbeing of the masses depends on three men: the priest, the doctor and the judge; these are the three authorities who can immediately make people conscious of the interplay of actions, interests and principles—the three great consequences brought about in a nation by events, property and ideas.

With the advent of Luther, the question at stake was not the reformation of the Church, but rather the undefined liberty of man, which means the death of all authority.

Authority can only come from above or from below. To attempt to find it half-way is to want to make nations walk on their belly, to lead them by the lowest interest of all, individualism.

There are no more than fifty or sixty dangerous men in a nation, whose minds are on a level with their ambition. The secret of government is to know who these men are, so that they can either be executed or bought.

A feudal aristocracy can be subdued by cutting off a few heads, but a hydra with a thousand heads cannot be subdued. No, unimportant people are not crushed; they are too flat under the feet!

When Europe is no more than a drifting herd of men, she will have no leaders and will be devoured by uncouth conquerors. Twenty times has the world presented us with this sight. Europe will repeat the process. Ideas eat up the centuries as men are eaten up by their passions. . . . When man is cured, humanity will be able to cure itself perhaps; but will man ever be cured ? . . .

The prophecy of the eagle plucked by diplomacy will be fulfilled before the eyes of a selfish generation, lacking in all religious sentiment, which is the principle of resistance, in patriotism, which has been destroyed by revolutions, and in fidelity to an oath, which is a peculiarly monarchical principle.

There are in the world countries which are no longer defended by their peoples: countries where individuals are no longer linked together and where *nationality* is replaced by *personality*. M. Lainé[1] has said: " Kings are disappearing." He might have added: Nations are advancing, but they advance from North to South. People who like to lie peacefully in their beds at night say: " Our industry is flourishing, our arms are equal to the enemy and nations do not easily let themselves be swallowed up." Does anybody think by chance that the invasions of the Goths, Franks and Saxons did not find flourishing industries and armed nations barring their way ? The interests of the fourth century were the same as those of the nineteenth. Only they took a different shape, and the barbarians found themselves faced by rival interests, just as we see today.

The day will come when people will say to each other: " Why not the Czar ? " as once they said: " Why not the Duke of Orleans ? " People do not care much about anything nowadays (1840). In fifty years time they will not care about anything at all.

If the Press did not exist, it would not be necessary to invent it.

___

[1] Vicomte de Lainé, Minister of the Interior under Louis XVIII, a leading Parliamentarian of the Constitutional Royalists and opponent of the " ultras."

We all know that newspapers outstrip kings in ingratitude, the shadiest business enterprise in speculation and cunning, and that they destroy our intelligence with the mental raw spirits which they sell us every morning; but all of us write in them, like those people who exploit a quicksilver mine, knowing that they will meet their death thereby.

There was once a journalist who confessed to having written the same article every day for twelve years. His now celebrated confession makes us smile, but ought on the contrary to make us shiver. Does not a mason always strike at the same spot with his pick-axe, in order to demolish a particularly fine building ?

II[1]

In order to destroy the principle of authority, the new political doctrines (an absurd phrase, since authority can only take one of two forms: aristocracy or democracy) claim that systems are born and grow, that a total philosophy would be an absolute science and an impossibility. This assertion is made by people who talk nonsense about free-will and liberty. The doctrine of authority is complete and final.

There is no absolute authority in the universe. The only absolute authority which the imagination has been able to conceive, the authority of God, works according to rules which He has imposed upon Himself. He can destroy all His worlds and return to His rest, but while He allows them to exist, they continue to be governed by the laws which together create order.

Politically speaking, man is the basis of society. It would be a mistake not to understand by man, three people: a man, his wife and child. " Man " means " family."

When man existed in a primitive state, did he live alone ? This question is very important, for many philosophers, in fact all who have wanted to apply their theories on man to society, and their theories on society to religion, have first begun by examining man in his primitive state, to find out whether he was naturally good or bad, and whether society corrupted or perfected him.

Hobbes said: Man is born bad and society perfects him.

[1] Extracts from the unfinished *Catéchisme Social.*

J. J. Rousseau said: Man is born good and society corrupts
him. Religion says: Man is born with the stain of original sin
and religion helps him to curb all his passions, so that he may
be made worthy of God, Who holds the secret of his destiny.

Imagine a fight between five Iroquis, a hundred leagues away
from their own country, and five Mohicans. They have had
nothing to eat for many days. The Iroquis kill a Mohican and
remain masters of the field and of the enemy; they proceed to
eat their prisoner.

It is an easy step to make a custom out of something which
was done once out of necessity. Custom can engender abuse,
just as it can in Society. The aim of religion is to curb bad
desires and inculcate good ones. Religion comprises the whole
of society. If it were not a divine institution, it would be a
human necessity.

Men have always wanted to discover the laws which govern
society in nature, but when we observe the laws of nature carefully, we find that they provide a complete justification for the
social laws, such as every society has always imagined them to
be, and which prove that Equality is the most terrible illusion.

The earth has no exact geometrical limits and cannot be
separated from the surrounding atmosphere. It has been proved
that none of her products, neither man, animal, nor plants,
could survive without this girdle of air, which determines their
food, their physical shape and their species.

Hence, nature has given all its earthly creations the *right* to
live on this sphere, the *right* to draw from it the elementary
substances which they need. Here we have a complete picture
of social rights. Social rights, taken in the broadest sense, really
mean the right to moral and physical life, in a given environment and in a given place, the whole regulated by a network of
customs. The analogy is not only an exact one; it is perfect.

What do we see as the result of the natural and visible law
which governs the creatures of the earth, and allows them to
develop in these atmospheric conditions? The most striking
inequality, and a variety of species which is the signal beauty of
the universe.

Man's free-will lies at the heart of any problem of his liberty.
If man has no free-will, the question of his liberty does not arise.
The problem is no longer whether he should be allowed to
gratify every whim, but what society allows him to do. If

nature has set limits to man's action, instead of giving him un-limited powers, and confines this action within a ruthless circle, society is not under a greater obligation to its citizens than man is to nature.

Free-will means then in its truest sense the power a man possesses to do what he likes, without any let or hindrance, and without being influenced in his decision by any moral or physical law.

Industry attracts workmen, and concentrates them in centres where they are not able to produce any food. Industry, while it doubles the population, does not increase agricultural products two-fold; on the contrary, by forcing up the price of labour, it forces up the price of food. A clash between industry and agriculture is inevitable, for industry, which is up against competition, wants food to be cheap, so that the cost of labour may fall, while agriculture cannot afford to sell food at prices below cost. This is a problem which modern politics finds insoluble.

The poverty of a certain section of the population is not only a reproach to a government, it is an indictment which will bring about its fall. When the numbers of the oppressed pass a certain limit, and they see how many rich people there are in the world, revolution soon breaks out. All revolutions depend on a leader, and on a contingency which suddenly precipitates it; every contingency has a leader, since every leader knows how to engineer the necessary contingency.

Religion is based on an innate sentiment in man, which is a universal phenomenon; no uncivilised peoples, tribes, hordes of savages, or men in a state of nature, have ever been dis-covered, who did not have a faith of some sort. This emotion, inborn in man, is the mine which has been exploited by all the philosophies of the world, and which has furnished them with weapons against the so-called sensualist and materialist schools of thought, etc. . . .

This sentiment, which is so strong in peoples who lived nearest in time to the disaster known as the Flood, pre-supposes a fall, a punishment, the result of a battle, a decline in the knowledge of a superior being and an angry victor.

The scientific knowledge which we possess today, thanks to progress and the indefatigable human brain, corroborates this feeling in man. Mammoth creatures belonging to the early life of the earth have now disappeared. Earth itself has perhaps fallen and become detached from a hierarchy of superior worlds. It has certainly undergone modification. Material science has vindicated the idea of religion, which is the common basis of all societies: in other words, divine revelation. The idea of reparation is almost universally accepted also.

These two general ideas, common to man, or this divine revelation, are at the root of Christianity. These findings, this conclusion of history, are beyond dispute. Whether God co-exists in the world, or is separated from His creation, whether He exists in Himself and for Himself, or is indissolubly linked to His creation or not, we can see that a part of that creation has been vitiated and punished, and while it has not been withdrawn from the whole, it has been condemned to undergo modification and purification, before it returns to the general stream.

Hence humanity can journey from worse to better (or from better to worse, if the globe has a life of its own, for it is going towards its death). Humanity has a future, and man likewise.

It is dangerous for man and for society to lose sight of these points. They contain the idea of obedience, which is fundamental to any society.

Catholicism is the most perfect religion of all, because it condemns the discussion of questions on which the Church has pronounced judgement, and because the Church admits those time-honoured practices of religious observance, which thereby bring us nearer to God. The fate which the various heresies have brought on Europe is an argument in favour of Catholicism. Revelation is always present within the bosom of the Church; it is restricted in the heretical sects.

When authority comes from the people it is vacillating; when it comes from God it is steadfast. It is either beyond all question, or it is no authority at all. Such is the lesson of history.

V.   FRIEDRICH VON SCHLEGEL

1772 - 1829

FRIEDRICH VON SCHLEGEL, poet, historian and translator of Shakespeare, together with his brother August-Wilhelm, the poet and philosopher Friedrich von Hardenberg (better known under his pseudonym, Novalis), Clemens Brentano, and Count Friedrich Stolberg—these are the Germans of the period who, as the result of the French wars, the Napoleonic conquests and the fall of the last remnants of the Empire, moved towards the eternal and central light of European history and culture, and who gave a Christian and European meaning to a belated German Renaissance. Certainly none of them is a major teacher of the Church, fighting the aesthetic-pantheist heresy of the nineteenth century (which was mainly German) in the sense that St Augustine fought the Manichean heresy, or St Thomas the Albigensians. All the same, the German convert thinkers of the Napoleonic era, by the very fact of their conversion, took up the struggle against all the perils of agnostic deviation from a firm system of truth, against the trend in German philosophy which reached its fullest expression in Hegel's dialectics, against all the pitfalls of a " historicism " which confuses all standards by its pantheism.

It was a Protestant historian, the Swiss Johannes von Müller, who first showed, with great brilliance and learning, that the law of Europe governing the relations between the individual states was originally laid down by the Papacy, and that the European concept of personal liberty is inseparable from the law of Christian morality. It was a Protestant publicist, the Prussian Friedrich von Gentz (who later became an Austrian, for some decades the theoretical organ of Metternich's policy), who showed the dogmatic—ultimately the theological—character of the common law of Europe. But the last consequences of the principles laid down by German political thinkers in the struggle against Napoleon were drawn by such Germans who, in the critical years of Napoleon's rise to hegemony, placed their hopes in Catholic Austria. For some years, Vienna was the centre of German thought and the German awakening. Johannes von Müller (born in Switzerland) and Friedrich von Gentz (born in Prussia) spent the most important years of their lives in the Imperial city, the birth-place of the " Romantic " school of thought and of art.

The central figure of the Vienna circle was a priest and preacher who, less than a hundred years after his death in 1820, became a canonised saint of the Church, the Redemptorist Father Clemens Hofbauer, whose Congregation, for forty years, replaced the dissolved Society of Jesus. From all parts of the German-speaking world, converts came to Vienna, the philosophers of a re-Christianised Europe: Zacharias Werner, Adam Müller and many other outstanding scholars and writers, some of whom were not only received into the Church, but even followed the priestly vocation among the Redemptorists of Father Hofbauer.

The following pages of Friedrich von Schlegel were written in 1827. They form the epilogue to his *Lectures on the Philosophy of History*, given in Vienna some twenty years earlier. Between these lectures and the epilogue, important events occurred in Schlegel's life: his failure to persuade his brother August-Wilhelm to follow him into the Church; his disappointment over Goethe's hostility to the " romantic " tendency and to Catholicism. There were also the years he spent on Metternich's staff at the State Chancellery of Austria, and his journey to Rome in 1819 in the Chancellor's company in connection with important negotiations with Pope Pius VII and Cardinal Consalvi. The close links which existed between Metternich and Friedrich von Schlegel allow us to consider the pages that follow as the foremost document of the political theory of a whole era of German and European history.

THE REGENERATION OF CHRISTIAN STATES AND NATIONS[1]

THERE are, in the history of the eighteenth century, many phenomena which occurred so suddenly, so instantaneously, and were so contrary to all expectation, that although on deeper consideration we may discover their efficient causes in the past, in the natural state of things and in the general situation of the world, yet there are many circumstances which prove that there was a deliberate, although secret, preparation of events, as indeed has been actually demonstrated in many instances. I must now say a few words on this secret and mysterious branch of illuminism, and on the progress it made during the period of its influence, and show the influence of this principle, both in regard to the origin and general spirit of the revolution (which in its fanaticism believed itself to be a regeneration of the world) and in regard to the true restoration

[1] Friedrich von Schlegel: *Lectures on the Philosophy of History* (Lecture XVIII). Translated from the German by James Burton Robertson, London, Henry G. Bohn, 1846 (slightly revised).

of society founded on the basis of Christian justice. One circumstance, however, is peculiar to this historical enquiry, that those who could best speak from their personal experience cannot always be considered the most reliable eye-witnesses; for we never know, or can know, what their particular views and interests may lead them to say, or conceal, or suppress. However, it has so happened that, in the universal convulsion and overthrow of society, many things have come to light on this mysterious and esoteric clue in modern history—things which, when combined together, furnish us with a not incorrect and reasonably complete idea of this mighty element of the Revolution, and of illuminism both true and false, which has exercised so evident and varied an influence on the world.

As to the origin of this esoteric influence, the impartial enquirer cannot doubt that the order of Templars was the channel by which this society in its ancient and long-preserved form was introduced into the West. The religious *Masonic* symbols may be explained by the traditions of Solomon connected with the very foundation of the order of Templars; and indeed the existence of these symbols may be traced in other passages of Holy Writ, and in other parts of sacred history, and they may very well admit of a Christian interpretation. Traces of these symbols may be found in the monuments of the old German architecture of the Middle Ages. Any secret spiritual association however, spread simultaneously amongst Christians and Mahometans, cannot be of a very Christian nature, nor long remain so. Indeed, the very idea of an esoteric society for the propagation of any secret doctrines is not compatible with the very principle of Christianity itself; for Christianity is a divine mystery, which according to the intention of its divine Founder lies open to all, and is daily exposed on every altar. For this reason, in a Revelation imparted to all alike, there can be no secrecy, as in the pagan mysteries, where, side by side with popular mythology and the public religion of the State, certain esoteric doctrines were inculcated amongst the initiated alone. This would be to constitute a church within a church—a measure to be as little tolerated or justified as an *imperium in imperio*; and in an age where worldly interests and public or secret views of policy carry far more weight than religious opinions or sentiments, such a secret parasitical church would unquestionably, as experience has already proved, be very soon transformed into a secret directory for political changes and revolutions. That in this society the unchristian principles of a

negative illuminism, disguised as they often were into sentiments of universal philanthropy, were reasonably modern in
date, all historical analogies would lead us to suppose. On the
other hand, the Christian opinions which survived in this order
(although in our day the adherents to Christian principles form
a minority in our society, agitated as it is by the quarrels of innumerable factions) assumed, in conformity with the historical
origin I have described, more of an oriental and Gnostic
character. The great, or at least not inconsiderable influence
which this society exercises in politics, we may discover in those
revolutions which, after having convulsed our part of the globe,
have rolled onwards to the New World, where the two principal
revolutionary factions in one of those South American states
whose troubles are not yet at an end, are called the Scots and the
Yorkists, from the two parties which divide the English Masonic
lodges. Who does not know, or who does not remember, that
the ruler of the world in the period we have just lived through
made use of this vehicle in all the countries he conquered, to
delude and deceive the nations with false hopes ? And on this
account he was styled by his followers the man of his age and,
in fact, he was a slave to the spirit of his age. A society from
whose bosom, as from the secret laboratory of Revolution, the
Illuminés, the Jacobins and the Carbonari have successively
proceeded, cannot possibly be termed, or in fact be, very beneficial to mankind, politically sound, or truly Christian in its
views and tendency. Still, I must observe here, that it has been
the fate of the oldest of all secret societies to have its venerable
forms, which are known to all the initiated, made a cloak for
every new conspiracy. In the next place, we must not forget
that this order itself appears to be split and divided into a multitude of different sects and factions; and on this account we
must not suppose that all those fearful aberrations and wild
excesses of impiety, all those openly destructive or secretly
undermining principles of revolution were universally approved
by this society. On the contrary, such a supposition would be
utterly false, or at least very exaggerated. A glance at all the
highly estimable characters, mistaken only on this one point—
most distinguished and illustrious personages in the eighteenth
century, who were members of this association—would be
sufficient to remove, or at least materially to modify, this
sweeping censure. From many indications, we may consider it
certain, or at least extremely probable, that in no country did
this esoteric society harmonise so well with the State and the

whole established order of things as in that country where all the conflicting elements of morals and society are combined in a sort of strange and artificial balance—I mean England. If now we turn our attention to the continent of Europe, and even to those countries which were the chief theatre of the Revolution, we shall see that there, among many other factions, a Christian party had sprung up in this society, a party which, although it formed a very small minority in point of numbers, possessed by its profounder doctrines and the interesting fragments of ancient tradition it had preserved, a great moral ascendancy; and this, many historical facts and many written documents which have since been published place beyond the shadow of a doubt. Instead of mentioning the names of some German writers less generally known, I prefer to quote in confirmation of what I have said the example of a French writer who is typical of the internal and more hidden character of the revolution. The Christian theosophist St Martin, who was a disciple of this school, stands quite apart in his age from the other organs of the then prevailing atheistic philosophy. He was, however, a most decided revolutionary (yet at the same time a disinterested fanatic whose conduct was entirely guided by high moral motives) because of his utter contempt and abhorrence for the whole moral and political system of Europe as it then stood—a contempt in which, if we cannot entirely agree with him, we cannot in many instances withhold from him at least a sort of negative approval; and secondly, he was a revolutionary by reason of his enthusiastic belief in a complete Christian regeneration of society, conceived it is true according to his own views, or the views of his party. Among the French writers of the Restoration, no one has so thoroughly understood this remarkable philosopher and so well understood how to appreciate him in all the depths of his errors, as well as in the many excellent things which his writings contain, as Count de Maistre.

This secret clue in the history of the revolution must not be overlooked, if we desire to form a due estimate of its character; for it greatly contributed to the illusion of a great many by no means ill-intentioned persons, who saw, or wished to see, in the revolution merely the inevitable and necessary, although in its origin harsh and severe, regeneration of Christian states and nations, which had then gone so far astray from their original course. This illusory notion of a false restoration of society was particularly prevalent during the imperial rule of that extraordinary man whose true biography—I mean the high moral law of his destiny, or the theological key to his life—still seems to exceed the critical powers of our age. Seven years were allotted to him for the growth of his power, for fourteen years the world was delivered up into his hands; and seven years were left him for solitary reflection, the first of which he misused by embroiling the world anew. On the use he made of the extraordinary power that had been granted him, of that formidable dominion which had fallen to his lot, history has long ago pronounced sentence. Never is it permitted to exercise such power, unless it is in a period of some awful reckoning to which it leads, for the purpose of a still more fearful probation of mankind. But if his restoration—that is to say, the restoration which his infatuated supporters attributed to him—was most certainly a false one, the question naturally occurs whether the restoration which his successors attempted to effect has been perfectly sound, or at least quite complete; and what are the defects in the new system and how can they be remedied ?

A mere treaty of territorial adjustments could not, and never can, constitute a great religious and international pacification of the whole of Europe. The re-establishment of subverted thrones, the restoration of exiled sovereigns and dynasties will not in themselves have any security or permanence, unless they are based on moral principles and maxims. After the severe and unexpected lesson which was again inflicted upon Europe, religion was at last made the basis of European policy; and we must not make it a matter of reproach that this principle still retained so indefinite a character; for this was necessary, at least in the beginning, in order to remove any misconception, or any possible suspicion of interested views. And not only does the stability and future existence of the whole Christian and civilised world depend on this bond of religious confederation —which we can only hope will be ever more and more firmly knit—but each individual great power is especially called upon to play its part. That the moral strength and stability of the Russian empire mainly depends on religion, that every departure from its sacred spirit must have the most fatal effects on its whole system, has already been stated by her late monarch, distinguished alike in adversity and in prosperity, and is an axiom of State policy, which can hardly ever be forgotten again. But in that country, where the elements of Protestantism (to use that word in its most comprehensive sense) obtained such weight at the outset of its literary refinement, and are incorporated to such a degree into the whole political system of the State, the toleration extended to every form of worship should not be withheld from that Church which is the mother-Church of the rest of Europe, including Poland; nor should the religious liberty of individuals be in that respect at all restricted.

It is equally evident that in that country of Europe where monarchy has been restored, the restoration of religion must go hand in hand with that of monarchy, and that the latter would lose all security if the former were removed. In the peace-loving monarchy of Austria, unchangeably attached as she is to her ancient principles, religion, rather than any other principle, has always been the recognised basis of her existence. As to the fifth Germanico-European monarchy of Prussia, recently created, the solid maintenance of religion is the only means of allaying the disquiet inevitably caused by such a State, and of securing its future existence. Any act of even indirect hostility towards the Catholic body—one half of the nation—any infringement of the liberty of individuals in that sacred concern —a liberty which must be guaranteed not only by the letter of the law, but by real, effective and practical measures—would not only be in complete opposition to those religious principles rapidly spreading as they are all over Europe and particularly in Germany but would violate and render insecure the great, fundamental and long-established principle of toleration, such as it has up to now been understood. It is only in England that Anglicanism has raised her doubts as to the utility of a religious fraternity among the Christian states and nations—doubts which are connected with the still exclusively character of the English constitution, and which on many occasions may lead England to a sort of schismatic rupture with the rest of Europe. On several occasions, we must regretfully note that mighty England, in the eighteenth century so brilliant and so powerful by the influence she exerted over the whole European mind, no longer seems to feel herself at home in the nineteenth century, and no longer knows where to find her place in the new order of things.

If we consider Europe as a whole, the maxims and principles of liberalism are but a partial return to the revolution—they can have no other tendency than to revolution. Liberalism will never obtain a majority among the well-thinking persons of any of the European states, except by some gross error, some singular degeneration in that party, which really does not constitute a party and ought not to be called such—I mean the men who in politics are attached to the monarchy, and in religion to Christianity.

The mere principle of a mechanical balance of power, to serve as a negative check on excessive power—a system which emanated from England and was in the eighteenth century universally accepted—has ceased to be applicable, or to be of any service in the existing state of things in Europe; for all the remedies which it can offer tend only to aggravate the evil, when once it has occurred. In religion alone are to be found the remedies, the safeguards, the emancipation and the consolidation of the whole civilised world, as well as of each individual State. The most imminent danger for our age, and the possible abuse of religion itself, are the excesses of the absolute. Great is the danger when, in a vindictive spirit of reaction, a revolutionary conduct is adopted by the legitimist party; when passion itself is consecrated into a maxim of reason, and held up as the only valid and just way of proceeding; and when the sacredness of religion itself is hawked about as if it were some fashionable opinion; as if the world-redeeming power of faith and truth consisted only of the dead letter and the recited formula. True life can only spring from the vivifying spirit of eternal truth. In science, the absolute is the abyss which swallows up the living truth, and leaves behind only the hollow idea and the dead formula. In the political world, the absolute in conduct and in speculation is that false spirit of time, opposed to all good and to the fulness of divine truth, which in a great measure rules the world, and may entirely rule it and lead it for ever to its final ruin. As errors would not be dangerous or deceptive, and would have little effect, unless they contained a portion or an appearance of truth, this false spirit of time, which successively assumes all forms of destruction, since it has abandoned the path of eternal truth, consists in this: it withdraws particular facts from their historical context and holds them up as the centre and term of a system, without any qualification and without any regard for historical circumstances. The true foundation and the right term of things, in the history of society as in the lives of individuals, cannot be severed in this way from their historical context and their place in the natural order of events. In any speculation or enterprise conducted by this passionate spirit of exaggeration, the living spirit must evaporate, and only the dead and deadening formula survive. What idols may successively be worshipped by the changing spirit of the age, which easily jumps from one extreme to the other, cannot be determined beforehand. It is even possible that for a while eternal truth itself may be profaned and perverted to such an idol of the day—I mean the counterfeit form of truth; for the spirit of the age can never attain the inward essence and living energy of truth, even if it assumes the appearance of it. Whatever may be the alternative idol, and the reigning object of its worship, or of its passionate rhetoric, it still remains essentially the same—that is to say, the absolute, as deadening to the intellect as it is destructive to life. In science, the absolute is the idol of vain and empty systems, of dead and abstract reason.

The Christian faith has the living God and His revelation for its object, and is itself that revelation; hence, every doctrine taken from this source is something real and positive. The defence of truth against error will then only be attended by permanent success when the divine doctrine, in whatever department it may be, is represented with intellectual energy as a living principle, and at the same time is placed in its historical context, with a due regard for every other historical reality. This calm, historical judgement of things, this acute insight into subjects, whether they be real facts or intellectual phenomena, is the invariable concomitant of truth, and the indispensable condition to the full knowledge of truth. This is the more so, indeed, as religion, which forms the basis of all truth and of all knowledge, naturally follows with an attentive eye the mysterious clue of divine Providence and divine permission through the long labyrinth of human errors and human follies, both of a practical and of a speculative nature. Error, on the other hand, is always unhistorical; the spirit of the age is almost always passionate; and both, consequently, are untrue. The conflict against error cannot be brought to a prompter or more successful issue by separating, in every system of moral and speculative error, and according to the standard of divine truth, the absolute, which is the basis of such systems, into its two component parts of truth and falsehood. For when we acknowledge and point out the truth to be found in those systems there only remains error, the stupidity of which it requires little labour, little cost of time or talent, to expose and make evident to every eye. But in real life, the struggle of parties often ceases to be purely intellectual, their physical energy is displayed in violent upheavals and in proportion as all parties become absolute, so their struggle becomes one of violent and mutual destruction, a circumstance which most fatally impedes the great work of religious regeneration— the mighty problem of our age—which so far from being brought to a satisfactory conclusion is not yet even solved. In this respect, it is no doubt a critical fact, that in certain parts of Europe, nay, even in some entire countries, parties and govern- ments should be more and more carried away by the spirit of absolutism. For this is not a question of names, and it is very evident that those parties which are called, or call themselves, absolute, are not the most so in reality; since now, as in all periods of violent party struggles, a whimsical mistake in names, a great disorder of ideas, and a Babel confusion of tongues, occur even in those languages otherwise distinguished for their clearness and precision.

. . . The dogmatic decision and definiteness of Catholic faith on the one hand, and the firmly rooted private convictions of Protestantism on the other, are very compatible with an historical judgement of historical events. Difficult as this may appear to the absolute spirit of our age, it is this very historical impartiality which must prepare the way for the complete triumph of truth and the consummate glory of Christianity. In the absolute spirit of our age and in the absolute character of its factions, there is a deep-rooted intellectual pride, which is not so much personal, or individual, as social, for it refers to the historical destiny of mankind, and of this age in particular. Actuated by this pride, a spirit exalted by moral energy or invested with external power fancies it can give a real existence to that which can only be the work of God, as from Him alone proceed all those mighty and real regenerations of the world, Christianity among them—a revolution in the high and divine sense of the word—occupying the first place; and in these plastic moments, everything is possible that man can wish or dare to hope, if, in what he adds for his own part, he does not mar in any considerable degree what the bounteous monarch of the universe pours out upon His earth from the overflow of His ineffable love. For the last three hundred years, this human pride has been at work, a pride that wishes to originate events, instead of humbly awaiting them, and of resting content with the place assigned to it among those events, and of making the best and most charitable use of those circumstances which Providence has decreed.

The idea of Illuminism is perfectly blameless, and it is unfair to pronounce on it an indiscriminate censure, and to treat it as an unqualified abuse. It was indeed a very small portion of this Illuminism of the eighteenth century that was really derived from the truths of Christianity and the pure light of Revelation. The rest was the mere work of man, consequently vain and empty, or at least defective, corrupt in parts and, on the whole, destitute of solid foundation, and therefore devoid of all permanent strength and duration.

But when once, after the complete victory of truth, the divine Reformation appears, then that human Reformation which has existed until now will sink to the ground and disappear from the world. Then, with the universal triumph of Christianity and the thorough religious regeneration of the age, the era of a true Christian *Illuminism* will dawn. This period is not perhaps so remote from our own as the natural indolence of the mind, which after every great occurrence loves to sink again into the death-sleep of ordinary life, is disposed to believe. Yet this exalted religious hope, this high historical expectation, must be coupled with great apprehension as to the full display of divine justice in the world. For how is such a religious regeneration possible, until every species, form and denomination of political idolatry is eradicated and finally extirpated from the earth?

Never was there a period that pointed so strongly, so clearly, so generally towards the future as our own. On this account, we should endeavour clearly and accurately to distinguish between what, on the one hand, man may by slow, progressive, but unwearied exertions, by the pacific adjustment of all disputed points, and by the cultivation of his intellectual qualities contribute towards the great work of the religious regeneration of government and science, and what, on the other hand, he should look for in silent awe from a higher Providence, from the new creative fiat of a last period of consummation, unable as he is to produce or call it into being. We are directed much more towards the future than the past; but in order to understand the problem of our age in all its magnitude, it is not enough to seek this social regeneration in the eighteenth century—an age in no way entitled to praise—or in the reign of Louis XIV and his times of false national glory. The birth of Christianity must be the great central point to which we must recur, not to bring back, or counterfeit the forms of past ages, which are no longer applicable to our own; but clearly to examine what has remained incomplete and what has not yet been attained. For, unquestionably, all that has been neglected in the earlier periods and stages of Christian civilisation must be made good in this true, consummate regeneration of society. If truth is to obtain a complete victory—if Christianity is really to triumph on the earth—then the State must become Christian and science must become Christian. But these two objects have never been generally or completely realised, although during the many ages in which mankind has been Christian it has struggled for the attainment of both, and though this political struggle and this intellectual aspiration form the purport of modern history. The Roman Empire, even after the true religion had become prominent, was too thoroughly and too radically corrupt to form a truly Christian State. The sound, unvitiated, natural energy of the Germanic nations seemed far better fitted for such a destiny, after they had received from Christianity a high religious consecration for this purpose. There was, if we may say so, in the interior of each State, as well as in the general system of Christendom, a most magnificent foundation laid for a truly Christian structure of government. But this groundwork remained unfinished, after the internal divisions in the State, then the divisions between Church and State, and lastly the divisions in the Church and in religion itself, had interrupted the successful beginnings of a most glorious work.

The ecclesiastical writers of the first ages furnish a solid foundation for all the future labours of Christian science; but their science does not comprehend all the branches of Christian knowledge. In the Middle Ages, undoubtedly, the foundation of a Christian science, laid down by the early Fathers, was slowly and in detail advanced; but on the whole, many hurtful influences of the time had reduced science and speculation to a very low ebb, when suddenly, in the fifteenth century, all the literary treasures of ancient Greece, and all the new discoveries in geography and in physics, were offered to philosophy. Scarcely had philosophy begun to examine these mighty stories of ancient and modern science, in order to give them a Christian form, and to appropriate them to the use of religion and modern society, when the world again broke out into disputes; and this noble beginning of a Christian philosophy was interrupted, and has since remained an unfinished fragment for a later and happier period. Such, then, is the two-fold problem of a real and complete regeneration which our age is called upon to solve; on the one hand, the further extension of Christian government and of Catholic principles of legislation, in opposition to the revolutionary spirit of the age and to the anti-Christian principle of government hitherto so exclusively prevalent; and on the other hand, the establishment of a Christian philosophy, or Catholic science. As I have already characterised the political spirit of the eighteenth century by the term Protestantism of State (taking that word in a purely philosophical sense, and not as a religious designation), a system which found its one main support in an old Catholic Empire—Austria; and as I characterised the intellectual spirit of the same age by the term Protestantism of science, a science which made the greatest progress and exerted the widest influence in another great Catholic country—France; systems in which nothing irreligious was originally intended, but which became so by their too exclusive or negative bearing: so I may here permit myself to say in like manner that the destiny of this age, the peculiar need of the nineteenth century, is the establishment of those Catholic principles of government and the general construction of a Catholic system of science. This expression is used in a purely scientific sense, and refers to all that is positively and completely religious in thought and feeling. In the certain conviction that this cannot be misunderstood in an exclusive or polemical sense, I will expressly add that this foundation of Catholic legislation for the future political existence of Europe may be laid by one, or more than one, non-Catholic power; and that I even cherish the hope that it is our own Germany, one half of which is Protestant, which more than any other country is destined to complete the fabric of Catholic science and of a true Christian philosophy in all the departments of human knowledge.

The religious hope of a true and complete regeneration of the age by a Christian system of government and a Christian system of science forms the conclusion to this Philosophy of History. The bond of a religious union between all the European states will be more closely knit and more comprehensive, in proportion as each nation advances in the work of its own religious regeneration, and carefully avoids any relapse into the old revolutionary spirit, any worship of the false idols of mistaken freedom and illusory glory, and rejects every other new form or species of political idolatry. For it is the very nature of political idolatry to lead to the mutual destruction of parties, and consequently it can never possess the elements of stability.

Philosophy, as it is the vivifying centre of all other sciences, must be the principal concern and the highest object of the labours of Christian science. Yet history, which is so closely and so variously connected with religion, must be by no means forgotten, nor must historical research be separated from philosophic speculation. On the contrary, it is the religious spirit and views already pervading the combined efforts of historical learning and philosophical speculation that chiefly distinguish this new era of a better intellectual culture, or as I should rather say, this first stage of a return to the great religious restoration. And I may venture to assert that this spirit, at least in the present century, has become ever more and more the prevailing characteristic of German science and on this science, in its relation to the moral needs and spiritual callings of the nineteenth century, I have now a few observations to make. Like an image reflected in a mirror, or like those symptoms which precede and announce a crisis in human events, the focal-point of all government, or the religious basis of legislation, is sure to be reflected in the whole mental culture, or in the most remarkable intellectual productions of a nation. In England, the equilibrium of a constitution that combines in itself so many conflicting elements is reflected in its philosophy. The revolutionary spirit was prevalent in French literature of the eighteenth century long before it broke out in real life, and the struggle is still very animated between the intellectual defenders and champions of the monarchical and religious Restoration and the newly-awakened liberal opposition. In like manner, as the German people were, and still are, half Catholic and half Protestant, it is religious peace which forms the basis of their modern intellectual culture in all literature, and particularly in philosophy. The mere aesthetic part of German letters, as regards art and poetry—that artist-like enthusiasm peculiar to our nation, the struggles which convulsed our literature in its infancy, the successive imitation and rejection of the French and English models, the very general diffusion of classical learning, the newly-enkindled love for our native speech and for the early history of our country and its older monuments of art—all these are subjects of minor interest in the European point of view which we take here, and form but the prelude and introduction to that higher German science and philosophy which is now more immediately the subject of our enquiries. Historical research should never be separated from any philosophy, still less from the German; as historical erudition is the most effective counterpoise to that absolute spirit, so prevalent in German science and speculation.

Art and poetry constitute that department of the intellect in which every nation should in general follow the impulse of its own spirit, its own feelings and its own turn of fancy; and we must regard it as an exception when the poetry of any particular nation (such, for instance, as that of the English at the present day) is felt and received by other nations as a European poetry. On the other hand, history is an intellectual field open to all European nations. The English, who in this department were extremely active and distinguished, have, in recent times, produced works on their own national history which really merit the name of classical monuments of the new religious regeneration. Science in general, and philosophy in particular, should never be exclusive or national, should never be called English or German, but should be general and European. And if this is not so entirely the case as in the nature of things it ought to be, we must ascribe it to the defects of particular forms. The example of the French language may convince us of this truth; for no one will deny the metaphysical profundity of Count de Maistre, or the dialectic perspicacity of the Viscount de Bonald. Although these absolute principles which appear to characterise the European nations at this time have much less influence on real life and on social relationships in Germany than in any other country, yet the false spirit of the absolute seems to be quite native to German science and philosophy, and for a long time has been the principal cause which has cramped the religious spirit and feelings so natural to the German character, or at least has given them a false direction.

That in this progress of mankind a divine Hand and guiding Providence are clearly discernible; that earthly and visible power has not alone co-operated in this progress and in the opposition which has impeded it, but that the struggle has been carried on in part under divine and against invisible might —this is a truth, I trust, which if not proved on mathematical evidence, has still been substantiated on firm and solid grounds. We may conclude with a retrospective view of society, considered in reference to that invisible world and higher region from which the operations of the visible world proceed, in which its great destinies have their root, and which is the ultimate and highest term of all its movements.

Christianity is the emancipation of the human race from the bondage of that inimical spirit who denies God, and, as far as in him lies, leads all created intelligence astray. Hence the Scriptures style him " the prince of this world," and so he was in fact, but in ancient history only, when among all the nations of the earth, and amid the pomp of military glory and the splendour of pagan life, he had established the throne of his domination. Since this divine era in the history of man, since the beginning of his emancipation in modern times, this spirit can no longer be called the prince of this world, but *the spirit of the age,* the spirit opposed to divine influence and to the Christian religion, which is apparent in all those who consider and estimate time and all things temporal, not by the law and feelings of eternity, but for temporal interests, or from temporal motives, change or undervalue and forget the thoughts and faith of eternity.

In the first ages of the Christian Church, the spirit of the age appeared as a beguiling sectarian spirit. This spirit attained its highest triumph in the new and false faith of a fanatical Unitarianism, utterly opposed to the religion of love, and which severed from Christianity so large a portion of the Eastern Church, and whole regions in Asia. In the Middle Ages, this spirit displayed itself, not so much in hostile sects, as in scholastic disputes, in divisions between Church and State, and in the internal disorders of both. At the beginning of the new era of the world, the spirit of the age claimed as an urgent need of mankind, full freedom of faith, the immediate consequence of which claim was only a bloody warfare and a fatal struggle of life and death, protracted for more than a century. When this struggle was brought to an end, or rather appeased, it was succeeded by an utter indifference for all religions, provided only their morality was good; and the spirit of the age proclaimed religious *indifferentism* as the order of the day. This apparent calm was followed by the revolutionary tempest; and now that this has passed away, the spirit of the age has in our days become absolute, that is to say, it has perverted reason to party-passion, or exalted passion to the place of reason: and this is the present form and last metamorphosis of the old, evil spirit of the age.

Turning now to that Divine aid which has supported mankind in its everlasting struggle against its own infirmities, against all the obstacles of nature and natural circumstances, and against the opposition of the evil spirit; I have endeavoured to show that in the first thousand years of primitive History, Divine Revelation, although only preserved in its native purity in the one original source, still flowed in copious streams through the religious traditions of the other great nations of that early era; and that troubled as the current might be by the admixture of many errors, yet it was easy, in the midst of this slime and pollution, to trace it to its pure and sacred source. Every religious view of universal history must begin with such a belief. We shall prize with deeper, more earnest, and more solid affection, the great and divine era of man's redemption and emancipation, the more accurately we discriminate between what is essentially divine and unchangeably eternal in this revelation of love, and the elements of destruction which man has opposed to it, or mingled with it. And it is only in the spirit of love that the history of Christian times can rightly be understood and accurately judged. In later ages, when the spirit of discord has triumphed over love, historical hope is our only remaining clue in the labyrinth of history. It is only with sentiments of grateful admiration, of amazement and awe, that we trace in the special dispensations of Providence for the advancement of Christianity and the progress of modern society, the wonderful concurrence of events towards the single object of divine love, or the unexpected exercise of divine justice long delayed.

VI. PRINCE CLEMENS METTERNICH

1773 - 1859

THE name Metternich signifies a European era. Without any exaggeration, we can, as many historians do, sum up the Europe of the nineteenth century under three names: Napoleon, Metternich and Bismarck. Yet it is true that this century can also be characterised—perhaps more adequately—by the one phenomenon which these three outstanding figures fought with only temporary success: the Revolution.

What was this Revolution, which was invincible until it was conquered by its own demon, and by that universal exhaustion, disillusion and fear in which the remainder of Europe still lives after the Second World War ? Metternich can best define it. He does so in the following pages, in a memorandum written for the personal use of the Czar Alexander I in 1820, a copy of which the Austrian Chancellor communicated to his own sovereign, the Emperor Francis of Austria, as " a not very diplomatic document."

Metternich is less often remembered for what he wanted than for what he feared. As his English biographer, Algernon Cecil, remarks, he dominated his era " not by the sheer force of genius, but by the highest quality of understanding."

The tragedy of genius in action is a spectacular fall. The tragedy of intelligence and understanding is that it encounters a lasting misunderstanding. So lasting has been this misunderstanding of Metternich, that posterity is inclined to see him as the merely negative force of his age.

Metternich's life spans a long era of European history, which has often been described, and which will no doubt still be written about, for landscapes change with every move of the sun and with every step the spectator takes, and the history of an era provides just such a landscape. The light changes with the passing of time. After the First World War, the Vienna Congress, over which Metternich presided, became a popular subject for study. Harold Nicolson's book, and the *Talleyrand* of Duff Cooper, were the outstanding contributions in the inter-war years to the popular analogy between the statecraft of the peacemakers of the " post-war " which began in 1814, and that which began in 1919. Metternich's policy of peace and reconstruction contrasted very favourably for its elevation of thought, genuine concern for true civilisation, humanity and understanding, with the meanness, ignorance and hypocritical

formalism of the parliamentary democracies. The new appreciation
of the policy came from a very unexpected quarter: it was suggested
by the Italian statesman Francesco Nitti, in his *Europa senza Pace*.
An Italian and a Liberal was indeed the last man one would have
expected to stir up a historical controversy in favour of Metternich.
Memory connected the name of the Austrian Chancellor with the
persecution of the secret patriotic societies working for Italian
unity, and there was hardly a name which was more synonymous
with anti-Liberalism, or with the authoritarian theory of the State,
than Metternich's.

But after the First World War events moved quickly in Europe.
The outlook changed. Interest shifted from politics to society, to
culture and religion. Once the crisis was diagnosed as a lasting
phenomenon, and once it was diagnosed in its full context as the
crisis of moral and social values, politics and political economy
receded into the background, and once more the religious issue
became apparent. Before political or economic remedies could be
applied, politics needed to be re-defined, and so did economics.
The very principles of social life seem now to be at stake, just as
they seemed to be to Metternich. Thus from Metternich, the peace-
maker of 1814, and his colleagues and antagonists at the Congress
table of 1814-15, interest has shifted to Metternich, the European
statesman of a long period, in which he was almost alone in per-
ceiving the central importance of the revolutionary phenomenon,
and in observing it with deep misgivings.

Was it out of fear for the material possessions of the governing
class to which he belonged ? This primitive and over-simplified
interpretation must be left to a primitive school of thought, or rather
to the Marxist school of thoughtless repetition. The usual classification, into those who defend and those who attack an established
order of State and society, discloses little of the figures of a period.
Were they right or were they wrong to attack a fortress, the
strength of which is anyhow a fading memory ? Is a " governing
class " wrong in itself ? Are we bound to take it for granted, and
on whose authority, that the will to preserve—the most fundamental
of social facts, whether we are dealing with the initial social phenomenon of the family, or the more complex and broader phenomenon
of the State and the nation—is in itself an evil, and that upheavals
and radical changes are necessarily an improvement on the principle of preservation ?

These problems of political philosophy inevitably arise when we
deal with the judgements which are still current on the most symbolical historic figure of the principle of preservation, or European
Conservatism. For Metternich was that figure, and neither praise
nor blame, nor any new historical interpretation, can turn him into
anything else.

What did Metternich see as the peril of the time and of the future, and for what, and against what, did he struggle ? He gives the answer himself in the pages which follow. Society is governed, in his view, either by an eternally valid concept of God and Man, or it becomes a mere administration of ephemeral needs: worse still an ambitious scheme of " politics," conceived according to lights which are not more than human. Metternich always discriminates very strictly between " government " and " administration." He distrusts administration as such, " bureaucracy "—a word which he was possibly the first to coin in criticism of the administrative machinery of Austria. This arch-enemy of " doctrinaires " in politics delighted in formulating axioms, in bringing experimental wisdom to its highest theoretical expression. He gives the primacy always to the " social principle," which he interprets in the same way as Bonald; politics take second, and administration the third place only. The social principle is that of the family, the principle of preservation and continuity. Once political institutions or administration intrude upon the first principle, which is the preservation of personal rights and the rights of the family, there is no limit to further incursion by tyranny.

In the political testament which he composed after his resignation in 1848, Metternich strongly protests against a confusion of his principles with " Absolutism." He rejected, he says, both Absolutism and Democracy, two different names to describe the same evil, namely the placing of the human will and human judgement above the facts established by history, above fundamental laws such as that of inheritance, the Christian religion, the unwritten moral code. To recognise no limits to the power of a ruler, to admit his claim to make himself the supreme authority in matters of religion and conscience, to admit his right to confiscate inheritance, to interfere with autonomous institutions, such as academies, universities, professional bodies, is bad enough—as the short experience of the rule of Joseph II of Austria proved in Metternich's youth. It was bad enough to concede such rights to monarchs, who are at least bound, by the very principle which brought them to their thrones, to recognise the rights of the family, and by the religious character of their hereditary office to preserve some amount of Christian morality. But it was infinitely more dangerous to vest these powers in assemblies and elected authorities, not bound by the principle of their existence to respect any inheritance, spiritual or material. Metternich saw that Liberty could be safeguarded only by dogmatic authority of a spiritual nature. He believed, perhaps with some exaggeration, that movements of national independence were usually a pretext to establish a power which would remove all religious and spiritual safeguards, in order to institute political tyranny over the individual.

This vision of the problem set by the nineteenth century can hardly be said to be out of date, judging from our present perspective.

We have the same problem today, and the statesmen of our day quote Metternich's arguments more often than they realise—although few share his strong, somewhat unconditional condemnation of " democratism " and " parliamentarianism " as the potential source of arbitrary power and tyranny.

If Metternich opposed German unity, it was because he saw that the autonomous regional institutions offered the only safeguard to German liberty, to Germany's real, historically established constitution. A German confederation of autonomous states would be at liberty to participate in the political transactions of Europe, and have a permanent interest in preserving a European order. It would also, he thought, be the only means of avoiding either a bellicose Germany (which, in her isolated, central position, would conceive ideas of domination) or a Germany which, seceding from Europe, would unite all the other powers in alliance against her. Who could say that Metternich was a bad prophet, when we read such an analysis of Germany's position in the world ?

His opposition to Italian unity must be understood in its historical context. His reference to Italy as a " geographical expression,"[1] more often quoted than correctly understood, was a warning against the possible consequences of a secular and national power threatening the perfect independence of the Holy See. The latter, with the accession of Pius IX in 1846, repudiated any protection on the part of Austria (which Metternich was bound to defend in theory) and turned towards the concept of an independent confederation, under Papal leadership and with the participation of Austria, the natural ally of Italy in the political and economic field. Once more, could a retrospective history claim that Metternich was wrong ?

And are we not bound to recognise that his fear of Russian expansion, and a return to Russian barbarism was legitimate, unless those two factors which acted as a brake on Russia, Christianity and the Monarchy, brought Russia into a European system of alliances ? If he considered such an alliance as the only means of curbing Russia, he did not consider it to be a perfectly safe means, as we know from his correspondence with Ambassadors and Plenipotentiaries in Constantinople and Athens. He was fully aware of the dangerous tendencies existing in Russia, and attributed them, again not so wrongly, to circles which propagated innovations from the West.

Metternich's thought seldom reached the summits of Catholic theology. To prove the truth of theology by human tradition, as it

[1] Metternich: *Mémoires*, Vol. VII, p. 415. *Dépêche circulaire*, 6.8.1847, to Count Apponyi, Imperial Ambassador in Paris. N. 1610:
" *L'Italie est une expression géographique. La péninsule italienne est composée d'Etats souverains et indépendents les uns des autres. L'existence et la circonscription de ces états sont fondées sur des principes de droit public général et corroborées par les transactions politiques les moins sujettes à contestation. L'empereur, pour sa part, est décidé à respecter ces transactions et à contribuer autant qu'il est en son pouvoir à leur inaltérable maintien.*"

is seen in the law of nations, is one-sided, and, as the Spanish
philosopher Menéndez y Pelayo remarks in his *Historia de los Hetero-
doxos Españoles*, the Church only tolerated the traditionalism of
Joseph de Maistre, Bonald and Donoso for the great merits of these
thinkers, preferring St Thomas's proof of absolute truth to that of
tradition alone. Yet, one-sided as this traditionalism may be, Metternich saw in it the source of political and social wisdom, as he says
in his despatch to Count Lützow, his Ambassador to the Holy See:

" *Je suis, Monsieur l'Ambassadeur, un homme d'église, un franc et sévère
catholique, et c'est pour cela même que je me crois à la fois un homme d'état
pratique. La vérité est une et l'Eglise en est le premier dépositaire. Entre les
vérités religieuses et les vérités sociales, il n'y a point de différence, car la
société ne peut vivre que par la foi et la morale religieuse.*"[1]

MY POLITICAL PROFESSION OF FAITH[2]

" Europe," a celebrated writer said recently, " arouses pity in
the heart of the thinking man and horror in the heart of the
virtuous man."

It would be difficult to give in fewer words a more exact
picture of the situation at the moment of writing these lines!

Kings have reached the stage of wondering how much longer
they are going to last; passions are let loose and are in league
to overthrow all that society has hitherto respected as the basis
of its existence: religion, public morality, laws, customs, rights
and duties; everything is attacked, confused, overthrown, or
made a matter of doubt. The great mass of the people looks
calmly on, in the face of so many attacks and upheavals,
against which there is an utter lack of any sort of protection.
Some of them are lost in vague dreams, whilst an overwhelming
majority desire the maintenance of a public order which no
longer exists, the very first elements of which seem to have been
lost.

What is the cause of so many disorders ? By what means
have they become established and by what means do they
penetrate into all the veins of society ?

Are there any means of halting the growth of this disorder
and in what do they consist ?

Such are doubtless the questions which are most worthy of
the earnest attention of any man of good will, any true friend

---

[1] Metternich : *Mémoires*, Vol. VII, p. 427; N. 1614, Oct. 10, 1847.
[2] Taken from *Mémoires, Documents et Ecrits divers*. Edited by his son, Prince
Richard Metternich (E. Plon et Cie. Paris, 1881).

of law and order, these two elements which are inseparable in their principles and which are the first necessity and at the same time the foremost good of humanity.

Has the world then not created any institution really worthy of this name ? Has truth then always been confused with error, ever since societies thought that they had the power of distinguishing one from the other ? Has all the experience bought at the price of so many sacrifices, and reiterated at so many different periods of history, and in so many different places, always proved wrong ? Has a torrent of light suddenly been shed over society ? Has knowledge in itself become an inspiration ? If a man could believe in such phenomena, he would still need to be first convinced of the reality of the fact. Nothing is as fatal as error, whatever the question at stake and it is our desire and intention never to abandon ourselves to it. Let us examine the situation.

THE CAUSES OF OUR DISORDERS

The nature of man is immutable. The first requirements of society always remain the same, and the differences we can see between them, when we reflect on the question, can be explained by the diversity of influences which natural causes exert on the race of men, such as diversity of climate, the barrenness or the richness of the soil, whether men live on an island or on the continent, etc., etc. These local differences no doubt produce effects which extend far beyond purely physical needs; they create and determine individual needs in a higher sphere; they finally settle types of legislation and their influence, even in the matter of religion, cannot be contested.

On the other hand, the same thing happens to institutions as to everything else. Uncertain in their origin, they go through periods of development and perfection, only to fall into decay, and conforming to the same laws which govern the nature of man, they have, like him, their infancy, their youth, their reasoned maturity and their old age.

Two elements alone remain at the height of their strength and constantly exercise their indestructible influence with a like authority. These are the precepts of morality, both religious and social, and the local needs of man. Once men begin to move away from these bases and to rebel against these sovereign arbiters of their destiny, society is in a state of unrest, which sooner or later will cause an upheaval. The history of every country can show blood-stained pages which tell the story of the consequences of such errors; but we dare to put forward this suggestion, without any fear of contradiction: that we should search in vain for a period when a disorder of this nature has spread its ravages over as vast a field as it has done in this present age. The causes underlying this state of affairs are natural ones.

History only embraces a very restricted lapse of time.

It only begins to deserve this name long after the fall of great empires. Where it appears to bring us to the cradle of civilisation, it leads us only to ruins.

We see republics come to birth and develop, fight and then suffer the rule of a fortunate soldier.

We see one of these republics pass through all the phases common to society and end in a Monarchy that was almost universal, that is to say that it conquered all the scattered parts of the then civilised world.

We see this Monarchy suffer the fate of every body politic; we see the original elasticity grow weak and bring about its own decay.

Centuries of darkness followed the barbarian invasions. The world however could not return to barbarism. The Christian religion had appeared on earth; imperishable in its essence, its mere existence was enough to dispel the darkness and re-establish civilisation on new bases, applicable to all times and all places, satisfying the needs of all on the basis of a pure and eternal law!

The Crusades followed the formation of new Christian states —a curious mixture of good and evil.

Three discoveries soon exercised a decisive influence on the fate of civilisation: the invention of printing, the invention of gunpowder and the discovery of the New World.

The Reformation then came, another event the consequences of which were incalculable, because of the moral effect it had on the world. From that time onwards, the face of the world was changed.

The communication of thought, facilitated by the invention of printing; the complete transformation of the means of attack and defence brought about by the invention of gunpowder; the sudden increase in the natural value of real estate produced by the great quantities of metal put into circulation following the discovery of America; the spirit of adventure which was encouraged by the opportunities of making a fortune in a new hemisphere; the modification which so many and so great changes had introduced into social intercourse—all this underwent still further development and in some measure was crowned by the revolution which the Reformation brought about in the moral order.

The march of the human spirit was therefore exceedingly rapid throughout the last three centuries. This march having progressed with a more rapid acceleration than the course of wisdom—the unique counterbalance to passion and error—had been able to take, a revolution, prepared by false systems of philosophy, and by fatal errors into which several sovereigns, the most illustrious of the second half of the eighteenth century, had fallen, at last broke out in that country which was one of the most advanced in intelligence, the most weakened by a love of pleasure, in a country inhabited by a race of people who can be considered the most frivolous in the world, considering the facility they have in understanding, and the difficulty they experience in judging an issue calmly.

We have glanced rapidly at the primary causes of the present state of society; now we must show in greater detail the nature of the disorder which threatens to disinherit it at one blow of a very real patrimony of benefits, the fruits of a real civilisation, and to disturb it in the enjoyment of these things. We can define this disorder quite simply in a single word: *presumption*, the natural result of such a rapid progress of the human mind in material improvements.

It is presumption which draws so many people today into the paths of error, for the sentiment has become widespread.

Religion, morality, legislation, economy, politics, administration, everything seems to have become common property, accessible to all. People think that they know everything; experience does not count for the *presumptuous man*; faith means nothing to him; he substitutes for it a so-called personal conviction and feels himself dispensed from any examination or course of study in order to arrive at this conviction, for these means seem too lowly to a mind which thinks itself powerful enough to take in at a glance a general review of problems and facts. *Laws* are of no value in his eyes because he did not help to make them and because it would be beneath the dignity of a man of his calibre to recognise the milestones traced by brutish and ignorant generations before him. *Authority* resides in himself; why should he subject himself to what is only of use to a man deprived of intelligence and knowledge? What had formerly, in his view, been sufficient at a tender age no longer suits a man who has reached the age of reason and maturity, that degree of universal perfection which the German innovators designate by the idea, absurd by its very nature, of the *emancipation of the peoples*! *Morality* alone is not openly attacked, for without it he would not be sure of his own existence for a single moment; but he interprets it according to his own fancy and allows everybody else to do the same thing, provided that the other man neither kills nor robs him.

By sketching the character of the presumptuous man in this way, we think we have drawn a picture of the society of today which is composed of similar elements, if the name of society can be applied to an order of things which only tends in principle to *individualise* all the elements which compose society, and to make each man the head of his own dogma, the arbiter of laws according to which he can deign to govern himself, or allow others to govern him and his fellows, in a word, the only judge of his faith, of his actions and the principles according to which he means to regulate them.

Do we need to prove this last truth ? We think we furnish the proof by calling attention to the fact that one of the most natural sentiments in man—*nationality*—has been erased from the Liberal catechism, and that where the word continues to be used at all, it only serves as a pretext for the leaders of the party to fetter governments, or else as a lever to encourage upheavals. The true aim of the idealists of the party is religious and political fusion and, in the last analysis, is no other than to create in favour of each individual an existence which is entirely independent of all authority and all will, except his own—an absurd idea, which is contrary to the spirit of man and incompatible with the requirements of human society.

THE COURSE WHICH THE DISORDER HAS FOLLOWED AND STILL FOLLOWS

The reasons for which the disorder which weighs on society has acquired such a deplorable intensity appear to us to be of two kinds.

Some are so intimately bound up with the nature of things that no human foresight could have prevented them.

Others must themselves be sub-divided into two classes, however similar they may appear to be in their effects.

Some reasons are negative ones, others positive. We place

amongst the first the weakness and inertia of governments.

It is enough to cast a glance at the course governments have followed throughout the eighteenth century, in order to be convinced that none of them had any conception of the disease or the crisis towards which the body politic was moving.

It was quite otherwise with some men, unfortunately endowed with great talents, who were conscious of their own strength and who were not slow to appreciate the inroads of their influence, and to realise the weakness or the inertia of their opponents, and who knew the art of preparing and leading minds to the triumph of their hateful enterprise, an enterprise all the more odious because they pursued it without any thought for the consequences they would bring about, giving themselves up completely to the one sentiment which moved them: hatred of God and His immutable laws!

France was the country which was unfortunate enough to possess the greatest number of these men. It is within her bosom that religion, with all its most sacred associations, that morality and authority, with all their implied power to govern men, were attacked by them with systematic method and fury, and it is in that country that the weapon of ridicule was used with the greatest ease and success.

Drag the name of God in the mud and the authority instituted by His Divine decrees, and the road is open for revolution! Talk of a social contract and the revolution is a fact! It was in the palaces of kings, in the salons and the boudoirs of various towns that the Revolution was already a reality, while the way for it was still being prepared amongst the mass of the people.

It is not possible to omit here any reference to the influence which the example of England had exercised for so long on France—this country of England, placed in such a special geographical situation that we feel ourselves able to affirm boldly that no forms of government, no habits or institutions that are possible in this State, could ever suit a continental State, and that where it is taken for a model the result can only be defective and dangerous, without a single advantage accruing from it.

The intellectual atmosphere was such in France at the time of the convocation of the States General, and the influence on public opinion during the previous fifty years had been such— an influence which in the last instance had been reinforced, and in some measure made peculiar to France by the imprudent aid which the French Government had recently given to the American Revolution—that all reforms in France which touched upon the very foundation of the Monarchy were necessarily transformed into a revolution. What ought to have been foreseen, and what had in fact been foreseen by practically everybody, with the single exception of the Government, came to pass only too soon. The French Revolution broke out and went through a complete revolutionary cycle in a very short period of time, which only appeared long to its victims and its contemporaries.

The scenes of horror which marked the first phases of the French Revolution prevented the rapid propagation of its subversive principles beyond the frontiers of France, and the wars of conquest which succeeded them inclined public opinion abroad to view the progress of the revolutionary principle with disfavour. That is why the first criminal hopes of Jacobin propaganda failed.

The revolutionary germ however had penetrated every country and was more or less widespread. It developed still further during the period of the military despotism of Bonaparte.

His conquests changed a great number of sovereignties, institutions and customs, and broke all those links which are sacred for all peoples, and which resist the inroads of time even more surely than certain benefits do which innovators sometimes impose upon them. As a result of these disturbances, the revolutionary spirit in Germany, in Italy, and later on in Spain, was able to hide beneath the cloak of genuine patriotism.

Prussia made a serious mistake when she called to her aid weapons as dangerous as secret societies always prove to be; a mistake which cannot be justified by the deplorable situation in which that Power then found herself. It was she who first gave a vigorous impulse to the revolutionary spirit in her State and this spirit made rapid progress, supported as it was in the rest of Germany by the growth of a system of foreign despotism from 1806 onwards. Princes of the Rhenish Confederation in particular made themselves the auxiliaries and accomplices of this system, to which they sacrificed institutions in their countries which had from time immemorial served as safeguards against arbitrary action and the rule of the mob.

The War of the Alliance, by setting limits to the preponderance of France, was enthusiastically supported in Germany by the very men whose hatred for France was in reality nothing more than a hatred of the military despotism of Bonaparte, and who also hated the legitimate power of their own masters.

If only governments had shown wisdom and firmness in their principles, the end of the war in 1814 could still have assured a perfectly happy and peaceful future for the world. Much experience had been acquired and the great lessons which had been learnt could have been applied to some useful purpose. But fate decided otherwise.

The return of the usurper to France and the completely erroneous direction which the French Government took from 1815-1820 amassed for the whole of civilisation new dangers and immense disasters. It was to the first of these misfortunes that the critical state in which France and the whole of the body politic lie is in part due. In one hundred days Bonaparte wiped out the work of the fourteen years during which he had exercised power. He let loose the revolution which he had managed to hold in check in France; he rallied men's minds, not to the time of the 18th Brumaire, but to the principles which the Constituent Assembly had adopted in its lamentable blindness.

The harm which Bonaparte did in this way to France and to Europe, the serious errors which the French Government made and into which other governments fell later on in their turn— all these fatal influences lie heavy on the world today; they threaten with total ruin the work of restoration, the fruit of so many glorious efforts and of a union between the first Monarchs of the world which was without any precedent in the annals of history, and foreshadow incalculable disasters for society.

We have not yet in this present Memorandum touched on one of the most active and at the same time most dangerous instruments of which revolutionaries make use in every country, with a success that none can deny. These are the *secret societies*, which constitute a real power, all the more dangerous because it works in the dark and undermines all parts of the body politic, depositing everywhere the germs of a moral gangrene which will soon mature and bear its fruit. This scourge is one of the most real which governments who are the friends of public order and of their peoples should watch carefully and fight.

CAN THIS EVIL BE REMEDIED AND BY WHAT MEANS?

We regard it as a principle that every evil has its own remedy, and that a knowledge of the true nature of the one leads to the discovery of the other. Few men, however, take the trouble to make a deep study of the evil against which they propose to fight. Few men are exempt from the influence of various passions and nearly all are blinded by prejudice; a great number are guilty of a fault which is even more dangerous because of its flattering and often brilliant exterior; we mean those who are animated by *intellectual pride*; this pride, which is invariably in error, but which is indefatigable, audacious, insensitive to any rebuff, which satisfies the men who are imbued with it (for they inhabit and administer a world of their own), is all the more dangerous for the inhabitants of the real world, so different from the one created by intellectual pride.

There is another class of men who, seizing upon the outward form only of an evil, confuse the accessory manifestations with the evil thing itself, and who, instead of directing their efforts towards the source of the evil, are content to combat a few passing symptoms.

Our duty is to endeavour to avoid both of these two reefs.

The evil exists, and it is an immense one. We do not think we can give a better definition of it and the primary cause of it, which is perpetually at work everywhere and at all times, than we did when we used the word *presumption*, this inseparable companion of half-digested knowledge, this driving force of boundless ambition, which is easily satisfied at times of stress and upheaval.

The middle classes of society are the ones which are chiefly infected by this moral gangrene and the real *coryphées* of the party are only to be found in this section of society.

This gangrene is powerless against the great mass of the people and has no hold over them. The type of work to which this class—*the real people*—has to devote itself is too obvious and too positive for them to give themselves up to vague abstractions and the uncertain path of ambition. The people know that their greatest blessing is to be sure of the morrow, for it is only the morrow which brings them any reward for the troubles and the hard work of today. The laws which guarantee a just protection for the highest good of all, the security of individual families and the security of property, are simple in essence. The people distrust change, which is bad for trade and invariably brings in its train an increase of burdens.

Men of a higher class in society, who embrace the revolutionary career, are either ambitious hypocrites or perverted and lost minds in the widest sense of the word. Their career is for this reason usually short. They are the first victims of political reforms, and the part which the small number of survivors amongst them play is usually that of hangers-on, who are despised by their inferiors as soon as these latter have reached the highest dignities in the State.

France, Germany, Italy and Spain today offer many living examples of the theory we have just put forward.

We do not think that new upheavals of a directly revolutionary intention, other than palace revolutions and changes in the highest government posts, are to be feared today in France, if we take into account the profound aversion of the people to all that could disturb the tranquillity which it now enjoys, after so much suffering and so many disasters.

In Germany, as in Spain and Italy, the nations only ask for peace and law and order.

In these four countries, the dissatisfied classes comprise moneyed men who are really cosmopolitans, acquiring their profits at the expense of any existing order of things; civil servants, men of letters, lawyers and foolish professors.

The ambitious hypocrites belong also to these intermediary classes, few in number amongst the lower conditions of men, but more numerous amongst the higher ranks of society.

Furthermore, there is hardly a period in history when the various factions have not used some catchword.

Since 1815, the catchword has been *constitution*. But do not let us be under any illusion—this word, which lends itself to so wide a latitude in interpretation, is only imperfectly understood if we suppose that the various factions attach the same meaning indiscriminately to it under different forms of government. This then is not the case. Under autocratic Monarchies, it means *national representation*. In countries recently subjected to representative government, it calls itself development and guarantee of charters and fundamental laws.

In the one State which possesses an ancient national representation, it has *reform* for its objective.

Everywhere it means *change and disturbance*.

Paraphrased, it means under a despotic Monarchy: " Your heads too must suffer the levelling process of equality; your fortunes can pass into the hands of others; your ambitions, which have been satisfied for centuries, can give place to our impatient ambitions, which up to now have been denied."

In States subjected to a new régime: " Let ambitions which were satisfied yesterday give place to those of tomorrow, for we belong to tomorrow."

Finally, in England, the only country to be placed in the third class, the catchword—reform—combines the two meanings.

So Europe presents a deplorable and curious picture to the impartial observer.

We find peoples everywhere who desire only the maintenance of law and order, who are faithful to God and their Princes, and remain strangers to the increasing seductions and attempts made by factions who call themselves their friends and try to draw them into a movement against their will!

We see governments which have lost confidence in themselves, and are frightened, intimidated and routed by the catchword of this intermediate class of society, which is half-way between the kings and the peoples, which breaks the sceptres of the former and usurps the voice of the latter—seizing every avenue to the throne—of this same class which has so often been rejected by the people, when it presumes to speak in the people's name, yet is listened to, caressed and feared to excess by those who, with a single word, could drive them back to obscurity.

We see this intermediate class giving itself up with blind fury, and with a desperation which betrays its own fears far more than it reveals confidence in the success of its enterprises, to all the means which it thinks will assuage its thirst for power; applying itself to persuade kings that their rights do not go beyond sitting on a throne, while the caste has the right to administer and to attack all the sacred and positive things which the centuries have bequeathed for the respect of men; finally we see this class denying that the past is of any value and declaring that they are the masters and can create a future. We see them assuming any sort of a mask, uniting or forming splinter groups according to need, helping each other on the day of danger and tearing each other's throats on the morrow of each new conquest. That is the class which has seized control of the Press, which runs it and only uses it for the sole purpose of extolling impiety, disobedience to the laws of Religion and the State, and has even forgotten itself to such an extent that it preaches murder as a duty *for any man who is sure of what he wants.*

One of their leaders in Germany gave this definition of public opinion: " *The will of the strong man in the mind of the party,*" a maxim which is put into practice all too often and is all too little understood by the men whose right and duty it is to save society from its own errors and weaknesses, and from the crimes which factions commit when they claim to act in its interest.

The presence of the evil is evident; the means used by the disruptive faction are so much to be condemned on principle, they are so criminal in their application, they even offer such a total of dangers for the faction itself, that what short-sighted men, whose heads and hearts are shattered by circumstances which are stronger than their own calculations or courage, look upon as the end of society, can become the first step towards a better order of things. These weak men will be proved to be right, unless men stronger than they come forward, close their ranks and make sure of victory.

We are convinced that society can be saved only by strong and vigorous determination on the part of governments which are still free in thought and action.

We think also that it can still be saved if these governments face the truth squarely, if they cast off their illusions, if they close their ranks and stand firm on a line of correct principles, from which all ambiguity is absent, and which are frankly upheld and stated.

By acting in this way, Monarchs will fulfil the first of the duties imposed upon them by Him who, by giving them power, charged them to uphold justice, the rights of each and all, to avoid the byways of error and to tread firmly the path of truth. Placed as they are outside the sphere of passions which rend society, it is above all during times of crisis that they are called upon to strip reality of all false appearances, and to show themselves for what they are, fathers invested with all the authority which rightly belongs to the head of the family, to prove that in times of disaster they can be just and wise and therefore strong, and that they do not abandon the people, whom it is their duty to govern, *to the sport* of factions, to error and its consequences, which inexorably bring about the ruin of society. The present moment, when we put down our thoughts in these pages, is one of those moments of crisis; the crisis is grave; it will be decisive according to the party-decisions we make, or refuse to make.

There is a rule of conduct common to individuals and to States, sanctioned by the experience of centuries, as well as by that of every day; this rule states: It is not in the stress of passion that we ought to think of *reform*; wisdom decrees that in such moments we should confine ourselves to *preserve*.

Let Monarchs adopt these principles whole-heartedly, and

let all their resolutions bear the imprint of them. Let their actions, the measures they take, and even the words they utter, state this determination to the world and prove it; they will find allies everywhere. When governments establish the principle of *stability*, they in no wise exclude the development of anything that is good, for stability does not mean immobility. It is, however, for those who are burdened with the heavy task of government to improve the wellbeing of their peoples! It is for the governments to decide the pace, according to needs and to circumstances. It is not by the concessions which the various factions think they can impose on the legitimate authority, and which they have neither the right to demand, nor the power to restrain within just limits, that wise reforms can be achieved! Our most ardent wish is that the utmost good should be done; but do not let what is not good be confused with what is good, and even let real good only be done by those who combine under the law authority and the means to do it. Such should also be the sincere desire of all peoples, who have learnt only too well at their own expense how to appreciate the worth of certain words, and the nature of certain caresses.

Respect for all existing things; liberty for every government to watch over the wellbeing of its own people; an alliance between all the governments to fight factions in every State; contempt for words devoid of meaning, which have become the catchwords of mischief-makers; respect for the progressive development of institutions according to the law; refusal on the part of every Monarchy to help or succour dissident elements, in whatever disguise they may appear: such are happily the thoughts of every great Monarch; the world can be saved if they are translated into action, it is lost if they are not.

Union between Monarchs is the fundamental basis of the policy which must be followed to save society from total ruin.

To what particular end should this policy be directed ? The more important this question is, the more necessary it is to resolve it. A principle counts for much; it only acquires real worth when it is applied.

The primary causes of the evil which overwhelms the world have been summed up by us in this little work, which does not claim to be more than a sketch. The progressive causes of this evil are here indicated; if in its relation to *individuals* it was defined as *presumption*, we think that when we apply this word to society as a whole, it also describes the evil which exists in that *vagueness of thought which is due to an excess of generalisation.* Let us see what disturbs society today.

Principles which have hitherto been considered as fixed are now attacked and overthrown. In religious matters, *private judgement* and *examination* of the subject replace *faith*; *Christian morality* is to take the place of the *law of Christ,* such as it has always been interpreted by the relevant Christian authorities.

In the Catholic Church, Jansenists and a host of isolated sectarians who desire a *Religion without a Church* devote themselves to this enterprise with eager zeal; in the Protestant sects we have the Methodists, themselves subdivided into almost as many sects as there are persons, then the enlightened promoters of Bible Societies, and the Unitarians, or promoters of a fusion between the Lutherans and the Calvinists in an evangelical community.

The common aim of these men, irrespective of the sect to which they ostensibly belong, is no other than to *overthrow authority.* In the moral field, they want to *set souls free,* just as those men amongst the political revolutionaries, who do not abandon themselves exclusively to a calculating personal ambition, want to *set people free.*

If the same elements of destruction which today convulse society have existed in every century—for every age has seen the birth of unscrupulous and ambitious men, hypocrites, hotheads, pseudo-intellects and builders of castles in the air—our own age however, by the single fact of the licentiousness of the Press, possesses more possibilities of contact, of corruption and of influence, which are greater and more easily set in motion, and more susceptible of working upon this class of men, than any other age.

We are certainly not alone in wondering whether society can continue to exist when *the liberty of the Press* prevails, this scourge which was unknown in the world before the latter half of the seventeenth century, and only practised until the end of the eighteenth century, with few exceptions, in England, in this part of Europe separated from the Continent by the sea, as much as by its language and its individual customs.

The first principle which Monarchs, who are united in will as well as by the uniformity of their desires and their judgement, ought to proclaim is the stability of political institutions, in face of the disintegration which has taken hold of men's minds; the rigidity of certain principles, in face of the mania for *interpreting* them; and *respect for existing laws*, instead of the *over-throw* of these laws.

The hostile section is divided into two very distinct groups.

One consists of the levellers, the other of the doctrinaires.

United on the day of revolution, these men are divided when they play a merely passive rôle. It is the business of governments to know who they are, and to keep them in their place, in accordance with their real value.

Among the class of levellers, there are to be found strong-willed and determined men. The doctrinaires never count such men in their ranks. If the first category is more to be feared on the day of revolution, the second is more dangerous in those deceptively calm days which precede a storm in the social order, just as they do in the physical order. Constantly in the grip of abstract ideas which it would be impossible ever to apply to real issues, and which are ordinarily even in contradiction with those issues, it is men of this class who perpetually stir up the people with imaginary or simulated fears, and weaken governments in order to force them to deviate from the right path. Men want to be governed by facts and in accordance with justice, not with words and theories; society needs first and foremost to be upheld by a strong authority (any authority which lacks real strength is unworthy of the name), not to govern itself. If we calculated the number of disputes in which the various groups in mixed governments, and the number of just grievances to which an aberration of power in a Christian State can give rise, the result of this comparison would not be in favour of *modern theories*. The first and most important matter for the overwhelming majority of the nation is the stability of the laws, their continuity, and by no means their overthrow. Let governments govern then, let them maintain the fundamental bases of their institutions, ancient as well as modern; for if it is dangerous in any age to alter them, it is certainly not a propitious time to do so today, amidst the general unrest.

Let them acquaint their peoples openly with this determination and let them prove it by acts. Let them reduce the doctrinaires within their States to silence, and let them show their contempt for those who are beyond their frontiers. Let them not give colour by their demeanour, or by their acts, to the suspicion that they are either favourable to error, or indifferent to it; let them not give the impression that the lessons of experience go for nothing, and make way for experiments which, to say the least, are hazardous. Let each one of their words be precise and clear, and let them in no way try to win over by concessions those groups whose only aim is the destruction of all authority which is not in their own hands, who could not be won over by concessions, and who would become the more emboldened in their pretensions if they were granted concessions.

Let them be more cautious in troubled times than at any other time, in their approach to the questions of reforms which are genuine, and not demanded imperiously according to the exigencies of the moment, so that the very good that they do will not be turned against them—a contingency which can easily happen, if a government measure appears to have been granted out of fear.

Let them not confuse in this way concessions made to rival groups, with the good which they can confer on their peoples by modifying, according to *acknowledged* requirements, any particular branch of their administration which could benefit by such a measure.

Let them devote the most careful attention to the state of the finances of their country, so that their peoples may enjoy, by a reduction in taxation, the benefits of a period of real and not illusory peace.

Let them be just but firm; kind yet severe.

Let them uphold religion in all its purity, not suffering any attack upon dogma, or allowing morality to be interpreted according to the *Social Contract*, or the visions of simple sectarians.

Let them suppress secret societies, this gangrene which preys upon society.

Finally, let all the great Monarchs come closer together and prove to the world that if they are united, it can only be beneficial, for union between them will assure the political peace of Europe; that they are only firmly united in order to maintain public order at a time when it is menaced on all sides; that the principles they profess are as paternal and as much intended for the protection of good citizens, as they are repressive for dissident factions.

Governments of lesser Powers will see in such a projected union the anchor of their salvation and will hasten to associate themselves with it. Peoples will regain confidence and courage, and the deepest and most salutary pacification which the world has ever witnessed in all its long history could be established,

for such a peace would first of all include all those States which
are still left standing; it would not remain without a decisive
influence on the fate of those which are threatened with imminent subversion, and even on the restoration of those which
have already suffered the scourge of revolution.

Every great State which is determined to survive the turmoil
of the time still has a good chance of salvation.

A firm union between States on the principles which we have
just laid down will vanquish the turmoil itself.

VII. JUAN DONOSO CORTÉS

1809 - 1853

A FEW years before the European Revolution of 1848, which, in a very short time, had shown in a concentrated and spectacular form all those modern trends which for good or ill have dominated Europe ever since—Germanism and Slavism in the East and the social conflict in the West—one of the principal prophets of the Slav awakening, the romantic poet Kollar, who brought home to his Slovak mountains a somewhat rough, but still unadulterated, version of Hegel's philosophy from his Lutheran theological studies at Jena, wrote: " In the East, amongst the Slavs and for the Slavs, the sun is rising. Over the Germanic lands it is broad daylight. Over England it is high noon, over France and Italy the sun is already setting, over Spain and Portugal it is dark night."

The Slav poet, Lutheran in his religion, Hegelian in his philosophy, and Liberal in his politics, was not alone in considering the Spain of the post-Napoleonic era as the country of dark night. This opinion was general and most believers in the ingloriously, although somewhat slowly, expiring deity called the *Zeitgeist*, concurred in seeing in Spain nothing but a ruin and a past.

Few, far too few, eyes turned towards the " Far West," as some modern Spaniards like to call the Iberian peninsula and its trans-atlantic extension. The Spanish *ochocientos* presented a disturbed, almost chaotic picture of changing dynasties and ephemeral political régimes, of military upheavals and conspiracies, of a society near to disintegration, which the keenest observer was discouraged from penetrating and understanding. Yet, can we forget that Napoleon's first failure was in Spain, and that the whole historical and ideological trend symbolically summarised by the Battle of the Nations began on the Peninsula ? It was in Spain too that the conclusion of the great European crisis was summed up in terms of the philosophy of history, in terms of an eschatological interpretation of State and society, and above all in those deep accents of prophecy which only posterity appreciates at its full value. Two meteor-like figures of thinkers stand out in this post-Napoleonic generation in Spain: the philosopher-statesman Juan Donoso Cortés and the theologian and philosopher Jaime Balmes. Neither of them lived to be old. Donoso died when he was only forty-four, the great priest of Catalonia, Jaime Balmes, at the age of thirty-eight.

The Battle of the Nations at Leipzig in October 1813 was to some

extent prepared and summarised by a philosophical movement in
Germany which had an immense importance for the rest of Europe.
Fichte and Hegel, and their common master Immanuel Kant,
revolutionised European thought by the importance which they
achieved as the ideological masters of their people during the
national resistance to Napoleon. They educated Germany in the
rôle she was to play from the time of the French Revolutionary wars
to Napoleon. The great German innovation consisted of a new
metaphysical approach to History, to art and human society, a new
emphasis on the subjective, ethical conscience and on emotion, a
neo-Platonic emphasis on the transcendental and symbolic significance of all earthly phenomena: "*Alles Vergängliche ist nur ein
Gleichniss*," as Goethe says in *Faust*—this line could almost stand as
the device of the whole ideological movement of post-Napoleonic
Germany.

Overwhelmed by German ideas, or rather by the new German
emphasis, the European mind paid little attention to a philosophical
movement which was hardly less intense, and which came from a
different corner of Europe. This was the philosophical renaissance
occurring in Spain, in the same context of a national awakening
born out of resistance to Napoleon. Europe hardly noticed Spain
in the nineteenth century. Power shifted to the East and to the
North, as a result of the Napoleonic Wars. Almost every well-
informed person considered in 1815, and in the years following,
that the chief political factor of the present and the future was
Russia, counter-balanced by Russia's only potential rival, England.
The country producing new intellectual impulses was thought to
be the Germany which emerged from the Battle of Leipzig, while
France continued to dominate European civilisation by her
language, and like a barometer registered the variations in pressure
of the highly disturbed political, social and cultural atmosphere of
the time.

The life-work of Donoso Cortés constitutes a spiritual link of
considerable relevance between Spain, France and Germany. Born
in 1809 in a convent of the Estramadura, where his mother was
confined during the flight of the family from the French invaders,
Juan María Donoso Cortés achieved a most brilliant literary,
political and diplomatic career. As a child he was recognised to be
an infant prodigy; at the age of twenty, he was a Lecturer at the
University of Salamanca, where regulations had had to be waived
in order that he might take his degree before the required age.
Before he was thirty, he was elected by his native province to the
Congress of Deputies, where he soon was called to a junior Cabinet
post. Later on he held an important diplomatic post in Paris at the
time of Louis Philippe and Guizot and was raised to the peerage
with the title of Marquis of Valdegamas; in 1849 he was Ambassador Extraordinary and Minister Plenipotentiary to Prussia. He

was again posted to Paris as Ambassador during the Presidency of Louis Napoleon and the beginning of the Second Empire. He died in Paris when, as we have seen, he was only forty-four.

Yet these external events of a short and brilliant career are but a feeble indication of the background to the pages which follow. More important in Donoso's life than his political career was his decision to renounce it early, for as he says in one of his letters to Louis Veuillot, he became convinced that prayers were more efficacious in good causes than anything politics had to offer.

As a young man, Donoso was a Catholic Liberal, attached to the service of Queen Isabella, as were all the Liberals—Moderados— during the years of the dynastic crisis, when Don Carlos rallied the party of the strict legitimists—Apostolicos—to the cause of the Salic Monarchy. His early writings, comprising a treatise on *The Law of the Nations*, an *Essay on Diplomacy*, a *History of the Eastern Question*, literary and political chronicles and comments on Spanish, French and world events of the 1830's and 1840's, do not show him yet in the light in which he stood after the European Revolution of 1848-49—a prophetic voice announcing with deep, mystical insight " the doom of the Kingdom of Philosophy " and the coming of the Kingdom of God amidst Revolutions of cosmic proportions and all the signs foretold in the Apocalypse. It was in Prussia— which under Frederick the Great had been the favourite country of foreign " philosophers " and again in 1813, the country of a German philosophy, the principal tenet of which is individual judgement, that spiritual and ethical inheritance of Protestantism —that Donoso became convinced of the impending " final dissolution of modern civilisation," the impending catastrophe which would overwhelm Europe, for some unrevealed, but certainly glorious, purpose of Providence.

In the history of post-revolutionary Christian thought and philosophy, Donoso represents a landmark of the greatest relevance, which few contemporary observers sensed, although their number is less important than their quality. Louis Veuillot, a close personal friend during his Paris years, was one of them; Barbey d'Aurevilly did not hesitate to place him beside Joseph de Maistre and Bonald as one of the " Lay Fathers of the Church "; Schelling, head of the German philosophers since the death of Hegel, greeted in him a new and unexpected luminary of the century; old Metternich did not hesitate to declare that " After Donoso Cortés, one has to put down one's pen, for nothing more and nothing better can be said on the historical transition we are witnessing."

Donoso Cortés says the final word on the Parliamentary Liberalism of the early part of the century—this political reflection, he says, of the Deist philosophy. He is, if not the first, certainly the most important Christian voice to comment on the deeper (and not merely political) Revolution through which Europe was, and still is, passing. The pantheist negation of God and authority has only one social expression, Communism—Donoso was the first to be fully aware of this—and when the belief in Divine privilege vanishes, the actual consequence of privilege, political and personal liberty, will also vanish. His *Essay on Catholicism* (1851), a masterly comment on the European Revolution of 1848-49, was perhaps the first, and at any rate for some time to come, the most elaborate and profound Catholic analysis of revolutionary Socialism and Communism. Time has also justified Donoso's vision of Russia and Germany as the two future centres of good and evil for Europe, as those quarters from which more deadly revolutions than the French one may come.

Prophecy has seldom been more conscious than in the speech on " Dictatorship " which Donoso delivered in Madrid in the Spanish Congress of Deputies on January 4, 1849, and which appeared in full soon afterwards in *L'Univers* and also as a brochure. We republish it here, omitting a few contemporary allusions which have now—especially outside Spain—lost their importance. Donoso's powerful and frightening image of a coming tyranny, on a scale yet unknown in the annals of mankind, which would come upon them in days not too far removed from their own, is the counterpart of the classic prophecy on the horrors of subversion to be found much later as an image of the future in Dostoievsky's *The Possessed*. Even without the *Ensayo*, it would raise Donoso from the level of the merely political theorists of his generation to that of the visionaries who saw spiritual doom in the age of material progress, such as Kierkegaard or Dostoievsky. Because of his Catholic vision, he uses better arguments concerning Authority and Faith and is a more systematic and more rational defender of spiritual truth than the other prophets of the modern Apocalypse.

1. THE CHURCH, THE STATE, AND REVOLUTION[1]

GENTLEMEN,

The long speech which Señor Cortina made yesterday, and to which I am going to reply by considering it from a certain angle, in spite of the vast implications it contains, forms but an epilogue: an epilogue to the errors of the Progressive party, which in their turn form but another epilogue: the epilogue to the errors which were invented three centuries ago and which rend in varying degrees every human society today.

At the beginning of his speech, Señor Cortina confessed, with

[1] Donoso Cortés' speech on Dictatorship to the Spanish Parliament, January 4, 1849 (*Obras Completas*, Tomo II, p. 187; *Biblioteca de Autores Christianos*, Madrid, 1946).

that good faith which distinguishes him and which enhances his talent to such a degree, that it has even occasionally happened that he wondered whether his principles might not be false and his ideas disastrous, when he saw them always in opposition but never in power. I will tell the honourable gentleman: if he reflects but a little, his doubts will become a certainty. His ideas are not in power, and are in the Opposition, precisely because they are the ideas of an opposition rather than of a government. They are barren ideas, Gentlemen, disastrous ideas which we must fight until they are laid to rest in their natural tomb, here beneath this dome, at the foot of the tribune.

Loyal to the traditions of the party which he leads and represents; loyal, I repeat, to the traditions of this party since the Revolution of February, Señor Cortina included three things in his speech which I shall term inevitable. The first is praise of his party, praise based on a recital of its past merits; the second is the dissertation on its present grievances; the third, the programme, or a statement, of the services it could render in the future.

Gentlemen of the majority, I come here to defend your principles; but do not expect the slightest praise from me: you are the victors, nothing is so becoming to the victor's brow as a crown of modesty.

Do not expect me either to speak of your grievances: your business is not to avenge personal insults, but those which traitors to their Queen and country have cast on society and the Throne. I shall not draw up an inventory of all the services you have rendered. What would be the object? To tell the nation about them? The nation does not forget.

It has not escaped your memory, Gentlemen, that Señor Cortina divided his speech into two parts. The Honourable Member dealt with the foreign policy of the Government and designated the events which have taken place in Paris, London and Rome as of great importance in the foreign policy of Spain. I, too, shall touch upon these questions.

The Honourable speaker then approached the question of domestic policy; and domestic policy, according to Señor Cortina, can be divided into a question of principles and a question of facts, a question of method and of application. By the voices of the Secretary of State for Foreign Affairs and the Home Secretary, who discharged their task with their accustomed eloquence, the Cabinet replied to the question of facts and of policy, as was fitting, considering that they have all the relevant data for this. The question of principle has been barely touched upon; I shall confine myself to dealing with that one question, and if the House gives me leave, I shall go into fundamentals.

What principle inspires Señor Cortina ? This principle, if I have analysed his speech correctly. In home affairs, the form of the law; everything by the law, everything for the law, always the form of the law; the form of the law in every circumstance, the form of the law on every occasion. But I, who believe that laws are made for societies and not societies for the laws, I say: Society, everything through society for society; society always, society in every circumstance and on every occasion.

When the form of the law is sufficient to save society, the form of the law is best; when it is not, let us have dictatorship. This formidable word, Gentlemen—less formidable than the word Revolution, the most formidable of all—this formidable word has been pronounced by a man here, known to us all, and who assuredly is not of the stuff of which dictators are made. I myself understand them instinctively, but not in order to imitate them. I find two things impossible: to condemn dictatorship and to exercise it. Incapable, I recognise in all frankness, of governing with a lofty nobility, I could not in conscience accept the responsibility of government. I could not do so without setting one half of myself at war with the other half, my instincts with my faculty of reason, my reason with my instincts.

So, Gentlemen, all those who know me can bear witness : nobody, within or without these precincts, can say that they have rubbed shoulders with me along the crowded path of ambition. On the contrary, I shall always be found, and have always been found, in the modest path of the good citizen; and when my days are accomplished, I shall go down to my tomb without feeling remorse at having failed to defend society when it was barbarously attacked, or without feeling the bitter, and for me unbearable, sorrow of having done evil to any man.

I say, Gentlemen, that dictatorship, in certain circumstances, in given circumstances, such as those in which we find ourselves, for example, is a legitimate form of government, as good and as profitable as any other, a rational system of government, which can be defended in theory as well as in practice. Let us examine in what the life of society really consists.

The life of society, like human life, is composed of action and reaction, of the ebb and flow of certain forces which attack, and others which resist.

Such is the life of society and the life of man. Now the attacking forces, which we call disease in the human body, and by another name in the body politic, although in essence it is the same thing, appear in two forms. In one form they are spread here and there over society and are only seen in individuals; in the other, in the state of advanced disease, they take a more concentrated form and are seen in political associations. Very well, then, I say that the forces which resist, only present in the human body and in the body politic in order to repulse the attacking forces, must necessarily be in proportion to the actual strength of the latter. When the attacking forces are disseminated, the forces which resist must likewise be disseminated; they permeate the Government, the authorities, the Courts of Law, in a word, the whole body politic; but should the attacking forces be concentrated in political associations, then necessarily, without anyone being able to prevent it, without anyone having the right to prevent it, the forces which resist are concentrated into the hands of one man. This is the theory of dictatorship, clear, luminous and indestructible.

This theory, which is a truth in the rational order, is a constant factor in the historical order. Quote me one society which has never known a dictatorship, just one. See, on the contrary, what happened in democratic Athens, what happened in aristocratic Rome. In Athens, this sovereign authority was in the hands of the people and was called ostracism; in Rome, it was in the hands of the Senate, who delegated it to a prominent citizen bearing the rank of Consul, and that was called dictatorship, as it is in our own country. Look at modern societies; look at France amidst all her vicissitudes. I will not speak of the First Republic, which was a dictatorship of gigantic proportions, unbounded, full of blood and horror. I speak of a later time. In the Charter of the Restoration, dictatorship had taken refuge, or if you prefer it, had sought refuge, in Article 14; in the Charter of 1830, it was to be found in the Preamble. And where is it to be found in the present Republic? Do not let us talk of it: What is it, except a dictatorship disguised as a Republic?

Señor Galvez Cagnero quoted here, somewhat inappositely, the English Constitution. As it happens, Gentlemen, the English Constitution is the only one in the world (so wise are the English!) where dictatorship is not an exception in law, but is part of the common law. The matter is quite clear. In all circumstances, and at every period, Parliament possesses, when it likes, dictatorial powers, for in the exercise of its power it only recognises the one limit which bounds all human authority—that of prudence. It can do anything, and that is exactly what constitutes dictatorial powers; it can do anything except change a woman into a man, or a man into a woman, say its jurists. It has the power to suspend *habeas corpus*, to outlaw by a bill of *attainder*; it can change the constitution; it can even change the dynasty, and not only the dynasty but even the religion of the people; it has the right to oppress consciences; in a word it is all-powerful. Who has ever seen, Gentlemen, a more monstrous dictatorship ?

I have proved that dictatorship is a truth in the theoretical order and a fact in the historical order. Now I am going further: if I may say so without impropriety, dictatorship could be said to be a fact also in the divine order.

God has given the government of human societies into the hands of men, up to a certain point, and has reserved exclusively for Himself the government of the Universe. God governs the Universe, if I can so put it, and if I can use Parliamentary language for such an august subject—God governs the Universe constitutionally. Yes, Gentlemen. It is as clear as daylight and proved by evidence. The Universe is governed by certain precise and indispensable laws, which are called secondary causes. What are these laws, except laws analogous to those we call fundamental in human society ?

Now, Gentlemen, if God is the Legislator of the physical world, as certain men are legislators, although in a different way, of human societies, does God always govern according to the same laws which He has imposed upon Himself in His eternal wisdom and to which He has subjected us ? No, Gentlemen, for He sometimes manifests His sovereignty directly, clearly and explicitly by breaking those laws which He has imposed upon Himself and deflecting the natural course of events. Now, when God acts in this way, could we not say, if human language can be applied to divine things, that He acts dictatorially ?

That proves, Gentlemen, how great is the folly of a party which imagines that it can govern with less means of doing so than God, and refuses to use the means of dictatorship, which is sometimes necessary. That being so, the problem, reduced to its real terms, does not consist in knowing whether dictatorship is justified or not, or whether in certain cases it is a good thing, but whether such circumstances are present, or have been present in Spain. This is the most important point and the one on which I shall concentrate my attention exclusively. In order to do so, and in this I shall but follow those speakers who have preceded me in the tribune, I shall have to glance briefly first at Europe and then at our own country.

The February Revolution, Gentlemen, like Death, came unexpectedly. God had condemned the French Monarchy. In vain had this institution undergone profound transformation, in an attempt to adapt itself to circumstances and the times; it was of no avail; it was irrevocably condemned, its fall was inevitable. The monarchy of the Divine Right of Kings came to an end with Louis XVI on the scaffold; the monarchy of glory came to an end with Napoleon on an island; hereditary monarchy came to an end with Charles X in exile; and with Louis Philippe came to an end the last of all possible monarchies, the monarchy of prudence. What a melancholy and pitiful sight does an institution so venerable, ancient and glorious present, when it cannot be preserved by divine right, legitimacy, prudence or glory!

When the startling news of this great Revolution reached Spain, we were all plunged into consternation; we were all terrified. Nothing could compare with our consternation and our terror, unless it was the consternation and terror felt by the defeated monarchy. Yet that is not all; a greater consternation and a greater terror existed than that felt by the vanquished monarchy—in the victorious Republic. Even today, ten months after their triumph, ask them how they won, why and with what forces they conquered, and they will be unable to tell you. Why? Because it was not the Republic which conquered: the Republic was only the instrument of victory in the hands of a higher power.

This power, once its work was begun, destroyed the monarchy with such a tiny thing as this Republic; do you doubt, Gentlemen, that if it was necessary, and in its own interest, it could not overthrow the Republic in its turn with the shadow of an empire or a monarchy? The cause and the effects of this revolution have been the subject of wide comment in all the Parliaments in Europe, and particularly in the Spanish Parliament, and I have marvelled at the deplorable frivolity with which the deep-seated causes which bring about such upheavals have been treated, here as elsewhere. Here as elsewhere, revolutions are always attributed to the mistakes of governments; men forget that universal, unforeseen and simultaneous catastrophes are always providential; for such, Gentlemen, are the characteristics which distinguish the works of God from the works of man.

When revolutions betray these symptoms, be sure that they come from Heaven and that they come as a result of our mistakes and for the punishment of us all. Shall I tell you the truth, Gentlemen, the whole truth concerning the causes of the last French revolution ? The truth, then, is that the day came last February of the great reckoning with Providence for all classes of society, and that on that dread day all classes were found to be bankrupt. I go further: the Republic itself, on the day of its victory, confessed that it was bankrupt. The Republic has said that it was going to establish in the world the reign of liberty, equality and fraternity, three dogmas which were born, not in the Republic, but on Calvary. What, Gentlemen, has it accomplished since then ? In the name of liberty, it has made necessary, proclaimed and accepted dictatorship. In the name of equality, in the name of the republicans of yesterday and tomorrow, of men who were born republican, it has invented a curious sort of aristocratic democracy bearing ridiculous coats of arms. Finally, in the name of fraternity, it has restored the fraternity of pagan antiquity, of Eteochus and Polynices: and brother cut the throat of brother in the streets of Paris, in the bloodiest battle the centuries have ever seen within the walls of a city. I give the lie to this Republic which calls itself the Republic of the three truths: it is the Republic of the three blasphemies, the Republic of the three lies.

Let us now touch on the causes of this Revolution. The progressive party always finds the same causes for everything. Señor Cortina told us yesterday that revolutions occur because of certain illegalities and because the instincts of the people make them rise in a uniform and spontaneous way against tyrants. Señor Ordax Avecilla told us previously: If you want to avoid revolution, give the hungry bread. Here, in all its subtlety, is the progressive theory: the causes of revolution lie, on the one hand in poverty, and on the other in tyranny. This theory, Gentlemen, is contrary, absolutely contrary, to historical fact. I challenge anybody to quote me one example of a revolution which has been started and brought to a conclusion by men who were either slaves or hungry. Revolutions are a disease of rich peoples, of free peoples. Slaves formed the greater part of the human race in antiquity: tell me one revolution these slaves ever made.

All that they could do was to foment a few slave wars: but deep-seated revolutions were always the work of wealthy aristocracies. No, Gentlemen, the germ of revolution is not to be found in slavery or in poverty; the germ of revolution lies in the desires of the mob, which are over-excited by leaders who exploit them for their own advantage. *You will be like the rich*— such is the formula of Socialist revolutions against the middle classes. *You will be like the nobles*—such is the formula of the revolutions made by the middle classes against the aristocracy. *You will be like Kings* is the formula of revolutions made by the aristocracy against Kings. Finally, Gentlemen, *You will be like gods*—such was the formula of the first revolt of the first man against God. From Adam, the first rebel, to Proudhon, the last blasphemer, such has been the formula of every revolution.

. . . I have always believed, Gentlemen, that in governments and peoples, as well as in individual cases, blindness is a sign of perdition. I believe that God always begins by making those He wishes to destroy blind, that He confuses their minds so that they do not see the abyss which stretches beneath their feet. Applying these ideas to the general policy pursued for some years by England and France, I can say here that I have long foretold great misfortunes and catastrophes.

It is a historical fact, recognised and incontrovertible, that the providential mission of France is to be the instrument of Providence for the propagation of new ideas, whether they be political, religious or social. In modern times, three great ideas have taken possession of Europe: the Catholic idea, the philosophical idea and the revolutionary idea. Now in these three periods, France was always made man in order to propagate these ideas. Charlemagne was France made man to propagate the Catholic idea; Voltaire was France made man to propagate the philosophical idea; Napoleon was France made man to propagate the revolutionary idea.

Similarly I believe the providential mission of England is to maintain a just moral equilibrium in the world by serving as a counterbalance to France. England is like the ebb and France the flow of the sea. Imagine for one moment the flow without the ebb and the seas would pour over all the continents; imagine the ebb without the flow, and the seas would disappear from the earth. Imagine France without England and you would see the world shaken only by convulsions; every day a new constitution and every hour a new form of government would appear. Imagine England without France and the world would vegetate indefinitely under the· charter of John Lackland, that unchanging type of every British constitution. What is the significance then of the co-existence of these two powerful nations ? It means progress within the bounds of stability, and stability quickened by progress.

For some years then, Gentlemen—I call contemporary history and your own memories to witness—these two great nations have lost all recollection of their traditions, all consciousness of their providential mission. France, instead of spreading new ideas in the world, has everywhere preached the *status quo*—the *status quo* in France, in Spain, in Italy, in the East. And England, instead of preaching stability, has everywhere preached revolt: in Spain, in Portugal, in France, in Italy and in Greece. What has been the result ? The inevitable result has been that each of the two nations, playing a rôle which was never hers, has played it very badly. France has tried to transform herself from devil to preacher and England has tried to transform herself from preacher to devil.

Such, Gentlemen, is contemporary history; but to confine myself to England, for it is with her alone that I wish to deal at present, God forbid that the disasters she has invited by her mistakes should ever overwhelm her, as He has overwhelmed France! No mistake is of such magnitude as the one England has made by supporting revolutionary parties everywhere. Unhappy country! does she not realise that when danger comes, these parties, with a surer instinct than her own, will turn against her ? Has it not already happened ? And it had to happen, Gentlemen; for all the revolutionaries in the world know that when revolution becomes serious, when the clouds pile up, when the horizon grows dark and the waves grow higher, the vessel of Revolution has no other pilot than France.

This then has been the policy of England, or rather of her Government and her agents during the last few years. I have said, and I repeat, that I do not want to go into this question; grave considerations dissuade me. Consideration for the public good, first of all, for I solemnly declare: I desire the closest and the most complete union between the Spanish and the English nation. . . .

When he dealt with this question, Señor Cortina, if I may say so frankly, suffered from a kind of vertigo: he forgot who he is, where he was and who we are. Although he spoke in Parliament, he imagined himself to be a lawyer; speaking to Members, he thought he was speaking to judges; addressing a Consultative Assembly, he imagined he was addressing a Court of Law; dealing with an important political and national subject, he acted as though he were pleading a case; a case there certainly is at stake, but two nations are the interested parties. Now, Gentlemen, was it right of Señor Cortina to constitute himself counsel for the prosecution against the Spanish nation ? Is that by any chance, Gentlemen, what we call patriotism ? Is that the way to be a true patriot ? No indeed. Do you know what patriotism really is ? It means, Gentlemen, loving, hating, feeling as our country loves, hates and feels.

Gentlemen, neither the state of home affairs, which was so serious, nor that of foreign affairs which were so involved and so full of peril, can soften the Opposition of the honourable Members seated here. What about liberty? they say. What, is liberty not to be prized above everything else ? Should we not respect individual liberty and has it not been sacrificed ? —Liberty, Gentlemen! Do those who pronounce this sacred word understand the principle they proclaim and the name they pronounce ? Do they realise the times in which we live ? Have the reverberations of the recent disasters not yet reached our ears, Gentlemen ? Do you not know that Liberty is dead now ? Have you not followed its tragic passion in your mind's eye, as I have ? Have you not seen it persecuted, mocked, treacherously struck down by all the demagogues in the world ? Have you not seen its long-drawn-out agony in the Swiss mountains, on the banks of the Seine, beside the Rhine and the Danube and alongside the Tiber ? Have you not seen it mount to its Calvary on the Quirinal ?

This word makes us shudder, Gentlemen (but we ought not to hesitate to pronounce such words when they express the truth, and the truth I am determined to speak) : liberty is dead. It will not rise again, Gentlemen, on the third day, nor yet in the third year, nor perhaps in three centuries' time! You are alarmed at the tyranny we endure. You are alarmed by small things: you will see far worse things. And now, Gentlemen, I ask you to engrave my words in your memory, for what I am going to tell you, the events which I am going to predict are bound, in a future which cannot now be far distant from us, to come to pass.

The cause of all your errors, Gentlemen, lies in your ignorance of the direction which civilisation and the world are taking. You believe that civilisation and the world are advancing, when civilisation and the world are regressing. The world is taking great strides towards the constitution of the most gigantic and destructive despotism which men have ever known. That is the trend of our world and civilisation. I do not need to be a prophet to predict these things; it is enough to consider the fearful picture of human events from the only true viewpoint, from the heights of Catholic philosophy.

There are only two possible forms of control: one internal and the other external; religious control and political control. They are of such a nature that when the religious barometer rises, the barometer of control falls and likewise, when the religious barometer falls, the political barometer, that is political control and tyranny, rises. That is a law of humanity, a law of history. If you want proof, Gentlemen, look at the state of the world, look at the state of society in the ages before the Cross; tell me what happened when there was no internal or religious control. Society in those days only comprised tyrants and slaves. Give me the name of a single people at this period which possessed no slaves and knew no tyrant. It is an incontrovertible and evident fact, which has never been questioned. Liberty, real liberty, the liberty of all and for all, only came into the world with the Saviour of the world; that again is an incontrovertible fact, recognised even by the Socialists. Yes, the Socialists admit it; they call Jesus divine, they go further, they say 'they continue the work of Jesus. Gracious Heaven! Continue His work! Those men of blood and vengeance continue the work of Him Who only lived to do good, Who only opened His lips to bless, Who only worked miracles to deliver sinners from their sins and the dead from death; Who in the space of three years accomplished the greatest revolution the world has ever witnessed and that without shedding any blood but His own.

Follow me carefully, I beg you; I am going to present you with the most marvellous parallel which history can offer us. You have seen that in antiquity, when religious control was at its lowest point, for it was non-existent, political control rose to the point of tyranny. Very well then, with Jesus Christ, where religious control is born, political control disappears. This is so true, that when Jesus Christ founded a society with His disciples, that society was the only one which has ever existed without a government. Between Jesus Christ and His disciples there was no other government than the love of the Master for His disciples and the love of the disciples for their Master. You see then, that when the internal control was complete, liberty was absolute.

Let us pursue the parallel. Now come the apostolic times, which I shall stretch, for the purposes of my plan, from the time of the Apostles, properly speaking, to the period when Christianity mounted the Capitol in the reign of Constantine the Great. At this time, Gentlemen, the Christian religion, that is, the internal, religious control, was at its zenith; but in spite of that, as always happens in human societies, a germ began to develop, a mere germ of protection and religious liberty. So, Gentlemen, observe the parallel: with this beginning of a fall in the religious barometer there corresponds the beginning of a rise in the political barometer. There is still no government yet, for government is not yet necessary; but it is already necessary to have the germ of government. In point of fact, in the Christian society of the time, there were no real magistrates, but there were adjudicators and arbitrators who form the germ of government. There was really nothing more than that; the Christians of apostolic times engaged in no lawsuits and never appealed to the Courts: their disputes were settled by the arbitrators. Notice, Gentlemen, how the scope of government is enlarged with the growth of corruption.

Then came feudal times. Religion was still at its zenith during this period, but was vitiated up to a point by human passions. What happened in the political sphere ? A real and effective government was already essential; but the weakest kind was good enough. As a result, feudal monarchy was established, the weakest of all kinds of monarchy.

Still pursuing our parallel, we come to the sixteenth century. Then, with the great Lutheran Reformation, with this great scandal which was at the same time political, social and religious, with this act of the intellectual and moral emancipation of the peoples, we see simultaneously the growth of the following institutions. In the first place, and immediately, the feudal monarchies became absolute. You believe, Gentlemen, that a monarchy and a government cannot go beyond absolutism. However, the barometer of political control had to rise even higher, because the religious barometer continued to fall: and the political barometer did in fact rise higher. What did they create then ? Standing armies. Do you know what standing armies are? To answer that question, it is enough to know what a soldier is: a soldier is a slave in uniform. So you see once again, when religious control falls, political control rises, it rises as high as absolutism and even higher. It was not enough for governments to be absolute; they asked for and obtained the privilege of having a million arms at the service of their absolutism.

That is not all: the political barometer had to continue to rise because the religious barometer kept falling; it rose still higher. What new institution was created then? The governments said: We have a million arms and it is not enough; we need something more, we need a million eyes: and they created the police. That was not the last word in progress: the political barometer and political control had to rise to a higher pitch still, because in spite of everything, the religious barometer kept falling; so they rose higher. It was not enough for the governments to have a million arms and a million eyes; they wanted to have a million ears: and so they created administrative centralisation, by means of which all claims and complaints finally reached the government.

Well, Gentlemen, that was not enough; the religious barometer continued to fall and so the political barometer had to rise higher. And it rose. Governments said: A million arms, a million eyes and a million ears are not sufficient to control people, we need something more; we must have the privilege of being simultaneously present in every corner of our empire. This privilege also they obtained: the telegraph was invented.

Such, Gentlemen, was the state of Europe and the world when the first rumblings of the most recent revolution intimated to us all that there is still not enough despotism on the earth, since the religious barometer remains below zero. And now the choice between two things lies before us.

I have promised to speak today with complete frankness and I shall keep my word. . . .

In a word, this is the choice we have to make: either a religious reaction will set in, or it will not. If there is a religious reaction, you will soon see that as the religious barometer rises, the political barometer will begin to fall, naturally, spontaneously, without the slightest effort on the part of peoples, governments, or men, until the tranquil day comes when the peoples of the world are free. But if, on the contrary, and this is a serious matter (it is not customary to call the attention of Consultative Assemblies to questions of this nature; but the gravity of events today is my excuse and I think I have your indulgence in this matter); I say again, Gentlemen, that if the religious barometer continues to fall, no man can see whither we are going. I cannot see, Gentlemen, and I cannot contemplate the future without terror. Consider the analogies I have put before you and weigh this question in your minds; if no government was necessary when religious control was at its zenith, and now that religious control is non-existent, what form of government is going to be strong enough to quell a revolt? Are not all despotisms equally powerless?

Have I not put my finger into the wound, Gentlemen? Yes, I have, and this is the problem which faces Spain, Europe, humanity and the world.

Notice one thing, Gentlemen. In the ancient world, tyranny was fierce and merciless; yet this tyranny was materially limited, since all States were small and formal relations between States were impossible from every point of view; consequently tyranny on the grand scale was impossible in antiquity, with one exception: Rome. But today, how greatly are things changed! The way is prepared for some gigantic and colossal tyrant, universal and immense; everything points to it. Observe that already moral and material resistance is at an end: all minds are divided, all patriotism is dead. Tell me now whether I am right or wrong to be preoccupied with the coming fate of the world; tell me whether, in dealing with this question, I am not touching upon the real problem.

One thing, and one alone, can avert the catastrophe: we shall not avert it by granting more liberty, more guarantees and new constitutions; we shall avert it if all of us, according to our strength, do our utmost to stimulate a salutary reaction —a religious reaction. Now is this possible, Gentlemen? Yes. But is it likely? I answer in deepest sorrow: I do not think it is likely. I have seen and known many men who returned to their faith after having separated themselves from it; unfortunately, I have never known any nation which returned to the Faith after once it was lost.

If any hope had remained in me, the recent events in Rome would have dispelled it. And now I am going to say a few words on the same subject on which Señor Cortina spoke.

No words can adequately describe what has happened in Rome. What word would you use, Gentlemen?—Deplorable?

All the events I have discussed are also deplorable. What has happened in Rome is worse than that. Would you use the word horrible ? It surpasses even horror, Gentlemen.

There was—there no longer is—on the throne in Rome the most eminent, just and the most evangelical man on earth. What has Rome done to this just and evangelical man ? What has this town, where once reigned heroes, Caesars, and Pontiffs, done ? It has exchanged the throne of the Pontiffs for the throne of demagogues. Rebellious to God, it has fallen into the idolatry of the dagger. That is what it has done. The dagger, Gentlemen; the demagogic dagger, stained with blood, is today the idol of Rome. That is the idol which overthrew Pius IX. That is the idol which the Caribbean hordes are parading in the streets! Caribbeans ? No: Caribbeans are fierce, but they are not ungrateful.

I have determined to speak frankly, Gentlemen. I say now that either the King of Rome must return to Rome, or, with all respect to Señor Cortina, no stone will remain standing in Rome.

The Catholic world cannot, and will not, consent to the virtual destruction of Christianity by a single town which has been delivered over to frenzy and madness. Civilised Europe cannot, and will not, consent to the ruin of the edifice of European civilisation, just because its cupola has been laid low. The world cannot, and will not, consent to the accession to the throne of a strange new dynasty, the dynasty of crime, in the Holy City. And let nobody say, Gentlemen, as Señor Cortina says and as the Members who sit on the left say in their newspapers and speeches, that two questions are at stake, one temporal and the other spiritual, and that the matter under dispute concerned the temporal Prince and his people; and that the Pontiff is still alive. Two words, two words only, will explain everything.

There can be no possible doubt that spiritual power is the principal attribute of the Pope: temporal power is accessory to it; and this accessory is essential. The Catholic world has the right to expect that the infallible mouthpiece of its dogmas should be free and independent; and the Catholic world can only be certain that its spiritual head is independent and free when this head is a Sovereign; only a Sovereign is dependent upon nobody. Consequently, Gentlemen, the question of sovereignty, which is universally a political question, is furthermore a religious question in Rome; the people, who can be sovereign everywhere else, cannot be sovereign in Rome; Constituent Assemblies, which can exist in every other country, cannot exist in Rome; in Rome there can be no other constituent power except the power already constituted there. Rome, Gentlemen, and the Papal States do not belong to Rome; they do not even belong to the Pope; they belong to the Catholic world. The Catholic world has recognised that they are an attribute of the Pope, so that he may be free and independent, and the Pope himself cannot divest himself of this sovereignty and this independence.

I will stop, Gentlemen, for the House must be tired and I am very tired too. I tell you frankly, I cannot go on any longer, because I am not well and it is a wonder that I have been able to speak at all; however, I have said most of what I wanted to say.

I have dealt with the three external problems touched upon by Señor Cortina and now I conclude with the internal problem. Ever since the beginning of the world until today, men have discussed the question as to which is the better course, in order that revolutions and upheavals may be averted—to grant concessions, or to offer resistance; but what had always been a problem from the year of Creation to the year of grace 1848 is no longer one today, it has been resolved; and if I felt strong enough, I would prove it to you by passing under review all the events which have occurred from last February up to today. I will limit myself to recalling two. In France—my first example —the monarchy offered no resistance and was conquered by the Republic, which scarcely had the vitality to set itself in motion: and the Republic, which scarcely had the vitality to set itself in motion, conquered Socialism, because Socialism offered no resistance.

In Rome—my second example—what happened ? Was not your model there ? Tell me, if you had been artists and wanted to paint the model of a king, would you not have chosen the features of Pius IX ? Pius IX tried to be magnificent and generous, like his Divine Master; he found outlaws, gave them his hand and returned them to their country; he found reformers, and granted them the reforms for which they asked; he found Liberals and granted them liberty: each word of his conferred some benefit. And now, Gentlemen, answer me this. Do the present ignominies he now suffers not equal in number the benefits he conferred, or do they not rather surpass them ?

Faced with this result, Gentlemen, is not the problem of a course of concession resolved?

If it were a question here of choosing between liberty and dictatorship, we should all be agreed. Which man, in fact, possessing liberty, would prostrate himself before a dictatorship? But that is not the problem. It is a fact that liberty does not exist in Europe: the constitutional governments which represented it in these last few years are today, in nearly every country, no more than structures lacking any solid foundation, bare bones deprived of life. Cast your minds back, Gentlemen, to Imperial Rome. Here in this Rome all the institutions of the Republic still survived: all-powerful dictators, inviolate tribunes, senatorial families, eminent consuls: all these people still existed; only one thing was lacking and only one thing was superfluous: what was superfluous was a man; what was lacking was the Republic.

Such, Gentlemen, is the state of nearly all the constitutional governments in Europe; and quite unconsciously Señor Cortina proved it to us the other day. Did he not say, and rightly so, that he prefers the example of history, rather than that of theory? I call history to witness. What, Mr. Speaker, are these governments with their legal majorities, which are always conquered by turbulent minorities; with their responsible ministers, who have nothing to be responsible for; with their inviolable kings, who are always violated? Thus, as I have said, Gentlemen, the choice does not lie between liberty and dictatorship; if that were so, I would vote for liberty, just as all of us here would do. The problem, and my conclusion, are as follows: we have to choose between the dictatorship of insurrection and the dictatorship of government; of these two alternatives I choose dictatorship on the part of the government, as being less onerous and less shameful.

We must choose between a dictatorship which comes from below or one which comes from above: I choose the one which comes from above, because it emanates from purer and more serene regions. Our choice must finally lie between the dictatorship of the dagger and that of the sword: I choose the dictatorship of the sword, because it is more noble. As we vote, Gentlemen, we shall divide on this question and in so doing we shall be true to ourselves. You, Gentlemen (*the Opposition*), will, as always, follow the most popular course and we (*the Government supporters*) will, as always, vote for what is most salutary.

2. SOCIALISM[1]

THE most consistent of modern Socialists appears to me to be Robert Owen. An open and cynical rebel, he breaks with all religions which are depositaries of religious and moral dogmas, rejects the idea of duty by his denial of collective responsibility (which constitutes the dogma of solidarity) and of individual responsibility, which rests on the dogma of the free-will of man. Then, having denied free-will, Robert Owen denies sin and the transmission of sin. So far, no one can doubt that these deductions are logical and consistent; but the contradiction and the extravagances begin when Owen, having denied sin and free-will, makes a distinction between moral good and evil, as if there could be any good or evil where free-will is non-existent and as if evil and sin were not synonymous. Furthermore, he differentiates between good and evil, while denying the penalty which is the necessary consequence of evil.

Man, according to Robert Owen, acts in consequence of certain deep-rooted convictions. These convictions come to him in part from his peculiar heredity and in part from his environment; and as he is the author of neither his heredity nor his environment, it follows that both have a fatal and an inevitable effect upon him.

All this is logical and consistent, but it is completely illogical, contradictory and absurd to postulate good and evil, when human liberty is denied. Absurdity reaches grotesque proportions when our author attempts to found a society and a government in conjunction with men who are irresponsible: the idea of government and the idea of society have no meaning apart from the idea of human liberty; denial of the one follows from the denial of the others and if you deny or affirm them all, you deny or affirm one and the same thing. I do not know whether the annals of mankind show a more striking proof of blindness, inconsistency and madness than that which Owen gives, when, not satisfied with the extravagance of affirming the existence of society and government, after having denied individual responsibility and liberty, he goes still further and falls into the inconceivable extravagance of recommending benevolence, justice and charity to those who, being neither responsible nor free, can neither love, nor be just, nor be benevolent.

[1] Donoso Cortés, *Essays on Catholicism, Liberalism and Socialism.* Wm. B. Kelly. 1874. Translation by Rev. William M'Donald, Rector of the Irish College, Salamanca, *revised.* Pp. 279 *et seq.*

. . . This shameful contradiction in terms which is the essence of Socialism is so palpable that it will be easy to set it in relief, even on those points on which all these sectarians appear to be united in agreement. If one single negation is common to them all, it is assuredly the denial of the solidarity of the family and of the nobility. All revolutionary and socialistic masters of doctrine are unanimous in their rejection of this communion of glories and misfortunes, of merits and demerits in generation after generation, which mankind has recognised as a fact throughout the ages.

Now these same revolutionaries and Socialists affirm quite unconsciously by their practice the very thing they deny in theory in other people. When the French Revolution in its frenzy and blood-lust had trampled all the national glories underfoot; when, intoxicated with its triumphs, it believed final victory certain, a mysterious aristocratic pride of race took hold of it, which was in direct contradiction to all its dogmas. Then we saw the most famous of the revolutionaries, as proudly as any feudal baron of old, behave with great circumspection, so that the privilege of entering their family was only accorded with reserve and at the cost of many scruples. My readers will remember that famous question put by the doctors of the new law to those who presented themselves as candidates—" What crime have you committed ? " Who could not but sympathise with the unfortunate man who had committed no crime, for never would the gates of the Capitol, where sat the demi-gods of the Revolution, terrible in their majesty, be opened to him. Mankind had instituted the aristocracy of virtue, the revolution instituted the aristocracy of crime.

. . . Examine all the revolutionary schools one by one and you will see that they all vie with each other in an effort to constitute themselves into a family and to claim a noble descent: Saint-Simon the aristocrat is the ancestor of one group; the illustrious Fourier of another, and Babeuf the patriot of a third group. In each one you will find a common leader, a common patrimony, a common glory, a common mission; each group is distinct from the other, then breaks away from the others to form a splinter group, all the members of which are linked together by a narrow solidarity and seek out of the depths of the past some famous name as a rallying cry. Some have chosen Plato, the glorious personification of the wisdom of the ancients; others, and they are numerous, carrying their mad ambition to the heights of blasphemy, do not fear to profane the sacred name of the Redeemer! Poor and abandoned, they would perhaps have forgotten Him; humble they would have scorned Him; but in their insolent pride they do not forget that poor, wretched, and humble as He was, He was a King and that royal blood flowed in His veins. As for M. Proudhon, that perfect type of Socialist pride, which in its turn is the prototype of human pride—carried away by his vanity, he goes as far back as he can to the remotest ages, in an attempt to seek his ancestry in those times which bordered upon Creation, when the Mosaic institutions flourished amongst the Hebrews. As a matter of fact, his lineage and his name are still more ancient and illustrious than he thinks; to discover their origin, we must go back still further, to times beyond the pale of history, to beings who in perfection and dignity are incomparably higher than men. At present, suffice it to say that the Socialist schools of thought tend inevitably towards contradiction and absurdity; that each one of their principles contradicts those which precede or follow; and that their conduct is a complete condemnation of their theories, as their theories are a radical condemnation of their conduct.

. . . The fundamental negation of Socialism is the negation of sin, that grand affirmation which is, as it were, the focal point of the Catholic affirmation. This denial logically implies a whole series of further negations, some of them relating to the Divine Person, others to the human person, others still to man in society.

The most fundamental of them all is this: that the Socialists not only deny the fact of sin, but the possibility of sinning; from this double negation follows the negation of human liberty, which is meaningless if we ignore the power given to mankind to choose between good and evil and to fall from the state of innocence into a state of sin.

The denial of free-will leads to a disclaimer of human responsibility; the responsibility of man being denied, penalties for sin are also denied, from which follows on the one hand the negation of divine government, and on the other, the negation of human governments. Therefore, as far as the question of government is concerned, the negation of sin ends in nihilism.

To deny the responsibility of the individual in the domestic, political and human spheres is to deny the solidarity of the individual in the family and in the State; it is to deny unity in the species, in the State, in the family and in man himself, since there is such complete identity between the principles of solidarity and unity that one thing cannot be conceived in isolation without reference to the principle of solidarity and vice-versa. Therefore, as regards the question of unity, the negation of sin ends in nihilism.

Unity being denied absolutely, the following negations are implied—that of humanity, of the family, of society and of man. The fact is that nothing exists at all except on condition of being " one," so that the existence of the family, of society and of humanity can only be postulated on condition that domestic, political and human unity is affirmed. If these unities are denied, the negation of these three things must follow; to affirm that they exist, and to deny unity between them, is a contradiction in terms. Each of these things is necessarily " one," or it cannot exist at all; therefore if they are not " *one* " they do not exist; their very name is absurd, for it is a name which does not describe or designate anything.

The negation of individualism also follows from the negation of the principle of unity, although by a different process. Only individual man can, up to a certain point, exist without being " one " and without having any solidarity with his fellows: what is denied in this case, if his unity and solidarity with mankind is denied, is that he is always the same person at different moments of his life. If there is no bond of union between the past and the present and between the present and the future, it follows that man exists only in the present moment. But in this hypothesis, it is clear that his existence is more phenomenal than real. If I do not live in the past, because it is past, and because there is no unity between the present and the past; if I do not live in the future, because the future does not exist and because when it will exist it will not be future; if I only live in the present and the present does not exist, because when I am about to affirm that it exists, it has already passed, my existence is manifestly more theoretical than practical; for in reality, if I do not exist at all times, I do not exist at any time. I conceive time only in the union of its three forms and I cannot conceive it when I separate them. What is the past, unless it is something which no longer is ? What is the future, unless it is something which does not yet exist ? Who can halt the present long enough to affirm that it is here, once it has escaped from the future, and before it relapses into the past ? To affirm the existence of man, denying the unity of time, amounts to giving man the speculative existence of a mathematical point. Therefore the negation of sin ends in nihilism, as regards both the existence of individual man, of the family, of the body politic and of humanity. Therefore, in every sphere, all Socialist doctrines, or to be accurate, all rationalist doctrines must end inevitably in nihilism. Nothing is more natural and logical than that those who separate themselves from God should end in nothing, since there is nothing outside God.

Having established this much, I have the right to accuse present-day Socialism of being timid and contradictory. To deny the Christian God in order to affirm another god; to deny humanity from one point of view in order to affirm it from another; to deny society in certain of its forms in order to affirm it in different forms; to deny the family on one hand and to affirm it on the other; to deny man in one of his aspects in order to affirm him in other and contradictory ones—is not all this to enter upon the path of conflicting actions, the consequence of timidity and irresolution ?

. . . Present-day Socialism is a kind of semi-Catholicism and nothing more. In the work of the most advanced of its doctors, there is a greater number of Catholic affirmations than Socialist negations; with the result that we have a Catholicism which is absurd and a Socialism which is contradictory. If we affirm the existence of God, we fall into the hands of the God of the Catholics; if we affirm the existence of humanity, we must accept the humanity one and indivisible of the Christian dogma; if we affirm the existence of society, we must come sooner or later to the Catholic teaching on social institutions; if we affirm the existence of the family, we are bound to affirm everything which Catholicism lays down and Socialism denies on the subject; in a word, that every affirmation concerning man, whatever it may be, is finally resolved into an affirmation of Adam, the man of Genesis. Catholicism can be compared to those huge cylinders through which the whole must pass, if a part has done so. Unless it changes its course, Socialism with all its pontiffs and doctors will pass through this cylinder, without leaving any trace.

. . . Catholicism is not a thesis, consequently it cannot be combated by an antithesis; it is a synthesis which embraces all things, contains all things and explains all things, which cannot be—I will not say conquered—but even combated, except by a synthesis of the same kind, which like it should embrace, contain and explain all things. All human theses and antitheses find their place in the Catholic synthesis: it attracts and resolves all things into itself by the invincible force of an incommunicable virtue. Those who imagine that they live outside Catholicism really live within its orbit, because it is as it were their intellectual climate. The Socialists have met the same fate as the others: in spite of the gigantic efforts they have made to separate themselves from Catholicism, they have done no more than to become bad Catholics.

VIII. JAIME BALMES

1810 - 1848

IN Jaime Balmes, whom Donoso considered to be the master of his mind, we miss the poetic note and the prophetic vision. He was, above all, a theologian. His mind was of a more scholastic formation, and he lived to see only the beginning of those events in Europe which raised Donoso's thought to its highest level. Though less striking as a literary personality, and less of an original thinker than Donoso, the importance of Balmes in the history of apologetics cannot be, and indeed never has been, overlooked.

It had been usual, ever since Montesquieu's day, to postulate the social good in the political theory of Europe, and to relegate theological truth, not only to a secondary plane, but to deny that dogma had any justification at all. Montesquieu and his successors still recognised Christian morality as the best foundation for society. Yet he protested at the same time that a definite system of Christian dogma was not necessary to produce that moral good which society derives from Christian beliefs. According to him, that religion is best which fully meets the circumstances and requirements of the time and the place: Catholicism is best for Monarchies, Protestantism for Republics and even Islam for the East, although in his view Islam is less promising as a religion when we consider " our welfare in this world and the next " (*Esprit des Lois*).

The historical schools of the early nineteenth century—Guizot, Michelet and Quinet in France, and especially Macaulay in England—went much further, and saw the Protestant Reformation as a step forward on the road of the inevitable and salutary progress, a phase in the " emancipation " of mankind. Macaulay identified material progress with Protestantism and thought that such progress was incompatible with Catholic civilisation.

During the three decades following the Napoleonic Wars, two political influences were at work in Spain, the country which had played such a tremendous part in frustrating Napoleon's plan to dominate and conquer Europe. Both Britain and France attempted to make the Peninsula an outpost and an extension of their own power: Britain almost in the spirit which we know from George Borrow's *Bible in Spain*, and France in the spirit of Guizot, who was not only the foremost ideological influence in the reign of Louis Philippe, but for some years was also a leading statesman, especially at the moment of the treaty of 1846,[1] which seemed to establish French influence in Spain for some time to come, to the dissatisfaction of Palmerston. The Spanish supporters of the British and French influence in Spain hoped to bring material prosperity to Spain and to " emancipate " the " backward " Spanish masses through Liberal institutions.

Balmes wrote his *Protestantism* as a reply to these widespread arguments, which were found in the 1840's in the Spanish Press and Parliament. He went part of the way with Bossuet, who in his *History of Variations* showed that every " variation " from the unity of dogma is bound to lead, sooner or later, to the vague and hardly Christian doctrine of the " Unitarians " of Socinius, and he wrote his monumental book to establish the necessity of a precise and authoritative dogma.

Balmes accepts discussion with his opponents, on ground of their own choosing, not in the field of dogmatic truth, but in that of history and culture, which they consider to be of primary importance. He proves with historical arguments that Luther's break with the Church was, far from being an act of progress and emancipation, a great retrogressive step. Denying as it does any other basis for theological truth except individual judgement and personal interpretation of a text, Protestantism rules out spiritual authority. This way leads either to anarchy or to despotism, to an undue buttressing of the secular and temporal authority, which Luther called to his aid when some of his followers attempted to push his doctrine to its extreme, although logical, consequences. Deprived of the consecration which the Church conferred on temporal power, and limited to temporal purposes by the very nature of its own legitimacy, Protestantism had to find some other grounds for the justification of the authority of the law and for social order. Thus we find Calvin justifying the inheritance of wealth through the doctrine of Grace, and Luther proclaiming Adam, and not Christ, to be the father of the temporal order, which therefore is bound to remain under the stain of original sin, and the despotic excesses of which —as Hobbes, developing Luther's argument later on in a more systematic way, explains—are bound to be the punishment for original sin.

Anarchy or despotism is the Protestant alternative to the Catholic synthesis of Authority and Liberty. Balmes is naturally ready to recognise that a great deal of the Catholic inheritance survived the Reformation of the sixteenth century, and extenuated Protestant practice, just as he is ready to admit that the Catholic political order often fell short of the ideal. But with his critical analysis of Protestantism as the religious origin of spiritual anarchy and temporal tyranny, he brought a new and immensely important element

---

[1] This treaty arranged the marriage of the Duc de Montpensier, youngest son of Louis Philippe, to the Infanta sister of Queen Isabel II.

into the historical and political controversy of the time. It is enough to recall the sociological school of the German Liberal Protestant scholars, such as Max Weber and Ernst Troeltzsch, in the first two decades of the present century to show that Balmes' analysis of Luther and Protestantism fell on fertile soil in Luther's own country, Germany.

Almost everybody who has tried to analyse seriously the causes which led Germany to the virulent crisis of the First World War and to the diabolical rule of Hitler has seen the origin of the German tendency to anarchy and despotism in Luther's attitude to temporal authority—more often than not in unconscious imitation of Balmes.

Balmes is the teacher of the Church on Order and Liberty, a master in the controversy against political and social Protestantism, as Bossuet was the master in the controversy against theological Protestantism. Thus he stands—with Donoso Cortés—at the threshold of the new, glorious and historical rôle which fell once again in the post-revolutionary age to the Christian and national genius of Spain.

FAITH AND LIBERTY[1]

THE supposed incompatibility of unity in faith with political liberty is an invention of the irreligious philosophy of the last century. Whichever political opinions we adopt, it is extremely important for us to be on our guard against such a doctrine. We must not forget that the Catholic religion stands high above all forms of government—she does not reject from her bosom either the citizen of the United States, or the inhabitants of Russia, but embraces all men with equal tenderness, commanding all men to obey the legitimate governments of their respective countries. She considers them all to be children of the same Father, participators in the same Redemption, heirs to the same glory. It is very important to bear in mind that irreligion allies itself to liberty, or to despotism, according to its own interests; it applauds unstintingly when an infuriated populace burns churches, and massacres the priests at the altar, but it is always ready to flatter monarchs, to give an exaggerated importance to their power whenever they win the favour of this power by despoiling the clergy, subverting discipline and insulting the Pope. It cares little what instruments it employs, provided it accomplishes its work: it is Royalist when it is in

---

[1] Taken from *European Civilisation, Protestantism and Catholicity*, John Murphy & Co., Baltimore, 1868. Translated by Messrs. Hanford and Kershaw (*revised*).

a position to influence the minds of kings and expel the Jesuits from France, from Spain and from Portugal, and to pursue them to the four corners of the earth without giving them any respite or peace; it is Liberal when it shows itself inside popular Assemblies, which exact sacrilegious oaths from the clergy and send into exile, or execute, those priests who remain faithful to their duty.

The man who cannot see the strict truth of my argument must have forgotten history and paid little attention to very recent events. When religion and morality are present, all forms of government are good; without them, none can be good. An absolute monarch, imbued with religious ideas, surrounded by counsellors whose doctrines are sound and reigning over a people who share the same doctrines, can make his subjects happy and is bound to do so, as far as circumstances of time and place permit. A wicked monarch, or one surrounded by wicked advisers, will do harm according to the extent of his power; he is even more to be dreaded than revolution itself, because he has better opportunities for laying his plans and carrying them out more rapidly, he is faced with fewer obstacles, can assume a semblance of legality and can claim to serve the public interest, so that he has a far greater chance of success and of achieving permanent results. Revolutions have undoubtedly done great injury to the Church; but persecuting monarchs have done her as great injury. A whim of Henry VIII established Protestantism in England; the cupidity of certain other princes produced a like result in the nations of the North; and in our own days, a decree of the Autocrat of Russia drives millions of souls into schism. It follows that an absolute monarchy is not desirable unless it is a religious one; for irreligion, which is immoral by nature, naturally tends to injustice and consequently to tyranny. If irreligion is seated on an absolute throne, or if it takes possession of the mind of the occupant of that throne, its powers are unlimited; and for my part, I know nothing more horrible than the omnipotence of wickedness.

In recent times, European democracy has been lamentably conspicuous for its attacks upon religion; a state of affairs which, far from furthering the cause of democracy, has injured it considerably. We can indeed form an idea of a government which is more or less free, when society is virtuous, moral and religious; but not when these prerequisites are lacking. In the latter case, the only possible form of government is despotism, the rule of force, for force alone can govern men who are without conscience and without God. If we compare the American and the French Revolutions carefully, we find that one of the principal differences between them is that the American Revolution was essentially democratic and the French was essentially impious. In the manifestoes which inaugurated the former revolution, the name of God and of Providence appears everywhere; the men engaged in the perilous enterprise of shaking off the yoke of Great Britain, far from uttering blasphemies against the Almighty, invoke His assistance, convinced that the cause of independence was also the cause of reason and justice. The French began by deifying the leaders of irreligion, overthrowing altars, watering churches, streets and scaffolds with the blood of priests—the only revolutionary sign recognised by the people is Atheism hand in hand with liberty. This folly has borne its fruits—it spread its fatal contagion in other countries which have recently experienced revolutions—the new order of things has been inaugurated with sacrilegious crimes; and the proclamation of the rights of man was preceded by the profanation of the churches of Him from whom all rights come.

Modern demagogues, it is true, have only imitated their predecessors the Protestants, the Hussites and the Albigenses; with this difference, however, that in our day irreligion has manifested itself openly, side by side with its companion the democracy of blood and baseness; while the democracy of former times was allied with sectarian fanaticism. The dissolving doctrines of Protestantism rendered a stronger power necessary, precipitated the overthrow of ancient liberties and obliged authority to hold itself continually on the alert, and to be ready to strike. When the influence of Catholicism had been weakened, the void had to be filled by a system of espionage and compulsion. Do not forget this, you who make war on religion in the name of liberty; do not forget that like causes produce like effects. Where no moral influence exists, its absence must be supplied by physical force: if you deprive people of the sweet yoke of religion, you leave governments no other resource than the vigilance of the police and the force of bayonets. Think of these things and make your choice. Before the advent of Protestantism, European civilisation, under the aegis of the Catholic religion, was evidently tending towards that general harmony, the absence of which has rendered an excessive use of force necessary. Unity of faith disappeared, leaving the way open to an unrestrained liberty of opinion and religious discord: the influence of the clergy was destroyed in some countries and weakened in others: thus an equilibrium between the different classes no longer existed and the class which was destined by nature to fulfil the rôle of mediator was deprived of any influence. By curtailing the power of the Popes, both people and governments were loosed from that gentle curb which restrained without oppressing, and corrected without degrading; kings and peoples were set at variance one with the other, without any body of men possessed of authority being able to mediate between them in case of conflict; governments lacking a single judge who, as the friend of both parties and with no personal interest in the quarrel, could have settled their differences impartially, began to rely upon standing armies, and the people began to rely on insurrection.

It is no use alleging that in Catholic countries a political phenomenon was seen familiar to the one we see in Protestant nations; for I maintain that amongst Catholics themselves, events did not follow the course which they would naturally have followed if the fatal Reformation had not intervened. In order to reach its full fruition, European civilisation required that unity from which it had sprung; it could not establish harmony between the diverse elements which it sheltered within its bosom by any other means. Its homogeneity was lost immediately the unity of faith disappeared. From that hour, no nation could organise itself adequately without taking into account, not only its own internal needs, but also the principles that prevailed in other countries, against the influence of which it had to be on its guard. Do you imagine, for instance, that the policy of the Spanish Government, constituted as it was the protector of the Catholic religion against powerful Protestant nations, was not powerfully influenced by the peculiar and very dangerous position of the country ?

I think I have shown that the Church has never opposed the legitimate development of any form of government; that she has taken them all under her protection and consequently that to assert that she is the enemy of popular institutions is a calumny. I have likewise placed it beyond doubt that the sects hostile to the Catholic Church, by their encouragement of a democracy which is either irreligious, or blinded by fanaticism, have, in fact, far from helping on the establishment of just and rational liberty, left the people no alternative between unbridled licentiousness and unrestrained despotism. The lesson with which history thus furnishes us is confirmed by experience and the future will but corroborate the truth of this lesson. The more religious and moral men are, the more they deserve liberty; for they need less external restraints in that case, having a most powerful one in their own consciences. An irreligious and immoral people stand in need of authority of some sort, to keep them in order, otherwise they will constantly abuse their rights and so will deserve to lose them. St Augustine understood these truths perfectly and explains in a brief and beautiful way the conditions which are necessary for all forms of government. The holy Doctor shows that popular forms of government are good where the people are moral and conscientious; where they are corrupt, they require either an oligarchy or an autocratic monarchy.

I have no doubt that an interesting passage in dialogue form that we find in his first book on Free Will, Chapter vi, will be read with pleasure.

Augustine: You would not maintain, for instance, that men or people are so constituted by nature as to be absolutely eternal, subject neither to destruction nor change ?

Evodius: Who can doubt that they are changeable and subject to the influence of time ?

Augustine: If the people are serious and temperate; and if moreover they have such a concern for the public good that each one would prefer the public interest to his own, *is it not true that it would be advisable to decree that such a nation should choose its own authorities to administer their affairs ?*

Evodius: Certainly.

Augustine: But imagine that these people become so corrupt that *the citizens prefer their own good to the public good; supposing they sell their votes, that corrupted by ambitious men they entrust the government of the State to men as criminal and as corrupt as themselves;* is it not true that in such a case if there should be a man of integrity amongst them, who possesses sufficient power for the purpose, he would do well to take away from these people their power of conferring honours, and concentrate it in the hands of a small number of upright men, or even in the hands of one man ?

Evodius: Undoubtedly.

Augustine: Yet since these laws appear very contradictory, the one granting the right of conferring honours and the

other depriving them of that right; since moreover they cannot both be in force at once, *are we to affirm that one of these
laws is unjust, or that it should not have been made ?*
Evodius: By no means.

The whole question is contained here in a few words: Can
monarchy, aristocracy and democracy all be legitimate and
proper ? Yes. By what considerations are we to be guided when
we wish to decide which of these forms is legitimate and proper
in any given case ? By considering existing rights and the condition of the people to whom such a form is to be applied. Can
a form of government, once good, become bad ? Certainly it
may; for all human things are subject to change. These reflections, as solid as they are simple, will prevent all excessive
enthusiasm in favour of any particular form of government.
This is not a question of theory only, but one of prudence. Now
prudence does not decide before having considered the subject
carefully and weighed all the circumstances. But there is one
predominant idea in the doctrine of St Augustine: the idea,
which I have already indicated, that great virtue and dis-
interestedness are required under free government. Those who
hope to build political liberty on the ruins of religious belief
would do well to meditate on the words of this illustrious Doctor
of the Church.

How do you think people could exercise extensive rights, if
you prevent them from doing so by perverting their ideas and
corrupting their morals ?

You say that under representative forms of government,
reason and justice are secured by means of elections; and yet
you strive to banish this reason and justice from the bosom of
that society in which you talk of securing them. You sow the
wind and reap the whirlwind; instead of models of wisdom and
prudence, you offer the people scandalous scenes. Do not say
that we are condemning the age and that it progresses in spite
of us: we reject nothing that is good, but perversity and corruption we must condemn. The age is making progress, it is
true. But neither you, nor we, know which direction it is taking.
Catholics know only one thing on this subject and that is that
good social conditions cannot be formed out of bad men. They
know that immoral men are bad, and that where there is no
religion, morality cannot take root. Firm in our faith, we shall
leave you to try, if you so desire, a thousand forms of government. Apply your palliatives to your own social patient;

impose it upon him with deceitful words. His frequent convulsions, his continued restlessness, are sufficient evidence of your lack of skill. It proves that you have not succeeded so well in securing his confidence. If ever you do secure it, if ever he fell asleep in your arms, " All flesh will then have corrupted its way " and we may fear that God will have resolved to sweep man from the face of the earth.

IX. LOUIS VEUILLOT

1813 - 1878

THE following pages, which comprise the Foreword to Louis Veuillot's *The Freethinkers*, published amidst the upheavals of the Revolution of 1848, tell us almost all there is to know about the author and about the part played by him in his time. Veuillot appears here at his best.

The Freethinkers is a monumental image of a period, and is a landmark in the history of post-Revolutionary apologetics, just as the year which saw its publication was a landmark in the post-Revolutionary history of France and of Europe. What La Bruyère's *Characters* was for the seventeenth century, Veuillot's *Freethinkers* might deserve to be for the nineteenth century. The first is a grandiose satirical panorama of human weaknesses in an age of social and national splendour; the second a polemical and satirical dissection of human stupidity disguised as intellectual pride, in an age of social crisis and national decadence. And La Bruyère may be said to have outlined the principal theme of *The Freethinkers* in the final chapter of his *Characters*, when he describes the *Esprits Forts*:

" Do strong minds realise that this name is bestowed upon them ironically ? What greater weakness is there, than for a man to be uncertain as to the principle which guides his existence, his life, his senses and his attainments, and to what it all leads! What greater discouragement can there be for a man, than to doubt whether his soul is not as much matter as a stone or a reptile, or whether it is not as easily corrupted as these vile things of clay ? Do we not show more strength and greatness by accepting in our minds the idea of a Being, superior to all other beings, Who has made them all, and to Whom all must return; of a Being Who is sovereignly perfect and pure, Who has neither beginning nor end, in Whose image our souls are created, and if I may so express it, a part of which is, as it were, spiritual and immortal ?

" The docile mind and the weak mind are both impressionable; the one receives good impressions, the other bad ones; in other words, the first is convinced and faithful, while the second is obstinate and corrupted. Hence the docile mind accepts the true religion, and the weak mind does not accept any religion, or else accepts a false one: now the strong mind has no religion, or else invents one for itself; therefore the strong mind is really the weak one."

These " strong minds," just numerous enough to be noticed in the century of Louis XIV, invaded the French scene a hundred years later, and became the masters. After the great Revolution and the Napoleonic epic, Victor Hugo and the Romantics brought down to the level of the profane crowds the majestic mysteries of the language of Pascal and Bossuet, and by an often cheap and vulgar melodrama, the precursor of the cinema, and by their easy rhetoric, precursor of the Press and modern propaganda, they became the symbol of an age which it is the lasting merit of Veuillot to expose and reject.

Veuillot was a man of the people, son of a poor, working-class family, grandson and great-great-grandson of peasants. This gave him the right to reject with indignation and horror the sugary spiritual poison which was offered as food for the " people " by those who claimed to be the people's friends. Veuillot was a son of the poor. He had an incontestable right therefore to reject the unwanted advocates of the people who schemed to detach the poor from the protection of Christ the King, to withdraw from the poor their right to persevere in their allegiance to Christ and His Vicar on earth. There is hardly a writer more at war with the authorities of his time than was Louis Veuillot. Hardly ever has a writer said worse things about authorities than this untiring defender of Authority, not of course because constitutional monarchs, royal ministers, Parliaments, academies and universities, and last, but not least, bishops of the Church, were autocratic in his eyes, but because they did not always have the courage of their authority, and courted popular favour by bribing the anti-Christian forces and pseudo-ideas of the age with cowardly concessions.

Balzac knew the Holy Ghost mainly under His aspect of Prudence. Veuillot derived from Him mainly the virtue of Fortitude. Both are one-sided, of course, just as Bonald, who saw God mainly as the author of Law and Order, and Joseph de Maistre, who saw Him mainly as Providence in action, moving History through events which seem a chaos to uninformed human eyes, were one-sided before them. Yet fully enlightened wisdom on the workings of God—which is not yet full knowledge—is the privilege of the Church, guardian of God's name among men. Her lay defenders have done enough for the salvation of their time, and possibly enough for their own salvation, if they proclaimed loudly enough the inseparability of any particular human virtue or understanding from the Creator of all fortitude and all knowledge.

Joseph de Maistre—and especially Bonald—are still near to the Cartesian method. They are still trained in Descartes' school; in their meditations on the State and its upheavals, on nations and their destinies, their chief concern is to find a law and a rule, and in the great Revolution they mainly see aberration and deviation from Truth and from Law. Veuillot, at first sight merely a chronicler who found his subjects for meditation in the futile and ephemeral events of the town, inaugurates a different and a new approach. Bonald and de Maistre fight false ideas, errors and aberrations; for Veuillot, the principles and forces of evil appear in their personal incarnations, in their human forms. Veuillot is the chronicler of a society at a period of crisis.

Bonald and de Maistre saw the nations in error and tried to restore the Law. Veuillot knows—for he lived to see it—that restorations do not help much, and when they were tried, proved to be ephemeral. Society itself is in dissolution, the people themselves are cast out—perhaps for centuries—into the desert, where they will have no kings, no prophets and no sacrifices, as Nehemias said of the Jews; the fall of Crowns, once given to crown the glory of Christian nations, was but a beginning. Veuillot sees his time as the beginning of the Rejection. In this prophetic vision, which is no more Cartesian, in this vision which is formed and inspired by the Old Testament and the Apocalypse alone, and not by any method of reasoning derived from Descartes or Leibnitz, Veuillot was confirmed by a great Christian visionary, who began as a philosopher and a political thinker, but who was changed into a mystic and prophet by the first European Revolution—by Donoso Cortés. From a simple chronicler of Parisian characters and events, Veuillot reaches the much higher sphere of the Absolute, after the Revolution of 1848 and the years spent in Donoso's company, until the death of this latter in 1853.

Perhaps he never fully reached this sphere. We do not need to defend Veuillot against the opponents of his day. Most of them were the enemies of the Church and of Christ, or, worse still, they were those modern Pharisees who, like the sweet-tongued and benevolent Renan, were prepared to recognise a moralist and a poet in the Lord and Redeemer. But he had Catholic opponents too: not only politicians like Falloux, Berryer or Montalembert, but Liberal and slightly Gallican bishops, Mgr. Sibour or Mgr. Dupanloup, who would have preferred *L'Univers* to be an organ of day-to-day politics in the interest of the Church in France, and complained that Veuillot spoilt chances of Parliamentary compromise on practical matters such as legislation for the schools. Veuillot considered himself to be the Pope's soldier, and the direct personal approach which Pius IX always readily granted him was sometimes the object of complaint or objection by the French hierarchy.

We do not need to defend Veuillot from Victor Hugo's biting rhymes in *Les Châtiments*, which made him out to be the defender of all tyrannies because he was prepared to accept the protection of any legal order against revolutionary terror and disorder. Victor Hugo was perhaps the only temperament and the only master of style who could treat Veuillot with a polemical talent worthy of his own, but as Veuillot answered Hugo with a series of replies which he collected into a whole volume—which has the merit of re-vindicating the best of Victor Hugo for Christian inspiration and makes good fun of the rest—we may consider this debate as closed. We can dismiss as much below the level of literary debate such opponents of Louis Veuillot who thought fit to assert that he was personally employed by Pius IX to spy upon the bishops who were opposed to the Bull of Infallibility!

Nevertheless, we must try to find an explanation of the disappointment Veuillot caused to men like Barbey d'Aurevilly, Ernest Hello, and Léon Bloy; for it was Veuillot's fate to disappoint those whom he inspired and for whom he was in a certain sense a precursor and a master. He wrote from day to day for some forty-five years, of which he asked posterity to discount the first fifteen. Before being overwhelmed by the *Soirées de St Pétersbourg*, and "before being moved by Joseph de Maistre to seek his peace in the Church through confession to a Jesuit," Veuillot was, as he says, a "condottiere of the pen" at the service of the Liberalism of Louis-Philippe and Guizot. He asks us to consider all that he wrote in his early years for other reasons than the glory of God and the truth of the Church as unwritten. In fairness to him we may do so, although he probably judged himself more severely than we may do. Even before his irrevocable engagement in the cause of the Church, Veuillot was not an enemy of God's cause, any more than was King Louis-Philippe, or the Protestant statesman and historian Guizot. But a life of daily polemics in the turbulent, revolutionary street life of Paris did not allow him to show God in His glory, consoling the solitude of sad hearts. A good soldier in all battles for God's honour, he was not—like Léon Bloy—a poet of God's glory.

As we said in the Introduction the history of apologetics is a history of answers; it begins with the Redeemer's own answer to the Rabbis and Pharisees, whose reasonings on the Scriptures He has for ever defeated. In France, Pascal was a reply to Montaigne. The great humanist's aphorisms on the relativity of everything human was defeated by a greater humanist, who, through a more masterly exposition of human relativities, concluded that *Jesus Christ will suffer agony to the end of the world; we must keep watch until then.* Joseph de Maistre was a reply to Voltaire; to Voltaire's paradoxical wit, the Church riposted with a more brilliantly paradoxical wit. To oppose Montesquieu's wise and stoic search for harmony and equilibrium in human institutions, the Church found Bonald, a greater teacher of harmony, order and perfect equilibrium.

Mazzini's and Proudhon's burning desire for justice and for the "People" found its reply in Louis Veuillot.

Then, a little later, when the idol of "the People" was replaced by the aesthetic idol of artistic perfection and inventive genius, the Church found her reply in Barbey d'Aurevilly, Léon Bloy, Ernest Hello and Charles Péguy, as it found her doctors of objective science, this other idol of the age, in Cardinal Newman and Lord Acton, and as the eternal agony of Christ found its voice, amidst the pleasant and shallow declamations of the aestheticism of a prosperous age, in Kierkegaard and Dostoievsky. *Opportet ut fiat scandala.* Louis Veuillot—this is his immense merit, while it is perhaps also his limitation—was the Christian scandal for the strong minds of popular " Enlightenment."

THE TRUE FREEDOM OF THOUGHT[1]

I UNDERSTAND by " free-thinkers," as they call themselves, those men of letters (or people who imagine themselves to be such) who, in their writings, their speeches and their daily lives, cunningly endeavour to destroy revealed religion and its divine system of morality in France. Professors, writers, legislators, bankers, gentlemen of the Bar, industrialists and business-men—they are ubiquitous, they have a hand in everything, they are our masters; it is they who have placed us in our present position, which they exploit and aggravate.

I have tried to paint their portrait in this book, not, I confess, in admiration. A Catholic and a son of the people, I am doubly their enemy, from the time when I began to *think* too, that is to say from the time when, by the grace of God, my mind was freed from the yoke which they had placed upon it for so long. " Free-thinkers " sounds as unpleasant to my ears as " Jesuit " does to theirs. But being a Catholic meant that I had to conform to certain obligations. It would have been wrong of me to *burlesque* a single portrait. I have copied from life; yet if I have not allowed myself to embellish anything, I have not drawn a veil over much. If a character seems to be far-fetched, he has been taken from an original which was even more brazen. The way in which these gentlemen present us on their side is a matter of common knowledge. The reader will judge whether the Jesuit's pencil is nearer to the truth than the free-thinker's paint-brush.

I began this book several years ago, laid it aside and picked it up again many times, until finally I had it ready for the printer, when the adventure of last February[2] intervened, so that publication was postponed. I publish it now without altering anything; I only omit a few chapters whose argument

[1] Foreword to Louis Veuillot's *Libres Penseurs*, Paris, Jacques et Cie, 1850.
[2] The February Revolution of 1848, which replaced the Constitutional Monarchy of Louis-Philippe with the Second Republic.

was riddled by the bullets which overthrew Charter,[1] Throne and Parliament. If only it had enabled me to tear up the whole book! The anger, the sorrow, and the fears which filled my heart when I wrote it would have vanished. I should have lost my misgivings over the terrible dangers I tried to foretell. But these dangers are still present in our principles and the Revolution at most has only changed our laws.

. . . I expect to have one reproach levelled at me. Nearly all the free-thinkers belong to that class of well-dressed people of formal education which is known as *bourgeois*; and I have not been able to deal with them without bespattering the *bourgeoisie* with mud. I shall be told that this is not the time to stir up criticism against the middle classes, when their very existence is threatened.

Granted that their very existence is threatened. But when I wrote my book they seemed to be flourishing; and I wanted to give a warning that, on the contrary, they were running a great risk.

Who spoilt everything for them ? Neither I nor my brethren. Exceedingly badly treated by the Government, the Administration, Literature, Philosophy, Legislation and *bourgeois* predominance; cavilled at, insulted, oppressed, imprisoned, fined, we have rendered good for evil. We have never failed to raise our voices to point out the dangers which we were incurring; we have never asked for anything but justice and liberty; nobody can quote a single word or action of ours that has been seditious.

Others did not observe such self-restraint. Nevertheless, the *bourgeoisie*, and only the *bourgeoisie*, is responsible for the danger in which they stand. The plots which have finally overthrown the middle classes were either hatched in their midst, or only achieved anything because of their support; the *bourgeoisie* loaded the muskets and sharpened the sword which struck them down; they undermined the ground on which they stood, so that now they have lost their grip and are breaking up. I think I am doing the *bourgeoisie* a particular service by trying to make them understand these facts, which they seem deliberately to refuse to recognise, and which it is high time that they should know. If they do not understand what I am trying to say, I am confident that their enemies will understand me even less. I speak a language which is not current in the red

---

[1] The Charter granted by Louis XVIII, on his restoration in 1814 after Napoleon's fall, which formed the constitutional basis of the new Monarchy.

suburbs; I have not the smallest fear that any workman will spend three francs on my book, in order to find arguments which popular hatred no longer finds useful, alas, and those which it would find in it are hardly suitable for its purpose. I will add that few *bourgeois* have gone on as many patrols as I have since February 26th, or mounted guard more often. I served with the National Guard during the latest riots. I shall go to the barricades as often as it is necessary. I think I have done my duty; in any case, I could not do more. I shall go to the barricades with an aching heart, to save the State from a present and very real danger; not in the least to bear witness that I think all is well, and will go well, within the State. Thanks to the recent painful victories, something is still left standing; the vessel has not foundered, there is a ray of hope, a miracle may happen: God is so good! I fight sorrowfully therefore against the misguided workers, because of all the misfortunes which threatens them, the greatest and the most irreparable of all would be their own triumph. If the sacrifice of my life could postpone by one day this fatal triumph, I would gladly give it; but with my dying breath I should say to my companions in the fight: Do not wrap my body in your flag! I came amongst you with very different aspirations from yours. It is your doctrines which have fermented these frightful passions. You must take your share of the blame for this impious warfare.

Pray do not confuse me with those flatterers of the people, those depraved men, who assert that intelligence and virtue are only to be found in the ranks of those who are corrupt and ignorant enough to follow them! All my life I have fought the ambition of these so-called democrats, devoid as it is of talent and above all, of conscience; they represent in my eyes *bourgeois* vice at its worst. Since I first began to study them, I never remember discerning in them any noble or sincere impulse; I have always found them to be violent, lying, deceitful and insolent; the only argument they know how to use is the Moloch of steel, the triangular axe, which they call *liberty, equality and fraternity.*

But if I am not on the side of the revolutionaries and cutthroats, neither do I belong to the ranks of polite sceptics, blasphemous men of letters and swindlers, whose folly and greed have dug the abyss confronting us. There is one thing which is as intolerable as the vile unscrupulousness of men who flatter the populace: it is the imperturbable flow of words with which the multitude of advocates pleads the complete innocence of the *bourgeoisie*, asking: " What crime have they committed ? "

Free-thinkers, and free-doers (a man cannot be one without the other)—I accuse the free-thinking *bourgeoisie* of having hated God and, as a logical and premeditated result, of having despised Man. This is their crime, if they really want to know. They propagated and imposed this crime—yes IMPOSED it by example, by cunning and by the laws they made—on a section of the people; that is the danger which confronts them, and at the same time, it is their retribution.

Men of letters, statesmen, learned gentlemen of the middle classes, what is your achievement since you came to power ? You found the Church to be superfluous in this world. Not only did you steal its wealth, destroy its institutions and reject its laws; but we have seen you tireless in preaching, teaching and commanding a like scorn and a like revolt amongst the poorer classes; certainly they never wanted you to take away their religion, for irreligion strips them bare and kills them. You wrote books and newspapers; you supported black-hearted pedants and obscene mountebanks, so that they could help your laws to loosen the remaining hold which Catholicism still had over the masses; madmen that you were, you did not realise that each victory they achieved was one more stone torn from the frail bulwark of your treasure and your power. When low murmurs coming from the hearts of the multitudes, like gusts of wind, precursor of the storms already brewing in those innermost depths, brought before your very eyes some fragment of the new dogmas, which were still being propagated in whispers, you burst out laughing and said: " It is madness." And if somebody called out to you: " Take care! It is madness; but you are dealing with barbarians and God alone can save you! "—then you paraded your police, your soldiers, your penal codes, your subservient law courts and you answered: " What is God ? "

There were several apostles of this gospel of revenge and frenzy amongst you, wearing moreover your own livery. You crowded round them, applauded them, cherished them. " He is a poet, he is saying something new; he rants, but his anger is amusing; he is a sophist, but he is eloquent! "—And you loaded them with almost as many favours as you give to a clever dancer.

You welcomed everything that these buffoons said, prophets several degrees lower down the social scale than yourselves.

They indicted you, they called curses down upon you, they even calumniated you. . . . But while they cursed you, they cast insults at the eternal Christ; that was enough, you recognised your own kind. If a priest said the same things to you, inspired by faith and the promptings of charity, you stoned him. Combalot, servant of God, missionary of the people, who spent his whole life preaching forgiveness, reconciliation and hope; Combalot was fined and imprisoned because he gave a true description of University teaching. Who condemned him ? This same *bourgeoisie*, in the name of whom, and for the benefit of whom, a newspaper proprietor paid Eugène Süe 100,000 francs a year to teach Communist doctrines.

Is all this true, or am I accusing people falsely ? Have the " thinkers," from Voltaire to M. Süe[1]; the statesmen from M. de Choiseul to M. de Thiers; the legislators and administrators from the last Judicial Courts and the last Provincial Assemblies of Royal Absolutism, down to the last Chamber of Deputies and the last Prefects of Departments of the Constitutional Monarchy (I say nothing of the rest), been anything else but *bourgeois*, or faithful supporters of the *bourgeoisie* ? Did they not hate the Church, impede her action, misrepresent her doctrine and pour scepticism in full measure into the hearts of the people ?

Well, they succeeded! The people—not the whole of the people, through the grace of God, but an appreciable section of them, the workmen, the townsfolk, those who read and discuss politics—this part of the people lost their faith. They are only a minority. They would have liked to win over more, and had hoped to do so; but nevertheless, there are still one and a half million able-bodied men who have arrived at " free thought "—in other words, who have ceased to believe in God.

The Church, deprived of her institutions and her liberty, cannot teach them any more; deprived of her wealth, she cannot succour them any more; dishonoured in their consciences by the calumnies of the " philosophers," made ridiculous in their minds by the gibes of Voltaire, she can no longer bring them back within her fold. Hence all Christian links have been broken; every Christian habit has been lost. The people are outside the bosom of the Mother of all charity; they have ceased to drink from her breasts, from which they used to draw faith and hope. That is exactly what was wanted.

[1] Eugène Süe, 1804-1857, fashionable French novelist of the time, of naturalistic tendencies and style.

Unfortunately, other, unforeseen phenomena have developed, parallel with the successful issue of the *bourgeois* plot. The people are suffering, they are becoming a nuisance and are getting out of hand. Their lowly station, which they once accepted as a dispensation of Providence, in return for alleviations which this same Providence had designed for them, and which were distributed by the Church, they no longer accept with resignation, now that it is dependent upon inexorable chance, which brings no attendant alleviations. They begin to ask dreadful questions: they wonder if all men were born equal or no, and why some men are rich and others poor. They are told that they are sovereign, they point to their masters; they are told that their condition is improving, they reply that they are hungry; books full of fine reasoning and beautiful statistics on the inevitable inequality of the human State are cast at them, they do not bother to read them. They prefer to listen to the insane doctrines which are ventilated in the darkest recesses of their infinite poverty. Instead of the Gospel of God, which used to be their consolation, and of which they have been robbed, they accept other doctrines which drive them to frenzy. Like a dog which has gone mad, because it was tied too long to its leash, they threaten to destroy the material order, to hurl themselves upon society and loot it. What an uproar they make, more alarming than peals of thunder! What strength there is in those bare arms, more relentless than a hurricane! All the brilliance, all the glory, all the authority of the body politic is vanquished within an hour. These straws which take flight in the wind and disappear—they are the King, the Charter, Parliament, the Judiciary and the Army. The victors stop short in their progress, themselves amazed at their conquest. They had not realised there would be a battle: they had merely been giving vent to their impatience.

Terror (a legitimate terror!) rises in the hearts of the mighty of the earth; they ask: What shall we do? What is going to happen to us ? With perspiring brows and white faces they hastily construct a new government. They try a thousand different means to push the people aside, those frightening actors who had appeared prematurely on the stage; but the people themselves are determined to play the rôle for which the *bourgeoisie* had long trained them. In vain do the *bourgeoisie* try to throw them off. With unrelenting rage, they lay siege to a bulwark which they know is too weak to withstand them. In vain are promises, decrees, millions of francs thrown out to them from within the

gates; they shout for the *bourgeoisie* and repulse the sops which
are offered them in panic and fear: *What I am after is your life's
blood*, they jeer. They are still with us, their eyes haggard, their
hearts full of hatred, their hands threatening fire and destruction, brooding over the bitter memories of their wrongs.

Their wrongs! Have they suffered then so cruelly? Some
there are who deny it. Well-written books and eloquent
speeches testify to perfection that the people are freer, more
respected, better paid, better fed, than at the time when they
had no grievances. Granted; but all the same, the people are
discontented.

The truth is that they are under a delusion, vile flatterers
have led them astray; the truth is that they have given themselves up to absurd dreams and a savage pride. . . . Alas,
who has brought them to this pass, and what remedy can you
suggest?

My father died at the age of fifty. He was a simple workman,
without any education or pride. Countless obscure and cruel
misfortunes had marked his days, which were spent in toil;
amongst so many trials, only the joy he took in his virtues, un-
shakable though quite unconscious, brought him some slight
consolation. For the space of fifty years, nobody had paid any
attention to his soul; never, except in his last moments, had
his heart, ravaged by anxiety, rested in God. He had always
known masters who were ready to sell him water, salt and air,
to claim a tithe of the sweat of his brow, and to require the
lives of his sons in war; never had he known a protector who
could defend and succour him; never a guide who could
enlighten him, or pray with him, or teach him how to hope.
At bottom, what had society said to him? What had all these
rights, which are written so pompously into charters, meant in
his case? "Work hard, be obedient and honest; for if you
rebel, you will be killed; if you steal and are found out, you
will go to prison. But if you suffer, weep alone, we cannot help
you; if you have no bread to eat, go to the workhouse, or
starve; it is none of our business." That is what society had
said to him and nothing more; and whatever promises are
written into constitutions, it cannot do or say anything else.
It only provides bread for the poor in the workhouse; it cannot offer consolation and self-respect anywhere. Heavens!
what good does it do to deceive ourselves and follow a will-o'-the-
wisp? Every day I listen to the speeches deputies make, and I
have just followed most carefully the debate on the right to

public assistance and to work; not a single legislator who does not look on the poorest citizen as his brother, I am sure; but what lies at the end of all these homilies ? Nurses at the work-house and the bolted doors of the asylum of Bicêtre!

So my father had worked, suffered and died. Standing at his open grave, I conjured up in my mind's eye the long-drawn-out trials of his life, every one of them, and I thought of all the joys his heart, which was truly created to love God, in spite of the state of servitude in which he lived, ought to have known: pure and celestial joys, which cannot be told in words, and of which he had been cruelly and criminally deprived by society. Then from the tomb of that poor workman there came to me as it were a glimmer of truth from the grave, which made me under-stand, and call down a curse . . . not on work, on poverty, or on suffering, but on the great social crime, the crime of irreligion, which robs the disinherited of this world of the com-pensations by which God has offset their lowly fate; I felt a malediction rise up from the depths of my grief.

Yes, it was at that precise moment that I began to under-stand and judge this society, this civilisation, these so-called wise men who had denied God, and by denying God had rejected the poor and took no further interest in their bodies and their souls. I said to myself: This social structure is iniquitous, it will crumble and perish.

I was a Christian by that time: if I had not been, from thenceforth I should have joined the various secret societies. I should have reasoned, like so many others to whom the light from on high has not been transmitted: Why should other people be well-housed, well-clothed and well-fed, while we are covered with rags, huddled together in garrets, forced to work in sunshine or in rain to earn scarcely enough to die on ? This dangerous problem would have made my head reel; for if God gives no answer to it, no man can do so. When I was a child and one of my father's employers would come along and roughly give him his orders, without bothering to remove his hat, my heart would thump as I felt a frantic longing to humble this insolent creature, to humiliate him and crush him. I would say to myself: Who made him the master and my father the slave ? My father, who is good, decent and strong, and who never did harm to a soul; while this man is puny, evil, dis-honest and leads a scandalous life! My father and this man represented the whole of society in my eyes. Now if I had remained as ignorant as working people usually do, does anybody imagine that the *Short Treatises of the Academy of Moral and Political Science* would have meant anything to me, and that I would have accepted as inevitable that unequal division of the world's goods of which I was fated to have such a small part? The logic of passion works differently. Either I would have done my utmost to seize a larger portion or I should have shouted with the crowd: Let us break up the lion's share, so that at least there will be equality of poverty! Perhaps I shan't get any benefit out of it, but I can't lose anything by it either— at least I shall have the satisfaction of taking my revenge and I shan't be insulted any more.

There lies the wound in the people; it is in their soul; it is a deep one, septic and fearful to behold. Constitutions will not help much, guns not at all. Society is threatened with complete ruin if it does not spit out the poison which it has been imbibing for the last century, a poison which traitors and fools are still offering it, even in these crucial days when everything seems to be breaking up.

Let society lose no more time! Perhaps it only needs one last dose, one last law against Christ and His Church, before it is utterly destroyed.

I point out in my book, as well as I can in my weakness and obscurity, some of the men who are trying to poison society, in order to give the public a warning. They are the same today as they were seven months ago: revolutionaries wearing the Republican cap, just as once they wore the livery of the king.

Liberty, equality, fraternity! Vain words, even fatal ones, now that they have acquired a political sense; for politics have changed them into three lies. Liberty really means justice; equality is humility and fraternity is another word for charity. We shall have liberty when we dispense justice; we shall accept equality, when we have all bowed our heads to the level of the Cross; we shall practise fraternity when we adore OUR Father Who is in Heaven, and when we have asked Him to give us the grace to love our brothers with the same love which He gives to His children. Until that time there will be nothing in our souls but selfishness, covetousness and pride; and the Republican device will only mean, as in the past, a bullet in our guns or the blade of the guillotine in the hands of triumphant factions.

I end with the words which the universal Church in her faith sings on this very day (The Feast of the Exaltation of the Cross):

Dominus ostendit Moysi lignum: quod cum insisset in aquas, in dulcetu-dinem versae sunt. This wood which the Lord shows to the leader of the people, and which, cast into the waters, makes them sweet where once they were bitter, is a figure of the Cross. Only the Cross can save the world.

Job, the Servant

The servant Job whom Holly hires for the little Leo reveals by his name that he is a servant of God, a suffering human being striving towards consciousness.[48] Haggard describes this servant as a rather unsophisticated spirit whose education consisted in working in a horse stable and whose interest was limited to the care and training of the body. Culture and empathy are replaced in him by rules of law. Haggard's novel describes him as the shadow-aspect of a narrow, puritanical Protestantism, based largely on the Old Testament and its Ten Commandments. Job thus brings with him a strengthening of the masculine, legalistic viewpoint; he is a rigid, simple-minded spirit who now joins Holly and Leo, the "father" and the "son." In his role of servant to the heroes, he portrays the limitedness of the human ego or, more specifically, the negative shadow-aspect of Holly's gentlemanly, conventional view of life. Expressed more concisely, Job is the body-person, the body-ego, which previously had served the instincts (symbolized by the horses) but which now assumes the task of caring for "the heavenly child," for the germ of a new wholeness.

The Message in the Trunk

Leo's youth passes inconspicuously. As is the case with other "heavenly children," it evolves in one instant. Suddenly the young hero is grown. For a god, twenty-four years are like one day. On his twenty-fifth birthday, the trunk, his father's legacy, is brought forth.

A second trunk made of black wood is found inside this outer iron trunk which the dying Vincey had given to his friend Holly. Inside this interior trunk rests a still smaller one made of silver with four sphinxes as feet and a fifth sphinx on the curved cover. Within this silver trunk is a fragment of a Greek amphora, covered with ancient Greek writings. Next to the Greek text are found a Latin

and two English translations, one of the latter by Leo's father. In addition there is a picture of Leo's mother, a beautiful Greek woman, and a scarab with the Egyptian seal "Royal Son of the Sun."

The inscription narrates that Amenartas, princess of Egypt and spouse of Kallikrates, a priest of Isis, had bequeathed the contents of the trunk to her young son Tisisthenes (the powerful avenger). It further tells of her flight with Kallikrates, whom she induced through her love to break his priestly vows, into the interior of Africa, during the days of Nectanebes. It clearly describes the path they had to follow, starting from a rock shaped like the head of an Ethiopian, on the east coast of Africa. The path led them to a white sorceress-queen, who fell in love with Kallikrates and wanted to kill Amenartas. A sorcery-charm possessed by Amenartas prevented it.

Thus the white sorceress-queen led Kallikrates and Amenartas into the cave containing the pillar of life, the fiery column of life. She then placed herself within the flame and emerged unscathed and more beautiful. Thereupon she promised Kallikrates that he too could become immortal on the condition that he kill his wife Amenartas. When Kallikrates refused to obey her, she murdered him with her magical power. She subsequently mourned his death and sent Amenartas away. The latter eventually reached Athens where she bore a son. This child was enjoined to discover the queen's secret of immortal life and then kill her. Should he fail in this task, the obligation would pass on to all his descendants, until one day a courageous man was found who would dare to bathe in this fire and would later ascend the throne of the Pharaohs. Further notations on the amphora indicated that Vincey's ancestors had moved from Greece to Northern Italy and, around 1400, to England, thus alluding to important transitions within Western cultural history.

Twenty-five years have passed but only one day for the gods. This day started with the first appearance of the "heavenly child" in the form of a vaguely recognized but often ignored inner birth. The acquisition of the knowledge necessary for the recognition of the task and the attempt to meet it gradually emerged from this inner birth.

Opening the trunk and removing the external wrappings portray

a progressive penetration into a mystery which, unknown to the grandson, had become an ever-recurring problem to the ancestors. Yet the latter remained without a satisfactory answer to this fundamental question of every human life.

First the iron trunk is opened. Iron is the metal of Mars. It symbolizes the forcefulness of the ego, strife and aggressive daredevilishness, force and sexuality in its primitive form. This is the rough outward wrapping, while the hidden treasure, the Anima's message, is contained within. One is not allowed to stop with such youthful, inconsiderate aggression but must penetrate further into the meaning of the task. The middle, wooden trunk is like a small coffin which hides within it a silver trunk with its curved cover and five sphinxes. The initial black gloom with which Haggard started to write the book brings forth a shiny vessel. This trunk is not of gold but of silver, not like the light of the sun, but more like the cool moonlight which illuminates the African nights. It is connected with the night, the moon, and the feminine principle. The sphinx is winged like the birds and has the same relationship to the air and the spirit as does the dove. This birdlike aspect is linked to a female upper torso, a lion's body and, sometimes, in the Hellenic period, a dragon's tail. In Egypt the sphinx guarded temples and graves; in Thebes her name was Phix, analogous to the nearby mountain of which she was the worthy mountain-goddess. She is a dreadful, man-eating monster, a frightening, deadly mother, related to the Gorgons.[49] Hera places her upon the road that leads Oedipus to the city of his parents where, as half-animal and half-feminine unconscious, she confronts him with her riddles.

Not without reason does the sphinx stand at the beginning of the "quest." Like Oedipus, Haggard descends from a family of red-haired, hot-blooded strongmen. Like Oedipus, he remains a "mother's boy." Haggard himself mentions that there was never a day on which he did not think of his mother. To her he dedicated his novel *Cleopatra,* the one following *She.* Nor was Haggard ever able completely to suppress his rancor towards his father. In the novel, Leo is pondering, like Oedipus, the question of the sphinx, namely, the dangers of his yet undifferentiated and unconscious instinctual side. The silver trunk is a valuable container. In the shape of a cube it points towards the realization of the feminine principle in the world. The curved cover symbolizes, like the sky, the en-

compassing view which culminates in a fifth sphinx, the quintessence of the feminine, instinctual soul. Yet all this is but an unrealized possibility, a mysteriously dangerous question and challenge.

The valuable silver container holds a clay fragment with a guiding inscription, concluding with a sphinx with two feathers. Holly had previously seen this symbol but only with kings or with bulls. Jacobsohn[50] illuminates the meaning of this inscribed sphinx. On a banner he had seen was a sphinx with a double-feather crown which represented the Royal Ka. This "Ka," he states, links the king with the gods and ancestors during festivities. For Jacobsohn, the Ka is the power of the Pharaoh's soul.[51] It is incarnated in the Apis, the live and spiritually creative principle which, emerging from the god Horus, disperses itself in the world and its creatures.[52] The guiding inscription is an appeal that originates in the spiritual and creative power of the soul, in the principle which Leo would have to integrate before becoming a "Horus" or, in more modern terms, a "god-man."

The inscription is written upon a fragment of clay, a broken amphora. The amphora is a vessel to collect and store water, the greatest treasure of arid countries. Vessels are always symbols of femininity, symbols of nourishing, enveloping, receiving, and rebirth. In many cultures, the vessel symbolized the mother.[53] Leo receives only a fragment of this symbol. This underlines the fact that once again the feminine aspect is lacking. Two thousand years before, the feminine principle had lost dignity and power as a result of the decline of the great goddess's cult.

We can assume that the inscription is a message from the unconscious, directed not only at Leo but also at the writer Haggard himself. It alludes to the conflict between two women, to the fight between two queens, and thus also between two principles. Kallikrates, which in Greek means "mighty through beauty," is the priest of Isis in Egypt and is hopelessly caught between his wife Amenartas, the daughter of the Pharaoh, and the priestess of Isis, "She," who represents the goddess here on earth. Thus the external queen stands in opposition to the internal one. The outer material world stands against the inner world of the gods and of the soul. On one side stands the love for and faithfulness to the mother of his unborn child, respect for conventions, and obedience to the ex-

ternal law. On the other, there is the promise of inexhaustible vitality and of unimaginable creative energies.

The inner queen, however, demands Kallikrates' exclusive love as the price for this gift of interminable superhuman power. The goddess does so with considerable justification, since Kallikrates, as priest of Isis, had made marriage vows to her priestess prior to his marriage to Amenartas. Thus right opposes right; duty opposes duty; the external, concrete obligation conflicts with the inner, religious one. The situation is further complicated by the fact that the priestess demands the priest for herself, inasmuch as she represents the goddess here on earth. Amenartas, however, will not let go of Kallikrates. She cannot allow herself to deliver him to the priestess for absolute possession, since as his wife she must defend marriage, the other pole of the feminine principle she represents, i.e., the external demands of life. Yet Kallikrates himself shies away from the priestess-goddess and refuses to murder his wife. When he does not relinquish her, the flame of wrath flares up in the priestess, and she slays her beloved. Neither of the two women grants him to the other. Neither is willing to relinquish any of her claim, and thus he is lost to both of them. Just as Isis and Nephtys grieve over the dead Osiris, so "She" and Amenartas mourn over their dead lover. He is torn from both, though he continues in his yet unborn child.

The message on the clay fragment modifies the drama of Isis and Osiris. It is a drama of the gods, an archetypal conflict. As mentioned, the wife, Amenartas, embodies worldly station and renown in her role as daughter of the Pharaoh. "She," on the other hand, is the incarnation of the goddess and simultaneously the "mistress soul" who promises superhuman happiness, glory, and powerful spiritual creativeness. Her legal claim on Kallikrates is older than that of his wife. In the guise of his soul she was, like Isis with Osiris, united with him in heaven before their births. Haggard points this out in one of his last books, *Wisdom's Daughter*.

Carl Spitteler, the Swiss poet, found himself confronted with this same dilemma some time before Haggard. He chose unequivocally his "severe mistress soul," thereby renouncing much natural, human happiness.[54] The Greek Kallikrates stood, like Haggard, for consideration, law, and outward respect, renouncing glory and immortality because of the justified fear of the demands of the im-

pulsive, heathen soul personified by "She." Two thousand years ago her powerful urges had to be denied and overcome, for the sake of a higher, spiritual law, namely, the Christian ideal of morality and humanity. This goal became a universal value as the result of the Christian influence on consciousness. Kallikrates had to make a one-sided decision. However, the longing for completion through the Anima, the longing for inner unification with the natural soul, continues to live and eventually reaches Leo by means of the message of the clay fragment. Leo then begins his quest for the lost treasure.

The trunk contains, in addition to the message, the picture of Leo's Greek mother. It is his mother's picture that summons him to search for the Anima, the image of the soul.

As evidence of his mission, he obtains the scarab with the inscription "Royal Son of the Sun." The scarab is a dung-beetle that rolls a black sphere through the sand. This characteristic made it into an Egyptian symbol of the black sun's nightly sea journey. The black sun travels in the form of a scarab on the sun-boat from west to east where it rises again. Thus the beetle also becomes the symbol of rebirth. Leo is challenged by his scarab to bring about a new consciousness by means of a sea voyage. Confronted with both death and resurrection, he will have to find his wholeness, his inner balance, within this conflict.

The Twin-Heroes

Holly remains skeptical in the face of the clay-fragment message, but Leo is immediately ready to accept the task and to leave in search of the queen and the swirling column of life. This reveals the basic difference between the two. Leo is the active hero, bursting forward in quest of adventure and renewal. Holly, on the other hand, is the prudent individual who hesitates and reflects; yet he is too close to Leo to let him take this voyage alone. Holly decides that, even though there may be nothing to the message, he will at least have a fine opportunity to hunt. Job, the servant, does not want to remain behind when his masters face grave risks, though he has forebodings about this affair. Thus Job represents

the human being who is drawn, half-willing, half-resisting, into the adventures of gods and heroes, whenever the time arrives for the transformation of consciousness. We have viewed Leo and Holly as archetypal figures, representing, as it were, the sun and its shadow.[55] Shadow here is not meant in a moral sense but in the sense of orientation and attitude. Leo is youthful optimism and conquering spirit, Holly aging, moderation, moral reflection, and depressed-saturnal mood. In short, Holly is that aspect which Haggard grew to know only too well in the course of the advancing years. As a youth, Rider had a lot in common with Leo, but the aging Haggard prefers to identify with Holly. Even so, the older Haggard could at times be more youthful and radiant than many others and additionally had known periods of depression in his youth.

The friendship of Leo and Holly has many precursors in mythology and fairy tales. Kerényi points out the hidden link, if not identity, between Zeus and Hades, between the illuminated god and the hidden, concealing god.[56] He mentions an analogous hidden identity and relationship between Apollo and Dionysus who are, respectively, light and underworld aspects of the deity.[57] The identical, and later the dissimilar, twins date back to the period of the astrologic religions.[58] Margarete Riemschneider found symbols of the twin-god and of the twins as far back as Susa and Ur.[59] The two symbolical eyes of the Eye or Twin-God are interpreted as sun and moon. Gilgamesh and Enkidu are equally a pair of friends belonging to this series. Like Leo, Gilgamesh is the new sun, the regenerator of consciousness, and Enkidu, his hairy, animal-man companion, has striking similarities to Holly.

Yet, considering the more advanced cultural evolution which affects the relation of the opposites, we find that Holly is, not pure instinct like Enkidu, but also knowledge and reason. He can be seen as related to Mephisto, the animal-human shadow-brother of Faust, who is intellectually quite sophisticated. Only his hoof and his whispered suggestions recall his rootedness in animal instinctuality. Yet Haggard himself, the hero's companion, developed from animal to hunter to farmer, and he eventually succeeds in turning these energies towards the humanities. Thus he recapitulated human evolution. In college he reached the contemporary limits of science and then faced a challenge to further widen his consciousness, lest he remain stuck in Victorian rationalism. Usually

at this point in development, the ancient pair of twin-gods appears showing that deeds are in the making, and a new phase of life opens up. As an example, we learn that the Asvins, the Indian twin-gods, carry in their chariot "Ushas," the dawn, as their shared bride.[60] Sons of the sun, they are the precursors of a new day, rescuers and healers. At one and the same time, they create in the world and augment consciousness. At this point Haggard conceives of Leo and Holly as rescuers and helpers. As such, they are the complementary aspects of their culture: Leo portrays the Englishman's self-confident, individualistic spirit of enterprise; Holly represents the conservative, ascetic, sober tradition.

The Night Sea-Journey

Holly and Leo, accompanied by Job, begin their journey. They sail along the east coast of Africa and plan to reach this shore in their own "whaleboat." At the moment of their arrival, in the middle of the night, they are hit by a violent hurricane. Only Leo, Holly, Job, and the Arabian steersman, Mohamed, survive. Risking their lives, they overcome the heavy surf and reach the quiet waters of the mouth of a river.

This storm is a sign that the foursome has lost contact with the conscious world of controllable, rational choices and is ready to deliver itself to the unconscious with its "perils of the soul." As if out of a clear sky, they are caught by the uproar of the elements, by wild emotions erupting from primitive depths. The large boat, their last link with England, and the crew, their human partnership, become victims of these emotions. Commonly, the first approach to the unconscious goes hand in hand with a sudden, dangerous commotion during which old values and relationships perish. At such a moment, it is essential to have a friend and guide like Holly. Once the hurricane has torn the heroes away from the security of their traditional world view, they must pass the trial of water. This is their first engagement with the unconscious.[61] Without Holly, that is, without a reflective consciousness, Leo, the young sun, would be lost. He would be swallowed by the darkness back into the primitive, undifferentiated universe. Leo is un-

conscious when he is rescued from the raging waters and is carried through the surf to shore in a small boat. This is the characteristic image of the night sea-journey of the sun which descends into the ocean in the west in order to re-emerge in the east. According to the text of the Egyptian book of the dead, the deceased Pharaoh also travels in the sun-boat towards his resurrection. Similarly, the dismembered Osiris floats down the Nile River in his coffin, as did Moses in a woven basket.

Mother Nature

With the destruction of the large ship, the heroes have also lost the soil of Europe as well as the foundations of Christian tradition. Fortunately, they have their own little boat in which they now begin their separate quest. Only four men are left. Of them, as is implied by their names, Holly represents the Nordic ancestors, Leo the Greco-Roman inheritance, and Job the Old Testament. They form a trinity widened by Mohamed, the representative of Islam, into a quaternity. Mohamed joins them as delegate of the dark continent which they are approaching. This male quaternity might create the illusion of a self-satisfied, self-contained masculinity.[62] Yet for complete wholeness, they are lacking the "feminine" and the "shadow." Admittedly, Job and Mohamed are shadows of the heroes, Job because of his conventional limitations and Mohamed because of his connection with the dark continent. Yet what is lacking, what would be truly complementary, announces itself for the first time in the vision of a woman in the sea, torn by suffering:

> Presently the moon went down, and left us floating on the waters, now only heaving like some troubled woman's breast. The moon went slowly down in chastened loveliness, she departed like some sweet bride into her chamber, and long veil-like shadows crept up the sky through which the stars peeped shyly out. Soon, however, they began to pale before a splendour in the east, and then the quivering footsteps of the dawn came rushing across the newborn blue, and shook the planets from their places. Quieter and yet more quiet grew the sea, quiet as the soft mist that brooded on her

bosom, and covered up her troubling, as the illusive wreaths of sleep brood upon a pain-racked mind, causing it to forget its sorrow. From the east to the west sped the angels of the Dawn, from sea to sea, from mountain top to mountain top, scattering light with both their hands. On they sped out of the darkness, perfect, glorious, like spirits of the just breaking from the tomb; on, over the quiet sea, over the low coast line, and the swamps beyond, and the mountains beyond them; over those who slept in peace, and those who woke in sorrow; over the evil and the good; over the living and the dead. . . .

The shipwreck corresponds, as we mentioned, to the loss of security within the European realm. Inasmuch as a ship is a technological instrument built by human beings for crossing the sea, it may also symbolize one's habitual world-view which offers security against the sea of the unconscious. In *Psychology and Alchemy* Jung states, "The ship is the vehicle which transports him/her across the sea and the depths of the unconscious. As human construction it has the meaning of a system, of a way, of a method (e.g., Hinayana and Mahayana = little and large vehicle: the two forms of Buddhism)." Our Nordic churches were built according to the model of a ship, which is the reason for their lateral entrances and for naming the long structure "ship."

In place of the collective security afforded by the protective ship as well as by the Mother-Church, we now witness the emergence of an older mother-image. The heaving ocean becomes a symbolic image of the all-encompassing Mother Nature's suffering. Wasn't the great goddess originally also the mistress of the waters?[63] Her suffering is more than the personal suffering that drove Vincey to his death. It is the suffering and enduring as passive, feminine principle far removed yet from consciousness. Because of the emergence of the great goddess, the archetypal myth of the youthful god's rebirth out of the original maternal waters resounds. The storm's turbulence gives way to a wonderful, cosmic vision. The torment of the Great Mother subsides. The god rests in her womb from which he must be born again. The moon resembles the chaste bride who hurries into her chamber, to the *Hierosgamos,* to the holy marriage, while the angels of dawn bring forth the new day. The exclusively masculine consciousness which is about to enter the realm of the unconscious meets the vision of a multiplicity of

feminine figures who are supposed to give birth and bring forth the new day. In the story this vision remains like a poetic foreboding, vague and unreal, a cosmic image still unreachably distant for the human being.

The Ethiopian Head

With the break of day, the men discover the omen of the land, the rock with the Ethiopian head. Job, frightened at the sight, exclaims that this is the portrait of the devil.

In early Christian usage, the term "Ethiopian," like the term "Egyptian," was used for the devil.[64] In alchemy he is the black "prima materia"[65] with which the alchemistic opus begins. The first and most important task of any dialogue with the unconscious is becoming aware of one's own blackness, of the shadow, of the dark reverse side of our self-satisfied consciousness. We dislike seeing our own inadequacies, our selfish motives, our evil impulses and thoughts. Of the shadow Jung says,

> It is a moral problem which challenges the entirety of the Ego-personality, inasmuch as no one is capable of confronting the shadow without a great amount of moral decisiveness. In fact this confrontation demands that we recognize the dark aspects of our personality as being unquestionably present. This is the unavoidable basis for any genuine self-knowledge and meets, therefore, considerable resistance. If psychotherapy aims for such self-knowledge, considerable difficult work is needed which may require a long time.[66]

The evil which we ignore reappears as a projection, as a "splinter in the brother's eye."

In the head of the Ethiopian, not only do the three white men see a dark, hostile, dangerous consciousness, but also Job perceives the quintessence of evil. Laurens van der Post, in *The Dark Eye of Africa,* states: "It is because the whites in Africa see in the blacks their own nature, that the prejudice against the black skin has become so entrenched. . . ." The Ethiopian's threatening

head anticipates that which our heroes are to expect in terms of primitive cruelty from the depths of their unconscious, from the abyss of human nature.

The Animals

The morning after the storm, the men row between swamps up the river and tie their boat to a magnificent magnolia tree with reddish blossoms.[67] The pendulum has quickly swung from the black devil towards the other side, the rose-colored tree. Flowers and blossoms symbolize feelings, and this is particularly true of a reddish color. The dark, evil world which the men enter contains not only evil but also the delicate miracle of naturally growing feelings.

They find an ancient port, which indicates that once there had been a commercial route. Later they navigate between hippopotami, hundreds of crocodiles, and thousands of swamp birds. The first animal they shoot is an unusual wild goose with two spurs on its wings and a spur on its nose. No one had seen one before, and Job names it a unicorn-goose.

The unicorn-goose has three spurs; it (in German "she") is a unity and a trinity.[68] Jung's extensive writings about the unicorn explain that it personifies a demonic–divine nature-power, which has connections with the "holy spirit." The horn on its forehead is a creative, spiritual quality. As a white bird, the unicorn-goose belongs to the same category as the swan or the dove. In contrast to the dove, the symbol of the holy spirit, the goose is a nature-spirit. Yet like the dove, the goose is sacred to Aphrodite and thus belongs to the world of femininity.

The natural spirit is projected into the wild nature of Africa. Leo had met it once before in the sphinx. Now, when the waters have calmed, Leo kills the goose as their first hunting booty. His ability to hit it ("her") indicates his intuitive understanding. He has somehow captured the bird-aspect of the sphinx from the otherwise still unknown nature-connection. Through this nature connectedness, Leo will be involved in a primitive, fundamental passion, in a non-dogmatic form of spiritual experience, in an instinc-

tual, vital state of mind which is to compensate for the intellectualism of Holly and the spiritlessness of Job.

Shortly thereafter, Job attempts unsuccessfully to shoot a water
buck. Holly must then kill it. As a buck it is related to the wild stag
and therefore also to Leo whom Haggard describes in the book's
introduction as a wild stag. Leo cannot grasp or understand his
own stag- or buck-like nature; hence, he needs the help of Holly,
the reflective spectator. An alchemical picture shows the buck as
soul, over against the unicorn as spirit.[69] The "natural" spirit and
the "natural" soul, in contrast to the spirit of the church and to the
Christian soul, must be brought back from their projection into
nature and re-integrated. The task is to become aware of and to
assimilate fleeting, seemingly aimless longings and ideas, of barely
conscious wishes and of subconscious thoughts. Such impulses and
feelings live hidden in the unconscious and, like shy, fleeing game,
are hard to hunt down. The buck is found near open water to
which he is driven by thirst. So it is that thirst and hunger give
body to the impulses and drive these feelings that are hard to grasp
towards a clearing, towards the edge of consciousness where we
can comprehend them.

During the night, the four men are awakened by a lion and
lioness. Leo kills the lioness; in the next instant a crocodile grabs
the remaining lion by its paw. A life and death struggle ensues, and
both animals succumb. The lion and lioness are royal animals. The
lion passes as the king of the virgin forest. In the horoscope, as
domicilium solis, he indicates the zenith of the sun and confers
royal bearing and the power to rule. The lioness is companion to
the God-Mother of Asia Minor. Lions pull the chariot of Cybele
and serve her as throne. Margarete Riemschneider points to
Sumerian seals and reliefs on which lions carry the goddess.[70]

The attitude and symbolism of the lion represent strength of the
body, heroic attack, self-assuredness, and royal rule. Yet they also
stand for rapacity and voracity. As an animal sacred to the mother-
goddess, the lioness combines royal nature with maternal
tenderness. Power and rapacity serve her primarily for the care of
the young. Obviously, the lion portrays the animal nature of the
sun-hero Leo. Thus by killing the lioness, Leo separates the
animal-parents. By killing the mother-animal who tenderly cares
for her young, he surmounts his own longing for security near

mother.[71] Later on, the lioness reappears in a new form, as the Royal Anima.

The lion and the crocodile are not killed by the heroes but rather fight and kill each other. They symbolize contrasting and conflicting forces within the unconscious. In Africa the crocodile stands for a lurking, great danger. Whoever receives the crocodile in an oracle is doomed to die.[72] Just as the lion is connected to Leo, the crocodile has a secret relationship to Holly who had the Cambridge nickname of Charon, death's ferryman. The lion is the hero's victory, while the crocodile is the evil outcome, the "No," the being pulled back into the unconscious. The two animals represent opposing life forces. Deriving from the animal-nature of the hero are the hot-blooded rapacity and greed for power of the lion, as well as the cold-blooded goal-directedness of the crocodile and serpent. Lion and crocodile embody life and death, progress and annihilation.

Yet, in which way are they related to Haggard himself? At twenty years of age, he was already viewed by the African natives as representative of the queen. As "Sompseu's child" and master of the highest court, he was given royal honors. When he traveled to supervise the execution of judgments, he sometimes brought death. This power that descended on him at such an early age awakened his "power soul" without his becoming aware of it. Crocodile and lion are not shot in the novel. The battle of these opposites remains a natural drama. This tension between unconscious opposites, parallel to the tension within the heroes themselves, remains hidden to them at this juncture. As a result, a certain amount of instinctual forces remains unrecognized and unavailable.

Haggard's inadequate insight into the instinctual aspects of human nature results in a frustration of his goals. It is important to keep in mind that Haggard was truly a pioneer. He did not have available, as we do today, any orientation to the unconscious as offered by modern psychology. Still he went a long step beyond the insights of his time. In this story, however, the absence of a conscious confrontation with the lion and crocodile diminishes the effectiveness of the hero's instinctual nature.[73]

The Swamp Belt

The following day, the four men row upstream and reach a man-made canal. Rowing against the current characterizes the journey as a struggle against the river. Not a life that devolves unconsciously and effortlessly, this is an undertaking in opposition to the ordinary course of things. The attempt to extract its secret from the unconscious, a heroic task, goes against nature. Yet the man-made canal which they reach and to which they must entrust themselves reveals that they are now following a path traveled in earlier times. In fact, there are ancient ways to penetrate into the hidden realm of the unconscious.

The swamp belt along the coast which they must traverse is one of the natural formations in that region. It also serves as a symbol of the chaotic condition of the initial state, well-known in alchemy. It is the initial period of the inner journey, when the firm ground of conscious orientation is left behind and when the conscious and the unconscious are no longer distinguishable. Here the unconscious threatens to flood the conscious human being with its contradictions. So the individual is repeatedly in danger of remaining stuck or of drowning in the inner disorder and disorganization.

The Old Wise Man Billali and His Tribe

After four days on the canal in this miserable region, our exhausted heroes awake one morning under the frightening gaze of savages who would have killed them instantly were it not for their queen. "She-who-is-to-be-obeyed" has ordered her people to spare the lives of the white men rowing up the river and to bring them into the interior.

The savages are good-looking, but their expressions are indescribably cruel. Their leader, an ancient white-haired man named Billali, brings the strangers in sedan-chairs to his tribe which lives in the fertile grassland of an extinct crater. The people dwell in

caves which, in fact, are ancient sepulchral vaults. They call themselves "Amahagger," the people from the rocks, and are matriarchally structured. This elicits Holly's comment that morality seemed to be a function of geographical latitude, since much of what is viewed as good and decent in one place turns out to be false and indecent in another.

Morality's becoming relativistic is the normal consequence of a clash with a different cultural group. Many people thereby lose the moral strength that they would otherwise have maintained in their own culture. Like the hero of *The Witch's Head* after his disappointment in love, they start drinking, gambling, or running around with women. Yet others try to cling all the more tenaciously to inherited standards, which leads to a progressive inner emptiness since the external behavior corresponds neither to the environment nor to the subjective truth.

The collision with another culture and another morality—a difficult problem and one that is very timely for many—demands a dialogue not only with the foreign consciousness but also with the contents of one's unconscious. The unconscious has mysterious connections with the environment and will be influenced directly by the instinctual patterns of a differently shaped environment. In order to achieve a viable adjustment to the new environment, one must seek a satisfactory position between one's traditional, conscious way of life and one's unconscious, which is being stirred up powerfully by the different culture and the subconscious instincts within it. Dealing with dreams and with spontaneous fantasies furthers understanding of the unconscious processes stirred up by the new environment and helps prepare for a new synthesis.

Haggard's position towards other cultures was open-minded. Yet in terms of himself and of the English youths for whom he wrote, he held fast to a strict, denominational Christian position and to the gentleman-ideal. The Christian example which he held up against an invasion by the unconscious prevents the breakthrough of Antichrist forces, as occurred later in Germany. However, his one-sided attachment to the gentleman-ideal so limits consciousness that the shadow cannot be integrated but continues to be projected, thus manifesting itself as an external peril.

Leo and his companions, representing a penetrating consciousness, are met by a commotion coming from the very center

of the dark continent, of the unconscious. Though previously confronting anything foreign with murderous intent, the unconscious now responds to this new approach with a sense of anticipation. The right "knights," with the right attitude, are arriving. They have unconquerable curiosity and are willing to die in order to discover the secret of the white queen. The lonely queen's deep longing to be redeemed supports their firm purpose. Thus she sends out her servant, Billali, so he can safely escort them to her.

Billali has a long, white beard, a hook-nose like that of an eagle, and eyes as sharp as those of a serpent. His behavior is instinctive, with partly bitter and partly wise humor. In contrast to academic knowledge, he personifies an instinctive insight and ability to deal with primitive nature. Without this quality, it is impossible to advance either into the inner Africa or the virgin forest of the unconscious. Billali is a nature-spirit, helpful but not dependable. That which the heroes met first in the sphinx and later in the hunted animals, namely, their unconscious impulses and instincts, returns now in a transformed way, as instinct-bound, helpful, unfamiliar knowledge.

Billal is the name of Mohammed's first *muezzin* or prayer-leader. In Cambodia all prayer-leaders are called Billal. Thus, Billali reveals himself to be a descendant of a Mohammedan in whom the recollection of the meaning of prayer and submission to Allah has remained alive. In the novel, however, Allah's servant has become the servant of the goddess who is banished to the unconscious. He has regressed to pre-Islamic matriarchy.

From the second novel concerning She—*Ayesha, The Return of She*—we learn that Holly is the reborn Noot, the wise, long-deceased, Egyptian priest and teacher of She. Yet only a limited amount of Noot's wisdom is reincarnated in Holly: knowledge, worldly prudence, morality, without priestly piety and wisdom. In modern human beings, piety as a basic attitude has become largely suppressed, and therefore unconscious and primitive, as a result of increasing technological acquisitions and greater, sharper knowledge. For modern humans the wise priest has died.

On the other hand, anthropologists are profoundly impressed to find in Africa genuine piety as an expression of the human being's dependence upon superordinate powers.[74] The European encounters in Africa this lost part of his being, namely, piety as a natural

instinct; here it is permeated by the sense of one's dependence, something that is still contained in the Mohammedans' concept of destiny. Without regaining some of this attitude, the European cannot become whole or wise. Billali and his long white beard embody another part of the heritage of the ancient wise man Noot. Job speaks of Billali sarcastically as "he-goat," underscoring the impulsivity of his spirit, his unpredictability, and his relatedness to the buck-hoofed Pan. As servant of She, Billali is subordinated to the feminine principle and conveys knowledge about instincts as well as the skill of dealing with nature within and about us. By means of this nature-piety, he offers a significant compensation for European intellectualism. Holly addresses Billali as "father." Billali possesses the older knowledge from which our own pragmatic science has evolved.

The First Crater

As head of his tribe, Billali lives in a small, extinct crater. The edge of the crater that surrounds the buried opening, which at one time reached the interior of the earth, is circular. This circle enclosed by high rocks is a first symbol for the "roundness," the "wholeness" that is grounded in itself, which comprehends the opposites and which Jung designates as Self.[75]

In the earlier phases of humanity's evolution, the wholeness does not realize itself in the individual but in the tribe with its complementary halves. Layard referred to this in his *Stonemen of Malekula,* and the same has been observed among the Pueblo Indian tribes. The four "quarters" of ancient cities also reflect the subdivision of the collective wholeness. The city of Kor where She waits for the heroes is similarly situated in a still larger crater surrounded by rocks. The crater of the "Amahagger," the rock-people, is a preliminary form, a barbaric shadow-aspect, of the Self's wholeness. Here it is achieved on a primitive level, whereas Leo's task is to achieve this wholeness, in conjunction with She, on an individual level.

Both Billali's crater and that of She are also gravesites: the heroes enter a realm of the dead. The Self includes generations, in

numerable layers of an impersonal past, all of which may announce themselves again in dreams and fantasies. The first encounter with the Self is often experienced as compensation for the
Christianity of consciousness, as an encounter with evil. The
crater shelters greedy, cruel, beastly human beings. Additionally as
compensation for the patriarchal orientation of our consciousness,
we find here matriarchy, which is common to many African tribes.

Ustane

At the first welcoming, a distinguished young woman kisses
Leo, whereupon Job mutters, "The hussy—well, I never!" Surprised and hesitant at first, Leo then returns the embrace, com-
menting that obviously some early Christian customs must still be
valid in this region. It turns out, however, that the greeting is a
marriage-ceremony of the Amahagger which is initiated by the
women and which a woman can dissolve at her discretion.
Another woman approaches Job with the same intention, but he
fends her off. His clumsy righteousness cannot tolerate such a
thing. Yet his rigid attitude will bring forth a bitter revenge. Not
only the rejected woman, but also the entire tribe, feels dishonored
and plans vengeance.

What Leo took for early-Christian brotherliness is in fact a
marriage-ceremony. While in his native country women are expected to behave passively, we find that here, in the unconscious,
activity originates in the woman. That which in England is
unalterable, i.e., marriage-law, is determined here by the variable
emotions of the feminine eros.

Leo's returning Ustane's kiss characterizes the harmlessness of
the sun-hero who sends his rays to all creation without allowing
himself to be impeded. Yet, as Leo returns what to him seems a
non-binding greeting, he consents to a different, local custom. It
becomes evident that his gesture is understood by feminine feelings
as a commitment. By returning the kiss, the sun-hero unexpectedly
finds himself tied in marriage to a black woman. In *King
Solomon's Mines,* Haggard couldn't yet conceive of a marriage
between a black woman and a white man; yet here it occurs,

against knowledge and will, even before Leo knows what has happened.

The male thinks he is to choose or to reject. He identifies with the sun-hero who strives towards his faraway goal: the white queen of his ideals. Yet things are decided differently in the unconscious. Unexpectedly, he succumbs to the embrace of his dark Anima. Thus marriage reveals a feature which men do not intend and do not wish to see, but of which some become painfully aware just before the wedding—namely, that viewed superficially he has been caught in a woman's net but that at closer view he has become a prisoner of his own nature. This occurs even more drastically in the colonies: consciously the white man thinks he is caught in a woman's trap. Yet in truth, the dark-skinned woman gains power over him only because he no longer is able to resist the dark side of his own nature which has been strengthened by the environment. Ustane's tie to Leo is primitive, the type of marriage people commonly live as long as no spiritual partnership is built upon it. Ustane cares for Leo, she offers him her feelings, nurses him during his illness, shares the nights with him; but missing is a genuine relationship based on mutual understanding.

Marriage as a binding but still primitive relationship is a preliminary form of the Self. Through the union of man and woman, marriage portrays an initial wholeness. It is the necessary basis for a relatedness to the feminine principle, a first step in helping the man to get closer to his nature and his soul and eventually to unite with it. At this point Leo gains a new experience of the "unconscious nature" which had appeared to him in the vision of the sea as a suffering woman.

Yet, in this layer of the unconscious, primitive impulses predominate. These impulses can become dangerous for the relationship and for consciousness. The feminine element which has been lacking in these heroes approaches them from the inferior, primitive, rejected side, thus bringing with it other contents. The young men clad in leopard skins also belong by nature to the matriarchal level. In Greece they are known as Corybants who, armed with swords and shields and clad in animal skins, dance around the newborn child of Rhea, the first mother.[76] Elsewhere, the Kabires and Daktyles belong to the mother-goddess's entourage: a large number of young men, warriors, dwarfs, phallic

creatures, or skilled blacksmiths. Here the male element is an anonymous, impregnating force, a universal, generative force, an energy which begins to differentiate itself by bearing arms and learning artistic skills. These are fervent, ardent men who have learned how to deal with and to use fire. On this level impulses begin to change into will; more accurately, here will is still composed primarily of impulse, and the essence of will shows itself in the form of spontaneous and sometimes destructive fire.

One evening, as Leo, Holly, and Ustane sit around a fire, the woman begins to sing: "You are my chosen one—I've waited for you since the beginning." But the song ends by telling how She, the white queen, proves herself the stronger and that something horrendous will separate Ustane from her chosen husband. Here, in the realm of the unconscious, Ustane may be free to take the initiative towards a man, but she does not have the rights that civil law grants a spouse to protect her against rivals. In "She-who-is-to-be-obeyed" she runs into a rival who is stronger and more beautiful.

The Incandescent Pot

Billali has visited She for five days in order to receive her instructions. Once within her sphere, the heroes are no longer free to act according to their own will. They have entered the soul's field of forces. Primary decisions now originate in the innermost center to which they are drawn as if by magic. They only retain the freedom to respond to the orders coming from within, according to their own insight.

The threatening thunderstorm comes to a head on the fifth day after Billali's departure. The two friends are invited along with Job to feast; and even Mohamed, the Arabian steersman, is brought in, trembling and pale, by the woman whom Job had rejected. An enormous fire lights the hall, and brandy is passed around in jugs upon which love-scenes are depicted in strangely childlike simplicity and frankness.

Naive simplicity and freedom in matters of love, but behind this

sits intoxication from brandy, and a great peril. "Where is the meat that we shall eat?" asks a voice, and all reply, "The meat will come!"

"Is it a ram?"

"It is a ram without horns and more than a ram; and we shall butcher him."

"Is it an ox?"

"It is an ox without horns. . . ."

Meanwhile, the heroes notice how the rejected woman begins to banter with Mohamed.

"Is the meat ready to be cooked?"

"It is ready, it's ready!"

"Is the pot hot to cook it?"

"It is hot, it is hot!"

"Great God," gasps Leo, "it was written on the clay fragment that there were people who put pots over the heads of foreigners."

Holly jumps up, seizes his pistol, and aims instinctively at the devilish woman who has grabbed Mohamed. The bullet hits her, and at the same time it kills Mohamed who is spared a more horrible death.

With the shot a general uproar begins. The white men defend themselves against the onslaught of the savages until finally Leo collapses. At this point, Ustane throws herself over him to save him. A terrible voice shouts, "Drive the spear through both of them; then they will be married forever!"

"Cease," a thunderous voice is heard through the hall as Billali appears.

After leaving the realm of water, the heroes have entered that of fire. The circle of fire is a place of the cannibals, of those emotions that are the more barbaric as they are rejected by our consciousness. Thus, this place represents an initial symbol of the Self's wholeness. The two rational Englishmen here run into the type of primitive, emotional nature that slumbers in each one of us and without whose richness and danger we would be but half human beings, simply surrogates without depth.

At the same time, the circle of fire is the place where marriages are contracted. Through marriage the emotional aspects of the Self are built into a culture. By declaring marriage a sacrament, the church affirms that emotions enter the human realm as something extra- or super-human, as divine power, as some formidable force

that must be guarded with care and veneration. Yet, all too often the other, dangerous, destructive side of the impulsive-divine energies breaks forth. Uncontrollable, negative affects originating from within may be turned against the "woman." Day-to-day married life offers many occasions for dissatisfaction over the spouse. Thus, the wife is commonly blamed for the husband's moods and fits of anger.[77]

Ustane, the black spouse, does not solely portray the married woman. As a member of her tribe, she also represents the dark, impulse-bound emotions in the man, his unrealized emotional dependency. Leo accepted the tie to his shadow-spouse which was forced upon him in the fiery circle of emotions. Yet Job, identified in the novel with law and conventionality, is no hero but an ordinary, narrow human being, who is simply the servant and shadow of the heroes and who rejects the appeal of the feminine side. For Job, marriage is an affair of the registrar's office rather than of the emotions. The tribe, however, cannot tolerate the rejection of a "natural emotion." This infraction against the law of the land brings forth a wild reaction. As is common in the case of infractions against the inferior side, this reaction becomes manifest only after several days.

During the feast to which everyone is invited, jugs decorated with love-scenes and taken from the graves are passed around. The decorations are somewhat like the Dionysian vase with pictures alluding to regeneration and rebirth.[78] It is not unusual to encounter such ancient jugs and Dionysian scenes also in dreams, whenever the process of exploration reaches the deep levels of the ancient soul. We are astonished when we discover that past rites and beliefs have been preserved by the unconscious and are reawakening in order to complete and revitalize our consciousness that has become too one-sided. From the graves, out of the memories of the ancestors, emerge pictures of a high culture in which free love belonged to the cult of the great goddess.

The savages in the novel and their cannibalistic customs probably represent a degenerated form of this high culture. While we educate the intellect, we leave the emotions to themselves so that they succumb to our primitive, barbarous side. Love, which in this region of Africa was expressed as a natural emotion, was refused by Job and thus turned into hatred. The incandescent pot which is to be put over the selected victim's head images the strong affects

that overcome him. His head burns, he turns crazy. He becomes the victim of cannibals. Psychologically, this means that one no longer deals with this one human being but with a band of enraged savages within him. "A ram without horns, an ox without horns, and more than an ox . . ." A man is the selected victim, a buck that has changed himself into a eunuch and who, therefore, also lacks will to fight and spiritual creativity. The split-off emotions will grow over the head of such a man if he gets too close to the unconscious. Whoever is unwilling to serve nature will become its victim.

As container and as cooking-pan in which the contents are transformed by heat, the pot can be viewed as analogous to two bodily organs, the stomach and the womb. In many persons, certain intense emotions are the source of burning gastric disturbances. Also the womb can be likened to a container within which warmth contributes to a creative process. As mentioned in connection with the message on the amphora fragment, the vessel is a primary symbol of the feminine. Erich Neumann states, "The feminine is experienced as the perfect vessel for good reason. Woman as a body-vessel is the natural expression of the experience that the feminine carries the child within herself, and that the male, in the sexual act, enters into her."[79]

The term *hysteria* is not accidental. The incandescent pot over the head is equivalent to the rising of hysterical affects. In fact, when a man rejects emotions because of rigid conventionality, the heat of this feminine side turns into an evil fire that consumes his brain. That which could have ripened towards creative involvement can change suddenly into hysterical rage which destructively inundates the entire person. It is Job, self-righteously defensive against the dark side of nature, who evokes this peril. Significantly, it takes several days before the tension leads to a discharge. The fury, however, does not aim at the conventional side, Job, but against the weakest point which in this case is Mohamed. As the most primitive among the four, he becomes the defenseless victim of the intense emotions. The uproar breaks forth from the collective unconscious like a mob. If the destructive rage cannot be stopped, reality will disintegrate. In such a state a man does not remember what he said or did. He will act surprised when he sees those around him responding defensively or fearfully. Most of all,

he does not recognize to what extent he has bullied the feelings of his wife and children.

The unconscious responds to rejection with a sudden attack of which Mohamed is the victim. Holly's bullet hits him and the black woman simultaneously, saving him from a cruel fate. Holly acts. Reason defends itself against affect. Just as Job is Holly's shadow, so Mohamed is Leo's. While Leo is induced to become active, Mohamed becomes the passive victim of primitive impulsivity. Holly's bullet unites the black woman and Mohamed in a gruesome death-wedding. Thus, an intuitive insight demands that the resolution of, and freeing from, hysterical explosions consists in the linkage (and transformation) of hostile opposites, even if at first only the most radical methods suffice to save the endangered consciousness.

When Leo is near defeat, Ustane throws herself protectively over him. She is not only nature but also love. Therefore, this pair is less imperiled than the other. Nevertheless, the same fate hangs over Leo and Ustane as over Mohamed: the danger of a brutal death-wedding. It is as though some primitive reason were attempting to arrest any further growth by Leo. The unconscious is trying to swallow back both Leo and Ustane. If the hero does not want to forget his task, he must defend himself with the weapons of his intelligence against the onslaught of his primitive, inner world. It becomes a matter of life and death, with the likelihood of an ominous result. A higher principle from the depths of nature must arrive and intervene. She, the white queen, must save him, since her own destiny depends on the hero's life and love.

Whenever a man on his inner journey confronts the shadow and the figures of the unconscious, he risks being flooded with the primitive, barbaric sides of his being. In such moments, he must, like Leo and Holly, defend himself with his intelligence, his will, and his superior knowledge. If a man yields to his primitive reactions when he projects his Anima upon a woman, he not only becomes arrested but also degenerates and in turn becomes more primitive. The goal then, as with Leo, is the acquisition of feelings and wisdom. It is necessary to know about the barbarous potentials lurking in each human being. Conscious dealing with the abysses contained in the soul protects one against being unexpectedly overwhelmed by the internal peril. Conscious awareness

renders one immune to contagion from psychoses which otherwise can lead an individual to lose track of his higher nature.

Billali, in the name of the queen, orders the uproar to cease. He explains to Holly later that it is a custom of the land to kill foreigners with the incandescent pot. It is a law of the unconscious to attack invaders suddenly. The unconscious then fills their heads with affects and passions, with everything that is suppressed, but not truly contained, by civilization and Christian veneer. Right below the surface of the gentleman is still the barbarian, not in his natural state, but degenerated towards unnatural evil. This barbarous layer—visibly in the open in the East—is right below the surface in Western cultures. There are various ways to deal with it. In Haggard's novels, the spiritual side fights against the barbarian in self-defense, because of compassion for the victims, and because of faithfulness to friends and idealism. Consciousness halts the destructive eruption of the unconscious at least until help from within rescues those who put up a courageous resistance.

The Mummy

Holly passes a restless night after the fire orgy. He dreams of a veiled, lovely woman who first turns into a skeleton, then regains her human figure and says: "That which is alive hath known death, and that which is dead yet can never die, for in the Circle of the Spirit there is neither life nor death. Yea, all things live forever, though at times they sleep and are forgotten." The following morning he learns that once the mummy of a beautiful woman had lain on the stone bench on which he slept. And Billali further tells him that, as a boy, he had felt drawn by this mummy and had loved her, and that wisdom had flowed from her into him. In her, he recognized the transitory nature of all things, the brevity of life, and the long duration of death. Billali's mother overheard him and cremated the mummy in fear that she was bewitching her son. Only a small, white foot remained untouched. Billali then brings it out from under the stone bench: "Shapely little foot! Well might it have been set upon the proud neck of a conqueror bent at last to woman's beauty, and well might the lips of nobles and of kings

have been pressed upon its jeweled whiteness." This is what Holly thought as he enclosed the relic in a military pouch.

The battle against the eruption of primitive emotions has not been fruitless. Holly has had a dream which brings an insight, transmitted by a mummy who becomes a beautiful, veiled woman, who reverts to a skeleton, and who speaks of eternal life in the sphere of the spirit.

Speaking of the mummy, Paracelsus claims that it [she] is an "antidote against mortality."[80] His treatise *De Vita Longa* begins with "Truly, life is but a kind of an embalmed mummy which protects the mortal body against the mortal worms."[81] And Hippolytos speaks of the "upper human being," of the "Protanthropos" whom the Phrygians called Papa (Attis), saying: "He is a messenger of peace and calms the battle of the elements within the human body. This Papa is also named Nekys [corpse], since he is buried within the body like a mummy in a shrine."[82] In the mummy Holly encounters an Anima which remains at the stage of a chrysalis. She is the still-veiled psyche, a seemingly dead remainder from distant times, for the Anima is the man's original experience of the woman. At this point she appears only as a ghostly figure. Yet through this she can manifest her spiritual, non-material being. Both the mummy and the ghost point to the appearance or reawakening of the supra-personal, spiritual Anima.

The veiled, invisible, or spiritual woman brings peace after the battle. She symbolizes the life that enlivens the body, the integration of the soul in the body that manifests itself bodily and then disappears without perishing. She is alternately nature and spirit. She speaks of the flow of things in the periodic alternation of becoming and vanishing, and of the fact that in the sphere of the spirit there is neither life nor death. In place of the opposites and their brutal battle, there appears to Holly the presentiment of another possibility: a rhythmically flowing alternation of existence in the spiritual realm with everyday reality, so that both remain related to each other. Here the opposites relieve one another without ever extinguishing each other.

Billali, the nature-spirit-father, received his wisdom from the mummy until his mother pulled him out of his seeming madness. With good reason she had suspected that this "spiritual Anima" might lead him into an unreal world. Now, only a foot of the mummy has been left behind, and Holly imagines the nobles and

kings of ancient times who submitted to the reality of the eternal feminine. Yet then he places the relic that brought this insight amongst the mundane objects of his pouch. Only a foot is left, but it suffices for reawakening the meaning of the whole.

Holly, representative of the undeveloped sensation function, is the one who receives the news concerning the mummy. This remnant of the mummy becomes a window into the past as well as into the realm of the eternally alive, creative spirit. In a matter-of-fact way, Holly takes the little foot as a keepsake, and whenever he will look at it, he will be reminded of his meaningful dream. The Englishman's dry reasoning and his belief in tangible facts render him particularly vulnerable to the compensatory attacks of the irrational side.

"In this country the women do what they please. We worship them and give them their way, because without them the world could not go on; they are the source of life. We worship them up to a point, till at last they get unbearable, which they do about every second generation." "Then," Billali adds with a faint smile, "we rise and kill the old ones as an example to the young, to show them that we are stronger." Here Billali expresses the unconscious wish of the man who would like to fight off the preponderance of the mother-complex.

Matriarchy is founded upon the biological function. Women are the fountain of life of the tribe. Now and then the man must or wishes to assert his greater strength against their biological importance, thereby maintaining a relative balance. Thus we noticed in the realm of fire the play of opposites on the biological level. The power of the biological assertion of life is seen against the strength and determination of the male.

Yet the mummy points beyond the sphere of fire, beyond biological life, towards death and towards life in the realm of the spirit, even beyond the center of fire. The little mummy foot is hidden in the realm of fire like a seed. The soul reaches all the way down to the foot, and here it touches the ground of reality. With the little white foot, the heroes gain a new standpoint which leads them on to She.

Ustane wants to accompany Leo on this journey. Yet in the presence of She, Ustane loses her rights. "The word of She," Billali states, "abrogates all other rights." "But what if Ustane will not let go of Leo?" asks Holly. Billali replies, "What if a storm asks a tree

to bend and the tree refuses, what happens then?" This is the cue for the next level of the journey. The heroes are going to the place of storms. She is a storm and as awesome as lightning.

The Land of Fever

The heroes are carried in sedan chairs through the swamps. Saved from the danger of the incandescent pot, Leo and Holly are racked by fever resulting from their battle wounds. "It is our own desires that stick in our flesh like arrows," says Jung.[83] One who is struck by Cupid's arrow is tortured by ardent desires. In Wagner's opera *Parsifal,* King Amphortas is ailing, wounded by his own spear that had fallen into the hands of his adversary. Behind the fever that befell Leo and which She will heal is probably Haggard's passion which drove him to write of an immortal woman and an immortal love. The same feverish passion drove Leo, the son of lovesick Vincey, to begin this journey. Leo refused the people in the fire-sphere, but the poison of their affects proved contagious. In his fever, Leo deliriously imagines that he is divided in two halves. Being torn internally is the fever's source. Leo is in the borderland between Ustane and She, and the inner division grows intolerable. In the novel *Jess,* John feels that he must sacrifice his relationship with the spiritual beloved for the sake of the more down-to-earth Bessie. Since both women are Anima-figures, however, his soul is torn. Each of the relationships offers him the experience of one side of his being. He cannot give up either of them. Not only Leo but also Job, the body-ego, is racked by fever. The body often becomes ill when the soul finds no solution to a conflict.

The Mandala of the Heart: Kor

As they journey from the swamps to the highland, they see in the distance a volcano which is ten times larger than the first one. It is the castle of She. Across the high rocks that seem to touch the sky

there are thick layers of clouds. Earlier inhabitants, in long forgotten times, had used canals to drain the lake which had formed in the crater. Inside the extinct crater is Kor, the city of the heart, circular and protected by nearly insurmountable rock walls. The Mandala[84] of the heart, almost inaccessible, is situated above the volcano of the emotions. This ground has been habitable only since the waters were drained off. This motif recalls some dreams in which the waters of the unconscious must be drained before the heart begins to function as a center of consciousness.

An American Indian tradition is that we think, not with the head, but with the heart. Europeans, however, long ago abandoned the heart in favor of the head as the center of consciousness. Yet She does not live in the head but in the heart, near abandoned temples and in old gravesites. She reigns over savages and is served by deaf and mute servants. "Mistress soul," the forgotten goddess, lives her existence dreadfully abandoned, in the midst of savage and primitive people. The realm of the heart is a realm of death. Deaf-mute servants come and go. There is nothing to hear and nothing to say, since the queen of the heart, the feeling aspect of the man, is condemned to be among the dead. Nothing can be voiced about her being, her suffering, or her wishes.

The Anima is found in a grave-city of an ancient or even prehistoric period. As the personification of the unconscious, she reaches far down into collective layers. Very much embodying these early layers, she appears in men's dreams as a medieval feudal lady, as a witch, or as a priestess, like Ayesha who represents an ancient goddess. She is yesterday's truth which has been repudiated by our one-sided consciousness. She is life as it always was, in varying garb. The queen of the heart, the mistress of emotional reality, dwells near the dead among the ruins of past civilizations. Many people live, as far as their emotions are concerned, in the past. Thus we see romantics, scientists, and ordinary human beings who live in the seventeenth century, in the Renaissance, or even in the Stone Age.

Leo seeks the city of the heart, knowing that for his father Vincey life without love was meaningless. Thus the son must find his way to complete the task passed on to him by his father. Haggard himself was compelled to undertake this journey since, like Oedipus, he is one of those mother-sons who are called upon to resolve a family conflict. During his early years in Africa, on his

lonely trips where he repeatedly confronted death, his unconscious awakened from its torpidity and fostered a life which was to burst the limits of his Victorian world. Holly, however, is unable to respond spontaneously to such reactivation of the unconscious. He limits himself to recording or collecting unusual, odd things or events and leaves it to Leo to become deeply affected.

She

The travelers are housed in caves containing graves. Leo is so critically ill that Holly fears for his life. When Holly is called by Billali to meet She, he picks up the scarab which in his delirium Leo had dropped on the floor.

Through a rock tunnel, Holly is led by Billali to the antechambers of She. Billali throws himself down and approaches She on his knees and then later on his stomach. Holly decides not to lower himself to that extent, since otherwise he would be expected to repeat the performance each time. Yet he, too, is overcome by fear when he senses that the gaze of the veiled, mysterious, strange figure is directed upon him. He has the impression of standing in the presence of someone uncanny. The mummy-like figure before him is a tall, lovely woman, revealing instinct and beauty in all her parts, with serpentlike graciousness, her movements flowing like waves over her body. Her raven-black hair reaches down to her sandals. "Why are you so afraid, stranger?" asks the sweet voice, one that, like the streams of the softest music, moves the heart.

"It is your beauty that scares me, O queen" is Holly's humble answer. Yet She replies with laughter that rings like silver bells, "You were afraid because my eyes explored your heart. Yet I forgive you your lie, since it was courteous." Chivalry calms the Anima and protects against her rage. She's reply shows that she knows what goes on in a man's heart. She is the truth within it.

When she notices Billali, her voice resounds clearly and coldly against the rocks, as she promises to sit the next day in judgment of the evildoers from the sphere of fire. Then she dismisses him.

The hall is filled with fragrance that seems to flow from She's hair and her white, transparent dress. "Sit down," she commands

Holly, "since you have nothing to fear from me. However, if you have reason to be afraid, you will not have to fear me for long, because I shall slay thee."

They converse about Egyptian, Greek, and Roman history; she knows nothing of subsequent periods. She speaks Arabic, Latin, Hebrew, and Greek but not English. Holly is aghast when he realizes that she has already been alive two thousand years. Yet She responds, "Do you really believe that all things perish? I assure you that nothing perishes, that there is no death, only transformation. What once lives will return. I, Ayesha, tell you that I am expecting someone whom I love and who will be reborn." "But," inquires Holly, "if it is true that we human beings are constantly reborn, how is it that you *never* die?" She explains to him that she has become one with nature: "Nature has its own life-spirit, and whoever finds this spirit and allows himself to be filled with it will live from it. He will not live eternally, since nature itself is not eternal. Nature, too, will die one day or, more accurately, will transform itself, but not for a long time yet."

She inquires about Leo's condition and suggests it would be better to wait another day and see whether he will not overcome the illness by himself.

Holly then begs her to unveil herself, yet she warns him that she is not destined for him and that he might consume himself because of a hopeless longing for her. But his curiosity is too intense, and finally she yields to his request. Her heavenly beauty, in spite of all purity and charm, is nevertheless frightful and dangerous. She is like the gods, sublime but dark—a miracle, not from heaven, but no less glorious. Her face is that of a woman of barely thirty years, showing the first blossoming of mature beauty, but it is also marked with unutterable experiences and deep acquaintance with grief and passion. Even her lovely smile cannot hide a shadow around her mouth that speaks of sin and sorrow. It shines even in the light of her glorious eyes; it is present in the air of majesty; and it seems to say, "Behold me, lovely as no woman was or is, undying and half divine; memories haunt me from age to age and passion leads me by the hand—evil have I done, evil shall I do, and sorrow shall I know until my redemption comes." Something radiates from her eyes which confuses and blinds Holly.

At this point she notices the scarab. She rises like a serpent who is about to strike. From her eyes a flame-like light breaks forth, and

Holly draws back, terrified. This helps her regain control: "Forgive me, my superhuman spirit becomes impatient over the slowness of your finiteness, and I am tempted to use my power out of vexation. But why do you have the scarab?" At this point, Holly is so confused that he can barely explain that he has found it.

Her face is that of a woman of barely thirty years. At the time of writing *She,* Haggard, too, was thirty years old. The Anima has caught up with him. She has reached his age and has turned into a conscious problem; she mirrors his soul, his experience, his suffering, and his passion. But She is more than that; She is two thousand years old. That is how old the soul is. She was born in the times when the gods died. Before then, she was far removed and dwelled, as the Great Goddess, in the "eternal place." Then, with the decline of the cult of the Great Goddess, the highest values disappeared from consciousness. Later on, a new vessel was discovered in the person of the Virgin. Other aspects of the original feminine image reappear in medieval chivalry, in the belief in witches, and in the Romantic period. Among Protestants the lost values and dangers manifest themselves in the form of projections upon actual women, since goddesses and nature-spirits lack any sense of reality for the enlightened, liberal mind.

The renouncing of a woman, which was the occasion for writing *She,* directed Haggard's focus away from the outer object towards the inner image. The image conjured up by Haggard is endowed with all the magic of an angel and of a serpent. Thus She is wonderful, fascinating, and dangerous; tender, lovely, and evil. She can be ruthless and cold when angered. She as a primary form of feminine nature is an enhanced, overwhelming, irresistible force of passion, a contradiction in the wealth of possible emotions that it contains. She is abysmal in destructive will, unmatched in pride and capacity to suffer. She is the blind will of nature, which is stronger than consciousness. Yet she is a light in nature, full of mysterious knowledge about nature. Not only is she nature and the spirit of nature, but also Soul, *Anima animata,* full of passionate psychic energy.

The name of She-who-is-to-be-obeyed is Ayesha, "the live one";[85] She is life in itself. Ayesha was also the name of Mohammed's favorite wife and daughter of his friend Abu Bakr. Married to the Prophet at the age of six or seven, Ayesha received over a thousand communications from him. After Mohammed's death,

she became "The Mother of the Faithful," and as such she was frequently consulted in questions of orthodoxy and of proper living. She involved herself in the political battles over the succession to the Prophet and was part of many intrigues. Furthermore, she was famous for the story about a necklace which provoked suspicions concerning her adultery with a young man.[86]

This Ayesha had both a niece and a sister-in-law with the same name. The latter, a younger sister of the Prophet, was a poetess. The niece, a granddaughter of Abu Bakr and daughter of Talka and Umm Kulthum, was famous for her beauty. It is said of her that she never veiled her face. When her husband Mus'ab reproached her over this, she allegedly replied, "Since God the Almighty stamped me with the seal of beauty, I want that all men may see me, so that they recognize his grace towards men; therefore I will not veil my face. There is indeed not one defect in me of whom anyone could complain." Since her husband could not master his jealousy, she refused herself to him, reconciling with him only when he returned victoriously from the battle.[87]

The three women with the name of Ayesha encompass the picture of the sister, daughter, and companion of the Prophet: the most beautiful, the most self-satisfied, the intriguing and the spiritual woman, namely, the woman who transmits spiritual values. In terms of historical tradition, this name is well-suited for the Anima. Margaret Smith mentions in her book about Rabi'a the Mystic several equally independent Arabian women who waged war on their own and concluded treaties. Such was Sajah, Harith's daughter, who proclaimed herself a prophetess and intended to attack Abu Bakr.[88]

Just such a daughter of an Arabian chieftain, untamed by patriarchy, is Haggard's Ayesha in her youth. Reared motherless, never taught to keep a household, she lives on her horse and rides into battle with the men. She is one with the active male instincts as an embodiment of the emotions that inspire masculine feats. Yet then she encounters Noot, the wise old priest, who ordains her as a priestess of Isis, as the earthly representative of the Great Goddess, of Mother Nature.

The Anima's turning towards the old wise man of whom she becomes a student reflects a change within man's soul which coincides with puberty. The Anima prepares herself for her future function: a mediator of inner, religious images. She is being withdrawn

from the exterior world, in order to turn towards the inner world and its spiritual contents. As priestess of the heavenly "Great Mother," she attains spiritual heights in which, however, she is unable to remain during the next developmental phase. If a man must create himself a place in this world, he cannot spare the Anima from becoming involved in earthly wishes, though for the priestess they represent sin. Only much later, in the second half of life, can these desires be taken up again after their first appearance during the storms of puberty. Rediscovery of the spiritual Anima and her development now become an inner task. Her relationship to "the old wise man" becomes meaningful only now, inasmuch as he administrates the wisdom of the unconscious. With his assistance one reaches maturity and therewith the fulfillment of old age.

Ayesha and the old Noot are a pair like Solomon and the Queen of Sheba. From the wise old man She has received her interest in the natural sciences. She possesses an alchemical laboratory. The wisdom of the Anima reveals itself in She's comprehensive knowledge and foreknowledge, as well as in her mastery of several ancient languages. When the aged Noot died two thousand years ago, all his knowledge—even the secret of the fire of life—went over to Ayesha.

Noot's death signifies that priestly wisdom has disappeared from the realm of conscious contents, thereby being taken up by the unconscious and the Anima. The Anima creates reality, like Maya, Shakti, and the spinning women of the Chinese.[89] It is unavoidable that Ayesha, in spite of Noot's strong warning, would try out on herself the fire of life that she was charged to guard. Her bathing in this fire results in her feeling superior to the gods, even to Isis, the great mother, and in placing herself beyond good and evil. Wisdom and the power of the gods and their priests have fallen to the unconscious and the Anima. Because of this, under the cover of Christian consciousness there occurs a self-glorification of man, who, Anima-driven, sees himself as the crown of creation and in his hubris no longer recognizes a law above him but thinks there are no limits to his intelligence and power.

In Haggard's mind Ayesha is a human woman who has usurped divine attributes. Just as the Christian receives his heavenly spirit through the baptism of water, so the Anima goes through a baptism of fire in which nature enters her. This fire-spirit finds not

a purified soul, but an ordinary human being tainted with original sin, a woman who, according to the story of the Garden of Eden, is far more accessible to evil than is man. The fire-spirit that takes hold of Ayesha increases in demonic proportions not only her natural beauty but also her "evil" nature. This She is not a savior figure, in spite of her baptism of fire. Rather, like Sophia who fell into Hyle, she herself is in need of deliverance from her inferior nature. She remains a sphinx, though no longer in the monstrous form of a beast, but as a soul who carries within herself the promise and peril of the potential inherent in the sphinx-animal: the deadly coldness of the serpent-body, the grabbing power of the lion-paws, the nourishing, healing fullness and warmth of the emotions, the distancing and seductiveness of the smile, as well as the wings that carry the spirit upwards.

The Anima, like the sphinx, is an iridescent figure. Depending on the man's disposition and his stage of development, she shows him a different face that compensates for or completes his consciousness. She can manifest herself on the most different levels, between animal and goddess, inasmuch as she encompasses life, impulsivity, eros, and spirit. With Haggard, the accent rests mostly on the subtler, immaterial aspects of the soul. Benoit's novel *Atlantide* shows the other aspect. In this widely read, turn-of-the-century novel, Benoit also sketches a fascinating, striking picture which in part is in startling agreement with Haggard's *She*. Benoit was unfairly accused of plagiarism. Inserted here is a brief chapter about Benoit's *Atlantide,* since this French novel completes the picture of the Anima in significant respects.

Benoit's Atlantide

Benoit offers the following etymological explanation for *Antinea,* the name of his Anima-figure. *Antinea* signifies the woman at the prow of a ship; thus she is a Nike or goddess of protection and victory. She can be a priestess, ancient; yet *Antinea* also means the blossoming-one, the striding and flowing-one, the one who spins or weaves, the one who gathers in.[90] These are all designations of the goddess of destiny. As *Nike,* the Anima incites to ac-

tion; she is the goddess of victory who furthers engagement and success in undertakings. As priestess she is the link to impersonal, spiritual powers. Ancient, she encompasses all the past; blossoming, she continues to offer promise for the future. She is the striding-one, life's journey towards a goal; she is the flowing-one, the life that flows from the inexhaustible depth of the collective unconscious. Spinning and weaving, she forms the texture of fate wherein a person gets entangled in good and in evil. As the gathering-one she prepares karma, guilt, experience, curses, and blessings.

Commonly, this destiny-shaping factor remains split-off from consciousness, in the unconscious, and tends to be projected. As long as the Anima is not recognized as part of his own desires and as an aspect of his own soul but, instead, is experienced as an unfamiliar, external event, the man will blame any woman he meets for his destiny. He is not aware that he is driven by internal forces to always select those women who correspond to his unconscious prejudices and that he pushes and influences them until they fit his destiny.

Antinea is the granddaughter of the god of the sea, Neptune. Her mother was a seductress. In this combination is revealed the ambivalence of the Anima-image which shows a different expression depending on how one approaches it. As Neptune's granddaughter, she is a nixie and a goddess, half-fish and half-woman. It is said of her that her body is willing but her soul inexorable. Though she passively offers her body to the daring young men who advance through the deserts towards her, her soul rules. The first queen who does not allow herself to become a slave on account of her passion, she is the only woman who succeeds in separating the two inseparable things: love and lust.[91] Since she is passion itself, she never becomes a slave but remains the mistress of the man whom she enslaves. She takes from the man as much as he is able to give. Through her the man gains experience of the woman who corresponds to his own ability or inability to love. Lust and love are separated in Antinea, because sexuality and feelings are split in the man. If the man seeks only the body, only nature without soul, then he cannot attain the feelings and the entire range of spiritual values. A victim of his own split, he turns into a Don Juan. He only finds as much as he gives or as he is able to receive. That which he really seeks, and that which he could only

find through a full connection of body and soul, eludes him. As long as his soul corresponds to that of Antinea, he cannot appreciate any other type of woman. He is compulsively enslaved by a vamp.

The men who are delivered to Antinea—namely, to this interior reality—are unrelated, incapable of committing themselves to a real woman. Once they leave behind what is for them the arid region of communal life, they begin to sense a fascination from within. They are assaulted by the interior image and irresistibly drawn into its circle. Alcohol and other drugs further this illusory dream life. Searching for a faraway ideal, these men escape reality and its responsibility; they strive for sensory satisfaction, when what they could have is an irrational spiritual experience. Such an experience could bring realization of the wholeness of their own being with its own ordering center. In *Atlantide* they find as the center of life a spring of pure water—the source of the spring of eternally self-renewing life—which flows from the depths of the desert. The center and the spring are in fact reached, but only through regression into death. In a large rock cave illuminated by copper pillars (copper being Venus's element) are already prepared the niches and caskets for 120 mummies, the corpses of the lovers, covered with orichalque.

Orichalque, according to Lippmann, is a copper-containing substance. In alchemy it is used for blanching the black "original matter" (prima materia).[92] The corpses of Antinea's lovers are mummified by being covered with a coppery substance, the metal of the love-goddess. The body as prima materia is ennobled through love and is thus transformed into an early stage of the stone of wisdom. As dead persons, the lovers put on the soul-dress.

The solution thus remains unsatisfactory and incomplete, since the body is conceived of too concretely, rather than symbolically as an image of the need to transform real life. Furthermore, transformation of the body consists only in superficial whitewashing by means of a substance. There is no transformation from within. The alchemical process terminates with the whitewashing, never attaining the goal—namely, pure gold. There is a hint that some insight is being gained into the nature of the previously black, and thus unconscious, contents, but the men remain subjected to the love-goddess Venus (copper), to the Anima, without having gained

wider consciousness (gold) and without having reached the Self. The material body gains in value. The heroes, however, are returned to earth as mummies, remaining there forever in a rigid, unconscious state. They become surrogates for the goddess. Enveloped by a strange glow, but unconscious and effeminate, they are eventually lost to life. Instead of the expansion of consciousness, a regression takes place.

It is significant that not even one of the heroes is wedded to Antinea, the bride: this would mean union of the opposites and achievement of individual wholeness. Instead, there are 120 lovers congregated around one center, approaching an eternal sleep within the magnificent cave. Return to the clan, thus accomplished, replaces the wholeness of the human being with the multitudes of a population relating to one deity. Though each person is distinguished from the next by name and number, nevertheless his destiny remains always the same: a return to the goddess Ishtar from whom already Gilgamesh freed himself, reproaching her for the innumerable lovers she had corrupted.[93] Every single one of Antinea's lovers has forgotten his family, his home, his honor, and everything consciously dear to him. Each loses all because of this addiction into which he drifts, which intoxicates him, to which he submits without battle and to which he succumbs.

The only exception is Morhange who resists Antinea for ascetic, Christian, moral reasons. His scientific curiosity had driven him into the desert. Yet his inexorable attitude is just as ill-suited for bringing forth a solution as is the blind fascination of Saint-Avit, the male protagonist of the story. Morhange's one-sided scientific passion is an expression of the type of extreme masculinity which suppresses and thereby perverts the emergence of eros.

Saint-Avit, "the Anima-possessed" man, searches for the untouched, virginal nature by fleeing from the city into the desert, from his own period into the pre-Christian past. He seeks it by whitewashing the body with orichalque. Though mummification is a rite of rebirth, it is arrested here at the level of overrating the body and thus does not lead to the purification, separation, and new synthesis of the natural human being's elements. In this longing for the "untouched and virginal nature" one recognizes Rousseau's call "back to Nature," which at the turn of the twentieth century brought forth nudism and fanatic vegetarianism, all of which are incomplete and superficial understandings. What was

truly intended was the return to the natural human being and the distillation of "silver" as the quintessence of this inner nature—namely, the conscious rendering of the innermost meaning of human nature.

Saint-Avit's other great longing is for a mysterious love; and he exclaims: "Shame on him who spreads the secrets of love. The Sahara desert encircles Antinea like an impassable barrier. . . . this renders her [this love] more chaste than any marriage and its inevitable publicity."[94] He searches for love as mystery, as a secretive union with the godhead, hidden like the *hierosgamos* (sacred marriage) in the ancient mysteries, segregated from any mixing with the world and its opinions, like the processes in an alchemical flask.

Yet the endeavor for nuptial union of the opposites fails because Saint-Avit murders the moral aspect of his person—portrayed by his friend Morhange, the Christian and scientific spirit—and thereby also fatally wounds himself. Antinea, the Anima, turns him into an assassin. She loves Morhange, the spiritual man, and avenges herself when she receives nothing but coldness and rejection from this ascetic, who unfeelingly remains true to his principles. This explains why Antinea appears as such a cold-blooded, man-killing monster. Benoit states: "Antinea must avenge herself. It is a very ancient struggle, a struggle that goes well beyond the present time. How many barbarous queens of antiquity were exploited by men who, driven by fate upon a foreign shore, became their lovers, only to abandon them or to return as conquerors with troops and ships!"[95] Antinea, the Anima, takes revenge for all faithlessness shown her by men. She is the compensating justice which reaches man from within himself and lets him find his ruin in a mirage, if he is unwilling to accept love as a commitment and responsibility.

Since, as Anima, Antinea has access to the wisdom of the past, she owns an immense library of rare manuscripts lost to the world. However, her wisdom, that of emotions and of the inferior functions, is of minimum interest to the man. In addition, Antinea has a predilection for languages and train schedules, knowing even the smallest details. This skill comes because she deals with time as a concrete reality and because she is so interested in France, her lovers' native land. Among Antinea's victims are the one-sided officers who only know their professional duties and scientists living

solely for research. Other victims were men like Gerard de Nerval[96] or St. Exupery,[97] idealist poets unable to reconcile the wonders of their dream-world with everyday reality, whose genius blew apart the dimensions of their actual life.

With inexorable consistency Antinea murders all her lovers until the mummies, shining like gold, close the circle around her. She lies down to sleep in the center, as if Briar Rose had never obtained the awakening kiss from her knight. As a result of addiction and fanaticism, the individual drifts back into the collective psyche. Longing has reached its goal, the Anima, only to perish, being unable and unwilling to carry back into the conscious, everyday reality the acquired increase of life. The heroes who had set out for the new land do not return.

All too often encounter with the Anima ends in such a disastrous way unless, through the ego's strength, dikes are erected against the eruption of the unconscious.

The Reverse Side of the Heart

Holly is frightened when he realizes that She must be two thousand years old, for this means that he is dealing with the primordial experience of the feminine, with the other half of creation and the godhead. Ayesha is everything that stands in opposition to the consciousness of his time. She is simultaneously liveliness itself and a continuous death-threat, nature as well as mediator to the spirit embodied in the aged Noot. She moves like a serpent; like a serpent she rises in anger. Like the serpent Kundalini of the Tantra-Yoga,[98] she is the energy hidden in nature. Ayesha is the unmediated inner experience and the inner truth as revealed in anger and desire when these are not deflected or hidden by prudence or by considerations of external rules. Neither good nor evil, she represents the reactions born directly from instinct, concerned with no law or moral beyond their own nature-given, stormy will. She stretches from the roots of bestiality to the glaciers of the spirit, from Kali up to Paravati, the golden mountain-goddess. Haggard's novel *She and Allan* speaks for her as "She who veils her head like the peak of a mountain."

The encounter with Ayesha shocks Holly. Though he has been a woman-hater since his early youth, he knows he will never forget those eyes. This woman's devilishness which terrifies and repels Holly attracts him at the same time. He feels close to madness, pulled back and forth by repulsion and admiration.

Suddenly, he remembers he must look after Leo whom he has almost forgotten because of his encounter with She. Holly finds Leo even sicker than before. As much as Holly is deeply affected by She, he does not want his friend to die, even if the latter should become an obstacle to his relations with Ayesha.[99]

An inner restlessness keeps Holly awake during the night. He leaves his room and discovers a hallway and a staircase through which he reaches Kallikrates' burial chamber. In front of the Greek's mummy, Ayesha convulses with longing and despair. Holly overhears her. Filled with blind passion and dreadful vengefulness, she hurls curse after curse against the Egyptian princess, Amenartas. He feels as if he has heard a soul in hell.

Holly is witnessing the secret of the mistress soul. The reasonable English gentleman, who raised Leo in a strictly Christian tradition, Holly must look down into the soul's abyss and discover that it is haunted by passion and vengefulness. It is no wonder that, in the secure university environment, Holly was more afraid of women than of a rabid dog.

Antinea takes revenge on men and turns them into playthings for her desires. Ayesha, on the other hand, curses Amenartas, her rival and wife of Kallikrates, since she sees in her the obstacle to the realization of her wishes. Deep down, however, it is not so much the wife who stops the husband from his own growth, but it is his own justified fear of an insoluble conflict regarding the dangerous wishes and demands of his Anima. Sometimes the Gordian knot is then abruptly cut by means of a divorce, when it would be more meaningful to remain faithful in one's commitment to marriage while not evading the conflict of the feelings within.

The following morning Leo is even weaker. Billali believes that he will not survive the evening. Meanwhile, Holly is summoned to Ayesha's court where She condemns the native evildoers to be tortured. If any survives, he is to be killed with the incandescent pot. Holly tries to soften her, but she replies that she reigns not by power but by terror and that, if she were not merciless, Holly's and Leo's lives would be in daily jeopardy. She adds: "My moods

resemble the small clouds which seem to drift aimlessly hither and thither; yet behind them blows the great wind of my purpose." The Anima of the heart avenges the transgressions of the primitive instincts.

Haggard was often reproached for the cruelty and bloodthirstiness of his books. He would reply that he simply presented reality as it was and as he had seen it in Africa. In the presence of savages, of a primitive tribe, where sovereignty is not based on genuine relationships or reason, one relies on cruel means to remain as ruler. Though European civilization fancied itself Christianized, its subjugation of foreign populations easily fanned and maintained the white Anima's fire of gruesomeness. Of the Boers, Haggard says they were disliked by all for their hardness and cruelty towards the natives. Yet he later recognized that in his youth he had judged them unfairly, by not taking into consideration the difficult conditions under which they had to live. In the Boers one clearly observes the effect of colonization upon the white people's soul. They lived widely scattered amongst warlike tribes without any protection from allies. Thus, they asserted themselves against the blacks only through violence.

Following the court session, She invites Holly to visit the burial caves, and in his curiosity he seems to forget Leo. It is possible to forget the present for the sake of the inner world of images, but also on account of collecting antiquities. Scientific interest can divorce itself completely from feelings.

Once they enter the city of the dead within the mountain, with its innumerable gravesites, however, Holly finally connects with his feelings. As Ayesha shows him a young couple united in death, Holly has a vision where the mummy before him is a pale young girl being escorted to wed an elderly man in purple clothes. Suddenly, a young man rushes out of the crowd and kisses her. In the same moment, guards fatally stab the youth, and the girl grabs the dagger and takes her own life. Although this is a fantasy image, Haggard asks himself at this point, "What is fantasy? Maybe fantasy is but the shadow of a truth that cannot be grasped; maybe it is a thought of the soul!"

Perhaps this vision mirrors Holly's own repressed wishes. Or it may cast Holly as a representative of tradition, where he sees himself as the old king. The young bride was to be given in marriage to the old man. The ancient ruler—the traditional, estab-

lished principle—demands that the soul, the feelings, unite with him. Yet the bride has grown up loving a youth who embodies the new truth, a not-yet-recognized form of consciousness. The new principle breaks through at the very moment the old principle wants to propagate itself unchanged. Since the times are not yet ripe for the new truth, the young couple's only possibility is union in death. This is indeed the bitter shadow of Rider Haggard's problem: a new order of things, a new orientation, seeks to assert itself within him, but the old principles and conventions are still too strong. His feelings have only the options of either bending before the predominant lifestyle or, as the inner, new truth breaks forth, showing allegiance to the new principle through self-sacrifice.

She is not ready to dismiss Holly so that he can attend to Leo. Holly has seen her torn by emotions during the night, yet ice-cold while in court and magnificently somber near the dead. Now she appears to him as radiant Aphrodite, as ecstatic life, as the quintessence of seductive femininity, and more perfect and spiritual than any other woman. Holly thus falls to her feet, stating he would risk his immortal soul to be allowed to marry her, for "who could ever resist her when she emanates her force."[100] Yet Ayesha laughs at him, saying that she is not destined for him but only wanted to demonstrate to an old bachelor her power. She is rich in changeable moods, like a mirror which reflects everything without changing itself. Later, She and Holly philosophize about religion. Here, too, She is a mirror of opinions that seem familiar to Holly, but he never finds out what She thinks, nor is he capable of convincing her of his position—for, in fact, She represents the possibilities that oppose consciousness. Just like Shakti mirrors the thoughts of Shiva, so Ayesha mirrors every imaginable concept. Like Maya, She is the variegated veil of wishes and illusions; if one follows her, one gets caught in the net of desires.

Finally, She and Holly visit Leo and find him drawing his last breaths. Caught up in the changing play of moods and discussions, the Anima has nearly forgotten the present moment: namely Leo, the beloved, for whom she has waited such a long time. Now she recognizes in him the reborn Kallikrates who again is at death's edge. Her mixed potion pulls him back to life. Like Isis, She has healing powers.

Then She sees Ustane at Leo's bedside and tries to turn her away,

but Ustane refuses to obey. Thereupon She presses three fingers upon Ustane's hair, marking her like Cain with a white sign. To this magic superiority, Ustane must yield. Leo's first question upon awakening is about Ustane, and Ayesha lies: "She wanted to leave!" The Anima may resort to lying to achieve her purpose. She suggests to the man what to believe, since she pleads her own truth and pursues her own goals which are often opposite to conscious intentions.

The Feast of the Animal Masks and Epiphany

A feast is celebrated to honor Leo's recovery. Mummies are piled upon a pyre and lighted; others burn as upright torches. In this awesome setting the savages play a game of murder and of being buried alive. Suddenly a woman is possessed by a demon. He asks for a black buck's blood and leaves her in peace only after he has obtained it. Thereupon begins a dance with animal-masks: lions, leopards, bucks, and even a serpent's skin which a woman drags far behind her. A leopard succeeds in gaining Leo's attention, enticing him into the dark. It is Ustane who wants to escape with him. But She discovers them immediately. Facing certain death, Ustane shouts to her enemy that even She will not obtain Leo as her husband in this life. With that she collapses, killed by the queen's will.

Leo attacks the murderous She with a curse. Ayesha cannot see any evil in the execution of her sentence; she has simply removed an obstacle to her love. And now, beside Ustane's corpse, she unveils herself for the first time in front of Leo, "like Venus who emerges from the waves, like Galatea who emerges from stone, and like a blessed spirit from the grave." In spite of his inner reluctance, Leo cannot escape this sorcery. Seemingly, all manliness is taken from him. Holly has already observed in himself how this woman destroys all his moral sense. Similarly, Leo senses that he pays with his honor in succumbing so rapidly to Ustane's murderess. He despairs and thinks of escaping, but he cannot sacrifice what he has finally achieved, since it has already taken possession of him. Stunned to see how quickly Leo becomes the

prey of this sorcery, Holly tells him that his sin will eventually return to haunt him. "Yet the temptress who seduces him towards evil is more beautiful than the daughters of human beings."

At the feast that She prepares for Leo and Holly, mountains of mummies burn in a large fire. Fire festivals, known in all cultures, expel evil and encourage the rebirth of light and the increase of fertility.[101] Such rites of spring we see preserved, for example, in the Zürich *Sechselaeuten*-festival. Closely linked to winter's death is the epiphany of the spring-godhead and her holy wedding. The old, rigid forms dissolve in the fire, transformed into new life. Masked festivals also belong to the winter and spring rites in Ur and Sumer where animal masks accompany the gods to the holy wedding.[102] In Egypt the gods themselves wear animal heads.

Even now animal and ghost masks are common in winter festivals and carnivals. The animal-mask festival, a primitive rite, reconnects us with the animal soul, thereby assisting life's renewal. Thus, the Anima brings to light the psyche's dark background. As the Great Goddess, she is also mistress of the animals.[103] The possessed woman's desire for the black-buck blood reminds one of the blood-intoxication which seized the Greek women honoring Dionysus. The god, in the guise of a kid, was dismembered, and the maenads (his female followers) tore apart young roebucks and drank their blood. Here the primordial, wild, ecstatic nature, repressed by patriarchal society, broke through. Worthy Athenian matrons, seized by blood-intoxication, streaked through the forest until, exhausted and then renewed, they returned to the narrowness of their homes.

In the animal-mask dance the unconscious's beastly aspect shows itself once again. As a game of the savages, however, it does not touch the heroes but ends without being interpreted. Nevertheless, it is a force that cannot be ignored, to which one must find a relationship if the quest is to succeed. Just as in fairy tales, it is the animals who often assist the struggling humans to solve a seemingly impossible task. The shaman must learn the language of animals to execute his journey into heaven and into the netherworld. In this quest, he must change himself into an animal by imitating animal voices and by wearing animal masks, feathers, and skins.[104]

When Ustane, in the shape of a leopardess, a fighting cat-

mother, undertakes to reach her lover again, she runs into She's jealous wakefulness. Ayesha had already marked Ustane with a sign on her forehead, thereby signaling her fate. Thus Ustane becomes the scapegoat and sacrificial animal. Unwilling to relinquish Leo voluntarily, she is simply destroyed by her rival. In the cases of Amenartas and Jess, faithfulness to the spouse and respect for universal moral laws led to the sacrifice of the beloved object and of inner truth. Now She strikes back and murders Ustane. In so doing, Ayesha obstructs the realization of her wishes. Ustane has prophesied that She will not reach, in this life, her goal of union with the beloved. Ustane represents the other, darker, earthier manifestation of the Great Goddess. Ayesha must also eventually reach the ground, the blood, the emotions, the earthly reality. By killing Ustane she separates herself, through guilt, from this ground. As goddess and Anima she denies her own dark, instinct-bound side. In other words, the Anima must not eliminate the wife.

Yet, "the seductress was more beautiful than the daughters of human beings!" The compelling force that flows from her destroys not only the man's persona but also his moral stance and thus his self-respect. If a certain woman provokes such moral danger, she does so only because the man's Anima is projected upon her. "More beautiful than the daughters of human beings": in these words we are reminded of the sons of god who descended from heaven to the daughters of human beings.[105]

Ayesha is her own law. Her natural will is so powerful that it challenges the entire human being to commit himself to the realization of her goal. Her will is also so ruthless that it recognizes no crime. The Great Goddess does not acknowledge morality in the male-patriarchal sense. The man, therefore, is justifiably afraid of Anima-possession. Her enticements must blind him to her ruthlessness. The greatest moral efforts are required to assert oneself against the Anima's unreasonable demands. A man must persevere in fulfilling his duties when he feels overwhelmed by his desires for love and life. The hunger for life that breaks forth from his unconscious must be confronted continually with conscious values and standards. He must attempt to find a balance—tolerable to the entirety of his person—between unconscious impulses and conscious morality. It is a matter of broadening the personality and

accepting conscious responsibility, a deliberate change from the previous tendency to let oneself drift or to shut one's eyes so as not to see what one is really doing.

Standing beside Ustane's corpse, Ayesha intones:

> "There is only one perfect flower in the wilderness of Life.
> That flower is Love!
> There is only one fixed star in the mists of our wanderings.
> That star is Love!
> There is only one hope in our despairing night.
> That hope is Love!
> All else is false. All else is shadow moving upon water.
> All else is wind and vanity."

And She concludes:

> "Crowned shall we be with the diadem of Kings.
> Worshiping and wonder-struck all peoples of the world
> Blinded shall fall before our beauty and our might
> From time unto times shall our greatness thunder on."

Because Leo falls in love with her (in spite of the murder), her intoxication with her victory grows enormously towards a fantasy of world-domination. Terrified, Holly and Leo try to enlighten her about the facts of external reality and to make it clear that her "blasting methods" would be unacceptable in England. Yet She simply laughs, claiming to be above any human law.

In an overwhelming and repugnant way, She is extremely possessive. This possessiveness has many roots which we must explore since intoxication with power is the great danger from the unconscious that assails individuals. As the feminine side, as emotion and irrational force, the Anima is suppressed by the man's consciousness, which aims for what is useful, prudent, and rational. But the Anima's natural and fundamental claim on life becomes immense and intolerable because nature, love, and emotions are disparaged.

Another root of Ayesha's greed for power lies in Haggard's own circumstances. At just nineteen years old, he became secretary to the highest authorities in Africa. Wherever he went with his

superiors, they received royal honors. When twenty-one, he became a high magistrate. Through all this he retained his human, Christian disposition. On the one hand an ordinary English citizen, he nevertheless was almost a king among both blacks and whites. When he returned to England, however, he had to act as if nothing inside him had changed. The power he had exercised fell to the unconscious, the Anima.

The third root of She's superior force is her bath in the fire of life, where she became one with the creative dynamics of the unconscious. The crown she promises to her beloved is the crown of wholeness, a symbol of the Self.[106]

Now a sinister scene follows. Ayesha leads the two men to Kallikrates' mummy, in order to demonstrate to Leo, in front of this image, her two-thousand-years-old love. She then destroys the corpse. By this confrontation with Kallikrates, Leo becomes aware that the age-old drama repeats itself, that his life imitates an archetypal event. The image of Kallikrates, wounded in his side and mourned by the goddess, reminds one of the precursors of the Pietà, of the mother-goddess of Asia Minor who weeps over her son-lover whose death, as a yearly sacrifice, she must decree. It is the drama of the Great Mother who never allows her son to grow up because she wants to retain all the power. She loves him as child and youth, as her creation. When he resists her in order to grow up, she slays him in anger.

Now that the beloved son is resurrected, however, the holy marriage is to be celebrated. Leo is bound no longer to a mother-wife but to a sister-beloved. To unite himself, as an equal, with the goddess, he is to be changed into a demigod by bathing in the fire of life. Holly, on the other hand, will renounce such a prolongation of life, as he would otherwise torture himself for millennia, longing for Ayesha.

The Temple of Truth

The following morning they start out for the fire of life. They cross the city of ruins, and in the evening they reach a temple in which they pass the night. Inside the temple, in the center of a

court, on top of a cubic rock on which rests a large sphere made of black rock, they find a colossal statue. This winged figure of a woman is naked except for her veiled face. Below, the inscription reads: "Is there no man who will draw my veil and look upon my face, for it is very fair? Unto him who draws my veil shall I be, and I will give him peace, and sweet children of knowledge and good works." And a voice cried, "Though all those who seek after thee desire thee, behold! Virgin are thou, and Virgin thou shalt be till Time be done. There is no man born of woman who may draw thy veil and live. By Death only can thy veil be drawn, O Truth!" These words recall the goddess of Sais[107] who, as an early Great Goddess, also held the keys to the netherworld, thus encompassing both aspects, life and death.

Here, at the beginning of the great adventure which Kallikrates could not master, we see Holly and Leo confronted with the Truth, with an image and symbol that is to prepare them to descend to the fire of life. In the sacred, enclosed court of the temple, upon a cube and sphere, stands a nude, winged figure. In the first place it is the naked truth of the body, human nature as such. However, it is not only the body but, as evidenced by the wings, also the soul. No longer does the sphinx rule here, for she has shed the animal body. Human reality points beyond itself to a spiritual realm: the Anima is an angel, a messenger from the air who barely touches the earth and who is always ready to fly to other spheres.

We may also view the dark sphere as the earth's and the figure as *Anima mundi* or "soul of the earth." Visible only in her naked body, as matter, the figure is veiled in terms of her deeper meaning. Only at death does she unveil her face, only when she carries the human being across into a world of spirit and meaning in which she participates.

The dark sphere, however, is also the great roundness, the encompassing whole made visible, the Self from its dark side resting upon the cubic rock symbolizing its realization in the world. The winged figure addressing the human being is simultaneously goddess and soul, the truth of the world and the truth of this individual human being, a mediator between the reality of the earth and the realm of the spirit. Here in the inner sanctum of the ancient temple, in the city of the heart, stands an effigy that points beyond time, beyond what has been achieved. For an instant the Anima's meaning becomes transparent. She is the inner truth, the

soul's immediate reality; as mediator she shows the way to the gods, to the primordial images, and to meaning. Sister of the paradisiacal serpent, She would like to seduce the man, that he may not only know good and evil but also recognize the truth of what he himself is in terms of good and evil. Yet the price and condition of recognizing the whole truth—not only the physical reality but also meaningfulness—is, as in the Garden of Eden, death.

"She-who-is-to-be-obeyed" is the live truth as a man experiences it in the heart's mandala. She is the changing play of his contradictory, subjective emotions which may act as compulsions and among which he often gets lost. He feels seduced, fascinated, repelled by his own abysmal potentials for irrationality and yearning. Whereas in his earlier experience the man was but the passive victim of his condition, however, he now can see what is being played and can value what happens to him. What has been transmitted from the past, religion and philosophy, gains in meaningfulness, though Holly does not know what to believe. Thoughts and emotions resemble drifting clouds which keep changing and convey somewhat deceptive meanings. Good and evil become relative. Real is the external environment by which one feels unavoidably trapped, as by Kor's rocky walls. Equally real are the drives which originate in the Anima and which represent a changing, iridescent, internal, instantaneous truth, in contrast to external reality.

Whereas She is the truth as a man finds it in Kor, in his heart, She is not yet the transcendent truth as it appears in the veiled/unveiled temple figure. Dominated by subjective wishes and greed for power, She wants to gain possession, no matter at whose expense. She becomes like a tornado which eliminates every obstacle in her path.

Yet also in Ayesha signs appear which point to a higher truth. "Like Venus from the waves, like Galatea from the stone, like a blessed spirit from the grave," so she too steps out from her dark cloak, and her presence is accompanied by fragrance and the silver bells of her laughter. During the celebration of the epiphany, everyday reality and matter are changed into divine presence.

The concreteness of spiritual presence, the truth to be unveiled already exist in the form of a presentiment. The journey to its realization leads through death. Omens of death have become numerous. In a vision, Holly has seen the death of the young cou-

ple; the spirit of Job's deceased father has appeared to him to announce his early death. Most of all, Ayesha has carried evil forebodings since she murdered Ustane.

Transitus

The next morning they start out before dawn and reach the crater of the volcano which towers before them as a steep wall of rock. Here they leave behind all the servants. Only Job begs to be allowed to proceed with them. Ayesha consents and has him carry a large plank. They come to a fissure in the rocks, a natural cave through which they reach an abyss inside.

This path was not cut by human hands into the volcano's ancient rocks. It was made by nature itself, either by the earth's convulsions or lightning blasts. Eruptions either of the innermost fiery nature or of cosmic energies have been at work. The heroes enter this very old rock formation—namely, the deepest foundation of being—following a path formed by natural forces. This path is neither found nor traveled without distress, as the soul's depth is approached only through massive upheavals.

A rocky ledge, stretching across the abyss to the crater's middle, quivers in the gathering storm. The travelers must cross this rocky bridge that juts out into what appears to be a void. They seem to be hanging between sky and earth in the midst of a dark, raging storm which whirls clouds and vapors around them. A sudden gust of wind carries Ayesha's dark coat into the void. Without her dark cover, the white figure seems to be "a ghost riding upon the storm towards the depths." Reaching the ledge's beginning, they cling to the trembling rock in complete darkness. Here they must wait until a ray of the setting sun breaks through a crack in the opposite rocky wall; in this narrow light-shaft, they will be able to see the entry into the inner crater. On the crater's edge rests a flat stone, balancing like a coin precariously placed on the edge of a water glass. They lay the plank, which Job has been carrying, across to this stone. Crossing over this wavering bridge, they reach the inner crater. Job, the last one to dare to cross, slips. Holly's grip keeps him from disappearing into the depths.

This dreadful crossing leads them towards still greater depths, while storms and clouds rage around them. The experience resembles that of Goethe's Faust when he descends to the "mothers." The heroes are caught in storms of the spirit, and no one knows whether this path will lead to death or rebirth. This precarious passage across the protruding ledge between sky and earth powerfully expresses the great risks one faces when entering total insecurity, the powers of the unconscious. There can be no simple return.

Here, in the midst of the raging storm, the Anima reveals herself as spirit. Similar to a light, she is the only one who knows about the path. Only She possesses the self-assurance that knows when to wait or to act, in order to reach the goal known only to her. She only knows that there will be an instant when the path becomes visible, when a light ray will fall, like a cutting sword, into the darkness and across the abyss: a moment of intuitive insight. When facing such an abyss that separates without and within, great care and all one's masculine courage are required to risk the transitus (the passing) and the complete renunciation of the external world. When on our internal journey we meet seemingly insurmountable difficulties, when reason fails, then we are entirely dependent on the light from within, on the advice, warnings, and explanations in our dreams. The Anima who previously seemed to be sheer seduction can then prove herself as a helpful light.

The crossing is possible only because Job carries the plank the way Simon carried the cross, or Attis the fir. He is the human aspect who takes upon himself the cross and death. When a hero seeks a new path, the human ego's load becomes heavy. Yet this load, this apparently impossible situation, eventually bridges the abyss, so that the inner center, the life-secret, is reached. The insoluble problem becomes the bridge between seeming opposites.

The balancing stone hovers on the crater's edge in a fashion that seems to contradict its weight. Haggard comments that it may be a glacial stone which is dancing on the narrow crest. This stone upon which they land is a place of contradictions where opposites paradoxically touch each other.

In his book *Shamanism,* Mircea Eliade describes how the above-mentioned situation belongs to "the complex of the difficult transition": the near-invisible entrance into the rocks, the narrow passage, the dangerous, nearly impossible crossing of the abyss on

a path "tread only by spirits and by the dead." He adds, however, that a few living individuals dare to make this transition: the shaman during an ecstasy, the hero through his force and courage, or the initiate through ritual dying and rebirth, or the old wise man.[108] Eliade quotes Coomaraswamy as saying that this paradoxical crossing can be accomplished only when one transcends an apparent dichotomy. The shaman who overcomes this difficulty proves he is a spirit and no longer an ordinary human being. He strives to reestablish the original condition where human and superhuman levels were not as yet separated, the original wholeness of the cosmos.[109] Eliade also describes the journey into hell, in contrast to the ascent to heaven. Descent to the netherworld, far more difficult, has rarely been described. Potanin pictures it as a long voyage south across a mountain range to the iron mountain which touches the sky and which the shaman climbs. On its other side he finds the entrance to the netherworld, the chimney of the earth, as smoke leaving from a man's abode. Across a bridge thin as a hair, passing skeletons and scenes from hell, he reaches Erlik Khan, the master of the underworld.[110]

The heroes travel the age-old, archetypal path which leads to the dead, to the ancestors, and to the gods. At this destination Leo is to unite himself with Ayesha, the spirit with the soul. The arduous path corresponds to the task's difficulty. Transition into the new condition demands a suspended balance between opposites, a balance jeopardized by Job who, through his fear, endangers the others. Holly's strength and skill save him. Job imperils the enterprise because of his rigidity and fear of anything unfamiliar; an overly narrow, Protestant, conventional attitude endangers Haggard. For a narrow-minded human being whose ego is chained to the everyday world, such a path is impassable. He requires the intervention of the transpersonal, archetypal figure, the hero or the wise man.

The travelers now descend into the crater and reach a rock hall where Noot, the wise old man, teacher of the Anima, died as a hermit two thousand years before. One of his teeth remains. This white tooth that has lasted throughout time is like the seed of Yang in the Yin of the Chinese cosmology, the seed of light in the darkness. Noot, the genuine wise-old-man, stands behind the Anima. With his intelligence, Holly represents only a small part of humanity's wisdom which is personified in Noot.

The Anima has received her knowledge from the archetype of the wise old man. Through him comes her power. He showed her the path to life's secret but he also warned her, just as God warned Eve in paradise about the fruits of knowledge. Ayesha, however, would not be Eve's daughter were she content with the knowledge. She must test it for herself. As the old man's daughter she turns his formidable knowledge into a dangerous, god-forbidden action. The renewal of life by the Anima does not stop at the head, at the accumulation of knowledge. It encompasses the entire human being, even his unconscious functions that are not subject to his will. If a man, urged by the Anima, tries to translate his thoughts into action, they become concrete and real. If he feels responsible for his thoughts, he becomes careful. If he acts with a conscious sense of responsibility, he can become wise.

Noot is dead, and She has usurped his secret. She owns "forces that act like electricity." Because these are a part of life's hidden fire, she becomes dangerous like sudden powerful flashes of lightning, impulsively driving a man to act before he is able to reflect. Whenever the Anima within him is touched, she reacts unreflectively and is therefore very convincing to him. He is in constant danger of being carried along by her moods and inhumanity. Only through great effort can he free himself of this Anima-possession, and only then is he capable of separating himself from his "compelling emotions" and from the so-called "power of the instincts."

Haggard relates that, during her two thousand years of exile, She was busy exploring the forces of nature. Though the goddess was no longer to be found in heaven nor in the temple, she could still be met in nature.

In Noot's hermit cave, She relates once more the tale of Kallikrates' death, of her guilt, and of her despair. Leo's love must become her door to redemption. She asks his forgiveness, and he forgives her to the extent that it is in his power. For the first time he is not only fascinated but also filled with love. Because he loves her, she is ready to submit herself to him. She bends her knee before him and kisses him to prove her womanly love. After this she forswears all evil and ambition, promising herself to Leo for all time to come. Her bridal gift is to be the "starry crown of her beauty," eternal life, unlimited wisdom, and boundless wealth. The mighty ones of the earth will bow before him, the beautiful women will be blinded by his looks, and the wise will seem small in com-

parison to him. He will lead others according to his will. Like the sphinx he is to reign over them for all time, and they will ask him to reveal the riddle of his greatness, yet he will respond with silence. With these offerings, She places the world at his feet; like a god he is to hold good and evil in his hands. She thus submits herself to him, to her master, the beloved of Ra, the master of all.

The instant Leo loves her, she becomes humble and subjects herself to him. She wishes to transfer her godly attributes to him, exalting him beyond any human measure and making him the worthy companion of the mistress of the cosmos. She promises him no less than deification. Becoming one with god is the aim of all mysteries and of all mysticism. Yet purification, sacrifice, and conscious subordination of the ego to the godhead must always precede this process. Ayesha, the consecrating priestess, however, feels superior to Isis. Since she entered the fire of life and united with it as with a god, she no longer feels responsible to anyone nor bound by any law. Only where she both loves and is loved in return can she give herself, offering to her beloved the exhilarating gifts of superhuman power, wisdom, and beauty. She intends to infuse him with her wishes and goals, thus turning him into an extension of herself. Her bridal gift is an inflation of cosmic proportions; it is the gift of her own godliness which, if misused, can lead to a boundless intoxication with power.

This scene has yet another aspect. In the last analysis She herself is the Great Goddess, and she wants Leo to become like her. Leo would have to allow himself to be reformed and deified in the fire of life so that all the earthliness would burn out of him. Leo and She are the divine couple, be it called Sol and Luna, Helios and Selene, or Isis and Osiris. Luna, who otherwise submits herself to no one, yields to the stronger light of Sol. Carrying within her all the life of nature and of the unconscious, she brings it to her beloved son.[111] Helios and Horus (both also sun symbols) are consciousness quietly hovering over the earth.

However, inasmuch as Leo is a human being and insofar as these ancient images of the god's holy wedding awaken within the human being's soul, there is not only the opportunity for renewal of life and consciousness but also the danger of hubris, of unbounded pride. A reflection of the superhuman figures falls upon the human being who experiences such events. It elevates and

transports him. Thus everything depends on his not allowing himself to be blinded or inflated by these powerfully meaningful images. If he is cognizant of his shadow-aspects, they can be a healthy counterweight against the enthusiasm that flows from these images. He must not forget his social position and his daily professional duties. On the contrary, he must pursue them with increased seriousness, fulfill them with added concentration, and devote himself with additional efforts to the care of his family. The inner experiences may entice the human being away from reality. Instead, they should serve to make him into a whole person, who devotes himself more fully than before and with his entire soul to his daily tasks. The internal wedding aims for the inner reconciliation of opposites, for the amalgamation of spirit and soul, for the connection of thinking and feeling, of rationality and irrationality. The powerful experiences must render the human being more, and not less, conscious, more fit for the fulfillment of his internal as well as external tasks.

In order to complete the marriage of Sun and Moon, the group takes the lamps and descends a stone stairway into the crater's depths to the fire of life, with Ayesha, light as a mountain goat, leading the way. The travelers descend the way Faust descended to the mothers. As he was guided by Mephistopheles, by the curiosity of eternally dissatisfied reason, so Leo is guided by Ayesha, the desire for heightened life. Mephisto and Ayesha are the two aspects of Mercury, of that spirit hidden in matter and in the soul who longs for consciousness.[112] Crawling on the crater's floor, Holly, Leo, and Job reach an immense cave where, in absolute silence, like lost souls in hell, they continue to follow the white, ghostlike figure of Ayesha. Through another passage they enter a smaller cave which ends in a third passage. A dim glow emanates from within.

"It is well," She says, "to prepare to enter the very womb of the Earth, wherein she does conceive the Life that ye see brought forth in man and beast—aye, in every tree and flower."

The caves through which they walk are graves. The path leads into the "untrod, not to be treaded." Mother Earth is also Mother Death: Cybele carries Attis, her son, in the form of a fir into a cave, there to mourn him.[113] Here everything that has been reaches its end, yet from the womb of Mother Death grows ever-

new life. A cave-like stable became the place of birth in Bethlehem,[114] and in Eleusis the mysteries of birth occurred in the darkness of a cave.[115]

Finally they arrive in the third cave, illuminated by a golden light. Threefold is the dark Hekate of the netherworld, three are the goddesses of destiny, mothers of what becomes and of what passes away. This threesome from the netherworld is mentioned by Mephistopheles advising Faust—"a glowing tripod will tell you that you are on the deepest, the very deepest ground." The small group has reached the place of the inferior threesome which stands over against the Trinity, the place of the earth's creative principle. Then with gnashing, thundering noise—so horrendous that everyone trembles and Job falls on his knees—there comes from the cave's distant end a dreadful, flaming fire-pillar, multicolored like the rainbow and bright like lightning. The pillar slowly turns about itself, and finally the awesome noise leaves behind only the golden light.

"Draw near," Ayesha calls to them. "Behold the very fountain and heart of life, the bright spirit of the earth without which it cannot live. Draw near and wash yourself in the living flames and take their virtue upon your poor bodies."

They follow her to the end of the cave, where the great pulse beats and where the flame dances. They are filled with such wild and wonderful intoxication, with such a great intensity of life, that whatever peak experiences they had had before seem flat in comparison. They laugh; they feel inspired. Holly speaks in verses of Shakespearian beauty, with ideas surging in him, and his spirit feels free, able to ascend to the very heights of its original potentials.

The flames come closer and closer as if all the sky's wheels of thunder were rolling behind the horses of lightning. The view is so overwhelming that all but She sink to the ground and bury their faces in the sand.

"Now, Kallikrates," She says, "when the great flame comes again you must bathe in it. Throw aside your garments, for it will burn them though thee it will not hurt. Thou must stand in the fire while thy senses endure, and when it embraces thee, suck the fire into thy very heart and let it leap and play around thy every part so that thou lose no moiety of its virtue. Hearest thou me, Kallikrates?"

"I hear thee, Ayesha," answers Leo, "but of a truth—I'm not a coward—I doubt me of that raging flame. How do I know that it will not utterly destroy me, so I will lose myself and lose thee also? Nevertheless I will do it."

Ayesha reflects for an instant, then she says, "It is no surprise that you hesitate; but tell me, will you also enter the flame if you see me unharmed inside it?"

"Yes," he answers, "I will enter, even if it slays me. I have said that I will enter now."

"See now, I will for the second time bathe me in this living bath. Fain would I add to my beauty and my length of days if that be possible. If it be not possible, at least it cannot harm me."

Yet She has a deeper reason for this decision. She would like to cleanse herself of the passion and hatred that is burned into her soul. Thus it is as if "Kallikrates" or Leo is to ready himself for death; for from the seed of this moment will spring forth the fruit of what he will be for endless time.

Now the rotating pillar of fire comes again, from far, far away. She drops her garments and stands there the way Eve stood before Adam. "Oh, my beloved," she murmurs, "will you ever know how much I loved you?"

With that she places herself in the column's path. The fire approaches slowly and surrounds her with its flames. The fire runs up her figure, and she lifts it like water and pours it over herself. She draws it in with her lungs. It plays like golden threads in her hair and shines from her eyes which are still brighter than the pillar. Suddenly there is a change. The smile disappears; the face becomes pointed; she turns old and shrivels. As she touches her hair, it falls to the ground. Now she looks like a poorly preserved, unspeakable old mummy with thousands of wrinkles.

She still asks, "How can the principle of life change?" and dying, she says, "Kallikrates, do not forget me, have pity on my shame—I shall come again and shall once more be beautiful."

Job falls down dead from the frightful shock. Leo and Holly, after having been dazed for a long time, shaken and exhausted, begin their way back. Leo's golden curls have turned gray. While they are waiting on the balancing stone for the sun ray which is to illuminate their passage to the external crater, a gust of wind brings back Ayesha's lost coat and covers Leo with it. Since the plank is gone, they must now jump across the abyss. As the last

one crosses, the balancing boulder crashes into the internal crater and forever closes off the path into the depths.

Eventually, they find Billali who guides them through the swamps. After many more adventures they return to their college in Cambridge.

The "pillar of fire" has such horrendous, frightful power that the heroes throw themselves to the ground. To explore its various aspects, we must first deal with the meaning of ordinary fire. Fire burns, destroys, and shines. In the hearth it warms and glows, and when used for cooking, it modifies foods. Fire is one of the foundations of human culture; its taming is an important but dangerous step which brings human beings closer to the gods. In Ustane's land we encountered hearth fire. From the viewpoint of psychological experience, this was the place of burning passions, of love, which all too easily can turn into burning hatred. When passion mounts to the head, "the brain is burned," consciousness is extinguished. This is the libido, the instinctual energy hidden within the body, which can either express itself in blind rage or transmute itself into purposeful will, thereby creating culture.

Yet the fire of life is more supernatural than natural. It lights up like lightning and roars like thunder. It burns dead matter, yet heightens life. The creative spirit inside earth's womb, it creates all life. It is both a cosmic fire and a spiritual essence with a hidden, creative mystery. Dwelling in the continually rotating motion at the center of the earth, at the innermost place, it becomes the fountain of inexhaustible energies.

If we look for parallels of this magic fire, we encounter them in Heraclitus and Simon Magus. For Heraclitus "fire metamorphoses itself into the All, and the All metamorphoses itself back into fire, just as gold changes itself into coins and coins change into gold." "This world, the same for everyone, was created by neither god nor human being, but it was, is, and will be forever a live fire which periodically lights up."[116] This same periodicity we see in the Indian myths of creation, where the world alternatively becomes visible and then vanishes, shaped by Shiva the destroyer and creator who dances in the circle of fire. Heraclitus states, "fire is want and satiety. It is desire, greed and fulfillment, it is glowing spirit which out of its want and desire creates the images of its greed as a reality." Simon Magus says, "And now the created

cosmos came forth from the uncreated fire."[117] The presence of God in the human being is fiery fulfillment; being seized with spirit manifests itself by a flame upon the head.

But also the devil deals with this power, tormenting souls in the fire of hell. In the book of Enoch, Enoch views God's house made of crystal and surrounded by fire; yet behind the mountains, where sky and earth end, "I saw an abyss with high pillars of fire, and I saw the pillars of fire fall down again. Behind this abyss I saw a place that had no heavenly vault over it, nor earthly ground below it; it was an evil, dreadful place. There I saw seven stars, like large, burning mountains. . . . Then Uriel spoke to me and said, 'Here remain the angels who became involved with women, and also their spirits which take on many forms and defile the human beings.[118] Here the fire is the place of punishment, the place of the fallen angels and of the unclean demons. The fallen sons of God burn in their own greed.'"

Fire, therefore, is the common element, belonging to the Trinity as the highest good, as well as to the devil as the epitome of evil; therefore, fire is a unifying symbol. It is the luminous form of divine persons as well as of the abyss; common to all of these is dynamic power, loveliness, energy, and captivating force. Impure greed devours the soul in hell for all eternity, and the purifying pain of remorse removes earthly remnants in purgatory. In the uppermost circle of purgatory, Dante must cross a circle of fire, so that his senses will be opened up for the song of the blessed in paradise.[119] After this crossing no more is said of fire in the *Divine Comedy*. Instead there is only talk about light. Under Beatrice's guidance, all passion and remorse have changed to longing and fulfillment, vision and knowledge.

The paradoxical aspects of these graded steps are well recognized in alchemy. Fire is simultaneously infernal and divine; "it is the secret fire of hell, the miracle of the world, the aggregate of the forces from above within the inferior."[120] "God has created this fire within the earth like the purgatory fire in hell. In this fire God himself glows in divine love."[121] "This Fire is the Holy Spirit and unites Father and Son."[122] The alchemical fire is identical with Mercury, for it is an "elementary fire," invisible, secretly acting, divine, and the universal and sparkling fire of the natural light that carries within itself the heavenly spirit.[123] Concerning the fiery

center of the earth, Jung quotes from alchemy: "Indeed all things come from this source, and nothing in the whole world is born if not by this source."[124]

Since Leo sees the fire of life in the shape of a column or pillar, we must investigate the meaning of this shape. In *The Faith of Ancient Egypt* Kees writes:

> Amongst the monuments best known for their symbolic importance in Egyptian culture there are three of particular importance: (1) the Obelisk in Heliopolis, (2) the Junu-pillar in Anan, and (3) the pillar of Djed in Busiris. At one time these monuments were independent deities, and because the idea that the origin of the world is linked to the obelisk in Heliopolis, such locations were called by the Egyptians "the place of the first time." Yet a pillar could also signify the bearer of the world, or the center of the world-edifice. In the Egyptian language, pillar also means support or poise.[125]

So it follows that the word *Djed* means "durable." The image of the Djed-pillar is a popular, protective symbol and a sign for enduring good-luck, which one wishes, along with life and power, to the divine king.[126] Later, the Djed-pillar was identified with Osiris and interpreted as his backbone.[127] In the region of Memphis it was taken over as symbol by the god Ptah, while in other places it symbolized the god Seth.[128]

We can consider the pillars, which Kees describes, ancient local gods endowed with supreme power—as original expressions of the godhead in his phallic or creative aspect. At a cultural level where natural and spiritual fertility are not yet separated, the pillar is symbolically imbued with divine power.

In his book *Shamanism,* Mircea Eliade carefully pursued the function of the *post* and of the *column* in the thinking of the earliest shepherds and hunters. Important evidence links them with the *tree* and suggests they symbolize the center of the cosmos. He notes that the cosmos is commonly viewed as three levels linked by a central axis. This world-axis was pictured concretely as a pillar holding up the hut, or as a post or tree standing alone, and was called "the pillar of the world." The post indicating the world's center is simultaneously the door into other worlds, the place where the world of ghosts touches upon this concrete world. Prayers are offered and sacrifices performed at the pillar's foot.

The Ostyaks from Tsingala call their pillars "human being" or "father" and offer them bloody sacrifices.

As the pillar or post is the middle of the hut, so is it also the center of the cosmos. For this reason the Mongols designated the polar star as the "golden pillar." The Kirgises call it the "iron pillar" and the Teleutes "sun-pillar." It is the cosmic axis around which the sky turns.[129]

The world-tree, too, links the three regions. The Vasyuagan-Ostyaks believe that its branches touch the heavens and its roots reach into hell. Other tribes speak of three cosmic trees: the first is in heaven, and human souls sit on its branches like birds, waiting to be born as children on earth; another tree is on earth; and a third one in hell. Speaking of the world-tree, Eliade states,

> The symbolism of the world-tree encompasses different religious conceptions. On the one hand, it portrays the universe in a process of continual renewal. It is the inexhaustible spring of cosmic life, and the true place of the saints. On the other hand, the tree symbolizes the sky and the planetary spheres. . . . In many old traditional beliefs the world-tree is linked with the ideas concerning creation, fertility, initiation and immortality. Enriched by numerous additional mythologic symbols (Woman, Spring, Milk, Animals, Fruits), the World-Tree appears as source of all life and as master of destiny.[130]

In his book *The Great Mother*, Erich Neumann asserts that *pillar* and *fire* were subsumed in the matriarchal layer of the mother-goddess.[131] Pillar and midpoint around which everything turns is the world-mother, from whom all life is born and to whom all created things return in death. In her womb is hidden the fire, the dynamic forces of life. In all times this fire was experienced both as devouring and destructive, and as the fire of transformation.[132] The Great Goddess is one with the tree of life which is rooted in the earth and from which the sun is born. She is the cosmic world and sky-tree, the light-tree of the night sky, the soul-tree of resurrection, on which every creature who dies enters the eternity of the great sphere in the form of a star.[133]

According to Hegemonius, the moon ferries the souls of the dead to the *Columna Gloriae* (The Column of Glory) which is called *vir perfectus* (perfect man). This man is the pillar of the

light, for the pillar is filled with pure souls and is the source of the souls' salvation.[134]

In Haggard's book we find that rotation around itself is added to the flaming and flowing movements of the pillar of fire. An expression of the collection of all energies, desires, and impulses flowing from one creative will, this tightly fashioned column rotates around an invisible center.

In nature, time is seen as circular motion, as eternal return,[135] as unchangeable, rhythmic alternation of becoming and fading. It is the unperturbed course of nature, where a new beginning follows upon each end. Circular motion aims at drawing the human being back into his rhythmic course of natural events.

From all this evidence it becomes clear that the pillar of fire is a primary symbol arising at a deep transpersonal level. It is mother and father, creative and destructive; like the great, all-encompassing goddess, it is the source of birth into the world, as well as the source for birth as a star in the sky—the higher, divine rebirth.

Let us now try to interpret the complex and paradoxical facts concerning Haggard's pillar of fire. "She," the Anima in Kor, the realm of the dead, represents the immortal aspect of the sacrificed emotions. In the guise of his soul, she leads the hero into his own depths and confronts him, not with the moral law, but with the fire of life. The latter is the innermost, destiny-shaping, fiery will of life which, from the very depth of nature, presses for ever new expressions. The pillar of fire manifests a frightful and wonderful god who glows in anger and love, a spirit who seizes us, gives us direction, and destroys old structures. In the end, it burns everything in order to let emerge anew the spiritual being, the essence. The pillar of fire is the time before time; it is the eternity of becoming and passing away; it is—like Shiva—creator and destroyer. This pillar stands for the *Anthropos* who carries within itself the souls of all the ancestors, as well as for the unconscious that releases all the new potentials. The fire of life, no ordinary fire dependent on matter, is rather a pure flame, a spiritual force, passionate manifestation, which goes along its path like "the thundering horses of lightning." The enthusiasm awakened by this flame finds expression in poetic inspiration and spiritual knowledge. For the human being this flame implies death and rebirth as well as the highest intensity of the creative instant.

Yet if one identifies too closely with it, it can bring hubris and

unrestricted greed. Leo experiences the rotating pillar as an archaic experience of the world's center, where heaven, earth, and netherworld meet. This world and the world beyond, inside and outside, intersect at this point. The world's center is also the soul's. It is the kernel of the personality where nature and spirit flow together, where god and human being become one. Consciousness is meant to penetrate to this center where the godhead becomes present. It is supposed to bathe in this spring from which flows all life, and it is intended to burn in the spiritual fire, to become one with the cosmos's will to life. Then it becomes wise through the elucidation of the unconscious and is seized by the kind of life in which experience and feeling, knowledge and action become one.

The Death in the Fire

Leo and Holly have reached their goal. The ancestral mother (Amenartas) has sent the son to avenge her on her rival (She), to bathe in the fire of life, and to place himself on the throne of the Pharaohs. Yet this revenge has turned into fascination by the ancestral mother's rival, into love for the Anima. Since She, as the internal goddess, guards the creative forces of nature and encompasses the entire range of emotions, She represents an experience that reaches far beyond one's individual life. As *anima mundi* she symbolizes transpersonal life that ruptures the limits of personal relationships.

She urges Leo to step into the fire to unite with the godhead, just as the Pharaoh unites with the divine Ka, with the transpersonal creative spirit who grants fertility. He is to become a "god-man," equal to the godlike Anima and capable of withstanding her lightning-like tension. Yet, should he, like the Anima, become a victim of this fire spewing out of the unconscious, there arises the danger of his feeling so superior that he would scorn all human considerations and become enthralled with suprahuman possibilities. If on account of this increased willfulness he no longer respects people, he becomes a totalitarian representative of the unconscious's passions. This great danger still threatens even well-meaning persons when they get in touch with archetypal images

and the hidden fire-quality of their passions. The only way to protect oneself against such a danger is to enter into dialogue with the internal powers, seeking a new midpoint between the views of the conscious and the unconscious, between conformist morality and the life-impulses originating in the depths. Once one reaches the realm of the ancient gods, one must repeatedly keep in mind one's human limitations, one's weaknesses and defects, as well as the social situation in which one lives and which must not be destroyed. We must bring sacrifices to the inner gods, we must assist them within our power, but we cannot permit ourselves to identify with them or, like She did, to disregard external rights and laws.

Though Leo is drawn to enter the fire of life, an all-too-justified doubt causes him to hesitate. He fears burning up and losing himself as well as his beloved. Then Ayesha shows him: She bathes in the fire as if it were water, she breathes it as if it were the life-giving air. As a consequence she dies, but first she becomes an ancient mummy, a shriveled-up, pitiful remnant of herself. She turns into what she would have become, after two thousand years, had she not once before bathed in the fire of life and attained infinite life. Dying, she speaks to Leo: "Do not forget me; have pity on my shame. I shall come again and shall once more be beautiful."

From the most beautiful, Ayesha becomes the ugliest. She is transformed from intense life to death and dust, from tangible, immediate reality to a vanishing ghost. The pendulum of nature of which she possesses the secret has swung to the other side. Nature is not only life and beauty, but just as much decay, decomposition, horror and death. It is for this reason that Leo, in a later novel, must recognize She in the guise of a death-mask. Kissing her, he must accept her reverse side. He can regain her blossoming life only if he accepts her antithetical nature.

Is She's ending in the fire a misfortune? Probably yes, inasmuch as the union (coniunctio) has been hindered and inasmuch as the development of the Self has been delayed for an indeterminate amount of time. There is no wedding; no child is born;[136] the new time will not come.

This event recalls a man's dream, in which the Anima went up in smoke after an explosion. The only thing left, a piece of silver ore, represented the end of an Anima projection and the return to his previous state. The woman upon whom the man had projected the

Anima had, in his eyes, prematurely reverted into an ordinary human being. What remained was but the projected feeling in a material form that could not be integrated by him.

Haggard himself said of *She:*

> It represents an attempt to show the effect of immortality on the inadequately cleansed, mortal human being. . . . The horrible end of She is also a type of parable; for what is science, knowledge, or the awareness of power and wisdom in the face of the Almighty? They all suffer the fate She suffered in her solitude; scorned and ridiculed they disintegrate and reveal what they truly are. At least, this is what I tried to communicate.[137]

She is a parable of the human being who becomes presumptuous. When consciousness behaves rationally and totally identifies with the powers of light, then the Anima allies herself with the godhead of the unconscious, with the creative fire, in order to misuse the soul's powers for her own egotistic purposes. She is filled, carried, and enhanced by the fire in which she consumes herself. She experiences a superabundance of passions which the man's feminine eros-aspect, his human relatedness, and eventually even his body cannot endure. Such an Anima becomes a man's downfall. She turns him into an inhuman super-being, since the unsolved Anima-problem stirs his ambition, driving him ever deeper into the excesses of his one-sided consciousness.

But *She* is more than an allegory. Ayesha is an ever-present reality which longs to be accepted, understood, and freed from her inhuman condition. In this regard She is different from Antinea, who acts only as a vengeful, ruthless vamp and drags the men into death. Benoit's Antinea is the kind of unconscious Anima of whom Jung says: "She is an autocratic being without genuine relationships. She seeks nothing but total possession of the individual, whereby a man becomes effeminate in odd and unfavorable ways. This shows itself in his moody and uncontrolled disposition which gradually spoils even his heretofore dependable and sensible functions, such as the intellect. . . ."[138]

The Anima is inclined to assume absolute power and to destroy man's judgments and morals, as long as the unconscious, feminine side is suppressed by consciousness. She is overly powerful and dangerous, probably because Haggard himself turned away from a

relationship with a spiritual woman of Jess's type. Since he lacked a relationship with a woman who could mirror and exemplify for him the world of eros, the inner factor gained control of him. Since he renounced love, love (or the Anima) changed into power; but in the hermitage of the old Noot, Leo is moved by love for the first time. As a result, the Anima becomes humble and ready to subordinate herself. In *She and Allan,* a later novel by Haggard, She says: "You should have worshipped me like a shrine, but since you failed to do this, the waters of salvation cannot flow for you."

The Anima expects of the man that he recognize her as a divine power inside himself. Haggard, as a matter of fact, knows that She has something to do with his own soul. But how could he ever reconcile her primitive and overwhelming emotional reality with his English consciousness? How could he ever conceive of integrating this dreadful world of emotions, when She murders Leo's wife, whereas he himself holds his wife in such high esteem? How could he ever accept his Anima who, in no way resembling his Christian conception of the soul, is a heathen goddess and *anima mundi* that tries to seduce him into seeking tyrannical power? She is both the mirror and the reverse of his one-sided consciousness, of his gentleman-ideal, which forces him to suppress feelings and nature and to tyrannize his surroundings. Yet, what would have happened had he accepted the Anima such as she was? What moral and religious conflicts would have overcome him had the goddess managed to seduce him to feel that he was beyond human morality? An insoluble conflict persists between his consciousness and the Anima.

The Anima is consumed by her own intensity, since she cannot yet be accepted in the guise in which Haggard meets her. She loses her shape and becomes a ghost, namely, unconscious. For Leo, transformation in the fire and communion with the godhead do not take place. The hero cannot renew himself. He loses the golden curls and becomes old and gray. Perhaps one reason for the undertaking's failure is that the attempted union was not preceded by sufficient purification and developing insight. In the vision of Zosimos, for example, Zosimos himself, as well as a dragon, is dismembered. This symbolizes the required analytic clarification of the contents of consciousness as well as of the unconscious. "In the later periods of alchemy one finds the 'slaying of the lion' along with the 'slaying of the dragon,' at least in the image of cutting off

the lion's paws."[139] Yet, in the beginning of the novel, the heroes were unable to dissect the lion and the crocodile on the river shore since—so it said—they were lacking the necessary tools. This means that they did not have the required prerequisites for a profound exploration of the unconscious. They stopped their self-examination at a safer and more superficial level, at that of the goose and the buck.

Thus the more primitive and powerful natural force manifests itself in its projection upon the Anima and renders her egotistical, power-hungry, greedy for possession, and vengeful. Contact with the fire would indeed have been dangerous to Leo's insufficiently purified nature. Haggard was justifiably afraid of his ancestors' passionate nature. Inasmuch as he was only partly successful in separating and identifying the contents of the unconscious, he was in danger of becoming a tool of a diabolically negative force, hidden in his body, which would be the reverse aspect of the godhead.

Nevertheless, the heroes brought back something from their long journey: the mummy's small foot and the Anima's dark coat. For Holly, for the reality-function, the small foot indicates a new, spiritualized vantage point. The coat is a symbol of being in the service of love to which Leo will consecrate himself henceforth. Reporting about the mysteries in Eleusis, Kerényi tells how the initiate was wrapped in the goddess's coat and was addressed with her name:

> The men also entered the form of the goddess and became identical with her. In Syracuse, in the shrine of Demeter and Persephone, the men also took the great oath, dressed themselves with the purple coat of the goddess and carried her burning torch. . . . In Pheneos there were the same mysteries as in Eleusis, and here the priests wore the mask of Demeter-Kidaria during the highest mystery. It was not a friendly face but rather a frightful, Medusa-like image.[140]

Thus some union with the Anima is accomplished nonetheless by means of She's dark coat. Leo is being consecrated to the goddess. The coat falls over him like a shadow and quells his youthful splendor. It brings him the presentiment that the Anima's shadow-aspect shades him too. At one time in his old age, Haggard said of himself that, like Ayesha, he was filled with changing moods. At times he tormented himself with guilt feelings. Yet he was never

completely free from his service to the goddess and from his efforts to redeem her priestess. Many of his books focus upon the same theme. In one, a captive white woman must serve a crocodile-deity. In another book, an elegant English lady is abducted by priests whose idol is a wild hermit-elephant. The Anima remains a prisoner of the unredeemed instinctual power of the chthonic godhead.

In *She and Allan,* Haggard continues the dialogue with She and his debate with the unconscious. She tells Allan, who embodies the Englishman:

> Had you been someone else, I would have revealed secrets to you and explained the meaning of much that I told you in pictures and various fables. Two things, Allan, are expected of a person who visits a shrine, reverence and faith. Without these, the oracles remain silent and the holy waters will not flow. I, Ayesha, am a shrine, but you offered me no reverence before I forced it from you by means of a feminine ruse. You had no faith in me, wherefore the oracle does not speak to you, and the redeeming waters do not flow.[141]

It depends upon the attitudes of one's consciousness whether and how the unconscious releases its secrets. Though Allan shuts himself off, by means of his common sense and skepticism, from a deeper understanding of the irrational nature of the Anima, she nevertheless offers him counsel for the future. "Therefore the wise will seek to turn those with whom Fate mates them into friends, since otherwise soon they will be lost for aye. More, if they are wiser still, having made them friends, they will suffer them to find lovers where they will. Good maxims, are they not? Yet hard to follow. . . ."[142]

Later Continuations of She

In the novel *Ayesha,* written twenty years later as a sequel to *She,* the actions take place in Central Asia. Here the rivalry between Amenartas, now called Athene, and the rediscovered She

continues. Athene is no longer Leo's wife but has turned exclusively into an embodiment of external might. Her husband is an Asian ruler gone mad who, haunted by distrust and jealousy, throws his enemies to the bloodhounds. Leo escapes from the insane ruler and takes refuge with a priestess who has her sanctuary on a nearby volcano. When he reaches her territory, a mummy on a pile of bones waits for him. Later on he must kiss this ghost-like being in order to awaken She to her former figure and beauty.

Her temple, hewn into the rocks, is at least three times larger than the largest cathedral, with equally enormous altars and halls. He is edified at the sight of the temple's Ankh-cross design, symbol of the life-giving Isis. The mighty halls are illuminated by tortuous columns of fire that arise from openings in the volcano. In the area of the altar, there is once again an image that anticipates the new inner condition which is to be attained: a mature, winged woman with a boy whom she consoles by promising him immortality. "All the love and all the tenderness have entered her picture, and it seems as if heaven was opening a path before her for her wings." Ayesha sits below this altar-picture with her priests and priestesses.

Now Leo is engaged to her. Yet the wedding cannot take place until Leo once more finds the fiery pillar and through it gains eternal life. Before the wedding She wants to punish Athene. As she takes off with her armies, Leo is ambushed. Ayesha and her troops, accompanied by storms and hail, lightning and thunder, overrun Athene's city and free her beloved. Leo refuses to wait any longer with the wedding, but new obstacles arise between him and his bride. Next to the corpse of Athene, who has taken poison during Ayesha's assault, She once again offers Leo power, success, and triumph over the entire world. Yet he does not want any power that is born of the murder. He wants only his bride's love, even if it should bring him death.

Ayesha senses that Leo is about to die, but she prophesies that death will no longer be able to separate them. She had previously spoken of love but had always remained unapproachable, like an icy mountain peak. Yet at this moment, a new transformation occurs in her: she becomes human. No longer is she the oracle of the shrine, no longer the Valkyrie of the battlefield. She is the happy bride. She would like to be nothing but woman. Up to this point she had not dared to yield to her longing, knowing well that Leo would be consumed by it. Yet now she wants to dare it, no matter

what might result. Holly is to give the couple to each other. In his hands, Holly feels the powerful, intense stream of life and heavenly happiness flowing from She to Leo in rapid, burning waves, and he has a sense of bursting. In passionate devotion She embraces her groom and kisses his mouth. She then sings him a love song, which stops abruptly, because Leo staggers and falls down dead.

Grieving, She takes leave of her priests and priestesses. She forgives the dead Athene, praising her for having played her role with greatness. She turns herself over to the benevolent, heavenly mother, from whom all were born and who faithfully accepts all back again. No longer is She the being filled with sin and pride which she had been. She is no longer the "fallen star," but, like long ago, "the star which is victorious over the night." Her soul is again one with her beloved, as it was in the beginning. In the evening she has Leo's casket brought to the crater and kneels beside him near the abyss. Then a flame twists upwards as if it had wings, and in the early dawn Ayesha and the casket disappear. As it becomes light, Holly recognizes two glorified figures rising upwards.

New in this second volume are the multitude of tortuous columns of fire which have turned into sources of light for the sanctuary. Especially new is the image in the cathedral inside the rock, the winged mother-goddess with her son: Isis with the Horus-child. No longer is the Anima exclusively woman and beloved, nor is she simply the self-satisfied soul; she is a mother filled with love and tenderness, caring and unselfish. Leo's love changes his Anima from a sterile virgin and bellicose goddess into a loving, mature woman. Only now does she experience herself again in harmony with the great heavenly mother, Isis. The feminine principle, mother and daughter, is reintroduced beside god-father and god-son. She becomes aware that her involvement in earthly possessions and earthly power was an error, since both Leo and Ayesha are spiritual beings, spirit and soul, which, cleansed and changed by means of the flame, strive towards heaven. She fought her own other aspect, her will to power, her involvement in the world, by fighting Amenartas-Athene.

Shortly before his death, Haggard wrote *Wisdom's Daughter,* dealing with She's early life. Here, in a "prologue in heaven," the

conflict between the two women is traced back to the strife between two goddesses. Isis is angry with humanity, because it has abandoned her altars in order to serve Aphrodite. Thus she orders her unborn daughter, Ayesha, to avenge her on earth and to depend only on her, the spiritual, heavenly mother. After this, Isis calls Aphrodite, who appears in her naked beauty and, laughing, alludes to the fact that she, too, is part of the great mother, Isis, and that life on earth would soon cease without her. Isis, however, seems to have forgotten this aspect of herself. She does not realize that her own increasing one-sidedness has brought forth Aphrodite, her antagonist. Enraged over the goddess of love, she leaves the field and thus delivers the unborn soul of Ayesha to her rival. Aphrodite brings her the consolation of love, with the lover in whose arms she is to forget the angry Great Goddess.

From birth on, the soul is weighed down by the striving of the two goddesses. The soul is forged by the split in the consciousness of the heavenly goddess, who has forgotten her own opposite side. Here Aphrodite takes on a role analogous to Satan. She is Lucifer's feminine aspect, the godhead's nature-side which makes creation possible. At first, She is the obedient instrument of the great mother. She grows up to be a priestess in search of wisdom. Then, however, she is overcome by love for Kallikrates, the beautiful young man. This interferes with her calling as priestess and awakens her calling as woman. Her love for Kallikrates first evokes the platonic love for the beautiful body, which widens itself to encompass the beautiful souls and eventually the eternal ideas.[143]

First, however, She gets involved in conflict and sin through her love. At the beginning of the Christian era, she stepped into the fire of life, in order to become one with that part of the spirit which, according to the Gnostics' teaching, had descended all the way down into matter. For the sake of the development of consciousness, the Christian orientation excluded this part of the spirit from salvation, viewing it as diabolical. Therefore, the Anima's ruthlessness grew larger and larger during the Christian era. Just as human consciousness identified itself with the Christian ideals, so our unconscious, natural side became one with the "lower deity." Like the Indian Shakti and Maya, She also weaves the texture of destiny. Now the time of this split-off, and therefore unrestrained,

anima mundi seems to come to an end. She has taken whatever she desired, under the motto "where there's a will, there's a way!" Under the name and the cover of Christendom, she violently converted, conquered, and colonized. Her mounting desires consume herself, and entire nations under her banner burn up by their own greed. The world-creating *anima mundi* turns to ashes and dust. Yet, if an individual struggles for the redemption of the Anima, she doesn't have to burn up, but can transform herself in the flames. The picture in the temple, the mother-goddess with her son, anticipates the birth of a transformed consciousness and of a new era.

We have repeatedly shown that "She" recalls the myth of Isis and Osiris. The column of fire with which She weds almost as a groom[144] in *Wisdom's Daughter* largely corresponds in mythological terms to Seth, the fiery, passion-driven, twin brother of Osiris. Through his literary work, as well as through his own inner conflict, Haggard became connected with the unconscious, and these archetypes were revived—the myth of the hostile brothers, of the evening- and the morning-star as the antithetical sisters, of their joint union, and of the dying and resurrecting son or brother lover. The story of *She* is linked to what has been valid at all times, but has been lost during a relatively brief period of our modern consciousness. Haggard reshaped in a more individual form the old myths, thus completing the first part of his task. His novel *She* was a world-wide success, since it satisfied a vague longing for the lost goddess.

We, too, should find anew the lost myth, when we arrive at a boundary from which we look for a new path. Yet, just like Rider Haggard, we cannot simply take the myth in its existing form and translate it into our life. We must wrestle with the old gods, like Jacob with the angel, in order not to become "possessed" by them. Our life must become changed through the inner experience, and our being must be completed by means of the contents of the unconscious. Yet this must occur without our drowning in the myth or our over-identifying with these internal, divine figures. What Haggard accomplished in the play of his fantasy and in his literary work should be carried a step further: namely, to the point where the two spirits united in the holy marriage of death return from heaven to revitalize the body they left behind.[145] This turn of

events is lacking in Haggard. He was capable of seeing the images, but remained unable to sufficiently understand them in terms of his own personal situation. He was not able to cope with the Anima-problem, with his emotions in everyday reality. As a consequence of this, we do not find a true solution of the problem even in his later works.

III. Summary of the Symbolism and of its Explanation

A pair of "Twin-Heroes" starts out to find the lost treasure: Leo, the sun-hero, beautiful as a Greek god, and Holly, the mercurial-saturnic satellite, capable of logical judgments, spiritual father and companion of the sun-child. Their servant Job is the narrow-minded human being with predominantly Old Testament views characteristic for a certain kind of rigid puritanism. Later on they are joined by a second shadow-figure, Mohamed, the Arabian steersman. We thus have a male quaternity, a preliminary male wholeness and self-sufficiency which, however, requires completion by means of the feminine principle that is suppressed by consciousness.

This feminine principle announces itself by a message in the trunk which Leo inherits from his ancestors, especially from his "primeval mother." Within a black cover, the trunk contains a silver-trunk with five sphinxes. They are the feminine symbol of wholeness, composed of a quaternity of silver and a fifth essential thing, a *quinta essentia,* in the middle. The sphinx, guardian of the tomb of the lost feminine side, symbolizes the riddle of life, which may confront us from within or from without, as a danger or challenge. She is the feminine-natural soul, still heavily contaminated by animal instinct, which must be redeemed from the unconscious. The inscription on the fragment of an amphora summons the heroes to a journey into the dark continent, where Leo is to find the white queen. Here he is to discover her secret, the pillar of fire, to take vengeance upon her, and to become Pharaoh himself.

Crossing the sea, Leo and Holly are surprised by a storm just when they approach the rock—described in the trunk—from

which the path leads into the interior. In his imagination, Haggard envisions in the stormy sea the suffering, great, original mother whose suffering diminishes only when Leo, the young god, sleeping in the small boat, approaches the coast. In their "night sea-journey," the heroes transcend the abyss which separated them, the representatives of the collective consciousness, from the deep layers of the collective unconscious. The moon crescent appears before them as a vision of the bride who prepares herself for the *hierosgamos,* the sacred wedding. Dawn's pink colors bring forth a radiant new day as promise of a new "world-day" that is about to be born. In the light of the new day, they discover the expected sign, the stony head of the Ethiopian, which looks so frightful that Job compares it with the devil. The initial encounter with the inner, hidden continent is thus an encounter with evil. The latter is an inner reality, repressed by consciousness, and therefore projected upon the blacks. The heroes then find a canal and tie their boat to a blossoming magnolia, symbol of the feelings that were also repressed by narrow, puritanical morality.

The animals they kill, unicorn-goose and buck, represent spirit and soul which had been projected upon nature as transient, instinctual energies. The killed lioness is the instinctual reality which was first experienced in relation with the mother, a relationship which is now to be transferred to the royal bride. Lion and the crocodile, which the heroes cannot kill as they lack the necessary tools, represent the original antitheses of the unconscious, the "yes" and "no" to life. Simultaneously, they are symbols for those instinctual layers which are farthest from consciousness and harder to recognize. Thus the heroes cannot accept them as expressions of their own unconscious.

The travelers are led into the interior by Billali, an old man with natural wisdom, and by his tribe of leopard-people who live in caves within the crater of an extinct volcano. A black woman, Ustane, chooses Leo as her husband. In this location, marriage is experienced as a matriarchal institution maintained by emotion and general consensus. The tribe of savages embodies a primitive level of consciousness where instinct can regress repeatedly towards blind impulse. It is a level that everyone passes through, that everyone carries within him/herself, and towards which everyone can regress if he does not try to become increasingly conscious of emotions and instinctual impulses. The danger that un-

controllable passions may gain the upper hand is portrayed by the incandescent pot which is put over the head of the victim. The pot here is a symbol for male "hysteria," occurring when he "sees red" as a result of being run over by the negative Anima. Such a condition can occur as the result of regression, when a positive but seemingly inappropriate emotion is turned away because of pride, rigidity or simply because of ignorance. The reaction to the suppression of the emotion is often delayed and can then be quite excessive, such as a sudden, violent explosion with little external occasion. Such an eruption of the unconscious is portrayed by the rebellion of the primitive tribe against the whites.

The white queen She, as the higher court of the soul in this region of the incandescent pots, stops this dangerous outbreak of primitive raging. She orders the foreign intruders to be brought to her, as she has already been waiting for them a long time. On the way, Leo develops a high fever and feels that he is being torn in two. He is plagued by an inner discord. On one side stands Ustane who, as wife, is sanctioned by the external world and upon whom, as a black woman, his primitive anima is projected. On the other side is She, the interior queen by whom he feels magically drawn, who encompasses all the dangers and fulfillments of the soul, and who surpasses the external world by being a compelling, inner force.

The fever which almost killed Leo is healed by She. Yet through ruthlessly murdering Ustane, She destroys the rights of marriage and all external responsibilities. In this she not only injures the man's morality, but she also undermines her own aims, because she destroys both the trust as well as the character of the man. It is a vicious circle, since the stern, Victorian world view only tolerates a rigid "either/or" and not the free development of feelings which are independent of rules. Thus this world view exiles Ayesha, "the live one," the queen of the heart, to the dead.

She seeks for a marriage with her beloved. Yet because she is not a human being but rather an inner archetype, a divine figure, the *anima mundi,* no earthly marriage can take place. What is intended is a *hierosgamos,* an ancient, solemn rite performed as a mystery in the temple between priestess and priest, the representatives of the godhead. This union must not be confused with an ordinary, mundane marriage. In order to separate the mystical

sphere from the mundane sphere and to prevent any degradation of the rite, there was the strictest rule of silence towards any uninitiated person, the disregard of which was punishable by death. The mundane marriage was an earthly reflection of this holy ritual performed in the most sublime place by the gods. This ritual conferring fertility and immortality was re-evoked in mythical tales, in order that human beings could experience and share in the fertility and immortality of the divine powers.

It is the superhuman quality of She, as well as of Antinea, that makes these two figures into archetypes in the novels. This archetypal quality reveals that we deal with compelling powers, belonging to the collective, rather than to the personal, psyche. They are powers that rule over life and death, for She guards the secret of the fire of life, and Antinea is near the spring of life. Both kill if they are offended. The Great Goddess of the Orient and of the Celts is revived in them, but in an altered form, half god, half human. Thus She is closer to us.

Originally the Great Goddess is Mother Nature, mistress of the animals, sublime mountain goddess, changing moon, Aphrodite born by the foam of the sea, love and fruitfulness of any kind, exuberant, and filled with intensity. Yet she is also mother death. In the form of her own daughter, she is simultaneously the promise of eternal life, since she is an inward psychological experience.

In her external appearances, She is subject to the creation and fading of matter, but not in her essential quality. Living in Kor, in the innermost heart, inaccessible to the world, hard to find and harder to attain, the goddess soul guards, as her most profound secret, the column of fire. This miracle rotates in the womb of the earth and is therefore designated as the secret of the Great Goddess or Gaia. Parallels from the Hebrews, from Greek sources, and from Christian and non-Christian literature show that it is a divine power. Whereas this power is seen from a Christian viewpoint as a predominantly angry and dangerous, as well as fascinating, aspect of God, it is revealed by sources originating or influenced by Greece as the divine logos, as the creative, spiritual fire.

Alchemy as well knows of this deity, incandescent with fire, abiding in the interior of the earth. It knows of her creative significance, her danger and her transforming power. Primitive parallels, such as those of the tree of life and of the world-pillar,

refer to the center of the world and of life, to the orientation according to an inner center and the re-establishment of the relationship with the gods.

Man's Anima guards the secret of the fire, of warmth, of light, of fertility and creation. She seeks a link with his spirit in order to become integrated into his life. What is initially but vaguely sensed in a man's mind—as an indefinite, instinctual urge, as a fleeting thought, or as a fantasy becomes a concrete form—can be realized when he finds the access to his soul and to this fire. His spirit is born into reality by his feminine soul in the fire of deep emotion.

Leo has found the access to the secret of life, but the path gets blocked by Job's clumsiness and Holly's and his own inadequate knowledge and understanding. In his own life, Haggard was able to accept the Anima only within narrow limits, because of her irrationality, her differing wisdom, and her need to love. Her heathen nature conflicted irreconcilably with the fading Victorian world view. Because of this, She was immoderate, power-hungry, and jealous. By her death in the fire, she demonstrates to Leo (the male consciousness) that he, too, must allow himself to be transformed by love or a sacrificial death. In a later novel he awakens the goddess, who had shriveled up into a mummy, with a kiss, and this time he does not hesitate to unite himself with her and her fiery fervor. By means of his love and sacrificial death, by means of the transformation of consciousness and of the spiritual attitude, the Anima is freed of her greed for power, of sin and pride, and of her entanglement in earthly desires.

His preoccupation with the Anima brought Haggard insights that were considerably ahead of his time. But Leo and She remain blessed spirits. After their transformation they do not return to earth. Haggard could not complete the task of realizing in his own life what he envisioned. The times were not yet ripe for the necessary consequences of his inward experience. This may well be the reason why, in spite of his outstanding personality, he did not always attain the outward results one might have expected from him. His plans for reforms, which were so close to his heart and which could have had a far-reaching significance for England, were thwarted. Even his continued mourning over the death of his only son may have had its deepest root in the fact that "the union of the gods" did not bring forth a "divine son." The new birth aris-

ing from a more profound internal vision remained but a hope for the future, a hope which might then be realized by a new generation in a new time.

SECOND PART
The Development of the Anima Portrayed in a Series of Dreams

I. Introduction to the Series of Dreams

It is the task of the first half of life to grow into life, to learn and exercise one's profession, to found a family and to care for the growing children. Viewed psychologically, this is the period in which the individual integrates him/herself in his environment by unfolding his talents and by developing his skills based mostly on his/her primary functions.[146]

A new task presents itself in the second half of life: the challenge is then to discover the "inner world" and to focus upon the deeper layers of the psyche, upon the unconscious which, in favorable situations, is complementary to the conscious mind. If the laws of the psyche are insufficiently respected, then the unconscious becomes an inner antagonist that thwarts our intentions and destroys our efforts. This inner antagonist announces him/herself in dreams. If one ignores dreams, then the unconscious appears in anxieties and neurotic symptoms. Usually, the impulse for a serious dialogue with the unconscious is provided by an inner distress-situation. The appearance of neurotic symptoms occurs if one does not follow either instinctively or consciously the laws of the psyche and its manifold demands.

At times, however, it is after a particular success that the unconscious announces itself. Once everything has been achieved that could be achieved, one's path does not continue in the same direction. The former purposes are outgrown and life seems to lose its meaning until a new goal can be found. Dreams become frequent during such periods of transition, because a transformation is occurring in the unconscious. In the middle of our life, an inner restoration and transformation can begin which is no longer focused primarily on instinctual forces but rather on insight. The

emphasis shifts from external expansion of power to maturation, away from one-sidedness towards wholeness and towards becoming the Self. It is difficult to relinquish one's old, habitual, and accepted ways of life and to find new goals on a different plane. Given our current extroverted environment which is so exclusively oriented towards external successes, it is usually only during periods of suffering that we are pushed to listen to our dreams and the call from our soul.

Yet, if we do turn our attention inward, we meet a new difficulty. In view of the good opinion we usually have of ourselves, our unconscious side, due to its compensatory function, will first show us our shadow[147] with all our limitations and contradictions. As one encounters one's shadow, one begins to doubt oneself and sees how questionable and selfish one's motives are, and how far they are from one's conscious ideals. In this confrontation with the shadow, dreams become most helpful, once it is seen that all dream-figures are actors on the inward stage of our being, actors who portray our various potentials.

If, with the beginning of the second half of life, a man begins to examine himself, he may possibly discover that he has become self-sufficient in his profession, with his knowledge and his skills, but much less so in his relationships to other people and to himself. He will dread acknowledging that he is subjected to unconscious motivations, childish dependencies, compelling emotions, pride and hypersensitivity. As he focuses on his dreams, many of the pressing external entanglements and inner problems can be clarified to the point where his everyday concerns are less predominant. Once the individual becomes aware to some degree of the shadow, deeper levels of the unconscious can begin to manifest themselves. Then a man may encounter in his dreams an unfamiliar woman. That aspect of his psyche which is foreign, distant, incomprehensible or unconscious reveals itself in this feminine figure. A woman discovers in her dreams of this period an unknown male partner who symbolizes her as yet incompletely developed spirit, whereas the unknown woman in the man's dreams embodies his yet unconscious soul and his potentials for genuine relationships.

The mother awakens the feminine soul-image, the Anima, early in man, while he is still a boy. Yet the Anima encompasses more than the mother's being; it is, as a psychological, archetypal image,

a condensation of all of man's experiences with women. For this reason the female figure in dreams can, in the course of development, reflect all the stages and aspects of woman, as the Anima corresponds to the image of the feminine godhead. Like the goddess, and like life itself, she has a kind as well as a frightful face. Which aspects of the image become operative in the boy's psyche depends in part on the constitution of the son and in part on the nature of the mother. The way the mother is, and the way she relates to her son, influences his feelings and judgments. He will form his own relationships by her example, and from her he receives his sense of religious devotion and faith.

Even if at a later time the boy runs away from her out of rebelliousness, he will have a hard time freeing himself from her standards and from her attitudes towards life which he had already incorporated. Liberation is seemingly achieved by denying her essence and by fighting her demands. In order to become a man and to dare to go out into the world, the youth will at times have to disregard the nurturance of an overprotective mother. Yet, if he becomes subjected to the inner, idealized feminine image, because of excessive ties to his mother (often coupled with a negative relationship with his father), he can end up a dreamer, inept and effeminate. The young man must therefore consciously separate himself, not only from the mother, but also from this idealized feminine image, just as Kallikrates had to leave the priestess in order to marry the "external" queen and become the father of a son. There are men who know exactly how the Anima, as the femme fatale, looks. They know that they must flee from this type of Anima, since they sense that they were not equal to the excessive power of this inner image projected onto an external woman. It is wiser for them to marry a woman who does not evoke this powerful inner image.

Growing into a marriage and into one's own family is one of the most important tasks of the first half of life. Marriage is a high value, shaped during thousands of years by means of strict rules and taboos. There are good psychological reasons that marriage was made an indissoluble sacrament in the Catholic church. Through this trustworthy base, the family and children, in the context of a home, find the necessary support. Grounded in the family, trust grows in the child's soul as a natural fruit of feeling sheltered, and it unfolds into affirmation of life and self-

confidence. Subsequent trusting relationships in one's community and country, and especially in close human situations, are founded upon this childlike trust that is gained within the family. Wherever the family—and thus the earliest reassurance and protection—fails, we find all too often that a person's ability to adjust to inward or external conditions also fails. We can now see that some of the early nervous disorders of childhood, and of later neuroses and psychoses, have a contributory cause in lack of love, insufficient security, and various tensions in the child's environment.

In marriage and in the family one feels accepted; and, during times of weakness, need, and illness, one feels supported. It is here that one learns to help and to care for someone else. The future of the generations depends upon each single, small family. Marriage is a test of endurance for both the husband and the wife, in terms of household management as well as human relations. Just as the church recognizes, not only the outward responsibilities of the parents for each other and for the children, but also a mutual responsibility for their souls and their salvation, so we too expect a marriage to be more than an economic union. Yet to be more requires the ongoing spiritual and psychological efforts of both partners, to insure that a marriage becomes a genuine relationship and friendship, as well as an inner, developmental journey. Marital bliss doesn't come by itself any more than does outward success. One must fight and suffer for it. Most of all one must not expect a marriage to flourish through the efforts of his or her spouse but rather through one's own effort.

The significance of marriage also consists in the fact that it forces upon young people choices and decisions, thereby making difficult any continued, indecisive rambling through life. When difficulties arise, the partners must solve them within the sanctioned institution of marriage. They must prove themselves in meeting unavoidable conflicts, adjustments and the needs of their children, which oblige them to educate themselves and thus to achieve another step in self-development. Marriage thereby provides the ground for individuation,[148] inasmuch as individuation cannot be attained without education, self-education and adjustment to one's environment. In his own life, Haggard achieved some degree of adjustment to his family. Where marriage is affirmed, and where it is held as a paramount value and continued obligation, as was the case with Haggard, it is likely that the sec-

ond half of life will bring up questions from the yet unconscious soul. These questions can only be followed successfully on the basis of holding true to one's previous commitments. However, if the projection of the still unconscious aspects of the Anima is misused in order to find grounds for divorce and remarriage, only calamities and guilts are sown, and nothing is gained. Anyone who gets a divorce in order to marry the "Anima" loses the inner value he seeks, as well as his wife, and gains another projected image. All who blindly chase after a new projection, believing that they can possess and tie to themselves their beloved, should listen to the words of Angelus Silesius: "Do stop! Where runnest thou, the heaven is in you, / If elsewhere you seek God, you miss him more and more."

The child's unconscious image of God is lost by the adult along with the feeling of parental protectiveness. Yet being of the highest internal value, it leads to such compelling longing that it is easily projected upon any halfway-suited partner. The man, as well as the woman, seeks in the other, without suspecting it, the lost image of God. The man looks for a wonderful partner who not only understands, like a mother, his innermost being but who also awakens his creative potentials; the woman looks for a spiritual example, a paternal guide and companion, capable of awakening her activity and her sleeping spirit. Inasmuch as the marriage-partner satisfies this deepest expectation only to a small extent—if at all (doesn't she suffer also from a similar longing?), a certain degree of disillusion in marriage is almost unavoidable. Yet all unfulfilled longing continues to live in hiding. The value one sees in one's partner and which makes the partner so desirable is, in the last analysis, a religious content which cannot be appropriated by tying a person to oneself. On the contrary, this approach would lead to the loss of this value, since the illusion of having appropriated it through the possession of the partner would interfere with becoming conscious of the projected content.

In the first half of life, the fascination emanating from the Anima easily becomes a peril for a man's masculinity; yet, if properly understood, it can become the agent for achieving wholeness in the second half. Encountering "the unknown woman" in his dreams, the man discovers in later years his yet undeveloped soul, his eros projected into nature and—sooner or later—upon a woman. In his dreams he discovers the creative depths that he

must explore. The development of this largely unconscious, feminine soul, of eros, of the potential for relatedness requires a great deal of the man. In all, it requires attentiveness and patience, readiness to look at things symbolically, chivalry, the commitment of his best forces. Slowly he will understand that it is not only a relationship to a woman that is called for (by the encounter in the dream), but mainly the establishment of a relationship with the inner, feminine side of his psyche, and thus to the feminine principle. The deep fascination produced by the Anima-projection resides in its religious origin. The religious images at its base are suited to compensate for the one-sidedness of the masculine world view. This will be illustrated in the subsequent dream-series, especially its second part. The gradual differentiation of the Anima makes possible a deepened, sensitive, and ethical—rather than only intellectual—appreciation of various human situations, and a more careful weighing of the pros and cons of one's own actions.

The forthcoming dream-series is meant to illustrate the development of the Anima. We deal with the experience of one person which, nevertheless, shows some generally valid patterns. Yet we must also be aware that Anima-development will show individual differences in each case. The dreamer was in his forties. The oldest of several children, he had lost his father early. Thus he became the hope and support of his mother and siblings. Raised Catholic, he married and had several children. He is an extroverted-intuitive type,[149] his feeling being his secondary function.

Let me, however, make a few preliminary remarks about this particular type. The extroverted-intuitive type puts his best efforts into his outward plans and tasks. With a fast eye, he catches new concrete and organizational possibilities which another type would notice only much later or not at all. Yet, on account of all these attractive goals, he easily forgets to tend his own field with sufficient thoroughness. Rarely has he the patience to wait for the harvest and to collect the fruits of his labor. Being full of ideas and vague presentiments, he has all too many irons in the fire. To use sensation, his inferior function, is difficult for him. In the case of our dreamer, thinking also belonged to the less developed functions, wherefore he is somewhat deficient in logical and systematic thoroughness. He is able to envision the overall, important connections, but he finds it very hard to work things out in detail. He

grasps new possibilities with great enthusiasm; yet once he has worked on them for awhile, he feels trapped by what he has achieved. He is an adventurer and initiator who spreads about him life, wit, and potentials. Yet often he finds himself empty-handed and feels, rightly or wrongly, passed over. People belonging to this type think they have wings which must carry them to the goal of their wishes. Just because he is always ahead of himself with his new ideas and wishes, he does not realize how another side of his being limps behind. For the sake of a faraway goal, he ignores himself and his environment. He constantly lives under high tension until his body rebels against this ruthless exploitation with depression and physical disease.

The intuitive disposition contributed to the fact that this man, whose dreams we are about to discuss, suffered twice as hard from the narrowness and poverty of the post-war situation. In this dilemma he obtained little support from his childhood faith that had been pushed into the background by the war. Like others, he had lost several times all his financial means. The lack of housing in the post-war years made it impossible, for a long time, to reunite his family. Trapped professionally and financially, his longings were for the faraway places, for the wide world, the large metropolis. Any idea of relationship and restriction filled him with fear.

Yet he recognized after a few psychotherapeutic meetings that limits were particularly necessary for an intuitive person like himself, and that it was important that he prove himself in a restricted situation. He understood that restrictions and limitations were an essential aspect of human existence. This insight offered a basis for accepting his reality as it was at that moment. Once he recognized that he didn't need to flee the narrowness that seemed to surround him, and once he saw that everything was the way it had to be, he accepted the work with his dreams as a novel form of widening his world by which the path towards his inner world would be opened up.

We may stress at this point that he had fulfilled the tasks of the first half of life. Efficient, talented and conscientious in his profession, he had little to improve in this area. During the war, he had great responsibilities which he carried out faithfully and in a humane way. He received no outward wounds, but, as will be

evidenced by his dreams, he was left with psychological injuries. He suffered from nervous tension, and his life seemed endangered by the predominance of the instinctual sphere that turned against him. After the war he had, at first, found a good position. Yet he soon realized that it would not further him in his profession. He gave it up for a new career where he had to start at the bottom. His precarious financial position required great sacrifices of him and of his wife in order to patiently hold to the goal he had set for himself. The series of dreams covers these eight long years of external restraint. Yet, shortly after the end of the dream-series, the dreamer attained his longed-for liberation, as he reached an independent and far better position.

Focusing largely on the dreams, the discussion initially dealt with his current life-situation. During the first period of elucidation of his history, he related the dreams without writing them down beforehand, and thus only a couple are included in this work. Dream One of the bugs portrays his difficult starting situation. The subsequent water-dreams, which referred to "catharsis," to self-knowledge and to the first insights into the personal shadow, are missing. Dream Two already brings to an end this first phase: a preliminary, symbolic death followed in the next dream by a rebirth experience. The plunge and death in a mountain stream portray not only a catastrophe, but also a kind of baptism, followed in the next dream by the birth of a new, inner person. The latter is confronted in Dream Four with the picture of "the royal couple" which is the new goal he must strive for.

The series contains sixty-nine dreams, starting with the dreamer's thirty-ninth year and stretching over a period of eight years. These are only the most important dreams pertaining directly to the theme; many others which did not refer to the Anima's development were left out. Even so, the series turned out quite long. However, if it were further shortened, it might give the impression that the inner path is a simple and straight affair. The reader must be able to participate in the stepwise development, rather than be confronted only with given facts. If one begins the adventurous inward journey, one must be prepared for detours, unpredictable difficulties, and reverses. One may benefit from orienting oneself with the markers left by predecessors, with the story of the journey to the Holy Grail, and with various myths and

fairy tales. Yet, it is unavoidable that each person must make the journey by himself, that each must fight his own, specific dangers, and find his own solution to his life's problems.

Considering the size of the series, it was impossible to interpret the dreams following all the rules of the art, since this would have strained the reader's patience. I was primarily interested in demonstrating the main line of development which, starting with an inner split, leads to a novel experience of nature and spirit, and eventually to a gradual synthesis and integration. Some dreams were easily explained; others at first seemed unintelligible. Yet looking back periodically and comparing the dreams helped solve many of the riddles. At times it was necessary to fall back on seemingly farfetched parallels. In fact, at all times it is possible to do only limited justice to the depth of the soul and to the many layers of its pronouncements. This multiplicity of the soul's layers is mirrored by juxtaposing dreams, dream-amplifications, subjective and objective interpretations. It renders a comprehensive presentation difficult, and it requires considerable integration by the reader. Still, I have dared to present the development of Anima as it unfolded in therapy, hoping the immediacy of the dream-language will be able to communicate part of the inner experience.

I shall not enumerate spectacular external successes. Instead, I will focus much more upon inward rather than outward events; yet I would like to avoid the misconception that the path of individuation, namely the journey to one's Self, is an exclusively internal affair. First, to be sure, the concern is with inner images and their meaning, followed by a stepwise change of attitudes, by fine nuances of differentiation of feelings, and by processes of transformation that require a great deal of time. Yet development would stop at any time that the new attitudes were not applied to the concrete, outward life. Only when a new level has been fully experienced and translated into living can it be sacrificed for the sake of transition to the next level.

Professional discretion prevents me from entering into the details of the external events that accompanied the inner development. May it suffice to repeat that the dreamer was an extroverted, intuitive person whose entire energy was by nature outer-directed and who quite independently did everything in his power to succeed and progress in his everyday life. Thus it soon

was possible to focus in therapy all the attention on the Anima, on rendering it conscious, and on differentiating the relationship-function. As stated previously, the dreams rarely deal with the outward life-situation or with deviant, pathological aspects of the psyche. They reflect primarily concern with the unconscious, the integration of which leads to individuation, to the wholeness of the personality.

In evaluating psychological development, one must keep in mind that, during the first half of life, progress can be measured by the degree of adjustment and—especially in men—by the amount of outward success. In the second half, this measuring by outward success is only of relative value. By discovering the unconscious soul and its existential as well as religious needs, one aims for an expansion as well as for a qualitative change of consciousness. This qualitative change cannot be measured or be described by means of rational concepts. Yet it manifests itself immediately in subsequent dreams in the guise of changed attitudes of the dreamer towards himself, towards religious problems, and towards his fellow human beings.

II. The Dreams and Their Interpretation

When this nearly forty-year-old man decided to discuss with a therapist his life situation and his dreams, he brought with him a dream which he had experienced some time earlier and which had both impressed and scared him deeply.

Dream One: Bugs

"A whitish-yellow gigantic head-louse comes towards me from a sand-cave on the slope of a mountain and tries to attack me. I'm smaller than the louse. With a long, thin lance I'm trying to parry 'her.' At that moment a beetle-like animal, of the same size as the louse, approaches the louse. They bite into each other doggedly and both fall down dead."

The dreamer is reminded by the louse of most unpleasant war experiences, of a life of filth and lice. The trauma of war was a contributory cause to his nervous tension. The louse (in German) is characterized as feminine through the article (*die Laus*) in opposition to the beetle *(der Kaefer)*. Thus we may surmise in "her" a first clue of a feminine aspect of the unconscious, of the feminine, instinctual soul. The latter has become negative, overpowering and dangerous, a gigantic, bloodsucking vampire. The small, thin lance of the dreamer, his limited human reasoning, his conscious will to defend himself are inadequate against such an internal threat.

Were it not for an equally gigantic adversary also arising from the unconscious against the louse, he would have fallen prey to the

superior power of the negative "Anima." The beetle—or scarab—rolling its black ball through the sand became in Egypt a symbol of the sun and of its voyage across the sea of the night, an image of the spirit's rebirth. At the time of embalming, a scarab was placed in the heart's space of the dead Pharaoh.[150] In this dream we may look at the beetle as an expression of the male aspect of instincts, as a yet preconscious impulse from which the individual spirit later emerges.

The two animals which doggedly bite into each other represent the unconsciously evolving battle of the opposites. Yet this eternal battle of nature no longer occurs undisturbed within itself. The louse comes at the dreamer and tries to attack *him*. The louse (she) is an autonomous, internal agent or factor which crosses and disturbs the ego's conscious efforts. The louse and beetle have no brain or spinal cord. They portray deep-seated, inarticulate instincts which become conscious only as vague irritability. For the time being, it remains unclear what the inner conflict consists of. The only thing we can know for sure is that the dreamer has become profoundly discordant with his nature and that he is being assailed by ugly, disgusting, anxiety-producing instincts. He therefore is not only irritable with himself and others, but even his life itself seems threatened by the predominance of the instinctual sphere that has turned against him.

This first dream was followed by others of similar nature, with attacking hornets and wasps which in the end, however, do not sting. These are again "insects," no longer larger than life-size, yet still potentially capable of killing a person if they attack as a swarm.

Unfortunately, the water-dreams that come next were not written down. Dreams that deal with water, especially with the sea, are indications of an approach between consciousness and the unconscious. Water itself symbolizes the phase of purification—alchemically speaking, of the *ablutio;* in psychoanalytic terms, of catharsis. In psychotherapy this is the phase of confrontation with one's own life, one's past, one's character, and one's shadow.

Dream Two: The Crash

"There is an airplane crash into a mountain stream. I'm dead, but I still become aware of the newspaper account about the accident."

When one habitually observes one's dreams, the inner process begins to flow. The "death" of the "death and rebirth" is being prepared. As an extroverted, intuitive person, the dreamer was used to passing lightly, as if flying, over situations. Inwardly he was always ahead of himself and lived in wishes and plans for the future. It was the discussion of his current situation that occasioned the crash into the hard reality of his *present* way of being, of his existence. With a plane he falls into a mountain stream, close to the source of his stream of life, where it all began and where in his youth the direction of his life was determined by his father's early death. The dreamer dies but is aware of the accident's announcement in the papers. Things cannot continue as before. Yet, fortunately the catastrophe takes place only in the dream. Part of himself is able to acknowledge the crashed ego, able to hear the news of the accident. Through this process comes the possibility of self-reflection.

This dream is followed by others contending with sharks. This points to the danger of being swallowed up again by the original, perilous lack of consciousness. Then, after additional discussions and other dreams, a dream occurred which, following the old ego's death, announces a new or reborn consciousness.

Dream Three: Sunrise

"I'm flying slowly with outstretched, unmoving arms, high above fields, forests and meadows. Wherever I fly, the shadow below me turns to sunlight. Though I do not have the sensation of being the sun, it is in effect as if I am. I see small trees and their shadows; I see how the sun penetrates into valleys in the morning. My light awakens cows sleeping on pastures and startles a pair of lovers at the edge of a forest."

Slowly, without even moving his wings, the dreamer drifts across the awakening world far below him. He doesn't have the impression that he is the sun, but rather that all the light comes from him. A light awakens in him which illuminates the world in a new way. It is the birth of a new consciousness. Having become quiet inside himself, he can again feel one with the awakening world. He becomes aware of awakening cows, feminine-maternal arch-symbols. At the edge of a forest a pair of lovers is startled. They reflect an awakening emotional relatedness at the very edge of consciousness. The dreamer is capable of a wide overview, as he is flying high above the earth.

"Deification always follows the baptism with water," said Jung. "The new person who has a new name is born at this point. We can observe this quite well in the Catholic sacrament, where the priest holds a candle during the baptism, saying: *Dono tibi lucem aeternam*—I give you the eternal light. The candle light represents the sunlight, for after the baptism we are related to the sun. We obtain an immortal soul; we are 'twice born.'"[151]

After the enthusiasm of his flight and the strengthening of his consciousness, the dreamer is again confronted, in the next dream, by his inner conflict.

Dream Four: The Image of the Royal Couple

"I'm walking between two fronts of a war-torn country, fleeing the enemy. I reach the gate of a park. A servant lets me in and guides me to a house where everything is peaceful, as if there were no war. But then I observe in the adjacent rooms people packing, getting ready for flight. I'm disappointed, as I'd hoped to have found a refuge. In a magnificent hall I notice a tiny picture of a married couple amongst precious Dutch paintings. The master of the house, a dignified, older gentleman, possibly an ambassador, explains to me that the couple was the king and queen. He tells me he has to leave; that I could stay but that he could not guarantee my safety. I renew my flight and reach a crossroad along with other refugees. I decide which way I will go."

In the first dream the dreamer found himself between a bug and a louse. In this dream he is between people at war, fighting each

other. However, a war concerns many people. This shows him that his conflict is universal, that he is not alone. In the house with the paintings he hopes to find peace by looking at his inner images. A tiny picture of a king and queen, a new form of the lost parental images, represents a distant goal. In the iconography of alchemy, king and queen stand for the quintessence of masculinity and femininity and for the matrimonial union of these opposites within the psyche.[152] In *Christian Rosencreutz's Chymical Wedding* it is a great honor to be invited to such a wedding, and the path to it is hard to find.[153] Thus the tiny picture embodies vocation and program, the dream's goal and the path towards that goal. Since the dreamer chooses the right path, he is led in the next dream to the King and Queen.

Dream Five: *The Royal Couple in the Country of Blacks*

"In Abyssinia, or another country of blacks, I am an ambassador dressed in a magnificent uniform, arriving at a ceremony of some sort. Very tall blacks with magnificent bodies, dressed in furs, golden necklaces, and white feather-tufts, stand in ranks and lower their weapons as a sign of greeting. Accompanied by dignitaries, I'm walking up wide stairs covered with leopard-skins. At the top of the stairs, before a throne, stand the king and queen. They, too, are most magnificent. I'm standing beside the king, turned towards the populace. It occurs to me that I have the honor of standing on the same level with the king."

As a messenger of consciousness, the dreamer penetrates into dark Africa, that is, into the unconscious. Here he is confronted by the living archetype, the original wholeness, represented by the opposites of king and queen which in the unconscious are not yet separated. Just as in Haggard's *She*, the journey to the "savages" leads across steps covered by leopard-skins.[154] These steps symbolize sacrificed bestial nature leading to the royal couple. The magnificence of this dream indicates its importance. The dreamer reviews within his unconscious that which he must later achieve on another level of consciousness. It occurs to him that he's given the honor of standing on the same level as the king. Thus he anticipates the possibility of reaching "the level of the king" in his in-

ner journey. The king is his unconscious Self. The next dream will remind him of how far he still is from this natural order.

Dream Six: Old Man

"An old man's life is saved by an operation after an abscess has perforated his intestine."

The dream makes clear that a severe disease caused by conflict can be healed through energetic, conscious intervention. The old man, like the old king in some fairy tales, represents absolute spiritual principles and diseased, antiquated views, inadequate for solving conflicts. These obsolete principles, however, are to survive for now. The old authority is to retain its legitimacy until a widened consciousness allows for a new orientation. The old man's intestinal disease indicates that everyday events could no longer be "digested" by the dreamer. Thus an abscess, a form of self-poisoning, had developed. By means of therapeutic dialogue, it has been possible to avert immediate danger.

Dream Seven: The Wedding Did Not Take Place

"The dreamer has been invited to a wedding which does not take place. He thinks that it is better this way, as he'd only have gotten drunk. When he leaves town, he is grazed by a war invalid on a motorcycle."

The dream recalls the theme of the "chymical wedding."[155] In alchemy one's intent was to separate, through chemical procedures, the opposing principles of silver and gold, sun and moon, masculinity and femininity; to purify them; and to fuse them into one. C. G. Jung explained that these processes were more relevant to psychic events than to physical objects. Alchemy, which deals with unknown substances with unknown properties, encouraged meditation and psychic projection upon chemical processes.[156] The relatively late alchemistic book *Chymical Wedding* clearly describes a process of inner development similar to that found in our dream-series. In the *Chymical Wedding,* Christian Rosen-

creutz is invited to a royal wedding. He must purify himself in order to be worthy to attend the celebration and be sufficiently mature to understand it. The small letter inviting Rosencreutz to the wedding contains the following warning:

> Take heed!
> Observe yourself.
> If you don't cleanse yourself carefully,
> the Wedding may harm you.
> Harm to him who fails in this,
> beware who proves too light.[157]

The dreamer realizes that he is not ready for this wedding. He comments that he'd only have gotten drunk during the celebration; that is, he would have become less, not more, aware.

The war invalid whose motorcycle grazed him is "the other" within him, his dark brother who had sustained internal rather than external wounds during the war. For some time the dreamer had been able to forget him, but the invalid is a part of him. He shows that he is back by his dangerous driving.

With this dream and the following one, the analytic work comes to a provisional closure. Up to here discussions have focused on assessing and clarifying the dreamer's external situation and his internal distress with its origins in family structure and childhood. The dream of the sunrise foreshadows a new development. The dreams of the royal couple show the dreamer his distant goal. The dream of the old man indicates a spiritual improvement caused by removing the source of pus. After the decrease in tension following the sunrise-dream, the dreamer is grazed by a war invalid's motorcycle at the end of Dream Seven. His shadow from which he seemed to have freed himself has caught up with him again. His hectic style of living is obviously associated with a psychic trauma suffered in wartime that continues to endanger him. In spite of the old man's recovery, the dreamer still carries within himself an invalid whose cure is not an easy matter.

Dream Eight: The Hand-Spun Coat

"I put my new hand-spun coat around my sister's shoulders. It turns into a warm cloak."

This dream concludes the first phase of analysis. The hand-spun coat symbolizes the dreamer's new orientation. This coat is not a factory production. Care and empathy have spun its thread. The dreamer will be able to approach his sister with greater warmth when he visits her the next day. While discussing this dream, he realizes that this sister is his Anima, a part of himself he is searching for and which will make him complete. The insight that the Anima is no longer projected on the mother, but meets him now in the person of his sister, fills him with joyful enlightenment. The Anima had appeared first in the tiny picture of the royal couple (Dream Four) and later as the queen of Abyssinia (Dream Five). In the latter the queen still represented the image of the Anima which the mother shapes in the child's soul and which unconsciously influences the son's way of life. The king embodied the leading spiritual principle, which the father awakens and which influences the child and the later adult without his awareness. The unconscious tie with the parents, especially with the mother, is indicated by the son's uncritical acceptance of everything traditional, that is, everything that was believed at home, including beliefs about emotions.

Now that the dreamer has transferred the inner image of the Anima from mother to sister, he will no longer be the child who still expects satisfaction of his wishes from women, who fears maternal strictness, and who attempts to escape the demands of an overprotective mother. He can now change from a mother's boy to a brotherly comrade who not only takes but also wants to give and be considerate. He becomes aware of his personal responsibility towards women. The transfer of the Anima-projection to the sister represents a first, important step in the Anima's development.

Up to this point, the dreams followed closely one upon the other. Due to outward circumstances, the next dream was only recorded about nine months later. This long interruption may not have been altogether accidental. Like growth in nature, the development of the unconscious is slow. Often it takes several

seasons, as does the development of the human fetus, before an insight is born into the reality of life.[158]

Dream Nine: The Horses Bolt

"With my brother who is slower and weaker, I'm standing in a stone-paved yard surrounded by a wall. It is open on one side. On another side, there is a smaller opening onto a rocky terrace which drops down hundreds of yards into the sea. Two black horses that have bolted away gallop through the yard. I fear lest they go beyond it and plunge into the sea. I run and catch one by the halter. My brother catches the other. The horses rear up and kick, but I manage to still them. They are saved."

The intuitive person's horses have taken off so wildly that he is in danger of being dragged into the depths, but beside him stands another, his younger brother. Being the older one, the dreamer had looked down upon him, but in the dream he is able to withstand the horses' onslaught only with his brother's assistance. Alone, his consciousness could not have held out against them. Because it is identical with extroverted intuition, it would have joined the onward rush. Yet his shadow-brother, usually a disparaged or unappreciated side of his being (reflecting one of his auxiliary functions), comes to his aid and saves him. Immediately after the discussion of this dream, another follows.

Dream Ten: Riding

"The next night I dream I am riding a wild, brown mustang. I'm sitting in the saddle. The horse makes the wildest leaps, but I have the wonderful feeling of remaining on top."

The dreamer is now capable of bridling his impulses. His horses, symbolizing his anger and desires, still bolt too easily, but it is a good feeling when he can subdue and guide his instincts and be carried by them.

In the analytic phase now beginning, the focus is no longer on clarifying the external situation, understanding family dynamics,

or finding causes for his being the way he is, but rather on developing internally. Now he must come to terms with his "animals," that is, his nature and instincts. He will meet on a different level those inner conflicts that were at first represented by an ugly louse and bug.

Dream Eleven: The Heath-Cock

"I'm sitting in the clearing of a forest. Ahead of me is a group of mighty firs. On the ground between the trees a heath-cock makes his mating call. A group of girls sits behind me whispering, snickering, and laughing. I'm angered because the heath-cock becomes suspicious. He stops his call, stretches his neck and flies away. A second one appears from between the trees. The same thing happens. Finally a third one comes. I get him into the sight of my rifle and am about to pull the trigger. I realize it is a hen, which one is not allowed to hunt. I put down the rifle. I realize that it isn't a hen either, but a little, shriveled-up, bearded woman with long, grey-white, stringy hair which partly covers her face and hangs all about her. She comes towards me slowly. I tell myself, 'Thank God I didn't shoot.' I awaken."

The two previous dreams dealt with horses that could be used for labor; that is, they dealt with more or less domesticated instincts. Now the dreamer finds himself in the forest, in nature which is not directly subject to his will. The heath-cock makes his mating call by instinct. He is temporarily deaf and blind to danger. Behind the dreamer's back, girls whisper and snicker at the blind instinctuality of animal nature and at the aggressive hunting instinct of the dreamer. The latter feels somewhat ridiculed by the women because of his instinctive reactions. The laughter startles the cock, and the hunter is not able to fire. The same thing happens with the second heath-cock. The third one, however, changes into a hen right in front of the hesitating rifleman. His conscience stops him from firing. Female game must be spared. As he continues to hesitate, the hen transforms into a troll. Intense anticipation and hesitation change an exclusively instinctive animal into a nature-spirit with human traits. It is nature-like but not instinct-bound.

Such miraculous transformations can be found in the sagas of the swan-knights.[159] In the Germanic epos, swans become swan-maidens who turn back into swans and fly away when hunters try to grasp them. If a knight succeeds in capturing a swan-dress, the maiden stays with him and bears sons who, because of an evil destiny, are again changed into swans. A similar metamorphosis is attributed to the white hind. She evades the hunter and leads him into distant, forlorn hunting grounds. As he approaches her, she turns into a radiant young woman. The passion for hunting pursues as game the shy, hard to find, hard to grasp nature-soul; it pursues the fleeting contents of the unconscious which promise fulfillment of one's deepest longings.[160]

If the hunter in this dream had fired prematurely, he would have permanently fixated his understanding of his instincts at an animal level. An assertion like "after all, it's only sexuality" would characterize a person with this fixation. The girls' mockery forces the hunter to reflect and evaluate himself. They mirror his still impersonal and indefinite Anima. His hesitation causes his impulsive-masculine aspect to be replaced by a passive-feminine, instinctual one. The latter is represented by a near-human nature-spirit with whom one may converse and establish human contact. The troll is a clearly defined figure in contrast to the vague, indefinite quality of the girls. In the next dream, the dreamer achieves the transformation he had observed in the third heath-cock.

Dream Twelve: The Bathing Suit

"I see hanging a woman's bathing suit which looks like a skin. When I put it on, it fits my larger body. I sense that I'm now simultaneously male and female."

The dreamer slips into the "skin" of the owner of a bathing suit. By identifying with a woman, with her attitudes and ways of reacting, he discovers that he is feminine as well as masculine. He finds that he is able to be passive-receptive. For the first time, it becomes clear to him that he must seek the feminine, not only outside in a woman, but also in himself. This decisive insight will help him to reclaim his Anima-projection. This dream is an anticipatory experience of his own wholeness.

It is important for the ego not to allow itself to be seduced into identifying permanently with the Anima, inasmuch as this would cause the man to become effeminate.

Dream Thirteen:
Young Hart, Poacher, Earth-Mother and Variegated Field

"Armed with my rifle I walk upward on a path through forests and meadows. Suddenly at a turn in the path, I see a young hart who has died of a gunshot-wound. Since it is illegal to shoot such a young hart, I call the foresters. We search through the forest until we find a dilapidated hut. We rush in with drawn weapons and arrest a surprised poacher. He is led away, and I leave the house with the arrested man's wife. At that moment a neighbor, an old, grey-haired, shriveled-up woman, comes out. She assumes that the poacher's wife will want to get rid of her property since her husband has been arrested and offers her $3000 for it. The offer seems quite high to me, and I ask her why she is willing to pay so much for a neglected hut. She answers, 'I need a variegated field which is on her property. It is worth it.'"

The heath-cock that changed into a hen is joined here by a young hart. Among the Germanic tribes, the hart symbolized the dying and resurrecting sun of New Year.[161] In alchemy a *cervus fugitivus*,[162] a fleeing hart, symbolizes an early, transitory form of spirituality. The goal of alchemistic skill was to transform the hart into the stone, symbol of the sun or the king. Unfortunately, before he can transform himself, the hart in this dream becomes a poacher's victim. This poacher represents the inconsiderate, lawless aspect of male activity. He breaks into foreign preserves and appropriates things which are not rightfully his. In his greed, he is as blind as the heath-cock during his mating calls. Lawless masculinity, the opposite of male courage and enterprising spirit, is arrested by consciousness and put behind lock and key.

After the poacher's arrest, the feminine side of the dreamer reappears. As in fairy tales, the troll of the previous dream appears, a bit more humanized, as the old earth-mother. For good money she acquires the poacher's property. Contrasting with the poacher in her willingness to pay for what she desires, she makes an offer

which seems excessive but is commensurate to the value of the variegated field. The dreamer explains that this field could produce a wide variety of fruits and plants. The field had belonged to the poacher, but instead of caring for it he had only exploited it. This field could produce several times more fruits and flowers if only it were cared for by the right person. Now it passes from the hands of the poacher and his wife, who represents primitive emotions associated with him, to those of this old woman who has detached herself from animal nature and from mere drive and instinct. The field will now serve a higher purpose.

Let us consider the poacher more closely. Among the Germanic tribes, poachers were accepted and rewarded by the god Odin who himself became a wild hunter.[163] Odin would attack men violently in order to turn them into either heroes or berserk people.[164] This "wild" masculinity was repressed, but not fully subdued, by Christendom. It continues to dwell in human nature in the guise of a shadow or "devil." A substantial part of psychotherapeutic discussions are devoted to the task of becoming conscious of the shadow.[165] Knowledge of the shadow becomes more important as one approaches deeper layers of the unconscious and the archetypal images found in myths, fairy tales, and ancient religions. The shadow is dangerous if it is not recognized; however, it contains energies without which we cannot attain the wholeness of our being.

The poacher is a universal shadow-figure. Faust,[166] for example, ails because he does not recognize Mephisto as his shadow, that is, as a part of himself. He is too willing to let the devil and his three wild companions—Fighthard, Robsoon, and Holdtight—comply with his wishes and projects. Their actions must, in the end, fall back upon Faust himself. Our dreamer, similarly, had not allowed himself to see that he was succeeding easily only through the poacher's assistance. Now he must take a further step and assume responsibility for his shadow's actions. Faust, convinced that he is an idealist with no evil intentions, yet becomes a poacher where Gretchen is concerned. At the end of the second part (of Goethe's work), he allows the devil and his cohorts to execute his plans for reforms, even though they cost the lives of Philemon and Baucis, a genuinely pious couple. To the very end, Faust wishes to claim new land, unaware that he is allowing his own grave to be dug.

In our time, Faust's quest has been repeated on a grand scale.

Obsessed by a Faustian urge, Germany made imperialist plans whose execution involved, as with Faust, Mephisto's helpers Fighthard, Robsoon, and Holdtight. Pious citizens were murdered. Their possessions, like those of Philemon and Baucis, were confiscated for the sake of "greater projects." Trenches turned to graves. Along with grave-diggers came "Want," "Worry," "Guilt," and "Misery," the somber personalities who afflict the blind Faust at the end of his life. Faust is, then, the symbol of Nazi Germany and of those of us who, driven by the Faustian impulse, ignore our shadow's actions.

Faust is rescued from hell through the intervention of the beatific penitents, women who show him the penance for which he never found time during his active, willfully masculine life. In heaven he is first changed by the example of the loving Patres into an admiring boy. Then the presence of his early beloved, Gretchen, pulls him upward to the Virgin, Mother, Queen, the epiphany of the eternal-feminine which will heal him through grace and love. Only now may he experience the *present* as fulfillment. This late fulfillment occurs in an otherworldly heaven, that is, in hidden strata of the unconscious, but leaves life on earth unchanged. A man will remain a victim of his untamed impulses and unlimited greed until he integrates the eternal-feminine into his being.

The feminine, however, does not approach him, in the beginning, in her heavenly glory, but as a modest, homely creature. For example, she appears in this dream as a troll; to Faust she first comes as a witch. We find in this dream the earth-mother of traditional fairy tales and ancient nature-religions. The Greeks called her Demeter, goddess of Eleusis. Her daughter was beautiful Kore. In the Eleusinian mysteries a ripe ear of corn, the golden fruit of the field, was presented as a sign of wealth and fertility. Corn and wheat became symbols for death and rebirth to new and eternal life. In agriculture the earth-mother teaches human beings to fulfill their needs through industriousness and effort.

Variations of this Great Goddess are Cybele, Anaitis, Astarte and Isis. The goddess is a mother or sister of a son- or brother-lover who dies and resurrects each year. In this sense, she is an early form of the Virgin Mary, whose godly son offers himself as a sacrifice for humanity. With the appearance of the earth-mother, one adopts the work of cultivating one's own field and waiting for the ripening of sowed corn, while sacrificing aggressive masculin-

ity, hunting instincts, and eagerness for combat. Among the priests of Cybele, this sacrifice took the form of self-castration. In the Catholic church, it is represented by the priest's renunciation of marriage and his obedience, even in thoughts and beliefs, towards the Mother Church. It requires of each Christian the imitation of Christ. This sacrifice is a denial of one's will as well as a renunciation of the ego's presumptuousness in favor of the superior impulses of the Self.[167]

In this dream the dreamer gains insight into his shadow and renounces primitive, masculine impulsiveness. In the following dream, he succeeds in remaining a passive observer and consequently discovers how nature, when allowed to follow its own ways, finds new solutions.

Dream Fourteen: Mouse and Corn-Hawk

"I'm walking along a broad forest trail. To my right and left are tall firs. Just behind me walks a feminine figure, possibly my sister. Ahead of me runs a mouse or mole. Along the path, above and slightly behind me, flies a bird of prey which I identify as a rare corn-hawk. I feel that he wants to aim towards the mouse but cannot see it, as I'm between them. I also have the impression that the mouse would like to be eaten by the bird of prey. I talk with my sister about that. The bird is quite colorful, as if he had blue and red laces or flowers pinned on his wings. I think that things would certainly work out if the mouse were decorated in the same way. I look at it again, and I notice that the mole, or mouse, now has colorful dots and lines, like those of the corn-hawk, in its pelt. At that very moment the bird of prey swoops down and grabs the mouse. Oh, thank God, all of us, including the mouse, are redeemed."

The awakening of the dreamer's feminine side is illustrated by the transformation of the heath-cock into a troll (Dream Eleven), the identification of the dreamer with the swimsuit's owner (Dream Twelve), the earth-mother's acquisition of the variegated field in the last dream, and now the Anima's transformation into an inward, sisterly companion. The mole or mouse represents chthonic nature, the soul's impulsive, instinctual aspect. The corn-hawk represents a spiritual aspect of the instinct. It is not holy but

rather wild, dark, and nature-like. In this dream the earth-bound instinct—the mouse—and soaring spirituality—the hawk—desire to become one. The union of drive and spirit is obviously longed for by the mouse. Earth-bound instinct has an innate drive towards the spirit by which it wishes to be recognized, grasped, and understood.

The approach of these opposite instinctual forces is mediated through the red and blue flowers and laces which decorate both hawk and mouse. Obviously, the variegated field of the last dream has brought forth blue and red blossoms. Blue may represent here the sky or rays of the spirit. Red may represent warmth, heat from a fire, or blood. Color as an expression of feelings is the mediating factor between seemingly unbridgeable contrasts. In this dream, the mouse is simply devoured, but a universal sigh of relief signals the correctness of this event. The fact that the mouse was devoured tells us that for the time being the spirit will be dominant, not by going its own ways, alienated from nature, but by feeding upon the chthonic instincts. The next dream will show how impulsive energies can now benefit scientific thinking and research.

Dream Fifteen: The Circus Athlete

"I'm in a circus tent. A female companion is right behind me. There is no audience. Up in front an athlete exercises on a high horizontal bar or trapeze. He's young and strong and has a pointed beard. My companion whispers to me: 'This is a scientist who does gymnastics here.' Two little boys, about four or five years old, work out with him. They lie on mattresses suspended in the air. The man swings the mattresses, and the boys must then make contrary motions. The child closer to the athlete repeatedly loses a rope, almost falling off. The other child has no problem and is no longer observed."

Dream Sixteen: Rotary Motion

"When I fall back asleep, my lady companion tells me, in connection with the boys' movements on the mattresses, that if I constantly turn from my back to my stomach, I will be able to solve

the scientific problem that has preoccupied my waking life. Then I dream I'm in a room with three young men whom I know from either high school or college. Each one of us lies on his own mattress. Before we have rotated ourselves ten times, I suddenly realize, 'Now I'm finished—I have solved the problem.'"

These two dreams demonstrate that the sharp-eyed bird of prey of the last dream anticipated an aptitude for scientific thought. In Dream Fifteen an athlete, whom the Anima-companion designates a scientist, hovers on a trapeze in a circus tent. Beside him are two boys on suspended mattresses. This arrangement is reminiscent of Mithras, the sun-god of the Roman legions, who is often pictured between two boys who may symbolize his rise and fall. With his pointed beard, the athlete/scientist calls to mind Mephisto. Thus, the scientist practicing gymnastics apparently is more than just a human being: he may be intellect manifesting itself as a demoniacal force. Thinking, as one of the dreamer's unconscious functions, is affected by the demoniacal aspect of the unconscious. The circus tent, with its round, enclosed form, is a first, though unstable, container for the roundness and wholeness of the Self.[168]

In Dream Sixteen we find four young people, including the dreamer, upon mattresses. They must practice the scientist's exercise in order to solve the scientific problem which actually preoccupied the dreamer at this time. Movements of the unconscious, represented visually by shifting bodily positions and counter-positions, reach consciousness. Now he is not simply the victim of opposites as in Dream One. He is learning to include opposites and move between them. Thinking in terms of contradictions still seems to him a circus trick; but it brings tangible results in his scientific work.

Three men exercise in the circus in Dream Fifteen. In the following dream, four men turn around on their mattresses. In this transition from a threesome to a foursome and in the tent's roundness, an approach to the wholeness of personality is expressed.[169]

Dream Seventeen: Spanish Riding School

"I'm riding a well-saddled horse. Then I see, in the guise of a tiny picture, the best horseman from the Spanish riding school on a white stallion."

Dream Seventeen concludes a series which began with Dream Nine. In the latter, there was a bolting black horse, but here the dreamer is on better terms with his instincts. He goes to work with greater interest and confidence. As a distant goal he envisions riding a white horse perfectly. The white horse illustrates the fact that his instincts have undergone a process of spiritualization, and spirituality can now become a supportive reality in his life.

The next dream is an epilogue to this series.

Dream Eighteen:
The Anima Warns against the Eleven Crows

"I was at a wedding. The couple, whom I know, and the other people were fairly well-off but primitive, uncultivated. We drove noisily in horse-drawn carriages to the inn where the wedding feast was held. In the midst of the crowd, I suddenly saw a woman who fascinated me. Looking at her with desire, I offered her a drink and a piece of cake. She declined politely but responded to my glance openly, without sensuality. I was again impressed. I realized that my approach was useless. Then the scene changed. I found myself in the office of a modern, neutrally styled house (or hotel). The door opened, and I stood again in front of this woman. She was well-dressed, unobtrusively elegant. She told me very intensely: 'You must always revile the eleven crows. They eat seeds and are to be chased away. You must always revile them.' (In the dream it was clear to me that, whenever I got angry, it was better to revile birds than people.) Then she left. I wanted to go after her and ask where I could meet her again. Just then she returned and said: 'If you need me, you can simply knock at my door. I live upstairs.' I was deeply impressed by her appearance and manners."

The dream had been triggered by a discussion about women

with a friend. Their talk is mirrored by the uncultivated wedding guests. Evidently, the feminine figure who had been following the dreamer for some time was also present during this discussion. Possibly because the dreamer was gradually able to respond properly, the Anima now appears to him for the first time in her distinguished, superior guise. He realizes that his covetousness will not accomplish anything. She cannot be reached by this type of behavior. Her influence is of such force that the dreamer finds himself transferred to a neutral setting, the office, where he discards his original, uncultivated viewpoint. Now, for the first time, the Anima exhorts him. Emphatically, she tells him of the eleven crows which eat all the seeds. In the dream he realizes that he must not revile people, when he loses his temper, but the crows. In the parable of the sower (Matt. 13) the Bible reads: "Look, a sower went out to sow. And as he was sowing, some seeds fell alongside the road, and the birds came and ate them up." The Anima wishes to remind the dreamer that the good seeds cannot grow roots because they are always swallowed by the black birds.

Black crows are dark thoughts tempting the dreamer to blame others instead of himself. Martin Ninck mentions the twelve berserk men of the Heidrek-saga and the twelve friends of Hrolf Kraki, the crow.[170] The berserk men are possessed swordsmen, followers of Odin. This Germanic god had, as companions, two ravens. For the Germanic tribes, the raven was a sign of battle and victory, as well as death. The crow was a messenger of bad news, and its name was a term of abuse.[171] The black birds of misfortune signal evil thoughts and primitive aggressiveness and depression. They are associated with an era in which disagreements were settled with weapons.

More difficult to explain is the number eleven. It can be seen as being made up of ten plus one, thereby pointing to a new beginning on a higher plane. Or it may indicate a tendency towards twelve, just as three tends towards four and seven towards eight. The two viewpoints need not exclude each other. Strangely appropriate is the following, seemingly farfetched association. The eleventh card of the Tarot, the ancient symbolic game of the gypsies, shows a beautiful young woman, richly dressed, wearing a pilgrim's hat. With her hands, she alternately opens and closes the jaws of a lion leaning against her. The card indicates self-assurance, self-confidence, trust, strength of character, triumph of

spirit over matter, courage, a good woman's influence, and patience in trials and sorrows. The lion symbolizes either refusal of masculine violence in favor of womanliness or animal nature kept in check by ethics.[172]

In the fairy tales of the Seven Ravens, the Twelve Brothers, and the Six Swans, we find common elements: bewitched brothers who have been transformed into birds and a young sister who redeems them by sewing shirts. In all three stories the sister is not allowed to utter a word for the several years in which she carries out this task.

A comparison between these tales and the present dream is instructive. In the fairy tales, the brothers are transformed back into knights only through their sister's silence. In this dream, the dreamer's Anima instructs him to keep silent when he feels tempted to revile others. She teaches him to come to terms with his anger and to humanize his spiteful, instinctive reactions (symbolized by the crows). She then tells him that she is always available as she is living in the upper story, the realm of the heart and spirit, as opposed to the lower realm of impulse and affect. The Anima indicates to the dreamer that she belongs to him. In fact, she is his own soul, but in order to integrate her refinement into his being, he will have to get rid of his concupiscence and change his wrath and anger into self-criticism and chivalry.

The dreamer had met his lower Anima in a previous dream in which she had begged him for protection in order to keep from drifting back to her earlier existence as a whore. At another time—the dreamer could no longer remember where these two dreams fit in the series—he heard a wonderful voice from a church altar singing the Magnificat: "My soul praises the Lord, as he has looked down upon the lowliness of his maidservant." The Anima of Western man is, as shaped by Christendom, split into a refined woman who has high, pure ideals and a primitive woman who is licentious and worldly. Instinctual compliance would jeopardize the development and transformation desired by the "whore-Anima." It would cause her to return to her former, primitive worldliness. Ignoring the whore-Anima's expressed wish would have been a tragic error, not only because it would have undone what she had already achieved, but also because primitivity is dangerous to the soul. It misleads people, especially men, to casually assume that they are moved only by instinct and not by

love. Such a misunderstanding occurs so easily, because in men feeling and instinct are two distinct, often irreconcilable realms. The resulting double Anima has been represented by a saint and a whore, by the madonna and by a cold-blooded nixie with a fishtail. Such an Anima does not have a human heart yet. In a double sense she is heartless. Fairy tales often state that she can gain a heart and an immortal soul only through sacrifice and suffering.

In *The Love-Dream of Poliphilo,* Poliphilo meets at the beginning of his journey a large number of nymphs.[173] At an early stage the Anima, because of her indefinite nature, is projected onto nature. At this stage she appears in the form of many kinds of women, such as the nymphs mentioned above. She may appear unexpectedly in new shapes as game. We find this, for example, in many fairy tales and in Hofmannsthal's *Woman without a Shadow.* Faust is at this early stage when he is rejuvenated by the witch, and Mephisto comments, "After this potion, you soon will see Helen in every woman."[174] In our dream-series, this initial stage of internal development is indicated by the heath-cock transformed into a hen and by the forest girls who snicker behind the dreamer's back (Dream Eleven).

In order for the Anima to transform herself and develop spiritually, the religious significance and value of her spiritual side must be recognized. As long as his Anima remains a vixen or a nymph, a man is justified in doubting whether that which he feels is truly love. If he persists in behaving in a primitive-masculine way, he will convince himself that his eros is nothing but instinctual hunger and thereby cheat and betray his soul which, like the whore-Anima, wants to love and be loved.[175]

One often finds two aspects in men: a "nature-boy" and an ascetic or spiritual man. If the "nature-boy" has been dominant, it is important that the spiritual aspect be developed in the second half of life. On the other hand, if the man has suppressed his natural masculinity, he has probably also disdained his Anima (inasmuch as she represents nature and life) as "evil." Because of this inner constellation, he has been tempted to regard himself as superior to women. He has felt that women are incapable of reaching his spiritual heights. Women have been branded as serpents and seductresses who are responsible for any arousal of his inferior nature.

When Mephisto states that Faust sees "Helen in every woman,"

he does so in the guise of "the force which wills evil and furthers good." Man looks for his lost nature-soul which, in antiquity, dwelled among the gods and was called Selene, Aphrodite, Psyche and, among the Gnostics, Sophia. According to the Gnostic tradition of Simon Magus, Helen was a "virgin of light" descended from heaven. She is at once goddess, moon, ennoia, idea, and prostitute. She is the divine soul which originated in heaven, was banished, infused into a woman's body, and lost on earth.[176] Man seeks his ancient soul. He longs for immersion in nature, for lost piety which venerated divine powers in nature, and for eternal ideas embodied in various goddesses. He seeks his ancient soul to compensate for, and to heal, his modern, one-sided consciousness. For this reason Faust descended to the netherworld of antiquity and returned with Helen.

There was, however, another reason for the revival of antiquity in Goethe's time, namely, the rediscovery of ancient art. The relationship between Faust and Helen is, therefore, a somewhat literary affair, from which Euphorion is born. Euphorion is full of fiery enthusiasm, but his life is short. His body disappears, and only his dress, coat, and lyre are left. For Faust poetry, in the form of an ancient garment, remains, but the reality of his experience of his feminine soul escapes him again when, after a brief period of intoxication, he embraces Helen for the last time. From her, too, he keeps only a dress and veil.[177]

Dream Nineteen: The White Bull and the Three Girls

"I'm inside a glass pavilion. I see an oversized, white bull running towards me. I'm frightened, aware of my vulnerability. The mighty bull snorts, stamps his feet, and lowers his horns in a threatening manner. Just as he is about to storm the glass wall, a wide glass door opens and he enters. A little girl appears and easily leads the bull outside. I'm saved. Then, I find myself in a spacious hall where young women are dancing. Three women approach me. I accept their offer, filled not by desire but by tenderness which I still feel upon awakening."

The glass house in which the dreamer lives symbolizes the struc-

ture of his ideas. The fact that it is made of glass and is, therefore, transparent indicates both vulnerability and spirituality. Though the house is more solid than the circus tent, the first container of his wholeness, he still cannot feel safe in it because of the gigantic bull which, snorting and stamping, threatens him.

In Mediterranean countries, the bull was venerated as a godhead. He embodied generative power, health, and fertility. Fertility flowed from the sacrificial sun-bull upon Mithras's altars.[178] The Egyptian Pharaoh, or god-king, was thought to be identical with the Apis-bull (also known as Ka), the incarnation of divine creative power. As "Ka-mutef" (bull of his mother), he procreates himself from his mother, the bull-god's wife.[179] Pasiphae, the queen of Crete, disguised herself as an artificial cow in order to conceive the Minotaur, the bull-god. Hathor is portrayed with the head of a cow. Hera is called the cow-eyed goddess. As a bull Zeus abducted Europa, and as a bull Dionysus was revered by his priestess. Being giant and white, the bull in the dream is, doubtless, a god against whom human knowledge and will are impotent. Thus, as if by magic, a large glass door opens before him. But then a little girl is able to take him by the bridle and lead him outside.[180] The virginal Anima succeeds where the man and his consciousness would fail. She leads the wild bull away as if it were a tame ox, thereby saving the man's newly-won spiritual stance.

The three women in the second half of this dream represent the feminine principle. They incarnate the three phases of Hekate (or Selene), the moon-goddess: growth, wholeness, and diminution. As the moon-goddess embodies both nature and the soul, this threefold succession indicates that both nature and emotions are subject to changing phases. When the fullness of life has reached its highest point, it must vanish in order to reappear like the moon's sickle in the evening sky. The three ladies offer themselves to the dreamer. Because the impulsive bull, the generative god of antiquity, had allowed himself to be led away, we find that the dreamer's instinctual impulsivity is replaced by trustworthy tenderness.

The white bull has still another aspect. Like the white stallion (Dream Seventeen), and unlike the brown stallion (Dream Ten), he represents a force of light or spirit. Like the Egyptians' Ka-mutef,[181] he embodies the universal, spiritual, creative force

which operates in nature and spiritual realms. Natural creative power and spirit are about to differentiate themselves. When the dreamer is able to avoid the impulsive violence of the god, his spiritual side emerges. In dreams that follow this one, but are not written down, he is brought into a new relationship with his father, the first effective spiritual factor in his life. He discovers new feelings of tender gratitude for his father whom he lost too early, but who, in one of these missing dreams, saves his life.

Because we have reached an essential developmental level, let us quickly review our dreamer's progress thus far. In Dream Eight he had turned with new warmth towards his sister, his Anima-projection. In subsequent dreams, he succeeds in withdrawing the Anima-projection from her. In the bathing-suit dream (Dream Twelve), he realizes that, although the Anima has appeared in the form of a woman, she is part of his own being. Therefore he is able to act in masculine ways and, psychologically, in feminine ways. Once he has withdrawn his Anima-projection from his sister, he is confronted by his animal side. At first the dreamer learns to tame his horses, so that they obey him when bolting. In a following dream (Dream Eleven), he is in a forest where he meets a still to-tally unconscious, instinctual aspect. There, his hesitating, careful attitude allows a heath-cock to change into a hen. This animal soul turns into a troll who later (Dream Thirteen) acquires, as earth-mother, an uncultivated field, an as-yet-unused part of his interior self. She plans to grow colorful flowers and fruits—namely, feelings and sweet nurture—on this land that had previously belonged to the poacher, the dreamer's shadow.

In the following dream (Dream Fourteen), we see how his dark, chthonic instincts allow themselves to be seized by the corn-hawk, his spirit in the form of his intellect. With this, a new spiritual movement sets in. The dreamer learns to think in terms of op-posites (Dreams Fifteen and Sixteen). In Dream Seventeen he foresees the time when he will achieve harmony with his spiritual instinct. His soul has now followed him for some time in a sisterly guise. Then, in the dream of the eleven crows (Dream Eighteen), she presents herself as his higher, spiritual Anima. She emphatic-ally warns him of his tendency to attack others angrily and ad-vises him to seek errors in himself. So strong is her influence that, in the next dream (Dream Nineteen), the dreamer is promoted to a

higher, spiritual level, the glass house. Now the Anima is able to stop the onslaught of the nature-god, the overpowering bull. Male impulsiveness is kept in check by emotion and feelings.

Meanwhile, the dreamer is able to rejoin his family. His wife, always his good comrade, now enjoys with him a loving closeness which he would never want to lose.

The girls in the forest (Dream Nineteen), symbolizing the nature-soul's indefinite quality, have been replaced by a sisterly Anima-figure through whom the dreamer is able to experience love as human relatedness. What had been instinctual ties can now become personal caring.

A few months later a new phase of development begins which is introduced by a super-personal Anima-figure and symbolized by a banner.

Dream Twenty: The Woman-Commander

"I'm looking at an Asian woman-commander. Behind her, to her right, stands her general. He is also Asian. She reviews her well-disciplined troops as they parade past her. I cannot see the troops. I only hear their steps and sense their enthusiasm and their dedication to their commander. The commander is tiny and neat. Her hair is black, her face round. She wears a silver-plated armor which half-covers her breasts. She also wears a precious, white bolero which reaches below her breasts. I'm exploring her face in order to figure out what it is about her that fascinates her troops, but I don't see anything noteworthy. In her right hand she carries a white and blue banner. With her left hand she grasps the upper end of the cloth and holds it tightly against her body. Only her head appears above it. When she puts her chin forward and stands at attention, I hear her troops seized by a fanatic enthusiasm. Meanwhile, her general has moved to the other side of the street. I hear him giving sharp orders. After a while, the commander plants the banner's pole into the ground and begins to pace back and forth, or in circles, with short, nervous steps. Occasionally, she draws figures in the soil with the tip of her foot. Then, her general stands again beside her. I become aware that it is improper to continually stare at her and leave with a female companion who stands behind

me. Before leaving, though, I turn around once more and nod farewell. The commander and her general acknowledge this gesture by nodding in a formal way."

The Anima in her personal aspect stands behind the dreamer, as she had in previous dreams. Now she seems to mediate the vision of a super-personal figure. Similarly, Gretchen draws Faust, Beatrice draws Dante towards a vision of the queen of heaven. The Eastern church has a song in which Maria is glorified as an army-commander.[182] The *High Song* reads: "You are beautiful, my friend, like Thirza, lovely like Jerusalem, fearsome like legions." To be sure, the dream's super-personal Anima is not a heavenly queen, but an Asian ruler and an Amazon.[183] She wears a silver-scaled armor. In alchemy, silver is regarded as feminine, moonlike. The scales remind one of the Anima's origin in the sea of the unconscious, the realm of fishes and vixens. The silver-scaled armor also implies that she is a moon- and war-goddess. Above the armor she wears a precious, white bolero, and in her hand she holds a blue and white banner. The latter has the light colors often found in paintings—Murillo's, for example—of the Maria Immaculata. The commander, however, has both feet on the ground. She rules the anonymous masses of Asia, not the saints.

The dreamer remarks that, for him, Asia represents "the other side," the anti-Christian world. Ever since the war, he has been terrified by the violence found in Asia. Because it encompasses the non-Christianized soul, Asia is for him a symbol of the collective unconscious. This realm, still foreign, is ruled by the feminine principle—a powerful, super-personal woman—and her general. One often hears that the East, Russia and China, has an *Idea,* and this *Idea* can move the masses. In the present dream this idea, embodied in the banner, is carried by a woman, the Anima, who stimulates imitation and enthusiasm. Mediator of super-personal, irrational ideas which oppose rationality, she has the power to exacerbate unconscious energies until they erupt into the Western world, that is, into consciousness. She is powerful because, like Haggard's She, she also represents the male Self, the still-unconscious male image of God. The general, her subordinate, is a shadow-figure of the male Self, under the Anima's spell. As emotional might, the commander is able to mobilize the compelling, impulsive energies of the dreamer and the masses. She acts as a

foreign power, opposed to consciousness, as long as consciousness does not approach her and display interest in her idea embodied in the banner. Later, the dreamer commented that the commander made him aware that it was time for him to learn about the East.

The blue and white banner combines the blueness of the sky and the whiteness of unrefracted light. Blue is the color of the heavenly sphere that encompasses and overlooks the world. This overview and knowledge of the world is linked with the logos, the white light of the cosmos. Knowledge of the world is transformed into detached insight, while, in an opposing direction, the light of heaven penetrates the earth. Like Prakrti and Sophia, the Anima is a mediator through whose being eternal ideas affect the world. Like the Chinese spinner or weaver, she actualizes destiny. However, she is also, like Mary and Kwan Yin, an intercessor who elevates human action and thinking into spiritual knowledge. Silver, blue, and white appear on earth with a feminine figure. That distant realm in which Murillo's Immaculata floats above the earth descends and moves the world. The goddess-soul moves the world through her quality of inner reality. She sets things into motion, with or without consciousness, knowledge, or approval. The general only transmits orders which originate from the woman-commander.[184] The dreamer comments that the general reminds him of the Korean Nam Il, a young man who represents, not tradition, but dangerous, impulsive actions. The dreamer's vision, then, extends beyond his personal problems to world events.

The flag indicates the dreamer's main concern. It announces, and symbolizes, a higher level of consciousness. In Tantric Yoga, blue and white belong to the visuddha-chakra,[185] the mandala located in the throat above the storms of the heart. The symbol of this chakra, a white elephant, is reminiscent of the white bull in Dream Nineteen. Jung reports that in this chakra ideas and concepts are integrated into one's own inner experience.[186]

Because the therapeutic goal, until now, had been differentiation of the ability to relate, the dreamer had progressed quickly. He became capable of relating with genuine emotion to a differentiated, cultivated woman who would expect a differentiated relationship. The next step, foreshadowed by the impersonal Anima figure dressed in silver and white, and by her blue and white banner, is far more difficult because it cannot be attained quite as directly. It involves sacrificing part of the dreamer's newly-achieved

personal relationship in favor of impersonal, spiritual contents. Relationships, at this stage, no longer exist for their own sake. They must lead to eternal ideas, to archetypal images, such as the truth about ourselves, and to the experience of God. We must now look differently at our friends and our enemies. We dislike our enemies only because we see in them the shadow that we refuse to recognize in ourselves. That shadow, the enemy within ourselves who places obstacles in our way and crosses our conscious intentions, is more dangerous than any external enemy. He is the "splinter in one's own eye" which impedes any agreement with the 'other.' Questions of acceptance or rejection will now move into the background. The only thing that matters is finding what we really are and how we will come to terms with our problems. Whatever happens to us can no longer be dismissed as accidental. Even the accidental event will be understood as providential and challenging.

Because every external event has an inner significance, the dreamer can no longer avoid even his fear of Asiatic people. He must seek their cruelty inside himself. This new, impersonal orientation will lead to a deeper understanding of the shadow.

The dreamer greets the strange, Asian woman from a distance, and by nodding her head she acknowledges that she, too, has noticed him. Yet there is an abyss between her Eastern way of being and his Western consciousness. However, unconsciousness is reaching consciousness. This is indicated by the quartet formed by the commander, her general, the dreamer, and his companion. Jung describes the "Wedding-Quaternio" as a symbol of wholeness.[187] Two pairs are linked within themselves as well as with the other pair, expressing the linking of opposites: the conscious with the unconscious and the masculine with the feminine. To be sure, the four persons in the dream are not yet linked sufficiently. The Europeans and Asians must approach each other, and the general is still subordinate to the commander. A genuine *quaternio* will be found only in later dreams.

Dream Twenty-One: The Sword of the Ancestors

"I'm walking through a grey city where misery reigns. I'm constantly approached by old beggars. On their backs they carry sacks

filled with precious family heirlooms, such as ancestral swords, which they offer for sale. I don't want to hurt their feelings, but I don't own anything with which I can pay them. I also fear that they may attack me in desperation. At a street corner I turn to the left. At the next corner, I turn to the right. At the end of this street is the house in which I dwell. I enter. In order to save electricity, I climb the broad, worn stairs in the dark. I reach a vestibule which leads into several apartments. My door is the last one on the right. It is a wide-open double-door. The light is turned on. Comfortable warmth exudes from the tile-stove. An old man who also has a sack with a sword over his shoulder is busy cleaning up. I'm genuinely happy that he has found work, and, thereby, warmth and food. The room is oak-paneled. Against the walls are antique chests. A small section of the room is set apart by a writing desk. This is my space, although it is only a small part of the entire room. The rest of the room belongs to my father. In the middle of my father's space, a large, evenly-grown Christmas tree stands on a table. It is decorated by numerous, elongated tin vases and two porcelain vases with designs of green leaves. As I turn one of the vases around, I see an inscription in gold letters. It is the name of the city of my father's ancestors."

The dreamer finds himself in a grey city plagued by misery. Wandering beggers try to sell heirlooms. Such widespread misery indicates a collective, rather than a personal, problem. The beggars offering heirlooms, particularly old, precious swords, for sale are unemployed souls of ancestors, psychological contents of the past which seek reacquaintance with people living today. Because no one takes an interest in them, they are in misery and, therefore, dangerous. The sword used to be an expression of the dignity and power of a family and an instrument for independent, masculine defense. For the dreamer, it is also the sword that Sigmund had to pull from a tree in order to begin his god-given destiny as a hero.[188]

The dreamer then finds himself in a pleasant, old-fashioned parlor, free from the sufferings of the war-ravaged modern world. Only a small part of his room is designated as his space. He is but a link in the chain of his ancestors. His ego is just a small, late-born descendant, a little segment of the unconscious Self which encompasses all his ancestors. The sword is still owned by an old man, now employed as a house-spirit. The old man, no longer

dangerous, is helpful and has a function with respect to the whole. His proximity allows the property of the ancestors, particularly their instrument, the sword, to gradually become the dreamer's conscious property. The sword represents an ability to make independent decisions and to judge for himself. By using the sword, the dreamer's consciousness should take over the unconscious functions of the Asian woman in Dream Twenty.

In the chamber of his father, that is, the chamber of the ancestors and the Self, is a wonderful, evenly-grown Christmas tree, symbolizing quiet, patient, even development; growth on barren ground; calm in the storm; light in the darkest periods; and union of naturally developed symbols with Christian tradition.[189] The tree is decorated with vases made from the metal used by the ancestors for their vessels. Vases are feminine symbols of receptivity and bearing. They are tangible forms of unconscious contents. Their golden inscriptions reveal the name of the paternal city. Love is thus channeled from woman, through the feminine vessels on the lighted tree, to the city, to which the dreamer would like to return some day. By means of the sword which endows him with the ability to make conscious decisions, he is to continue his father's and his ancestors' lives.

This dream redirects the dreamer's energies from the Anima to his spiritual and professional activities.

Dream Twenty-Two: The Little Daughter with the Ball

"I dreamed today of the beloved woman. I was enamored of her daughter, a child who playfully threw a soft, white ball towards me. I couldn't catch it, and it rolled into a neighbor's garden. At this instant the girl's dog, a playful, snow-white fox terrier, rushed and fetched it, but brought it back only to the border between the two yards where I picked it up myself. Then I was lying on a lawn chair. Ahead of me was a grove of mighty oaks. The woman sat at the end of my lawn chair, and I told her how utterly happy I was. I was filled with a sense of happiness and contentment which I had rarely experienced in actual life. The intensity of my emotion was reminiscent of the tenderness I felt in the dream of the bull and the three young women [Dream Nineteen]. On my left, by the way, was someone I was aware of, but whom I didn't see."

This dream occurred almost nine months after the dream of the bull. In some intervening, unrecorded dreams, the dreamer rediscovered his father who had died early in his life. Now, nine months after his encounter with the "three young women," he has become the father of an "inner" daughter. The sister-Anima is completed by a daughter-Anima. The sister-Anima feels and thinks like his real sister, but the daughter-Anima has her own spontaneity, immediacy, and lack of concern. She is joyful and lively like her little dog. She wants to play and to tempt the mature man to be childlike. By throwing the ball back and forth, she hopes to establish a mutual relationship between consciousness and the unconscious, between thinking and feeling. The dreamer, however, is clumsy and allows the ball to roll into a neighbor's garden. Maybe he unconsciously expects his neighbor, his shadow, to take on the troublesome, playful interchange with the little Anima, but the small dog, the newly-awakened playful instinct, does not allow this to happen. It knows exactly where the ball is and re-engages its master in the game.

After the quiet episode on the lawn, the dreamer finds himself in front of old oaks, sacred trees of destiny. Here he experiences happiness and satisfaction. He feels redeemed from problems that have troubled his family for generations. He now experiences the presence of feelings as an almost tangible inner reality. In Plato's *Symposium*, Diotima states that Eros would no longer be rough and barefoot if, like the dreamer's feelings, he could transform himself into a conscious, inner reality. Then he would no longer be the constant companion of need, a powerful, scheming hunter. Instead, he would be an enduring, inner acquisition, available when one is loved, when one desires goodness, beauty, or wisdom, and when a fellow human being is in need. Eros thus would obtain his rightful position, his home. He would be able to unite conflicting interests in the world of the discriminating and separating logos. Emotions would no longer be in opposition to Christian love as described in the first letter to the Corinthians: "Love does not behave indecently, does not look for its own interests, does not become provoked. It does not keep account of the injury. It does not rejoice over unrighteousness, but rejoices with the truth. . . ." The beginning of this transformation was first experienced in the dream of the three girls (Dream Nineteen). If the dreamer continues to care for his little dream-daughter, this transformation

will, through her, gradually become an integral part of his being. The following dream occurred eight months later.

Dream Twenty-Three: Bow and Arrow

"A youngster had laid down his bow and arrow as they didn't seem to function properly. They looked fairly miserable. As I lifted them up, they suddenly turned out to be very large, larger than myself. The arrow was as long and slender as a spear. It was made of soft, rough wood. I recognized the bow as an Australian aborigine's bow. It seemed to be made of antelope horns or of some special kind of tortuous wood. The youngster and a woman watched me as I bent it. I intended to pull hard and fast and to let the arrow fly. But then,[190] recalling the instructions of Zen Buddhist archery masters, I began to slowly bend the bow to its point of maximum tension. At this point my fingers let go by themselves. As in Zen, "it," not "I," shot. The arrow, made entirely of wood, without even a metal point, kept on flying for an infinite distance. I was quite surprised. It flew across the tops of a long row of trees before falling into a faraway village made entirely of straw-huts. I looked for the youngster and the woman, largely to gain recognition for my long shot. However, my pride was soon mixed with concern that someone in the village might be wounded. I told this to the woman, who was quite indefinite. She thought that no one was injured."

This dream reveals further progress towards less egoistic action, a development begun in the dream of the commander with her blue and white banner. Zen masters regard a quiet, calm state of mind, unaffected by success or praise, as exemplary. The masculine consciousness of the dreamer takes over the youngster's toy, his childlike wishes. In the man's hands, the bow and arrow become the wonderful instruments of our stone-age ancestors, the "original bow." The man now treats the bow and arrow not impatiently, as a boy would, but with complete calmness according to the dictates of Eastern wisdom. For a Western success-oriented person, this progression, made possible by familiarization with Zen, represents a great gain. The arrow reaches an unknown, dis-

tant goal, a far-off center. The following dream, which occurred several months later, brings the dreamer into a close relationship with the Eastern Anima.

Dream Twenty-Four:
The Chinese Girl in a Blue and White Dress

"A young Chinese girl, dressed in blue and white, was waiting at a bus stop. I stood beside her. My hip touched hers. She returned the light pressure. The bus arrived, full of people. We let it pass by. I left the bus stop. I sensed that the Chinese girl was following. Then I noticed that two people, a Chinese girl and woman, were following. A truck arrived. We climbed on. Several women sat in a circle around me. When I first saw the Chinese girl at the bus stop, I felt love, intimate tenderness for her. I felt as if I had finally found her. Now she was sitting on the floor of the truck, leaning her head against my left knee. There was infinite intimacy in her attitude and touch. I longed to kiss her, but, because of the other women, I could not. The Chinese woman sat on my right, loving me with cruel intensity. I felt no conflict between the two Chinese women. In order to be allowed to kiss the Chinese girl, I had to kiss all the others first, so I made the rounds. Among the women was a sinful, pretty blonde. The Chinese girl kissed me but briefly—she didn't want anyone to notice anything unusual—but with such longing that we both knew that we belonged together and would be together. I woke up."

In the past one could barely mention China to the dreamer because of his intense, largely war-related fear of that foreign, hostile country. He had to confront Asia for the first time in the dream of the feminine army-commander. In that dream, the Eastern Anima appeared as an overwhelming military power. Now she approaches him in a peaceful manner. He has, in the meantime, come closer to her by developing an interest in Eastern thought. Until relatively recently, China did not, like the West, focus upon casuality and upon controlling nature. It attempted, instead, to fit human beings meaningfully into nature, time, and the cosmic rhythm.[191] Eastern people attend to nature's uniqueness.

They perceive maxims of life by which they feel supported and against which it is dangerous to resist.

In the Chinese girl, the dreamer now finds the Oriental sense of life which he experiences as his long-sought inner complement. The girl is even more, because the shadow which surrounded the woman-commander is set apart as an elderly woman. The dreamer did not at first describe the older Chinese woman as the embodiment of cruelty and lack of restraint, the qualities which led him to fear the Orient. Only later did he reveal that the love of this older woman seemed to him cruel and dangerous because of its lack of moderation. To him the older Chinese woman appeared as the negative side of nature, as the perilous representative of the ruthlessness and cruelty which occur in Chinese novels and in war reports from all races. In the young lady, however, he encountered the blossoming femininity which is part of an ancient culture unfolding uninterruptedly from nature, a feature in which the East excels over the West. The older woman, on the other hand, represents the danger of lawlessness and barbarity of that collective unconscious that looms also within the dreamer. The young lady is the long sought-for bride, symbol of the forthcoming *coniunctio,* and a promise of inward confluence. She will eventually vanish as a figure and will become part of his psychological make-up.

The woman and the girl are opposites, but, paradoxically, they are also one. They are the one ancient and eternally young, dark and light soul. Sitting in a circle with the two Chinese are many other women. The dreamer must kiss all of them in order to reach the one he seeks. All, even the blonde, sinful, little woman, represent different aspects of women. The dreamer experiences the entire gamut of the nature-soul, from the ruthless cruelty of the older Chinese woman to various encounters and, eventually, to the tenderness of the young lady in the blue and white dress.

Eventually, he may reach that last step where the Anima can be withdrawn from his projections and become his soul's content, his inward completion. At first, however, the dreamer will have to confront many times the dark, dangerous side of the Anima and her shadow. As he gets closer to the collective unconscious, he is also more directly exposed to the collective shadow. As he gets in touch with impersonal, collective powers, it is imperative that he

build dams against their negative aspects. He must deal again and again with the shadow. First, however, we must briefly discuss a second dream in which the dreamer attempts to incorporate aspects of the Anima into his masculine being.

Dream Twenty-Five: The Runner

"I'm in a crowd, watching a runner. Enthusiastic over his performance, I go with a British officer to meet him. The officer asks what he must do in order to run as well. The runner demands to see the officer's feet. They are tightly bandaged and quite stiff. It is obvious that the officer tries to use them like machinery, to make them obey and run. The runner, however, insists that the bandages must be removed, as they are but an artificial cramp, that the foot must become soft and elastic, and that the movement of the muscles must occur playfully. With a touch of irony he adds that the officer is not likely to be able to learn this, since he's already too old and should have begun sooner."

Every experience communicated by the Anima is followed by its masculine counterpart. The dreamer now experiences, in a masculine form, the informal, open nature of the Chinese girl. Such male dream-figures as the runner or, earlier, the athlete in the circus tent demonstrate to him qualities that he should appropriate. In the bow and arrow dream, the arrow intuitively attained the distant goal which he is now to reach by himself. He must travel by foot, not by such modern means of transportation as the bus. What counts is the running, not the goal.

The victorious runner reminds us of runners in primitive tribes who, like animals, are one with their bodies and with nature. He wins, not because of an athletic feat, but because of natural elasticity. He is freed from cramp-like will because he does not force himself. Instead, he allows any performance to be as playful as the little Anima-daughter (Dream Twenty-Two).

With the feet we touch the ground of reality. The foot must be quite soft and elastic in order to adjust itself to any unevenness. For an intuitive person like the dreamer, it is extraordinarily difficult, only partly achievable, in fact, to adapt directly to concrete,

present reality. He is inclined to neglect the commonplace present with its many details in favor of presentiments and future possibilities. The dreamer had to force himself, both in military service and in his profession which required a great deal of precision, to acquire a self-discipline foreign to his nature. He wanted to advance and achieve high goals. He could not afford mistakes or negligence. These efforts and his ambitions created a cramp-like tension.

As a people, the English are predominantly sensation-oriented. Thus, the British officer is well-suited to represent the sensation-function. British officers in the colonies were frequently entrusted with distant posts and with the responsibility for heavy tasks. They were forced into tense individual performances and into a somewhat stiff formality. Thus, the officer in the dream may portray the dreamer's over-strained sensation-function. He admires the runner, but it remains doubtful whether he will ever be able to equal the runner's natural relaxation and flexibility.

Dream Twenty-Six: The Rats

"I see a rat come out of a pipe. It attacks our little dog, bites it, and kills it. I am disconsolate. I notice two women, one clad in black, the other in red. I know that they are the rats. I shoot them."

Rats multiply extremely quickly. They can barely be eradicated in their hideouts. They can become a frightful plague, both because they attack live animals and human beings and because they transmit illnesses. The rat in this dream is a seemingly insignificant, light-shunning, but extremely dangerous instinctual impulse. It is dangerous because of its greed and its tendency to invade domestic territory. In the dream the rat endangers the dreamer's dog, a cheerful, domestic, instinctual component. Undomesticated greed is about to kill the lively, charming aspect of instinct which benefits the family.

Then the dreamer has the sudden insight that two women are rats. As he is aware of their danger, he shoots them. Both women emerged from the older Chinese woman in Dream Twenty-Four. They are the gruesome and immoderate shadow of the Anima and

of the instinctual nature that now manifests itself. Years later, the dreamer still vividly recalled the malevolent, venomous red cloth of this dream-figure. In her he sees a perilous form of provocative sensuality. The woman in black impresses him as a threatening eruption of the shadow. He compares both women to the "Great Whore of Babylon," the symbol of unbridled covetousness in Revelation. He also compares them with "Everywoman" of the Middle Ages, who was portrayed, on one hand, as seductive and, on the other, as replete with sickness and vermin. The dream shows him that he must defend himself against a certain type of woman, namely, against this side of the Anima. As a result, he shoots the dream-figures. For the time being, he can protect himself from regressing to the level of the whore-Anima only through radical measures.

Dream Twenty-Seven: I Overtake My Mother

"I'm racing in a large sleigh. I'm supposed to win, but I find myself alone on the street. Then I notice my mother on a small sleigh ahead of me. I have to pass her on a curve without running over her and without being thrown out of my sleigh. I succeed. After overcoming a number of obstacles, including a bus, a skier, and a fence for animals, I realize that I'll reach my destination. It occurs to me that I will win first prize. At the same time I tell myself that this is entirely unimportant. The main thing is that I have done well and reached my goal."

Because of his earlier decision to fight the Anima's shadow-aspect, the dreamer is able to enter the race and reach the goal which he previously had been able to attain only with the far-flying arrow of his longing. Now, after overcoming the rats, the dark Anima, he is able to overtake his mother, the first bearer of the Anima-image, without disturbing her journey. In order to reach his new goal, the dreamer must leave his mother behind him. The mother represents the longing for childlike security from which the son's consciousness must become free. This time he succeeds in directing his attention entirely upon his task and his goal, without being distracted by ambition or desire to win.

The following dream portrays his personal struggle with super-personal, religious values.

Dream Twenty-Eight: The Church Collapses

"I meet an old professor, my former teacher, in a railroad-station. We exchange a few words. He leaves through a door with another old gentleman. With many other people I go along a hallway to a door. The Dictator was standing behind this door. I thought it was idiotic for him to stand there when his enemy was right outside the door. I entered and found myself in an enormous hall in the basement. My things were stored in a corner. I gathered them in order to climb out of this hall. Everyone else wanted to do the same thing, to escape from impending events. We reached the upstairs and found ourselves in Rome's cathedral of St. Peter. An officer yelled at the people and tried to chase them back. I swore at him. Suddenly I noticed some men in the cupola desperately trying to secure the bells and the bell-tower with ropes. Their strength left them and the bells plunged down, crashing through the floor and probably crushing people in the basement-hall where we had been. Then the cupola began to collapse. We turned and tried to get outdoors. All the walls began to crumble. I broke one of the church windows and managed to jump out. Just before I reached the door of a fence, walls collapsed behind me. A stone hit me in the neck. I still hoped to escape with a final leap, but square stones fell all around me. I realized I was trapped. I was crushed by stones before reaching the door."

After leaving his pious mother, the dreamer finds himself in a railroad-station, a new point of departure. There he meets a former teacher who soon departs with another old gentleman. The appearance of the old professor identifies this starting point as a place of men, of professionals, and of traditional conscious values. But the dreamer is moving beyond this place. He must distance himself, therefore, from his mother, his former teacher, and his scientific father. With many others, he now finds himself in a basement below St. Peter's Cathedral. Here the dictator stands, looking out for the approaching enemy. St. Peter's Cathedral is the

spiritual structure beneath which, in the unconscious, a power struggle between opposites (for example, between the lion and dragon portrayed by alchemy, between greed and might) takes place.

At the end of this dream, the dreamer sees himself transposed back to the end of World War II. He discovers that a power struggle between human consciousness, represented by the dictator, and primitive instincts, represented by the enemy, continues to rage within himself. At the same time, he discovers that his conscious world has been a netherworld. He has subconsciously drifted, with many others, away from the healing truths of the church, from that which the church signifies and presents as an ideal. But when he tries to escape the enemy, the eruption of unconscious powers, by seeking refuge in a church, he finds out that the church can no longer protect him from the enemy nor withstand an outbreak of primitive instincts. Worldwide political upheavals have undermined the grandiose structure of the church within the dreamer's soul. Within the church walls, he feels a lack of protection and an increased threat of collapse.

He had had a dream in which a church collapsed once before. In that dream he was able to save himself by fleeing in spite of his pious mother's pleas to stay. He was then able to avoid religious problems by not looking at them. How would he ever stand alone against the spirit of the age or find a remedy for its distressed condition? Was he not but one of the many victims of historical events? Was he not without a calling as religious reformer? In this last dream, however, flight is useless. Religious crises hurt him personally. The torch of the Second World War has revealed the power of the Antichrist. Subterranean conflicts have eroded the church's image. This is made clear by an earlier dream which we will discuss now.

Dream Twenty-Eight A: The Bomb

"I'm standing before a modern highrise building. Through a door I can see a court surrounded by residential buildings. A bomb hits the area behind this passage, and the buildings collapse. I know that my apartment and all my property, which I acquired

through great hardship after losing everything in the war, have been destroyed. I think of how hard my wife had to slave for our belongings. At that moment a priest in vestments comes out of the passage. Obviously, he has been with the wounded and dying. He carries the extreme unction with him. Suddenly, I'm overcome by rage against the cruelty of fate and God who controls fate. I raise my fist. I threaten the priest and curse God. Though I know that this is a horrendous sin, similar to that of the Titans, I continue to hate and to curse wildly and angrily. I am oppressed by my anger for many days, but I am also relieved that I have expressed it for once."

The trauma of war goes on. After people have re-settled in modern, utilitarian buildings, the peace and quiet are destroyed. A bomb may fall any time out of the clear sky and shatter everything. In his dream, in contrast to his real-life situation, the dreamer is simply one of many tenants of a large apartment house. The bomb affects him and all the others, destroying the calm, the peace, and the fruits of reconstruction. The dreamer's rebellion against God, who allows or causes such things to happen, and against the blindness of fate had been suppressed, but now it finally breaks through. He curses the priest, the sacrament, and God. He knows he is committing a mortal sin.

He internally confronts a problem which he had faced externally during the war. The highrise building, the modern, utilitarian apartment house which he inhabits in the dream, reflects his practical, modern attitude which he tried to accommodate to the world. But now this attitude no longer protects him. An internal bomb explodes his newly acquired peace. He must once more radically restructure the edifice of his views. His war experiences have finally driven him to the side of the Titans, towards rebellion against the gods in heaven. His suffering breaks down his Christian attitude, and he opposes the God-father of his childhood. He loses his sense of security. In the dream of the collapse of St. Peter's Cathedral he finds himself, therefore, between Scylla and Charybdis, between the dictator and the invading enemy, in a camp of mutually destructive forces of the Antichrist. Flight into the security of the church fails because deep down he left the church long ago. The men who make a last, strenuous effort to hold up the bell tower represent his desperate attempt to sustain

the edifice of his former Christian views. Bells are reminders which summon one for prayers and church services. They are the church's live voice. Falling, they act as the crushing Christian conscience. A similar function is found in the legend of the child who refused to go to church on Sunday and was, therefore, pursued by a bell.

The church is made up of a community of believers. In *The Shepherd of Hermas,* an apocryphal New Testament text, Hermas has a vision of the construction of the church. An old woman, personifying the church, explains to him the meaning of stones used for construction. White, square stones that fit together are the saintly, pure apostles, bishops, teachers, and deacons who live in conformity with God's holiness and who work for the benefit of God's chosen people. Broken, discarded stones are sinners. Those which are not discarded far from the church tower are likely to be useful for construction once they have made penance.[192]

The disintegration of this community strikes the dreamer with deadly force. The stone which hits him in the neck is his own, not yet hewn, self, his not yet resolved religious problem. He is not yet polished enough to fit into a religious community and help build it. His own religious problems overtake him and hit him hard; but what slays him is the failure of those whom he believed reliable but who, like himself, dropped out of the community.

That which, until now, was the highest, though not always obeyed, authority for him collapses. St. Peter's Cathedral is the symbol of the one and only *mater ecclesia,* Mother Church, built upon a rock. It is a visible symbol of the unification of opposites: the all-encompassing, protective Mother and the spiritual authority of the great Father, the Pope. Just as the individual stones in Hermas's vision symbolized the faithful, St. Peter's Cathedral symbolizes the fortitude and security one finds in the orthodox community. Until recently, religious questions were resolved by the Roman authorities. Now they are vital, personal concerns.

The dream of the church's collapse marks a radical change in the dream series. Up to now, personal problems—such as affects and emotions, approaches to the Anima, and differentiation of the latter's being—have been in the foreground. In the beginning, the relationship to the Anima was understood as a personal concern. There have been occasional attempts to experience the Self as an impersonal inner center—for example, in the dreams of the circus

athlete (Dream Fifteen), the lady commander (Dream Twenty), and the Christmas tree (Dream Twenty-One).

The collapse of the church, however, reveals that until now the dreamer still identified with the church and felt contained by it. With the cathedral's collapse, his "old Adam," his "old ego" must die once more. Because God has been nicely settled in heaven, and religion settled in church, the dreamer has been free to shape his life according to his own pleasure and traditional, local moral standards. Unconsciously identifying with the church, he believed himself to be personally free. However, with the collapse of the church, his sustaining and protective spiritual and psychological authority, he is confronted by religious problems. The following dreams have an increasingly open character. The inner dialogue centers more and more on the search for genuine religious insight. The death of the old ego, shown in the dream of St. Peter's Cathedral, at first hovers over the dreamer like a vague threat. Only gradually does he realize that this death signals the final relinquishing of an overly youthful, unreflective way of life. His unawareness must die in order to build the new, live world view of a responsible, free-thinking adult.

Dream Twenty-Nine: The Field on the Mountain Slope

"High in the mountains, surrounded by forests, there is a field on a grassy slope. It is filled with bushes and weeds. A man, possibly my brother, and I try to clear it. He digs up the bushes with his shovel, and I plow the field. It is hard work, but the result is a field of healthy, glistening, dark soil in beautiful furrows. Knowing that there is further work to do, we pass through a hedge to a field closer to the edge of the forest. This field, in contrast to the first, is well maintained. It is filled with various fruit trees planted in rows. The trees are relatively young. At a man's height their trunks are cut neatly, so that only the lower branches, some with apples, remain. All the trees lack tops. The other man states that, although it is a shame to dig the trees out, it would be better to do so. Being the stronger one, he begins to dig out the trees. We then become aware that there are rows of thick, heavy root-stocks of firs, cut about three feet above ground, between the thin stems

of the fruit trees. This is going to be a tremendous job, but I now recognize that the work must be done. The man tells me, 'When all the trees are removed, we will have a better shooting range. Also, we will be able to see deep into the forest.' I see only this second man, but I *know* that another man and a woman are here. At last the field is cleared and plowed like the other one. The four of us discuss what is likely to grow. We are full of confidence that there will be a good sowing. We don't sow, we leave this to the forest and the wind. When the field is ready, we find a dead mouse. It is as big as a rat. I think it *is* a rat. We know that this animal was killed by switches as it came out of its hole. We are glad that it is dead."

The field high up on a slope is probably the same as the colorful field in Dream Thirteen which was owned first by the poacher's wife and then by the old earth-mother. Now it is the dreamer himself who cares for this field. If the mountain symbolizes the highest goal attainable in this world, then caring for the field represents the dreamer's higher tasks. The front part of the field, full of bushes and weeds, reminds one of the parable of the sower (Matt. 13): "Other seeds fell among the thorns, and the thorns came up and choked them. Still others fell upon the fine soil and they began to yield fruit, this one a hundred-fold, that one sixty, the other thirty."[193]

The field is the soul. A good seed may not grow in it if there are many weeds. The field is an example of unadulterated, but also uncultivated, nature. It will yield a rich harvest once it is cleared and plowed. Behind the hedge, hidden and closer to the forest's edge, is another field with rows of trees. All the trees are cut at a man's height. The motif of topped trees is found in alchemy as a counterpart to the lion with cut paws.[194] It suggests a painfully incisive sacrifice. It is likely to suggest an additional meaning when it arises in an intuitive individual. Intuition induces the extroverted person to pursue new possibilities. What is new is more attractive to him than what is old, already-known, and close at hand. He lacks patience to wait until his trees bear fruit. Whatever has been started is truncated for the sake of a new goal. Because of his varied interests, and also because of pressing circumstances, the dreamer has changed his place of work and his career. He has

given up what he has achieved in order to continue his education. His versatility, restlessness, cosmopolitan skills, and lack of material success are both his strengths and his weaknesses. The truncated trees point to the repeated interruption of his development. The life flowing from the roots never achieves its crowning.

The roots of the firs between the fruit trees are reminiscent of the mystery of Attis. Every year Attis was carried in the guise of a hewn fir into the shrine of his mother who would weep over him. The remnants of the fir trees indicate that the dreamer lives his life as the beloved son of the mother-goddess and that he sacrifices his life over and over again for her. His consuming ambition is, ultimately, a concession to his mother. Her son is to accomplish that which her deceased husband was not able to do. He is to reach the highest rung of the professional ladder.

In the back of the field are two kinds of trees, firs and fruit trees. Not only Attis but also his mother-goddess was worshiped in the tree on the mountain. Jung quotes from the *Gnosis of Justin:* "The trees of the Garden of Eden are angels; the tree of life is the angel Baruch, the third of the paternal angels; and the tree of knowledge of good and evil is Naas, the third of the maternal angels."[195] The different trees correspond to these angels: the firs to the paternal ones; the fruit trees, bearing apples (like the tree of knowledge) and other sweet fruits, to the maternal ones. Growth of professional development as well as of the Anima has been repeatedly cut short. The truncated fruit trees represent a manifold Anima-experience which never allowed the fruits of knowledge to ripen. Even here, the intuitive individual keeps chasing different possibilities without realizing that he is caught in the mother-goddess's garden of Paradise.

We mentioned before that, as long as she remains in the natural state of paradisiacal ignorance, the Anima can be projected upon many kinds of women. Every possibility that appears on the horizon seems to promise the fulfillment that has been longed for since early childhood. Every attempt at becoming aware of the Anima is pushed aside by a new, false hope. The tree of internal growth was again and again truncated, and a new one was planted beside it. The dreamer never went beyond natural growth, devoid of insight and knowledge. What is missing in the dream is the upper part of the firs, the part that embodied Attis and was brought to his mother's sanctuary, and the upper part of the fruit trees, the

manifestation of the grieving or bridal mother, companion of her beloved son. The growth of the natural soul, depicted as an orchard, is halfway arrested. Denied maturity and fulfillment, it is incapable of growing into the spiritual regions. Spirit and nature remain separate. The church manages the spirit. In it the spiritual symbol is at home, but nature is not included and, therefore, must forego spiritual fulfillment.

Often alchemical work included caring for and growing one or more trees. The alchemical, or philosophical, tree must be planted in a well-protected garden into which nothing foreign may penetrate. This garden is the carefully purified inner earth, the "cleansed Mercurius."[196] It is said of the alchemical tree that whoever eats of its fruits will never be hungry.[197] Thus, alchemy replaces natural growth by planting a spiritual tree in the spiritual earth. Its prototype of this tree, according to Jung, is the paradise tree which bears moon- and sun-fruits instead of apples. These fruits allude to king and queen, the quintessences of masculinity and femininity.[198] The magnificent Christmas tree which the dreamer found in his father's apartment was also a kind of Paradise tree (Dream Twenty-One). It was both a legacy from his father and a happy childhood memory. Now he must plant a spiritual tree in his own inner garden.

The collapse of traditional, religious views forces the dreamer to turn towards his own "soul-garden." He discovers that it is full of wild weeds. A man, possibly his brother, shows him that his field must be cleared and plowed, if anything worthwhile is to grow in it. The earth within one's own soul is the *prima materia* that is transformed into "cleansed Mercurius." Four figures, three men and a woman, work in the garden. The dreamer comments that, although they are different figures, they may all represent himself. They portray those aspects of his being which, until now, he has not been able to differentiate.[199] As in the dream of the army-commander (Dream Twenty), the four figures indicate wholeness. This time, however, the male aspect predominates, since clearing the field represents a conscious activity requiring male initiative and man's spiritual capacity for discrimination. The dead mouse or rat discovered by the gardeners would then represent the greed of the impure *prima materia,* the tenacious gluttony which, in Dream Twenty-Six, appeared as the Anima's addiction. This greed has been expelled, as shown by the rat's death, by self-discipline.

The four persons, representing four different soul-forces, are hopeful that the forest and wind will bring forth good seeds. The forest, the unconscious, has predominantly feminine qualities; the wind, predominantly masculine qualities. The dreamer can prepare the soil, but he must leave the sowing to God or to the forest and wind, that is, to nature. He cannot rationally and willfully choose the right seed. His further development cannot be consciously predetermined, but the alchemical analogy of the garden with the sun- and moon-tree suggests that the dreamer's goal is attainment of the two lights, sun and moon—that is, the quintessence of masculinity and femininity, the union of spirit and soul.

The cut firs between the stems of the fruit trees show that the dreamer's immature spirit maintains an unrecognized, unconscious connection with the mother-goddess. When spiritual values were based in the church, he remained, as son, attached to unconscious nature. In the front part of the field, where male trees, symbols of his spiritual growth as a man, belong, only weeds prosper. Disorder and confusion have reigned here. This problem affects others than the dreamer. In Dream Twenty-Eight he was with others in the basement below the church. *Many* were buried by the collapsing, and *many* tried to flee with him. The people in the basement are the masses who are either not yet or no longer affected and guided by the church's eternal images and who, therefore, unconsciously lapse into paganism. They lead a life defined only by materialistic terms. The remedy for this state consists in cleaning up one's own soul-garden. This dream effected a change, a purification in the dreamer's everyday life. He decided to give up his heretofore superficial relations with women.

Dream Thirty: The Eagle

"I stood in a large room in a multi-story building. Below me I could see the tops of firs. Suddenly I saw an eagle rushing by, playfully shooting downwards and re-ascending. The eagle's wings were steel-colored with white tips. A boy was in the room and I called him to the window so that he could see the eagle. I protected him with my arm and we were standing behind the window, so that the eagle, soaring downwards, its wings rushing in the wind,

could not grab him. The eagle overtook a flock of birds but did not grab any of them. I was surprised. Then the arm of a crane moved swiftly out from the flat roof of the skyscraper and overtook the eagle. At first I thought that he had been captured, but then I realized that he submitted voluntarily. When he was brought into the room I noticed that he had his legs tied and was able to walk only with small steps, and was, therefore, unable to grasp the birds with his claws. In order to live, he had to allow himself to be captured."

The eagle is the larger relative of the corn-hawk in Dream Fourteen. He was Zeus's bird and abducted Ganymede into the clouds. He might prove dangerous to the boy at the window. He could carry the still weak Self of the dreamer up to the gods, alienate him from his daily tasks, and thereby turn him into an eternally immature companion of the gods, living on an unworldly Olympus.

Father Zeus is not mentioned, but the bird with his dark wings and white tips suggests a union of light and dark, good and evil. In ancient Egypt the Horus-falcon was the symbol of the highest celestial god. As a sharp-sighted and all-surveying celestial spirit, and as a manifestation of destiny, he corresponds to a concept of god more ancient than that found in the Old Testament. We find in Ezekiel (17:3) a riddle in which Jehovah also compares himself with an eagle. It reads: "This is what the Lord Jehovah has said: 'The great eagle, having great wings, with long pinions, full of plumage, which had color variety, came to Lebanon and proceeded to take the treetop of the cedar. He plucked off the very top of its young shoots and came bringing it to the land of Canaan; in a city of traders he placed it. . . .'" In his positive aspect, the eagle is an all-surveying, all-knowing spirit. As Horus-falcon he has the sun- and the moon-eye, a celestial consciousness, the precious gift which the dreamer needs to complete and crown his garden (Dream Twenty-Nine).

However, the eagle is also wild, sharp-eyed, greedy, predatory, presumptuous, and physically superior to the human being. His feet are tied in the dream. In order to live he must descend into the human realm, as he is no longer able to catch his own prey. It was probably the clearing of the field in the last dream which resulted in this restriction of the previously autonomous, knowledgeable, knowledge-hungry, instinctive spirit. In that dream, we found that

the dreamer cleared out all wild growth. He also killed the rat or mouse which had been the bird's food. This clearing of reality has restricted the freedom of the bird of prey, the rapacious instinct, and forced him to give himself up to the human beings. The bird is overtaken by the crane, by means of psychological control. Whereas the dreamer has experienced his life as subject to the whims of his curiosity and thirst for knowledge, he is now able to decide consciously what he wants to do. His hunger for life and knowledge will be subordinate to the conscious ego, to human responsibility.

Dream Thirty-One: The Woman in the Furrow

"War! I'm in a battle. I'm under cover in the furrow of a field. I notice a nude woman lying in the same furrow ahead of me. Then I find myself in a house with the same woman, and I'm told to marry her as she has only a few minutes to live. We are led into a room and married. Then the woman appears to be dead."

The dreamer finds himself again in war, in an inner conflict. His only protection and cover is the furrow he himself has plowed. He discovers a naked, unfamiliar woman in this furrow. The furrow is the open womb of the earth; the naked woman incarnates this earth. From above a celestial spirit, the eagle, had been approaching; from below appears the embodiment of earthly reality. The woman symbolizes unprotected, exposed life, nude and poor when deprived of all ostentatious garments. She is as bare as his field after he has cleared it of all weeds, trees, and incomplete growth. She is as poor as a soul deprived of all the benefits of the church. This woman is his life reduced to bare, human, natural facts. He is to affirm this reality and wed himself to her. His saying yes to her means saying yes to simple, untrimmed, and inescapable human nature. He accepts her, and thus she becomes his own truth. She dies in order to become a part of him.

Maybe the naked woman in the furrow is more than a human being. She may be the goddess whose dark aspect the dreamer has shot in the dream of the rats (Dream Twenty-Six). She is probably also a transformation of the mouse found by the dreamer clearing the field (Dream Twenty-Nine). As a rejuvenated goddess emerg-

ing from the furrow, she is also like a seed. She is the grain of wheat which through many transformations must die and resurrect.

Dream Thirty-Two: Divine Service in the Grotto

"I'm climbing up the side of a rock. Halfway up I reach a grotto. With great difficulty I pull myself into it and sit on its edge. Inside, numerous people are attending a religious service. I am surprised because they are also singing folk songs. They sing:

> With great longing
> I went to the Lord:
> May I, may I, may I,
> May I love the maiden?
> But of course, he says and laughs,
> Just for the boys I've made the girls."

In Dream Thirty a celestial spirit, in the form of an eagle, descended to the dreamer. In Dream Thirty-One the dreamer united with the earthy Anima. In this dream, the dreamer moves upward. The steep rock represents a great difficulty that he must overcome. In the course of the dream, it becomes clear that this difficulty is his distance from God which he must overcome. By his climb he reaches a point where a divine service, in which a question is addressed to God, is taking place. He has reached the level of a pre-Christian cult, a nature religion whose content and attitude have been preserved in a folk song and, by extension, in the folk consciousness. In the first two stanzas of this well-known song, a young man asks his mother and, later, his pastor: "May I love the maiden?" Both answer negatively. The mother believes he's too young for love. She wants to keep him for herself. The pastor, the representative of religion, would condemn the young man if he professed himself in favor of love. The community in the grotto sings only the third stanza which addresses the question directly to God. In the song, God answers that he has created the woman for the man. God accepts the dreamer along with his love. At this point, the formerly distinct realms of nature and spirit begin to approach each other. The nature-soul has spent its life in

the garden with weeds and truncated trees, and the dreamer has lived two lives, one Christian and one pagan. But the dreamer sets out to reach the level of Christian consciousness. The following dreams will tell more about this quest.

Dream Thirty-Three: The New Church

"A new church is being built. So far, only the scaffold has been completed. The church is going to be quite simple and modern. It will have a main ship with a high, slender tower on each side. The towers will be made partly of steel plates similar to those found in erector sets for children."

The dreamer has now also climbed the other half of the rock in the last dream. He is no longer in the cave, but in a place where a church can be constructed. The dream reveals a beginning attempt to build a new church, to reach a new understanding of religion. So far, only a scaffold exists which is to be gradually enclosed by walls. The two towers flanking the main structure are equivalent poles linked with each other, possibly logos and eros. This church is to replace the dome-like structure that collapsed in Dream Twenty-Eight. This dream is the direct consequence of that one.

Dream Thirty-Four: The Tabernacle

"I saw a tabernacle made of precious white and golden brocade. On top it had a border like one finds in tents.[200] When its curtains opened, I saw something resembling a bale of cloth in large folds flowing downwards. This material was grey and laced with silver. I was told, 'The tabernacle is the exterior life; and what it hides is the interior life. You must strive for the latter, taking care that it doesn't come outside.' I kept working on the material, lacing it with silver."

After the construction of the new church, its contents are to be understood in a new way. This dream, like Dream Thirty-Two, is concerned with the integration of nature and spirit. It states, "Your outward life is the tabernacle, and within it is contained, like the

holiest of holies, your interior life. Though it sometimes seems to you toilsome, miserable and worthless, this external life is the precious wrapping behind which the secret of your interior life is to remain hidden." In keeping with the dreamer's male consciousness, the external life is symbolized by white and gold. Gold represents the spirit's sun-quality; white represents the clarity of consciousness with which one strives for what is rational and morally good. The dreamer's inner life, however, is not represented by a silvery paten or the chalice, but by a silver and grey cloth, a symbol of the feminine aspect of the man's soul. This cloth is the vessel into which God descends. The dreamer intends to enrich the dark soul-material with silver, that is, with psychological insight. He is warned that this darker material must not become visible to the outside. The Anima's dark sides, her struggles, her depressions and irrational ideas, must not be visible on the outside. They must remain hidden behind a clear, correct, and conscious exterior attitude.

This dream locates the problem of the Anima in the dreamer's interior. The Anima becomes the inner reality, the content of his life. She becomes both the content of the tabernacle and the vessel for the incarnation of the living spirit. The dream sharply distinguishes between inside and outside. The outward life is laced with gold, with spiritual awareness, while the inner being is embellished with silver, with moon-quality, according to alchemy. Both the inner and the outer life are placed in relation to the most important mystery of the church. The dream elevates the human being and equals it to the central religious symbol.

Dream Thirty-Five: The Sapphire Ring

"I found myself in a large party with the British Queen and Prince Philip. However, they only spoke with each other. Later I could only see them through a pane of glass. The queen allowed me to choose a present, either a brooch with white and rose-colored rings, intertwined like those of the Olympics, or a ring with a setting of white pearls and a beautifully cut blue stone, which I could pick up outside the large window. The ring was too small for me, but I chose it anyhow, thinking that my daughter might be able to wear it. Only later did I discover that the ring was

contained within a sphere of golden filigree, a magnificent work of art."

At the time of this dream, the queen of England and her husband were in the news. In them the god-pair, sun and moon, take on human shape even though the queen of England outranks her male partner. The fact that the royal pair is removed behind a pane of glass suggests that they are a part of the inner, spiritual realm and are not yet within reach for the dreamer. One of the queen's presents is a brooch with white and rose-colored rings. Red and white, according to Jung, are the alchemical colors which correspond to sun and moon.[201] The interlaced rings thus symbolize the *coniunctio* of sun and moon, that is, the intimate, nuptial union of spirit and soul. This union is within reach of the dreamer, but he cannot yet grasp it. These two rings anticipate the next developmental step. The dreamer chooses the other piece of jewelry, the ring with the sapphire and crown of pearls. Jung quotes Rulandus in regard to the sapphire: "Its specific virtue consists in rendering the wearer pious and constant. In alchemistic medicine it was a heart medication."[202] These are the exact qualities that the Anima needs. The blue of the sky is crystallized into the solid, transparent sapphire.[203] This blue stone, spirit turned into a substance, reminds one of the heavenly throne of sapphire in Ezekiel's vision (Ezekiel 1:24) which is the seat of the divine, higher human being. We have previously mentioned, in discussing the woman-commander's blue and white banner in Dream Twenty, the blue and white vishuddha-mandala of tantra-yoga in which a white elephant personifies the spiritual drive that confers substance and concreteness to ideas.[204]

What is meant by the pearls? In the fairy tale of the goose girl at the fountain, we find that her tears shed during banishment turn into pearls. When she is delivered and has again become a princess, she receives her transformed tears as a dowry from the old earth-mother. These pearls then are the tears of princess Anima. When she was entangled in the world, she was forced to perform menial tasks. The salt of her tears and the bitterness of life which she tasted during this time, however, are later transformed into a softly glowing jewel. Alchemy speaks of the "pearl of love."[205] The ring with the sapphire and pearls is not meant for his

sister-Anima but for his daughter. The dreamer feels far more responsible for the latter than for the former. The ring symbolizes his connection with the daughter-Anima. The dreamer's relationship to women has undergone an additional change. From now on he will be able to meet women in a fatherly, responsible manner.

What appeared first in the guise of a banner and later in Dream Twenty-Four as the Chinese woman with a blue and white dress becomes the property of the daughter-Anima. She is to become the bearer of spiritual reality. At the dream's end, the dreamer notices that the ring is contained in a golden, filigree sphere, indicating that it belongs to the tabernacle. This dream reaches the acme of consciousness of the vishuddha-mandala. Subsequent dreams need no longer deal with blue and white. Now the dreamer must acquire the interlaced rings or produce the red and white stones. The white pearls are precious, but they have not yet attained the hardness and crystal-clear transparency of the alchemistic stone, or of the diamonds and rubies that decorate the royal rings. Alchemy speaks of the red slave and white woman who must be dissolved, purified, transformed, and united in the alchemical operation.[206] We already know that red stands for blood, fire, and passion. How can passion be transformed into a red stone? How can the nuptial union of the red and white essences take place? We do not know, for each and every individual's journey is new and unique. All we can do is entrust ourselves to the paths and wisdom of the unconscious.

Dream Thirty-Six: Brandy

"I was with many people in a church. I was in front, close to the communion rail, able to observe everything. The old bishop passed his office on to a younger one. Both were filled with profound piety, and I was deeply impressed. The service proceeded in the following way. The old bishop lifted the host, worshiping during the transubstantiation. He passed it to the new bishop who accepted it, full of reverence. At that instant, a priest with festive, priestly vestments came out of the sacristy. He held a chalice, into which he had poured a bottle of brandy, and passed it to the people who knelt down for communion. Soon, most of them were drunk and began howling. I went back to my bench where I knelt

down between two acquaintances, a woman and a man, and cried as I was horrified."

The dreamer finds himself in the church, a suprapersonal realm. He's in front, near the communion trellis. He is with the laymen, close to the priestly interchange that takes place in the interior room but which concerns him directly. The old bishop, the shepherd of the flock, has just lifted the host as he does during the transubstantiation. Thus, the dream starts at the center of the mass, the holy moment when God becomes present at the offering.

If we ask ourselves where and how the rites which preceded this high point of the holy service took place, we discover that previous dreams correspond, albeit in an individual and not easily recognized way, to these preparative steps.[207] In the dream of the rats, the dreamer shot the black and the red Anima, thereby sacrificing some of his former attitudes. As a result, he was able to overtake his mother in a race and reach a new goal (Dream Twenty-Seven). When he overtook his mother, he discarded a life without direction and began working deliberately on his problems. As a result, his former concept of the church as protecting mother collapsed (Dream Twenty-Eight). His new, increasingly aware, attitude led him to examine himself, to clear his field of weeds, and to plow rooted-out soil (Dream Twenty-Nine). In short, it led him to a cleansing of his life, which involved a sometimes painful process of letting go of old habits. Three men and a woman participated in rooting out the field. The number of workers suggested a four-fold differentiation or division of his being, as by a cross. (In the mass the priest makes the sign of the cross over the host.) In Dream Thirty the dark bird appeared with which the spirit is carried from nature into the human realm. Dream Thirty-One showed a woman lying in a furrow, a fruit of the field who must die in order to resurrect. After the dreamer's union with the sacrificial offering, he climbs a steep rock and is accepted, along with his natural aspect, by God (Dream Thirty-Two). This acceptance indicates nature's approach to the spirit. Like the first elevation of the bread during the mass, it suggests the spiritualization of nature.

A new church is built in Dream Thirty-Three. In this dream is gained a new concept of the church in which opposites balance each other. Dream Thirty-Four portrays the dreamer's outward life as a tabernacle which contains his inner life. Thus the dream links

his ówn inward experiences with the traditional symbols of the mass. In Dream Thirty-Five the king and queen appear. In alchemy they represent Sol and Luna, the god-pair. The terms *godfather* and *godmother* refer to this hidden meaning. Indeed, the queen and her consort appear as the communicant's godparents, his spiritual or divine parents. They give him a sapphire ring with white pearls, but he is not yet capable of accepting the intertwined rings, symbolizing the union of red and white, which they also offered. The daughter-Anima will receive the blue ring. As a virgin, as kore in Eleusis, and as rejuvenated fruit of the field, she corresponds to the sacrificed and prepared bread. The sapphire ring is the transformed substance offered by the divine parents, the pearls transformed tears, reminding us of the moon's soft glow. The sapphire, as solidified celestial blue, symbolizes a spiritual body. The offering of the ring signifies that insight into the nature of the unconscious can now occur, becoming hardened conviction and solid knowledge as symbolized by the sapphire. Eternal laws, archetypes, and religious truths will now become visible through various events.

Let us return to the present dream. The older priest passes the transubstantiated host to a younger one. The first part of the mystery, the transubstantiation of the bread, occurred in the series of dreams that we just discussed. Now something horribly sacrilegious happens. Another priest in full vestments emerges from the sacristy and pours brandy instead of wine into the chalice. Instead of giving the chalice, as is proper, to the priests, he passes it to the laymen. This brandy coming directly from the sacristy is not prepared by the ritual, expiated, mixed with water, or spiritualized. Moreover, it is not wine but highly concentrated alcohol. The laymen suffer the evil influence of this unholy beverage.

In his study of "The Symbol of Transformation in the Mass," Jung states: "Just as bread is the substance for physical existence, so the wine represents the substance for spiritual existence."[208] During the mass, wine transforms itself into Christ's blood. To partake of this wine is to be filled with Christ's spirit. Brandy, the soldier's restorative, however, has a devastating effect in this context. It produces drunkenness and a low spirit which profoundly saddens the dreamer. He returns to his seat and kneels between a man and a woman, the disunited opposites of his being. He

realizes that drinking this impure, unholy spirit will produce intoxication and loss of ego. He could try to reassure himself that this was but a diabolical temptation. Anyhow, the wine should be offered only to the priests. With such an explanation, he would abandon the solution of his next problem, the synthesis of red and white. (In the ritual this synthesis is illustrated by the mixing of wine and water.) However, because the priest appears in full vestments and approaches the laymen with great solemnity, we must surmise that this dream points to a future task for the dreamer. The following dream will confirm this possibility.

The older bishop passes the host to a younger one. The former represents a father, the latter a son. In a child's life, the father represents a phase in which spiritual tradition is blindly accepted as rule and law. As the son grows up, he learns to separate himself from his father and to confront him with his independent thoughts.[209]

After the collapse of the church in Dream Twenty-Eight, the time of the Father ends, and blind acceptance of spiritual tradition is no longer possible. In Dream Thirty-Three we witness the construction of a church with two towers. This construction symbolizes the separation of opposites. Psychologically, the phase of the son has begun. The son who no longer blindly subjects himself to his father's authority must now choose independently between good and evil. As a consequence, evil becomes more prominent. The third priest, representing the seduction of evil, reveals the contrast between good and evil. As carrier of an inebriating potion, he is a counter-priest and Antichrist. While the wine fills the priests with Christ's spirit, the brandy awakens the laymen's primitive, unredeemed, pagan nature. In the Dionysian mysteries, drunken emotions were incorporated into religious expression. In drunken states, people may try to burst the narrow limits of their existence. Alcohol, opium and other intoxicants are tempting because they promise transcendence of the everyday ego. The third priest attempts to awaken the impersonal depths of emotional nature in order to draw the laymen into the religious realm. His attempt fails because of their weakness and inadequate preparation. They lose their poise as well as their awareness of the solemnity and importance of the church. The potion effects a lowering of the mental level, a descent below the level of profanity.

The dreamer is not alone with his problem. About one year

later, he saw a movie which portrayed the same problem he saw in his dream. How to heal one's spirit, transform one's primitive, emotional nature, and unify one's self are not personal, but universal, human questions.

Dream Thirty-Seven: The Transition

"1. With many others I was standing in a church at the communion rail. In place of an altar, there was only a plain wall with many cracks. An older and a younger man stood on ladder-like wall-hooks trying to repair the cracks while new ones appeared. I feared lest they lose their balance and fall. I turned towards the people, mostly youths and uneducated persons, and began to preach. But my sermon was more like a lecture on physics or technology. It ended with a metaphor: 'A missionary must be like a sailboat which sails with full sails out into the dark sea.' A white-haired old man suddenly stood beside me. He told me that he had liked what he heard, especially the metaphor of the sailboat. Then he added that I better begin to preach, since I had promised it.

2. Near the small city in which I worked, one could cross a river by means of a ferryboat. On the other shore was a border-city named Nordlingen (Northlingen) where there was rich, Italian vegetation, with cypresses and Baroque churches. I wanted to visit. A man went with me. Inside the churches, there were museums with collections of prehistoric tools kept in glass closets. After viewing one of the collections of prehistoric tools and old wood- or wax-seals, we went to the ferry in order to cross the river. The old man sat in the front of the boat filled with people. He alone was allowed to row. Suddenly a motor started and propelled the boat. We hit a small ledge of sand which we had to cross on foot. The old man walked to my right, and beside him walked a younger woman. At first I wanted to lean on him as I was barefoot and my feet were hurting, but then I realized that it was up to me to support him."

A new threat to the church follows the disastrous distribution of brandy to the laymen in Dream Thirty-Six. The altar has disappeared. It is now necessary to seek behind it, behind all ecclesiastic symbolism, for the meaning of one's life. The wall behind the altar,

which separates the church from the world, is disintegrating. An older and a younger man, who probably represent, as in the preceding dream, a father and son, try to repair it. The dreamer, however, fears lest they fall down from the wall-hooks, the concepts, which sustain them. Thus he himself turns towards the waiting crowd, mostly young or uneducated people, and begins to preach. It is the younger and less educated ones, within himself and within the world, who sense deficiency and seek a new orientation. The dreamer's sermon is restricted by his natural-scientific schooling and his listeners' range of interests. He tries to convey some of his religious convictions through scientific parallels. He concludes: "A missionary must be like a sailboat which sails with full sails out into the dark sea."

His sermon, this last expression in particular, meets the special approval of an old man. It is not enough for a person to journey alone. He must take others with him. His insights must be transmitted in order to become alive, grow and deepen. If he feels called upon to help others, he must have the courage to let his own little lifeboat be driven by the wind (the *pneuma*) and to expose himself to the darkness and danger of the sea, the collective soul. Three events in this dream—the dreamer's sermon, his statement that missionaries must be like sailboats in a dark sea, and the old man's appearance—reveal a new developmental step. They show that the brandy, in contrast to its superficially horrendous effect in Dream Thirty-Six, has broadened the dreamer's consciousness. He speaks as layperson to the crowd about the necessity of allowing oneself to be moved by the spirit (*pneuma*). At that moment appears the old man, whom we may surmise is an archetypal old, wise man who embodies knowledge and wisdom accumulated through centuries of human experience. The appearance of the old wise man always signals a significant step in development.[210] Through him a man gains his personal spiritual orientation. After the old wise man becomes his companion, the dreamer relies more and more on his own "inner court." While he had previously been driven by his need for life and experience, he will now be motivated by his search for the meaning of his experience.

As long as the man is susceptible to his Anima's fascination and superior power, he must resist her seduction into fantasy and blind thirst for experience. Only conscientious execution of concrete

tasks, careful consideration of professional obligations, and genuine commitment to marriage and family can protect the dreamer from his Anima's inordinate demands. By the dreamer's gaining insight into her nature and limiting her demands, the Anima is induced to submit herself to the old wise man's guidance. A new attitude towards one's profession and everyday life, therefore, becomes necessary. The Self's suprapersonal archetype, the old wise man, confronts the dreamer with extensive possibilities which, if experienced as obligations, may become too demanding.

What is searched for but unknown always appears, at first, as projection upon the outside world. A man, especially an extroverted person, immediately believes that he must find the new values in his profession. He therefore attempts to improve in this area. He must, however, seek a much deeper meaning. In fact, in order to follow the path indicated by the old wise man, he must limit his outward activity and let go of everything inessential. He must also become less rigid in regard to rational rules and collective norms. If he does not fulfill these obligations, new insights will not prevail. The plenitude of new possibilities may also physically demand too much of the dreamer. He can protect himself only by a strict limitation to essentials.

In the second part of the dream, we find the dreamer on the shore of a river. Luxuriant Italian vegetation and Baroque churches are on this shore. On the opposite bank is Northlingen, which represents, to the dreamer, the Spartan poverty of the North. In other words, on the dreamer's side is Christendom, the good, the conscious world. On the other side is unknown darkness, the unconscious and its perils. In the North, according to Biblical tradition, the devil dwells. The Old Testament (Jeremiah 1: 14) reads: "From the North comes the boiling evil to the country's inhabitants." In the North, pagan gods dwell. At the North Pole, "behind the North Wind," is the castle of Arianrhod (silver-wheel), where dead pagan heroes and kings are placed, in contrast to ordinary dead people who wander disconsolately through its frozen grounds.[211] The next dream will take place in the North, the realm of evil, of dethroned gods and of lost masses.

In this dream the Baroque churches are museums. They are significant only as places where ancient symbols are stored. Remnants of ancient rituals do persist in the rites and customs of the

church. However, the dreamer does not tarry in these museums. He must find the meaning that has, for him, disappeared from the church.

The old wise man manages to ferry him across the stream. Crossing the island, the dreamer wishes to lean against the old man because the pebbles hurt his bare feet. He is painfully exposed to hard reality. He has lost his former attitude but has not yet found a new one. He tries to lean upon the wisdom of the unconscious, but realizes that he himself must fortify the ancient, though new to him, meanings that are still weak and uncertain. Consciousness cannot simply rely on help from within. It must provide enough active support so that the newly emerging contents can grow strong and expand.

Dream Thirty-Eight:
The Lay Priest and the Three Wart Fellows

"The rear of a large, empty hall is closed off by a wooden partition. I hear the sounds of wild jazz coming from behind it. I enter through a door and find myself in a room filled with people who are singing along with a recording of the crazed music. The people jerk their arms upwards in time to the music. A small area is fenced off by a rough table. An older man, obviously the lay priest of this community, stands behind the table and blesses the people. Three gigantic, muscular men stand beside the priest. Their naked torsos are ugly, covered with warts. They control the people by their glances. I don't participate in the singing or dancing. I don't want to. After all I do not have anything to do with it. One of the muscle-men looks at me piercingly and threateningly, but I withstand his glance and refuse to participate."

The dreamer has now crossed the river of Dream Thirty-Seven. Primitive dancing ceremonies channel instinctual energies into such activities as hunting, warring, cultivating the soil, harvesting and healing. Here in a hidden corner of the soul, energy is being produced as it has always been created in primitive cultures, but, as the frenzied music shows, it has become degenerate and dissonant through misuse. Whenever such energies are divorced from

their ritual, religious contexts, they discharge themselves in other ways and are easily converted into various excesses. The lay priest who blesses the activities seems to know that they were originally religious rituals which he would like to restore through his benedictions. The three muscular fellows beside him are devils. Their horrid warts remind one of dinosaurs and reptiles. The muscle- or nerve-energy that motivates the crowd's jerking movements derives from that part of the unconscious realm which is still related to reptiles. We have seen a manifestation of this level of the soul in the brandy dream. The dreamer refuses to take part in this excess and pretense. The three muscle-men who request this of him contrast too sharply with his consciousness and culture. The horrid, wart-covered figures also recall the masked devils who played crude pranks during Italian carnivals. These figures date back to the Saturnalia.[212] They are late caricatures of satyrs and fauns. These primitive, pagan energies were channeled by the Catholic church from carnival festivities into penitence and religious meditation during Lent.

Beyond the river, or behind the wooden partition, is a foreign world into which the dreamer enters, and into which a priest advances with his benedictions as a missionary who dares to sail alone into a stormy sea. He enters the devil's sphere where the wild, excessive dances and rituals take place. The dreamer discovers that which is directly opposite to the church, the heavenly sphere and the trinity. In the unconscious he meets a diabolical threesome. In *The Divine Comedy,* Dante, too, opposes to the heavenly trinity the three-headed devil of deepest hell. In the dreams, human beings are carriers of archetypal, divine and diabolical principles. As a representative of the higher principle, the old priest descends into an inferior realm. He attempts to bridge the two worlds which are now separated by a wooden partition.

The dreamer sees the dancers with their flailing arms impotently longing for happiness. The crazier they act, he comments, the more convinced they are that they can force benedictions. The primitive crowds try to achieve happiness, blessings and deliverance through excess and eccentricity. They will fail. Ancient wisdom dictates that deliverance can be achieved only through sacrifice, purification, transformation, and the placing of oneself

in a religious discipline. When the old priest's religious images and concepts fail to persuade the crowd, the dreamer turns away and refuses to participate.

The dream portrays the clash of consciousness and the unconscious abyss. It expresses a degree of over-excitation and strain which consciousness cannot assimilate. This unresolved stress causes complete exhaustion and an illness detailed in subsequent dreams (Thirty-Nine through Forty-One).

Dream Thirty-Nine: The Woman in the Violet Dress

"I'm at a party with many people. Our hostess has black hair and wears a violet evening gown. She is grossly sensual. Suddenly, the royal pair arrives. They are incognito, in plain clothes, but everyone recognizes them and bows. Everyone, that is, but the hostess, who turns them away because they were not invited. The queen orders a servant to have their coach driven up to take them home. The guests and I are aghast. We know what a frightful surprise it will be for our hostess. When she sees their coach, she finally realizes what an asinine thing she has done. All the guests begin to leave quickly."

The hostess in violet is equivalent to the red and black figures that the dreamer spotted and shot in Dream Twenty-Six. That shooting had stopped the immediate danger which threatened from without, but it did not resolve the dreamer's inward problem. The woman in violet is one more manifestation of that realm across the river or behind the wooden partition. She symbolizes the wild behavior which the dreamer rejected in favor of a cultivated consciousness. The rejected shadow now affects the Anima. Instead of being a helpful companion, she is a crude woman like the Whore of Babylon. Consciousness could not relate to this aspect of the unconscious which therefore refuses to subordinate itself to the royal pair, the ruling principle. The last dreams have uncovered a crack in the personality which cannot be immediately healed. As a result, subsequent dreams are gloomy.

Dream Forty: The Explosion of the White Powder

"Boxes filled with white powder are brought to a faraway place. They explode, producing a high, white, mushroom-shaped cloud. I find protection in a shed. I expect a few nearby horses to panic, but they remain calmly in place."

Dream Forty-One: Volcanic Eruption

"I am dangerously close to a volcanic eruption. Again, I do not have adequate cover. Ahead of me is a swarm of bees flying in perfect formation. As long as the bees are not disturbed, I am also protected."

What progress had been made is now threatened. The attempt to integrate red and white has failed. Both dreams reveal dangerous affective discharges that accompanied an illness with high fever. The calm of the horses and the perfect flight-formation of the bees allow us to surmise, however, that deeper instinctual levels were not affected by these disturbances. The next dream discusses a first attempt to deal with the opposite behind the wooden partition.

Dream Forty-Two: Faust and Mephistopheles

"We were at once two men and one person. The other was slightly older and heavier. We were performing *Faust* on a large stage. I was Mephistopheles, and the other was Faust. I knew, however, that we were one. He performed and spoke magnificently. I tended to stand on one side of the stage and to restrain myself. It was clear to me that he was better and more important. The enormous theater was sold out. We received stormy applause, but I know that it was mostly *his* achievements that deserved applause. We then went to celebrate our success. In the garden of an inn he sat down nonchalantly. He seemed to have the rough, friendly manners of my paternal, peasant ancestors. As soon as we had poured our drinks, people left the garden because of a police

curfew. We were angry. The other man called for the host, an unsympathetic, cunning type. To my surprise, my companion was on a familiar, first-name basis with the host. He complained, but the host did not yield. Then the other told him something very strange. He said that for once he would have liked to celebrate with me, his *dictator.* Suddenly, there was a large, black dog in the garden."

The dreamer and another man are in a colossal theater, obviously the theater of the world. They enact *Faust*, but their roles are reversed. The other plays Faust, the hero; the dreamer plays Mephistopheles, the shadow. A personality's dissociation into different characters is dangerous, though possibly essential to self-knowledge. In *Faust*, Goethe portrays an insatiable hunger for life.[213] Aware of his great abilities, Faust at the end of his life colonizes the world, barely conscious of the great responsibilities he is assuming. He is successful, thanks to his intelligence, his yearning for eminence, and his lack of consideration. His success is applauded. The dreamer enacts the story of Faust. He has not created the play himself, but has found the script and taken it over from his rough, friendly and ambitious ancestors.

During one's youth, one tends to identify with heroes and conquerors. One finds one's place in the world by adapting to collective ideals and expectations. One thereby becomes capable of channeling one's forces exclusively into one's purposes and goals and of accomplishing a great deal. As one becomes better in this role, Mephistopheles, the secret puller of the strings, the dark shadow of the collective ideal, becomes more dangerous. Faust starts to feel uneasy as he begins to recognize that the devil, his other ego, is his dictator. His name alone (Faust = fist) should alert us to the "rule of the fist" *(Faustrecht).*

Mephistopheles is our animal aspect paired with clever intellect. He represents given talents and skills such as drive and intelligence. He embodies physical impulses. He is also the despotic devil who craves power through possessions and knowledge. Because he represents drive and its extension, compulsion, he is a *dictator.* Goethe's Faust is aware only of his guiding ideals, but Mephistopheles knows the egotistic purposes they hide.

When the dreamer identifies with Mephistopheles, he becomes aware of his guilt. He is nearly crushed by the world's guilt which,

through this identification, falls upon him. If he blindly strives for success, he is bound to become overwhelmed by guilt during a depressive phase. Therefore, he must now separate both from Faust, the success-oriented person, and from his shadow, the devil.

Mephisto seduces through love as well as through power. In Goethe's *Faust,* he changes into his feminine counterpart when he dresses up as Phorkyas and when, after Faust's death, he becomes enamored of male angels. He shares with his brother, the alchemistic Mercury, a hermaphroditic nature.[214] He is dangerous in the same way as the power-hungry She. His ambition, greed and passion are consuming.[215] His is the danger of pleading life according to collective demands for inconsiderate self-affirmation and unconscious, instinctual impulses. In this dream, evil manifests itself, not as a quality of the Anima, but as a collective, male shadow figure, that is, as self-knowledge and insight into human potentials. It is this knowledge that keeps the dreamer from celebrating the theatrical success. It is police curfew. Faust's day is definitely ended. The host, without whom one cannot settle the bill, is the true shadow whom even the stage-Mephistopheles must obey and who announces Ash Wednesday, the end of the masks' festivities. Behind the host, a black dog, the poodle which Faust first encountered, appears. The dog is animal nature which the dreamer first recognized in the black and red figures, in the rats; which he rejected in the three warted devils (Dream Thirty-Eight); and which he finally repudiated in the violet hostess (Dream Thirty-Nine). Now his dark nature meets him as the shadow.

Faust, Mephistopheles, the host, and the black dog form a male quartet. The dreamer's ego, his consciousness, is overcome by the dark side. In spite of his earlier opposition, the dreamer has entered the realm of the three devils of Dream Thirty-Eight. In this dream the devils are differentiated into Mephistopheles, the host, and dog. Through the dreamer's identification with both collective roles, with Faust and Mephistopheles, his human ego is charged with the superhuman responsibility of the world's guilt and torn into the extreme opposites of good and evil. In the conscious, Christian conception of the world, good prevails. Yet here, on the side of the unconscious, evil prevails. The remedy for the painful condition into which the ego has drifted includes separating from the archetypal figures and defining one's limits with respect to the collective role. The ego must look within itself and accept its own

personal guilt, moral problems, and its obligations towards its own weaker sides. It must accept itself as a limited human being with limited possibilities. The ego is neither Faust nor Mephistopheles, but only the servant of the two superhuman, basically divine, figures. It only realizes the impulses that come from its light and dark sides.

This dream is significant for the dreamer's confrontation with the problem of *morality* through his identification with Mephistopheles and Faust. He must go one step beyond Faust and recognize that he is responsible for Mephistopheles's success. To identify with Mephistopheles is intolerable. However, identification with Faust is equally so. Mephistopheles is a figure of the collective unconscious, and Faust represents collective consciousness. Now, rather than continue the collective roles, the dreamer must modestly accept responsibility for his actions and claim the shadow, namely the host and the dog, as his.

Dream Forty-Three: Aida

"*Aida* is to be performed in an opera house with seats like choir chairs. I show several ladies to their seats in front. They invite me to sit with them. I gracefully decline and sit in the back of the hall with the crowd. I wear a white, flowing dress, reminiscent of the ancient Greeks or Arabs. It is made of fine white wool. It looks like a Dominican habit, but it is looser and more open. I think that the people will find it strange and effeminate, but, after some hesitation, I become indifferent to their possible criticisms."

Sometimes it is unusually difficult for consciousness to understand an inner necessity. In such cases, a dream may take the form of a play which shows and explains to the dreamer his next task. The place in which the play is performed is an opera house with choir chairs. It is half-profane and half-ecclesiastical. The dreamer doesn't exactly know where he belongs. The ladies ask him to sit with them, as if he were a woman, but he decides to join the ordinary people. He wears a strange dress, a version of a monk's habit, which strikes him as being somewhat feminine. A monk wears his cowl (like the Galloi of Cybele, the Great Mother) to show that he has sacrificed his masculinity. Just as the consecrated

follower of Cybele renounces his primitive, masculine nature in order to assume that of the mother-goddess, so the monk renounces his masculine nature in order to approach God with a receptive, feminine attitude. This attitude places the dreamer on the side of his unconscious. He no longer identifies with Mephistopheles, but partly with his feminine side, the Anima. Even the opera that is to be performed has a feminine name.

Aida is the story of the royal couple's death. Thus, the dream foreshadows the ritual death of the royal couple, one more conscious sacrifice of what has been achieved. If integration is insufficient because essential parts remain disparate, the current psychological-spiritual attitude, the royal pair, must die once more. In *Christian Rosencreutz's Chymical Wedding,* three royal couples and a Moor, representing their shadow, appear. They must all die once more in order to be melted into one pair through alchemy.[216] In his monastic outfit, the dreamer could be one of the Egyptian priests who sentence Radames and Aida to die. The white dress puts him in contrast to evil and draws him into the play.

In his white monastic outfit, the dreamer has cleansed himself of the world and evil, distancing himself from Faust and Mephistopheles. As a result, the religious problem reappears now in his dreams.

Dream Forty-Four: Three Priests and a Priestess

"I wish to attend a small, simple church in the country. Many people stand outside. Inside, many people stand in the hallways, but the pews are empty. I prefer not to sit down since I will have to get up and cede my place, maybe to a woman, when the rest of the people come inside. Also, I am not sure which side is designated for men and which for women. Everyone looks at me. I walk through the crowd all the way to the front. Here, the high mass is celebrated at the altar. The priests are in white and golden vestments, but, to my surprise, they are not, as customary, three priests, but four. The fourth is a woman. I wonder why a fourth priest was added, and why a woman priest. I think this situation is an earthly reflection of the situation in heaven. As is customary, the older priest is the main celebrant. He and one of the younger

priests are turned towards the altar. The other young priest stands on the side of the steps, his face turned towards the two in the center. On his dark head with short, trimmed hair he wears a small, golden crown. He sings the Epistle and the Gospel. The priestess stands in the middle and faces the public. In her hands she carries a large, white and golden book containing the Gospel and hands it to the priest with the crown to read and sing. She is joking and laughing. This bothers me, and I think that one should not have allowed women to participate in the service."

The dreamer enters the church, and the religious problem is explored further. He does not sit down because he does not know which side is the women's and because he would eventually have to give up his place to a woman. Thus, he feels uncertain about where he really belongs. His uncertainty about belonging to the women's side is a symptom of his remaining identification with the unconscious, the Anima, from whom, however, he is now able to distance himself.

Turning away from the women's side is also supported by the fact that the dream takes place in a church in which, because of the three priests, the male element predominates. Comparing it with the dream of the brandy (Dream Thirty-Six), we may notice some progress. In Dream Twenty-Six, the third priest played a most questionable role. Here he sings the Gospel and the Epistle; he has a function in the ritual. In comparison to the dream of Faust and Mephistopheles (Dream Forty-Two), we also find a great change. In that dream only one positive male figure, Faust, appeared, in contrast to two negative male figures (Mephistopheles and the unpleasant host), as well as the black dog.

In the present dream, there are three positive male figures, as well as a feminine one, who represents nature over and against the spirit. The third priest's crown signals a spiritual kingship. The dreamer associates the priestess, before her questionable behavior, with Maria, the heavenly queen. Later, however, her inappropriate behavior introduces darkness into the spiritual realm, almost as a complement to the old priest's bringing blessings from heaven down into the realm of darkness.[217] The dreams, thus, show a slow interpenetration between the two realms. The three priests represent the masculine principle of the logos; the priestess in-

troduces the feminine principle of eros. The mixture of evil, previously expressed as the pouring of brandy, reappears, in milder form, in the priestess's irreverent behavior. She takes the place of the grey-silvery cloth in the tabernacle's interior which would not blend properly with the white and gold of the priestly vestments (Dream Thirty-Four).

The four priests have different functions: the first, intuition; the second, feeling; the third, introverted thinking; and the woman, sensation, which, for now, is identified with the Anima.

Dream Forty-Five: The Adoration of the Queen

"I was part of a crowd, arranged in ascending circles, which was paying homage to the queen. I was quite close to the front, but I couldn't see the queen as I was kneeling and bowing with everyone else. A black man scantily dressed in native garb stood in front of me. He bowed his head all the way to the floor. I wanted to do the same, but, thinking it wouldn't be appropriate, I bowed less deeply. When we raised our heads, the queen was gone and a priest in a black cassock stood in her place. His back was turned towards me, and his arms were extended like those of a conductor. He made a quick, sweeping movement and the cheering stopped. He suddenly no longer had a head. Only a white collar protruded from his cassock. He left.

Next, I found myself in the black man's room. He was a student. He wasn't a black now, but a mulatto. We sat on the edge of his bed. I felt deep friendship and love for him, and I was sad that we had to part. The thought of returning to primitive conditions in Africa did not please him. He went to his washbasin in order to clean himself. He expressed the hope that we would see each other again."

In this dream the dreamer is on the side of the feminine and the shadow, yet he does not identify with these figures. The feminine principle, symbolized by the queen, is worshiped by a crowd. This dream occurred at the time of the papal letter proclaiming Mary as heavenly queen and mistress of all creatures. In his dream the dreamer participates in the celebration worshiping Mary as queen

(in fact he did so before he had actually heard of the papal declaration!). In his jubilation, he and his simpler nature are united with the crowd.

The horrid jazz music of the cosmopolitan city (Dream Thirty-Eight) has vanished. The beautiful black man with his genuine humility before the queen emerges from it. He may also be a precious aspect of Mephistopheles's black poodle (Dream Forty-Two). The dreamer shares this shadow-figure's humble and cheerful adoration of the queen. Mary, the queen of heaven, includes his inner, archetypal picture of the queen. The black man is "primitive" only in the sense of "spontaneous" and "genuine." As a primitive, he focuses upon that which is essential and practical. He is the dreamer's simple, unadulterated sensation-function. His European studies connect him to European consciousness. He has the runner's ability to relax which the officer in Dream Twenty-Five admired. The black man returns to Africa, his natural home. The dreamer, unfortunately, cannot stop him. Only during vacations (the dream occurred at the end of the dreamer's vacation) does the black man come into his own. During periods of work, he is exiled to Africa, the unconscious. The disappearance of the priest's head may mean that recognizing Mary as mistress of all creatures is not a task for the intellect. The crowd's rapture was a spontaneous experience that preceded the papal formulation of the new, dogmatic content. The dreamer is carried by this rapture, and thus linked to the black man with his genuine piety.[218]

Dream Forty-Six: The Convent with the Throne Room

"On overgrown paths I reached a magnificent old abbey, hidden in a garden. To my right is the path to the church's interior. Straight ahead is the entrance to a hall that looks like a treasury or museum. I enter through the path on my left. In the hall's foreground is a wonderful, large, white and gold throne. Moving on, I reach the cloisters surrounding a neglected, romantic garden. The sunlight which fills the garden and flows into the cloisters creates a unique, dusky-green setting. Proceeding in the arched hallway, I see, across the garden, the roof and tower of a church. The tower is large and impressive. At the end of the hall I meet a father. I'm a guest who desires to study and write. He shows and

offers to me several rooms. The first room, on the ground floor, is large, sunny and almost ostentatious. I don't want it because it is too grandiose and distracting, and because too many people will be walking through it. The second room, in the upper story, is very small and modest. I don't want it either, as it is musty like a prison cell and too dark and dusty. The third is a fine, medium-sized room with a window from which one enjoys a great view of green hills. I take that one."

Immediately the dream recurs in a slightly different form:

"I'm on the same path to the abbey, but I'm driving a mechanized vehicle which pulls small wagons filled with teenagers and children. I'm forced to drive very carefully as I must manage many curves in the road and pass underneath low tree branches. Then we are before the abbey and take the middle path into the hall. I want to guide the children towards the left in order to show them the beauty of the cloisters; I walk ahead and see the cloisters and the tower again. I turn around and find that no one has followed me. I return and find some of them in the hall. I feel a strong desire to sit down on the white and golden throne, but I don't. I want to show the children the beauties of the museum, but they disappear again. I look for them in the church interior. I enter a bright, high-ceilinged cathedral with white and golden columns. The boys are noisily entertaining themselves in a corner. The girls, on the other hand, have all climbed the stairs to the altar. From below I see them devoutly standing so close together before the altar that they wholly obscure it. They all wear the same white dresses and small red jackets. Meanwhile, the boys have left the church and are walking up a broad stairway to an adjoining room. It occurs to me that they should get something to eat. I plan to order some food, but I find that they are already eating happily and noisily in a dining hall. I'm just about to tell some of the big ones to watch out and keep order when it occurs to me that everything will be all right. All the boys are loud and cheerful. I don't need to do anything."

Here, the dreamer finds his way into a convent, a place of Christian meditation. The extroverted dreamer withdraws into a positive introversion. He discovers an inner place which was

cultivated, later neglected, by the ancestors. When the dreamer avoids the first, ostentatious room where he would always be interrupted by outsiders, he renounces an attitude that would induce him to work only for the sake of outward appearance. He also refuses the gloomy cell, the ascetic, depressive withdrawal, which he has also known. He chooses a room with an open view where he is free to work. This retreat is suitable and meaningful.

His free decision to immerse himself in introversion and meditation on religious matters brings with it a crowd of children: young, promising forces to whom he wishes to show the beauties of the old convent. He would like to seat himself upon the magnificent throne of the children's presence, but he resists the temptation. His ego renounces the king's place. This renunciation is of great importance and shows progress from the dream of Faust and Mephistopheles (Dream Forty-Two).

The children don't stay in the museum. They don't remain in the past. They live in the immediate religious experience. The boys display a youthful spirit of enterprise. They pass by the religious paintings without showing much devotion. The girls, however, stand devoutly around the altar. They retain the childlike openness and piety that are enhanced by the setting and by the hidden meaning of paintings. They are dressed in white and red, the union of soul and spirit, which was destroyed in Dream Forty and Forty-One, but which reappears with new freshness in these girls. This union is understood by the little Animas. They direct their warmth and immediacy towards the altar, the place of the holiest of holies.

The boys, the renewed spirit of enterprise in religious matters, soon find themselves in an adjoining room where the church offers them spiritual food. Since the dreamer renounced the tempting throne, he is now able to renounce the urge to impose order upon the boys. He realizes that he can allow their youthful eagerness freedom. He does not need to interfere; he can let things happen.

Dream Forty-Seven: The Round Church

"I'm in a church or a mosque. A central room is linked by open arches to similar rooms. I believe Constantinople's Hagia Sophia was built this way. One of these side rooms is an apse, in which the

altar is located. The altar is invisible to me, but I know it is there. In the middle of the central room is a horizontal wheel which almost fills the room. It moves clockwise very slowly. It has many spokes upon which many people, including myself, sit. As the wheel turns, I move, against my wishes, away from the altar. I look through the arches of the central room into the various side rooms. Each is built in a different style (Roman, Indian, Arabic, etc.). All religions are represented in these adjoining chapels. Finally, I come closer to the altar. I'm now at the periphery of the wheel. When I'm facing the altar, the wheel stops and slides, as if floating towards the altar. I'm completely immersed in the light of this apse. I'm quite close to the altar which is still invisible. Light flows over me and I hear a wonderful, tender music, similar to Christmas carols. I'm experiencing infinite devotion and bliss."

Dream Forty-Seven marks a high point in the dreamer's inner journey. In the previous dream he renounced the throne. Thus his ego became subordinate to a higher principle, an invisible center. In this dream, that higher principle takes the form of a wheel upon which the dreamer sits with many others. In its roundness the wheel represents perfection. Its circular shape is an ancient symbol of the godhead which manifests itself in the universe. The center is the invisible godhead; the circle represents the godhead's emanations in space and time. According to Plotinus, the soul turns in a circle around its center, the divine principle from which it emanates.[219] The nave of the wheel symbolizes the divine Self in the human being, the principle that is higher than the ego and encompasses opposites. As a symbol of the godhead's realization in creation or as a symbol of the Self in the human being, the wheel encompasses more than one individual human being.

All human beings belong to the Self. Our egos are but a tiny fraction of the infinite expressive possibilities available to the divine. In Buddhism the wheel symbolizes the doctrine, its proclamation, and the impulse for deliverance. In the dream the wheel turns clockwise, from unconsciousness to consciousness, and from ignorance to knowledge, reflection and self-awareness. As it turns, the wheel offers the dreamer insight into the world's religions and shows him that they all are related to the same midpoint. At first the dreamer is dissatisfied because the wheel's motion carries him

away from his goal, the altar. As he views the side-chapels, however, he gains the tolerance and universality which he is seeking.

The memory of the dream elicits from him a deeply satisfied exclamation, "Ah, indeed everything is here!" He now understands that he must distance himself from the faith of his childhood in order to experience the validity of all religious expression. The wheel carries him to the altar where he breaks through to another, hidden reality, one about which images speak, but which itself is beyond images. It is formless light, music, devotion and inner fulfillment. The altar of his religion and the Christmas songs remind him of his childhood's most blissful experiences. The piety of the girls in the preceding dream becomes, here, his own.

Dream Forty-Eight: Four Speeches

"I am supposed to give a speech at a large Christmas celebration. I propose instead that four speakers, including myself, present brief, but thorough, discussions of Mary to a small, select group. I suggest the following topics: (1) Mary, the virgin—a theologian is to discuss this topic. (2) Mary, the mother—this presentation is directed primarily to women. It should speak to the heart. (3) Mary, the queen—I reserve this topic for myself. I will include in my presentation a discussion of the dogma of Mary's bodily ascension and coronation. (4) Mary, the working woman—I insist that this topic also be included. This presentation should address workers and portray Mary, the wife of Joseph the carpenter, and the miserable conditions under which she gave birth to and raised a child. It should focus upon that part of her life which is hardly mentioned in the Bible. I emphasize that the portrayal of this important aspect of Mary has previously been neglected."

The preceding dream reawakened childhood memories of Christmas. Now, in celebration of the mother of God, Christmas is to be understood in a more conscious and profound manner. In place of a conventional party at which he would have been the sole speaker, the dreamer hopes to substitute a celebration during which urgent theological questions will be reflected upon and discussed by four speakers, the dreamer and three other men. He

no longer identifies with the unconscious, nor does his ego aspire to the throne. The four suggested speakers will discuss the four functions of Mary in order to arrive at a complete, comprehensive understanding of the Anima-problem. The first theme, Mary the virgin, is to be discussed by a theologian, that is, by the theologian who is inside himself and who his mother wanted him to be. Mary's eternal virginity is an irrational, supernatural phenomenon. It cannot be discussed rationally. However, intuition which grasps the meaning of dogmatic or symbolic statements can do it justice. The virgin birth of the savior is already anticipated in the great goddesses of the Near East.[220] It is found again in the many contemporary dreams which involve a virgin, or abandoned woman, who gives birth to a fatherless child, with the attributes of the mediator and the hero-savior. If we understand Mary as the Anima's archetypal image, we see that her "virginity" points to the ability to listen inwardly and to be fructified by the inner spirit.

The dreamer explains that the second speaker must address women. He addresses the problem of femininity through *feeling*. From early childhood, Catholics hear prayers to Mary in which she is presented as an example to and educator of mothers. A young girl can orient her behavior in accordance with that of the God-mother. Mary, the *mater dolorosa,* guides the girl through the joys and sufferings of motherhood. She takes her from possession to sacrifice and renunciation, from natural to spiritual motherhood. Men also experience these phases through prayer. Their feelings for mothers and their empathy for motherhood are imperceptibly developed. Viewed inwardly, Mary, the mother, dedicates herself with patience and devotion to the soul's rebirth. She embodies constant love and care for its inner growth.

The dreamer himself wants to discuss the third theme—Mary the queen. He attempts to complement knowledge acquired through *feeling* with knowledge acquired through *thinking*. He wants to learn the meaning hidden in Mary, the exemplary divine Anima. As queen, Mary wears a crown. Hers is the crown of human wholeness. The man who learns to worship her is no longer subservient to the discriminating logos only. He also submits himself to the heavenly queen, and by extension to the feminine principle, the forgiving and reconciliatory eros.

As queen of the earth and all its creatures, Mary shall, according to dogmatic pronouncements, overthrow Satan, the master of this

world. She will lift all creatures up to herself and will ascend bodily into heaven. Even the body, with its instincts and biological processes, will be deemed worthy to enter heaven. Matter will rise into the realm of the spirit. In Mary the entire material world wants to set out for the *coniunctio* with the spiritual realm. The split between spirit and nature need not persist forever. The human being is not forced to keep any part of himself separate. There is nothing so dark that it cannot strive towards the center and be understood by the spirit, and nothing so nonsensical that it cannot be transformed into meaning. By taking on the discussion of this theme, the dreamer attempts to grasp the eternal truth of contents that were formerly projected upon women. He seeks their archetypal, religious meanings that are valid independently of the particular woman in which they manifest themselves. Every individual woman is but an incomplete reflection of the queen, the archetypal image that is sought for within the soul.

The fourth theme is unusual. It outlines a future task. The dreamer meets some resistance when he proposes it, and the speaker's identity is unclear. This theme requires the dreamer's fourth function, *sensation*. This speech, addressed to laborers, is to describe Mary as one of their own. The dreamer comments that quiet, hard work is to be celebrated. The speech is also addressed to the people behind the wooden partition who suffer the surveillance of the three devils (Dream Thirty-Eight). In order to discuss this topic, a speaker must focus upon immediate reality. This discussion, neither abstract nor metaphysical, is concerned with human beings' relation to the eternal symbol of the heavenly queen. When Goethe's Faust addresses Mary as "Virgin, Mother, Queen," she seems unattainably distant. Here, however, she is addressed "Virgin, Mother, Queen—*and* simple woman." She is accessible for everyone. She is not in a distant beyond but can be found in the here and now.

For the dreamer, this means that the eros-principle must find access to his daily work. Even his occupational performance will require the participation of the *whole* human being. No longer are religious symbols confined to the church. They now transform everyday life. The *inner* child is born during everyday toil. The human being is the bearer and executor of the dogma. This dream paraphrases and amplifies the one in which the tabernacle represented the external life and the interior, dark, silver-laced

soul-material represented the Anima's activity (Dream Thirty-Four). If he learns from this fourth speech, the man will no longer require a "queen" who can speak to his feelings. He will be able to experience and worship the Anima in an ordinary woman. This is a parallel to Seuse, the mystic, who greeted the mother of God in every poor, little woman.[221]

Dream Forty-Nine: Riding Lesson

"The young imperial prince rides ahead of me. I'm unable to follow him at the same speed because my stirrup is knotted. I dismount and try to saddle the horse again. I notice that I cannot completely straighten the stirrup. I mount and continue to ride. The horse is young. It has a wonderful, soft coat that is brown like honey. I fear lest the young animal be unruly, but it allows itself to be guided by the slightest pressure of my thigh. On the street it trots softly. On the meadow it accelerates to a rocking gallop. It is just wonderful to ride this horse. Suddenly, I have two companions riding close to my left and right. They are imperial princesses whom I'm to instruct in horsemanship. Since I'm able to ride my horse without using the reins, I put my arms to my left and right around my companions' shoulders. I lift them in the rhythm of the trot and, thus, easily teach them proper, rhythmic riding movements. I feel uncomfortable since the imperial parents watch us from behind, incognito. They might notice that I can use only the left stirrup as I have only limited use of my right foot. Nevertheless, the ride continues easily. The princess to my left is older and more mature; the one on my right is younger and more childlike. I am most interested in the one on my left. She is friendly but unapproachable. The younger one on my right responds quickly to the slightest pressure of my hand upon her shoulder. After riding various types of paces, we finally stop. Carefully, I help the princesses dismount. I notice that the knotted stirrup became unknotted sometime during our ride. The entire saddle is in good shape now. I feel light and happy.

Later, I find myself in a large hall. There is a garden in front of the building from which one can see the front of a beautiful, new house. I know that the imperial family is visiting this house. I see them at the window and, later, the balcony. Two imperial princes

(one rode ahead of me at the dream's beginning), the two princesses and their parents are there. I salute. They wave back.

Then I find myself in a room with three other men. I can see one, but I know the others are there. The one I see wishes to either drink, celebrate or play a card game. I explain that we cannot do this because we have to go to work. He argues that we can always be reached by phone. I insist that we go to work, and we do."

The young imperial prince riding ahead of the dreamer represents the renewed and rejuvenated leading principle which is now embodied in the son, not the father. It is distinct from the traditional (paternal) spiritual attitude, but, because it is the *son*, it is closely connected to it. It is the organic continuation of the paternal world. That which in the church-dreams was expressed in the images of priests is now transferred to the secular world where emperor and princes are the leading powers. The renewal in the spiritual sphere has brought with it a renewal in the instinctual sphere. A wonderful young horse now carries the dreamer towards life. The velvety, soft coat of the young animal indicates health. Life forces have renewed themselves after an illness. The dreamer fears lest the animal be unruly, but it allows itself to be guided by the soft pressure of his thigh. A new accord and interplay between consciousness and instinct has been reached. As spiritual understanding changes, so does instinct. The instinct is no longer gruesome and destructive (as it was in the first dream) nor nervously overwrought (as in Dream Nine of bolting horses). The saddle-gear is still somewhat knotty, indicating a lack of agility and sureness in his new way of life.

Now the dreamer is to give riding lessons to the two princesses who appear at his sides. The two Animas are to learn to move in harmony with the instincts. The dreamer teaches them various riding paces. His own feelings are correlated with the movements. They don't bolt, limp behind, or get lost. The extroverted, intuitive man does not shoot beyond his target because of male capriciousness. He takes care that empathic feelings can keep in step. The dreamer is not identified with the imperial family nor with the Anima. His conscious ego establishes the pace and watches out for the unison of the different sides. He does this in sight of the imperial parents. He feels responsible to the superior court of

the Self, where the imperial, crowned couple represent the union of opposites.

He harmonizes easily with the younger princess. The youthful side of the Anima allows herself quite easily to be carried by the instincts. The older, more mature Anima, riding to his left, is more difficult to convince. The younger one may represent the youthful, personable, nestling feelings, whereas the older may manifest the type of relationship that has come up in the later dreams—for example, in the worship of the queen (Dream Forty-Five), the devotion of the girls at the altar (Dream Forty-Six), or the four speeches about Mary (Dream Forty-Eight).

In the course of the ride with the two positive Anima-figures, the knot in the stirrup disappears spontaneously. What initially seemed insoluble can straighten out by itself with the proper rhythm.

Later we find the dreamer back at work. The imperial family has settled in the beautiful, new building. Now we have three pairs—the parents, two princes, and two princesses—indicating that the dreamer's new masculine, spiritual attitude will benefit his profession and will be accompanied by appropriate emotional attitudes. This attitude, once attained, still depends on the proper understanding and "pacing." In other words, it must be practiced and maintained in everyday life.

The dream's postscript shows the other side of the picture. In place of the emperor and his two sons, the dreamer now has as companions three men who induce him to drink, feast and play cards. They try to seduce him into accepting the lower spirit. They are not demonic, like the three "wart-men" (Dream Thirty-Eight), but indolent. The emperor and the two princes represent their opposite. The dreamer as a *fourth* member stands between the upper and the lower threesomes. His ego remains free to choose his commitments.

Dream Fifty: The Hart

"I am the strongest hart in the entire forest. I'm lying down on soft moss, my legs drawn underneath myself. I'm protected by firs. At my side lies a hind. I stand up on my four legs. I wish to roam through the forest and drink water from a brook. The hind warns

me that the morning is already advanced and I must look out for human beings. I shake my antlers and feel them hit the tree branches. In order to get out from under the low-hanging twigs of the firs I must stoop. I walk around in the woods between the tall stems, but I soon return to the hind, because it has become light and I fear the hunter. Later, in the guise of a human being, I reach a trough below a stand of firs. I recognize the place. (After awakening, I know it was the same place where I have been as a hart.) I clear the ground of bark and twigs. I arrange the wood neatly so that something will always be at hand for making a fire. It is a good feeling to have this hideout and to know that I can return to it at any time."

In Dream Thirteen a young hart was killed by a poacher. Here, the hart is alive again, and the dreamer experiences his own nature by identifying with it. This extraordinary dream is a deep experience for him. Rarely do adults perceive their oneness with nature so intensely,[222] but a similar empathy was revealed in the dream of the riding lesson. The Anima, too, has become a hind. She does not pursue her separate, all-too-human path (as she did in the dream [Thirty-Nine] of the violet hostess). The dreamer and his unconscious soul journey from urban life to nature. He descends into the body's pre-human, animal nature and connects consciousness and instinct. Buddha suggests such connection in himself when he mentions his ability to recall prior incarnations as animals. As a result of education, civilization and culture, human consciousness has separated from its instinctive roots. In this dream, it is reconnected with these roots.

Later, the dreamer returns to the forest as a human being. He is happy to be able to find protection here. His fusion with his animal soul was so thorough that he actually *felt* his animal body (including his legs and antlers) and feared human beings. This fusion is a memory from which he can derive peace and protection. The dreamer's return to nature is highly significant. Many excesses and errors result from deviations from the laws of nature. The vivid experience of oneness with nature will lead one back to the laws of nature, provided that one listens carefully to what goes on inside oneself.

By examining the preceding dream of the riding lesson, we find how the hart and hind fit into the dream-series. In that dream, the

imperial parents appeared with the two princes and princesses on the balcony of a house. The princes and princesses are siblings linked to each other as same-sex and male–female pairs. Whenever two such pairs appear at the end of a fairy tale,[223] a satisfactory solution, an inner equilibrium, has been attained. This pattern of equivalent pairs, where one is closer to nature (the younger princess) and the other embodies a spiritual attitude (as expressed in the distinguished reserve of the older princess), finds two complements in these two dreams, a spiritual one in the parents and an earthly one in the animal pair. The imperial parents of the previous dream are above their children whose *spiritual* origin they represent. From this origin, the dreamer's renewed and widened inner structures have shaped themselves.

The hart and hind of this dream, then, portray both the *natural* origin and conclusion of the new pattern. They are its origin much as the nature-like Anima evolved from the heath-hen; they are its conclusion as the dreamer became a hart. The new internal structures which encompass the upper parental pair, the two princes and princesses, and the lower animal-pair represent a manifold link of *sol* and *luna,* king and queen, and white and red. That which was only alluded to by the intertwined rings has now become, in the four pairs, a living, inner symbol.

The dreamer has attained in this dream the quartet of pairs and, thus, the eight-fold link of the opposites. Now he must incorporate this wholeness into his waking life.

Dream Fifty-One: Your Will—Your Way

"I'm asked to speak at a meeting. My theme will be 'Your Will—Your Way.' I neither consent nor decline. Instead I wonder whether I have properly understood the meaning of the theme. Should it be 'your will—my way' (as in, quoting the Lord's Prayer, 'your will be done')? If so, my speech would be about the submission to God's will which determines one's path. Or does the theme 'your will—your way' mean that everyone is the forger of his own fortune? In that case, everyone would choose and follow his own path. These reflections continued beyond the dream and throughout the next morning. At first I considered the first version, adapted from the Lord's Prayer, more likely. Eventually,

however, I concluded that 'your will—your way' was correct. Therefore, my speech would not be a discussion of God, but a personal, direct appeal to my listeners."

Human beings possess the dangerous gift of free will. In contrast to animals, they are able to act against instinct. As a result, they must continually learn to submit to God's will and to recognize it in their fate. By doing this, they will be able to accept themselves and their fate and to understand life as meaningful. The first part of life's task may be expressed by the short phrase "your will—my way." In other words, "Let me recognize your will, so that I may choose my path accordingly." However, because the dreamer has reclaimed his instincts in his identification with the hart and experience of unity with nature, his task is reversed. After long reflection, he concludes that he must speak to his audience about a second phrase, "your will—your way." He recognizes that this formula emphasizes a human being's free will and personal responsibility. He has grown beyond the child's blind trust in God. He can no longer load his burden upon God; he must carry it himself. He must make a conscious decision and choose his own path. He must recognize that what happens to him from now on is a consequence of his own thoughts, decisions and actions. He can no longer accuse God nor argue with Him because he knows that what has happened to him in the past, what he experiences now, and what the future will bring are his destiny and responsibility.

But the phrase "your will—your way" can be understood in another, deeper sense. God's will, which expresses itself in the soul, is God's way, as expressed in the actions of human beings.

The next dream shows the dreamer a new path.

Dream Fifty-Two: Deliverance from the Water Tank

"I'm a prisoner. Escape to the streets is impossible. I must use the river. I and the 'Other' stand in a large, semi-circular water basin from which four rivers are flowing: two powerful ones to the right and two small ones to the left. The one on the far right is partly dammed up. The river on its side is a roaring torrent. The thin brooks to the left run through wooden culverts and pipes which carry very little water. I find myself swimming in the basin. I try to

swim to the right, but I'm constantly thrown back by a whirlpool. I'm totally exhausted. Suddenly a window opens in the dam. I hold on to its lower edge. Behind it are an old woman and a young girl. Both are quite friendly. The old woman gives me bread for refreshment. She advises me to seek passage through the small brook on the extreme left. I thank her and bless her. This makes her happy. I let go of the window frame and swim back to the point from which I began. Then I walk to my left on the edge of the basin. The 'Other' had remained on the rim of the basin without ever jumping in. He had wanted to go left from the beginning. Now we choose the path to the far left. The stream is quite shallow but rapid. It moves downhill in sharp curves through canals and wooden culverts. I am afraid, and in one of the sharp curves I cling to the rim. At that very moment a window opens before me in the wooden wall. Behind it are the old woman and the young girl again. The woman tells me to take off my shoes so I can swim better. She wraps the shoes in a package for me. I become aware that I am, strangely enough, wearing evening clothes. They look quite silly above my bare feet. I take off my white tie and give it to the young girl as a keepsake. As I have no gift for the old woman, I hope that she too will take pleasure in the tie. I continue to swim but lose the package with the shoes. At first I regret the loss, but then it loses its importance. The main thing is to escape successfully. The water flows through a covered canal. I wonder whether I'll get through. Happily, I do. On the other side, the river is large and quiet; I know I am now in my homeland, though not yet out of danger. I get out of the water. I want to continue on the road, but people I meet warn me that a checkpoint is ahead. In order to avoid it, I have to get back into the water and swim. Now the river is an offensive sewer. But there is no way out. In order to pass the checkpoint I even have to dive. Then, I am safe. The country is green. There is sunshine. The birds sing. I am free."

This dream returns to the dreamer's traumatic wartime experiences. These experiences, however, are presented as contemporary images. He has been imprisoned, and now he must free himself in order to survive. The escape which he attempts in this dream is as necessary, as difficult, and as vital as his escape from wartime captivity was. The dream reveals to him that he must follow the natural flow of energy. The old woman offering him

refreshments is the earth-mother. Her daughter represents life and promise for the future. The old woman advises him to follow the shallow brook on the far left, not the powerful river on the right. In other words, she advises him not to follow the path of the primary function—the easy, habitual path of intuition—because it is blocked.

The dreamer immediately accepts the interpretation that the four rivers may represent the four functions. He concludes that he must follow the tedious path of sensation, his fourth function—the path of accurate, factual observation—since his intuition no longer allows him to get ahead. The fourth brook is poorly contained. It is rapid, though shallow, and replete with turns and dark canals. The dreamer must entrust himself to his sensation even though it has poor foundations and little of the water of life. In the previous dream, he became one with his body, in the form of a hart. He must now do the same with the reality function close to his body. In the extroverted, intuitive person, this reality function, sensation, has an introverted or subjective connotation. Because of this connotation, he must painfully work through all the subjective sensations and fears that are evoked by external difficulties. And he must do so without knowing beforehand where this troublesome path will lead.

In his fear he clings to one of the curves, and the earth-mother and her daughter reappear. The woman advises him to take off his shoes—that is, to give up his former ways—in order to swim better. Only now does he notice he is wearing evening clothes, characteristic of the correct social attitude by means of which the extroverted, intuitive person tries to master his tasks and difficulties. This attitude is not appropriate here. Without hesitating, he gives away his white tie, the hallmark of a fine society dress; and when he loses his shoes, he shows little regret. What matters now is, not the proper, conscientious, social attitude, but the ability to endure in the fight against obstacles. Just when the canal leads into a large, quiet river and the dreamer assumes that his life will continue quietly and safely, he must dive into the water once more and traverse a disgustingly polluted section. Nothing is spared him on the path of the inferior function. But, finally, he reaches the green, sun-bathed, promising land: freedom.

This dream proved to be true even in its details. The struggle for survival became so hard that the dreamer had to temporarily give

up the fine social life to which he was accustomed. Deprived of all means of support, he eventually attained an independent professional position commensurate to his knowledge and skill. Finally, just when he thought he had reached his goal, a new delay with bitter privations was introduced.

By mentioning these details of his life, we are jumping ahead in our story. We mention them only to show that this dream of deliverance from a water tank anticipates external, professional deliverance. The homeland, the life-situation which is appropriate for him, symbolizes a return from constant tension and struggle to himself and his family. The end of the dream shows that escape was imperative and that the goal is promising. This dream gave the dreamer the strength and initiative to use his sensation-function as reality-function. It also showed him that perseverance was worthwhile. He concluded from this dream that from now on he had to develop his sensation. Doing so required restraining his intuition, basing his scientific work upon precise observations, repeated checking of details, and careful formulation. In order for him to adjust to life, developing his sensation-function meant keeping strictly to givens.

Dream Fifty-Three: Imprisonment in the Rocky Cliff

"I assume an unusual role in this dream. On the one hand, I'm an active participant, and on the other hand, I'm a spectator observing the various participants, including myself. I see three people. I am in the middle. To my right is a woman who belongs to me. We are quite fond of each other. To my left is a dark-skinned, muscular Egyptian. He walks about half a pace behind me. It is obvious that he is a constable. He urges me ahead, not forcefully, but I'm obliged to comply. I know that it is senseless to resist. I have done something that is against local customs and for which I am now being led to prison. With a white, cotton towel, the Egyptian dries his glistening, sweaty torso, arms, and face. In his movements I detect his superior force. The woman knows my fate and stands by me. She is such a calming influence that I don't even think of resisting. I see the three figures reach a vertical rock wall, and at the same time I experience this in the role of the prisoner. On the side of the rock, there is a small quadrangular opening

On the side of the rock, there is a small quadrangular opening through which I barely manage to crawl at the Egyptian's behest. Behind it is a cave. I can see through the small window that someone is inside. Simultaneously, I am inside the rock cave as a prisoner. Only this small window allows a view. On the floor of the cave, there are chains which the Egyptian orders me to place around my feet. I hear the chains' rattling. At the same time, I'm outside and the Egyptian is the prisoner. Once more he stretches his hand through the opening of the cave. Since he proffers it to me, I'd like to grasp it; but I fear lest he pull me inside and overwhelm me. However, I know, or trust, that he wouldn't do that, and I give him my hand. The events from the point where I cease to resist to the point where I give my hand to the Egyptian happen timelessly and simultaneously. No time distinctions can be made, though various themes can be separated. From this moment on, the process of deliverance begins. My cave in the rock is drilled into from both sides. Obliquely from the outside, the entire front of the cave is removed. Many drills and hammers are working. Soon, the cave will be, at best, a shallow deepening in the cliff wall. I admire the fine technical preparation of my rescue. I experience all this both as spectator and as prisoner."

According to the dreamer, the previous dream of his rescue from the basin referred to his external, professional life-situation. In contrast, he understood the dream of his imprisonment in the rocky cave as referring predominantly to a personal problem. The present dream shows him that, if he is to become professionally independent, he must submit to an inner judge. He sees that the journey to inner freedom requires insight into his personal guilt and voluntary submission to the decreed punishment. Imprisonment, then, is the beginning of deliverance. We are free only when we accept our finitude.

The split caused by the fact that the dreamer is both participant and observer is necessary because the dreamer must confront his empirical, acting ego. He must distance himself from his ego in order to recognize that this ego is the Egyptian's prisoner. The dark-skinned, muscular constable is reminiscent of the muscular men in Dream Forty-Five. At the beginning of the *Chymical Wedding,* a Moor lives with princess Anima in concubinage.[224] In our present dream, however, the Anima does not enter into a pact with

the shadow. She is clearly focused upon the conscious ego. The vigorous Egyptian represents the superior power of nature to which the ego may succumb. He embodies the dark shadow-side of nature and the danger of nature-religions. The situation in the dream is paradoxical. An error is condemned by an inner court. The dreamer must recognize his breach with traditional morality and allow himself to be imprisoned by the Egyptian.

However, it is his constable who is really the prisoner. Only his identity with the Egyptian in the rock prison keeps the dreamer captive. The handshake, by means of which he declares himself jointly responsible with the prisoner,[225] and his confidence that the shadow will no longer overwhelm him begin the process of deliverance. The cave in the rocks reminds one of *Aida* (Dream Forty-Three). In *Aida* Radames is buried alive with Aida, but here the dreamer is sentenced, as he says, alone to three years in prison. Three years of voluntary renunciation is a long time, but it can be endured. The Anima faithfully waits outside the prison. Psychological relatedness will outlast this period of suffering. Having renounced the arbitrariness of the ego, recognized his guilt, and accepted his punishment, the dreamer starts a period of submission to an inner court. The numerous drills mobilized to liberate the prisoner symbolize the spiritual activity of penetrating and understanding the supra-personal problem of matter and nature.

Several dreams follow in which the dreamer feels persecuted. He is called into court and condemned to be hanged. The ego hesitates when it is called upon to submit to the inner judge and accept restrictions of freedom. Accordingly, the dreams become threatening and speak of death by hanging. A radical change, symbolized by a state of suspension, is demanded.

It is said of Odin:[226]

> I know I hanged
> in the windswept tree
> for nine long nights,
> wounded by the spear,
> consecrated to Odin,
> myself to myself,
> on yonder tree
> whose root's unknown
> to everyone.

They offered me
no food nor drink;
Deep down I bent,
picked up the poles,
raised groaning them,
then down I plunged.
I began to wake up
and to thrive well;
Now I became wise;
Word led me to word
and another word.
Work led me to work
and another work.

Consecrated to himself, Odin, the roaming, captivating god, hung nine days from a tree. Tied to nature, prevented from roaming, he loses the ground under his feet. He must persevere, though pained by uncertainty, until he finds the right runes and attains wisdom through them. By remaining quiet and persevering, by renouncing the possibilities of the outer world, and by tolerating his own hindered nature, he achieves a state of concentration in which he uncovers the symbolic meaning of restlessness. Saint Nicholas of Flue was similarly stopped on one of his roaming journeys by a vision. He then returned to his cell where he transformed his urge to roam into inner reflection and spiritual meaning.[227] Hanging, not unlike the death on the cross, suggests self-sacrifice and, simultaneously, elevation and spiritualization.

The ego may continue to reject limitations on its freedom. It may not patiently accept any sort of suspension or heed the call to sacrifice willfulness and patiently wait and persist. If that happens, the symbolic dream-image could become an obsession. During the dirge for Attis, a picture of the young god was fastened to a fir or pine which was then cut and mourned as a god.[228] Death-masks of Dionysus were also fastened to trees. Both Odin and Dionysus are gods of intoxicating ecstasy who can lead human beings to their deaths. Both are also masters of the dead. Attis, the epitome of luxuriantly flowing life, dies, like them, when nature begins to wilt. He is sacrificed to the mother, and this sacrifice guarantees new life and fertility. Whoever is seized by the gods' ecstatic life must also accept, as conscious sacrifice, their end. Happy is he

who is able to take off the mask of a god and hang it, as a symbolic sacrifice, on a tree. When he returns her son's picture to the divine mother, he can recognize himself again as a human being, an actor in the god's mystery play who returns to his limited, everyday existence after the rite's performance. He who does not recognize as symbolical the wedding and the sufferings of the god, but instead identifies with the gestalt that seizes him, may fall prey to the compulsion of the death-wedding's archetype. He falls into a trance and, finally, death.[229]

Dream Fifty-Four: The Taming of the Anima

"In a jeep I'm driving with an old physician to an old woman's house. I carry with me the upright stem of a tree. A fox has killed hens here, but we cannot catch it. Then four foxes look up towards us from below the street. Later, I ride a fine red horse on a path beside a field. The horse is magnificent and large. It has a lot of pep, but with me it is quiet obedient and disciplined. Then a man comes riding behind me. He is leading another red, slender horse by the halter. This one rears up and is quite unruly. I had anticipated that my horse would behave in the same way, but I notice that it responds to me unconditionally. It is a pleasure to ride. I tell the man: 'Only one thing will help. You must hit this obstinate horse.' At this instant the horse turns into a nude woman. I am about to whip her across the back when she runs up a slope and threatens to hit me with a club if I come near her. She is just as unruly as the horse and needs to be whipped. In spite of her threatening attitude, I ride up the slope and manage to strike her just as she tries to duck. To my surprise she responds: 'Thank you!' She really means it and seems relieved. It is as if we were in a fairy tale and I had freed her from a spell. Another rider joins us. He is an Englishman riding excellently on a fine red horse. The woman has dressed herself by now. She is quiet and polite." (The dreamer added: "Maybe my Anima needs to be tamed.")

The dreamer's delivering the tree trunk to the old woman's house indicates his willingness to bring the sacrifice requested of him. This truncated tree symbolizes Attis who is carried as a fir trunk into the sepulchral vault where he will be mourned by his

mother. Instead of a priest, a physician accompanies the dreamer. He is the wise old man in the guise of healer. With the god's death and the sacrifice of the overflowing libido, all life sinks back into the grave. Even the dreamer's developed functions revert to a primitive condition. As in Dream Ten of the heath-cock, these functions take the form of shy, wild animals, in this case foxes.[230] Foxes confront consciousness rapaciously. They don't allow themselves to be ordered around.

But a new development is rapidly taking place. Barely has the dreamer looked at the foxes when one of them is transformed into a horse whose origin is betrayed by its color. The horse is a magnificent, well-disciplined animal on which the dreamer ascends. The instinctual energy that had regressed to its natural condition becomes again a supportive, adaptable, effective force that carries the dreamer towards his professional goals. His shadow-brother follows him on horseback. He brings with him a slender and unruly horse whose origin is obviously that of a hen-stealing type of fox. This unruly aspect of the instinct is also transformed by the dreamer. It becomes a nude, unruly woman, a primitive Anima.

Energy from the Anima can be utilized, but it brings an element of uncertainty to the inner economy of the man. The third horse, symbolizing the energy of the unconscious and the feminine soul, can be disturbed at any time by circumstances. If it is, it may derail conscious energies. In the meantime, the dreamer has learned *not* to identify blindly with the Anima or be induced by her to act rebelliously or with animosity. He is willing to tame the feminine side without false pity, but the Anima reveals her archaic nature by threatening the dreamer with a club, the most primitive weapon. The dreamer does not allow himself to be knocked out by her. Instead, he tames her the way he would tame a stubborn horse. And, lo and behold, she is thankful for it. By his firm opposition, he frees her from her dangerous, primitive nature. He achieves a deliverance similar to that in *The Taming of the Shrew* or the fairy tale of "King Thrushbeard."[231]

The transformation of a fox into a woman is a motif found in many fairy tales, especially those of China.[232] In the tale "The Golden Bird,"[233] the fox requests that the hero, whom he assisted in completing his tasks, kill it and chop off its head and paws.

Paws severed from beasts of prey symbolize the restriction of conceit, rage, and beastly nature. In "The Golden Bird," a fox is tamed. At first this fox with its sensitive nose is needed to obtain three treasures: the bird, the golden horse, and the maiden. Once the hero has obtained these treasures, he must sacrifice his own rapacious drives and the cunning of his instinct. In other words, he must kill the fox. The fox, after his death, changes into a prince who reveals himself as the maiden-princess's brother. Fox-prince and princess are variants of the original animal instinct.[234]

In this dream the Anima has again become unruly. She has fallen into the hands of the shadow, the second rider, who leads her by the halter. By being tamed, she is freed from her amalgamation with the shadow. After that happens, a rider with a proper attitude appears. The dreamer is rewarded for his responsible behavior by the restoration of his positive, masculine energies.

The Anima expresses her desire for guidance in this dream. The man recognizes that under certain circumstances he must resist the Anima. In fact, she will be thankful when he does not accept her unruly attitudes. Had the dreamer failed to tame her, the regressed Anima would have maneuvered him again into a primitive relationship. By his opposition, however, he enforces appropriate behavior. Thus he is able to direct the freed energies towards the transformation and spiritualization of his nature.

Dream Fifty-Five: The Communion Rail

"The church is filled with the devout. The priest says mass at the altar. Several men are crowded into the row of benches ahead of me. In order to create space, they carry the kneeler to the middle aisle. One of them pushes it with some zest, and it slips forward and hits the communion rail, which shatters. The priest, who has just reached the moment of the transubstantiation, seems to interpret the men's action as a personal attack and insult. He interrupts the transubstantiation, runs to the men, and starts to beat them. They defend themselves, gain the upper hand and chase the priest from the church. I am aghast. As he flees, I notice that he is bleeding from cuts on his neck below each ear. I run after him in order to help. I take him to his home. There, a very aged priest is

sitting at a table. He has been sleeping. He is the wounded man's superior. Dull and feeble, he looks up. I tell him what has happened, but he remains uncomprehending and indifferent."

Like Dream Thirty-Six, this one places the dreamer into the church at the very moment of the transubstantiation. The church is packed; longing for the church's healing truth is great. A few young men are too crowded. The enterprising, questioning, and researching side of the dreamer does not have enough space. Therefore, the young men place the kneeler into the middle passage. Maybe they are unable to show submission by kneeling. One of them pushes the kneeler so hard against the communion rail that it breaks. The dreamer comments that this action was not meant as an attack or insult. It was an impulsive action and an unconscious mistake. By their presence in the church, the young men indicate their interest in the religious service.

Their seemingly inconsiderate, disrespectful and involuntary action also has a deeper meaning. They wish to penetrate the separating wall and participate directly in the transubstantiation. The tradition-bound priest, or the tradition-bound side of the dreamer, experiences this attempted approach as an attack. In the men's clumsiness he can see only aggression and insult, and he retaliates in a most unchristian manner. The scene ends with a misunderstanding and brawl in which the priest is injured. The dreamer is deeply frightened by the young men's action and its consequences. He runs to help the priest. The cuts near the priest's ears tell us that his ability to listen and understand was injured. He is entirely incapable of understanding what is happening. Because the young men are unaware of the hidden purpose of their action, their attempt remains ineffective. Eventually, the dreamer seeks the assistance of the aged priest who embodies intellectual understanding of religion. But this priest is ancient, unrejuvenated. He has not adapted to the times. As a result, he is unable to understand or respond to the burning questions of the present. He is not even aware of them.

The fight between the church-goers and the priest symbolizes the battle within the dreamer's soul. His traditional beliefs conflict with his barely conscious wish to participate directly in the transubstantiation of the wine that takes place behind the separating rail. Like the dream of the brandy, this dream anticipated events in

the external world. A few years later, the dreamer heard of a decree of Pope Pius XII in which the symbolic separation of priests and laypersons was abolished and priests and laypersons were addressed clearly as *one* community. This dream, then, expresses a hidden longing of the collective folk-soul, one which eventually received a satisfying response from the highest court. Modern Catholic churches no longer build a separating fence between the choir and laypersons.

Dream Fifty-Six: Church or University

"There was a chapel with two doors: one closed, one open. Light came through its windows from inside. I wanted to go in. Beyond the open door was a second door which jammed. It did not open wide enough, and I could not get in.

I had a lot of time on my hands in a foreign city, and so I went to visit an old castle. In the castle's museum, rails—especially church-rails for doors, windows, graves, and altars—were on exhibit. I left the castle and went to a somewhat newer house which belonged to the university. Here I saw a collection of African artifacts, mostly weapons. Just then N came from a side room. He looked like Albert Schweitzer. Before I could speak to him, five blacks arrived. One or two were men, the others women. N spoke animatedly with them in their native tongue. As he spoke, his skin color darkened. I could not understand them, but I listened with pleasure to their fluent conversation with its strange smacking sounds. The blacks were very attentive, spontaneous, genuine, thankful, kind and sympathetic. I enjoyed their pleasure in chatting and their spontaneity."

This is the second time the dreamer fails to enter the sacred space of the chapel, the area of the mystery of transubstantiation. The first door to the church is open to all church-goers, but the second one is jammed and allows an opening too narrow for the dreamer to squeeze through. After this failed attempt to bring his problem into the church and resolve it in the traditional way, the scene changes. Now the dreamer finds himself in a foreign city where he has time to visit museums. He goes to a medieval castle in which different types of church-rails are displayed. The rails have

become museum pieces, indicating that exclusion and separation of the individual from the mystery of the transubstantiation is basically a carry-over from the Middle Ages.

The dreamer then visits a modern university which represents the scientific goal of universality accessible to every researcher, including the dreamer. The collection of African weapons which he finds here points to objective, factual interest in other people and their nature. Knives, spears and arrows symbolize the discriminating and penetrating qualities of thought. The collection of weapons thus stands for the natural person's ability to intelligently discuss and defend his or her own viewpoint. Explorer N embodies the scientific spirit of research which focuses on the primitive, natural human being. His helpful, empathic interest in the foreign black race is suggested by his resemblance to Albert Schweitzer. The resemblance also implies a medical attitude whose goal is the healing of conflicts and a Protestant demand for independent thought in theological questions. Indeed, Albert Schweitzer was an author of Protestant theological publications as well as a physician.

This humane, empathic and open-minded attitude of the representative of modern, scientific consciousness produces a change in the unconscious. The inert artifacts of the castle are replaced by lively, alert, sympathetic blacks who display spontaneous joy in chatting. The dialogue which could not be started in the church (Dream Fifty-Five) is now taken up in the university. The researcher changes his skin color in the course of the conversation. That is, he adapts to the blacks with whom he is conversing. The dream shows the process which the British call, albeit with a negative connotation, "going black." In the course of one's contacts with "primitive" people, one is unwittingly affected. By the same token, one's consciousness is changed by a dialogue with the primitive levels of one's own soul. Such a dialogue has important repercussions. On the basis of the mediating attitude of the researcher, an intermediate level is attained.

Dream Fifty-Seven: The Bird Griff

"I'm in a forest, close to the convent-school that I attended as a youth. I am stalking a deer when a large bird, a sort of 'griff,' ap-

pears above. He is quite ugly. He has a nude, red neck like a turkey. His body reminds me of the ill-shaped figure of the louse in the first dream. His colors are blue and red. I have my rifle, but I don't want to shoot it. Its horrid body might burst right over me if I did. I would rather that it fly away, and it does when I threaten it with the rifle."

The dreamer finds himself stalking a deer near his Catholic high school. He again tries to deal with his nature-side, but an ugly griff, or turkey-like bird, appears above him. This bird is the negative side of instinctive spirit. The turkey embodies blind rage. The griff (meaning "grasp") represents a dangerous, destructive grasping.[235] This new, disgusting and dangerous bird also belongs to the same archaic realm as the eagle of Dream Thirty. If the eagle is understood as an archaic image of God, then the griff is his negative aspect or that of the natural spirit. In his struggle to integrate his intellect and instinct, the dreamer must watch out for the negative side of nature and of the instincts.

Dream Fifty-Eight: The Cormorant

"The second one, a dark-haired and brown-skinned person, and I are in an unfinished house which is next to some horrible apartment houses. This house is similar to a small Japanese temple in that it has four corner pillars and a roof, but no walls. A black bird approaches rapidly. First I want to shoot it, but I know that I must leave it unharmed. I remember the ugly griff [of the preceding dream] which I couldn't shoot as I feared its stomach might burst. The reason I don't shoot this bird, however, is that it is a cormorant which the Japanese use for fishing. There are stone steps in the small temple. If one wishes to ascend them, one must first enter a pit with manure and garbage. Only from there can one begin the ascent. I hesitate, and the 'second one' encourages me to descend. I go ahead and then ascend the steps. Now I'm sitting with the 'second one' on the uppermost stone slab in the small temple. From here I can see that our little temple is situated on a magnificent bay with clear water and beautiful trees. It is pleasant. I can stay here."

In Dream Fifty-Five the dreamer could not gain access to the

mystery of transubstantiation in the church. In the university's collection of African weapons (Dream Fifty-Six), he resumed the dialogue with the blacks, that is, with the spontaneous, natural, primitive side of his being. In Dream Fifty-Seven he searched again for the nature-like spiritual soul. Paracelsus might say he was searching for "the light in nature." In his search, he discovered the darkness that sticks to the natural soul and that embodied itself in the "griff" or turkey-like bird. The rejection of this bird purified his natural soul. The griff reappears in Dream Fifty-Eight as a black cormorant, a positive, helpful bird. Meanwhile, the ugly and dangerous content has settled, as in the alchemical process, to the ground. It lies as garbage and manure in the pit before the small temple.

With his dark-skinned shadow-brother, the dreamer finds himself among horrid apartment houses which are, to him, the epitome of collective mass existence, present in all cities. Since the dreamer has set out by himself to find the inner treasure, he is no longer part of this existence. Before him he sees his own little house which could be a small Japanese temple. Above the garbage-pit, there are a few steps leading up to the four corner pillars. These steps, representing the stepwise increase of consciousness, are similar to the stepwise alchemical process which is based on the planetary steps. The four corner-posts symbolize the four elements or the four-fold and, therefore, total all-encompassing perception of reality. We found this earlier in the cubic form and noticed this already with the four sphinxes of the silver trunk in Haggard's *She*. [236] The roof represents a human construction that unites and surmounts the whole and that offers to the dreamer protection against sun and rain. It represents the basic design for his own world view which also offers protection against historical upheavals and generalizations that lead one into collective existence.

Here a black bird appears again, but this time it is a cormorant which the Japanese use for fishing. At first the dreamer wishes to shoot it, but then he becomes aware that he would be breaking the law since cormorants are protected everywhere. The cormorant is a positive hunting instinct, reminiscent of helpful animals found in fairy tales. The cormorant dives deep into the water for the fish; it brings the values of the unconscious to light.

Only now does the dreamer wish to enter the small temple. To

do so, he must first enter the garbage-pit which contains excreta from the bird of the preceding dream. The journey towards individual existence and towards a personal world view includes recognition of the shadow. Understandably, the dreamer hesitates at first, but he finally decides to pass through the garbage. As a result, he is able to reach the steps on which he climbs towards a conscious, all-encompassing view. Now he discovers that the temple offers a wonderful view of a bay with clear water and beautiful trees. The presence of the small Japanese temple in this dream emphasizes the Eastern, Zen-like qualities of natural piety, introversion and meditation in the dreamer's personal outlook. Zen confronts human beings with paradoxes, perils, and unexpected things in order to lead them to wholeness and spontaneity. If the student of Zen can remain calm in the face of any reproach, distraction, or danger, he will be able to live spontaneously. At the end of the dream of deliverance from the basin, the dreamer had to dive into a polluted section of the river. In that dream, he had to confront external difficulties. Here, however, he must recognize and accept human nature itself, in order to ascend towards a comprehensive view of life.

Dream Fifty-Nine: The Flying Hart

"I am hunting a hart who flies across the city like the symbol of a constellation or a wingless Pegasus. The 'second one' beside me doubts whether I'll be able to shoot the hart in motion. I fire. The hart is hit and drops. He falls into a river so powerfully that water splashes high across the city roofs. We run to the main bridge of the city, but the hart has sunk. He is lost. If I had known this would happen, I wouldn't have fired."

The day after this dream, a hunter told the dreamer about an old mountain goat that constantly stood upon the same rocky promontory. It was impossible to shoot him in that position because he would fall into a lake below and be irretrievable. This synchronicity or meaningful coincidence between a dream and external events alerted the dreamer to the archetypal quality and meaningfulness of his hunting dream.[237] Still, the dream seemed largely unintelligible. Only a year later was some light shed on it through an actual

hunting experience. While hunting, the dreamer had shot a heath-cock which had caused a lot of damage to other heath-cocks and had evaded rangers' snares for a long time. As a result, the rangers rejoiced. The dreamer, however, was unhappy. He continued to feel deep pity for the dead bird and felt as if his own youth had ended with the bird's life. The dream of the heavenly hart, then, refers again to the sacrifice required of the dreamer. In Dream Fifty the dreamer had become one with the hart and its instinctual, passionate nature. The hart in the sky represents an elevation—that is, a spiritualization and divinization—of this nature.

In the myths of Germanic tribes, there is a hart of the sun and of New Year's standing on the earth whose horns reach into the sky.[238] Waldemar Fenn hypothesizes that the constellation now known as the Big Dipper was the hart in prehistoric astronomy. A petroglyph depicts the hart near the pole at the summer solstice, its antlers formed by the four large stars of the Big Dipper.[239] In addition, a prehistoric cave painting, again above the zodiac at the summer solstice, shows the hart beside the hind. At the side of the animal pair is a human couple, who may represent life and death.[240] The constellation of the hart was above the pole in spring and summer. The descending or falling constellation of the hart clearly indicated fall and winter, the descending course of the year.

After postulating a connection between the hunt of the hart and the ritualistic murder of the king, Robert Graves asserts that the dying or falling hart symbolizes the spring- and summer-hero's death and, thereby, the end of youthful fertility.[241] The dream's end may represent such a sacrifice of the youthful hero. The hart in the sky becomes, through its loss, a sacrificial offering. The transfer of the hart into the sky reveals to the dreamer that what he had viewed as his own, personal instinctual energy is of a super-personal magnitude, placed above the ego. His hunting companion is clearly the dreamer's shadow-brother, the natural human being who would like to prevent the sacrifices that must be made in the second half of life.

In Dream Thirty-Five the dreamer faced the task of the interlaced rings, that is, of transforming blood and passion into spiritual captivation. This task has led to a lengthy struggle. At first, consciousness was not equal to the collision with the chthonian nature of the fourth one, the evil one (Dreams Thirty-Six through Forty-Two). In addition, such a transformation requires

broadening and deepening. The dreams of the Egyptian (Dream Fifty-Three) and of taming the Anima (Dream Fifty-Four) introduce the required distinction between the ego and shadow and Anima. In Dream Fifty-Five, the dreamer unsuccessfully seeks access to the mystery of transubstantiation. Here the sacred office is interrupted for the second time at the moment of transubstantiation. The dialogue with the natural side must thus be resumed (Dream Fifty-Six). The dreams of the griff and the cormorant indicate a further purification of that nature later elevated as the heavenly hart, which falls into the river as a sacrificial offering.

Identifications with the images of the unconscious, such as the dreamer's identification with the hart in Dream Fifty, introduce complications for which one is not immediately responsible. In the encounter with the unconscious, one repeatedly finds such identifications. They are essential to some extent. One must identify with these images in order for them to be taken seriously and rendered conscious. These identifications are also dangerous because they distract consciousness from reality.[242] If one struggles against identifying with these images, impoverishment and rigidity of the personality result. If one does allow a certain degree of identification with the internal figures, one must try to grasp their meaning. Only by this conscious effort is it possible to escape their fascination. The hart's sacrifice represents a sacrifice of the hart-nature and an attempt to be freed from unconscious compulsion and youthful instinct.

Dream Sixty: The Picture of the Ancestors .

"In a large, beautiful room, I'm working at a writing desk. On the wall behind me is a large picture in the style of the English portraitist Gainsborough. I'm portrayed as an old, famous, white-haired gentleman, like the old English aristocracy. I'm dressed in white satin and wearing knee-pants. It is an interesting experience. I observe this painting, and, at the same time, I know that I may be this person in some thirty years. It is not a fantasy, but an experience of simultaneity. I do feel at the same time like an old man."

The evening after this dream, the dreamer attended a perfor-

mance of Strauss's *Rosenkavalier*. In this opera, the Rosenkavalier was dressed in a manner similar to that of the old man in the dream-picture. Synchronicity, then, figures both in the relationship between the dream and external events and within the dream itself where space and time are suspended and present and future, ego-reality and picture interchange mysteriously. In his article "The Spirit of Psychology," Jung describes synchronicity as a psychologically conditioned relativity of time and space.[243] In the opera, the Rosenkavalier, who in fact is a woman dressed as a gentleman, wears a white and silvery suit, whereas the dreamer in the picture is dressed in white satin. The dreamer envisions the possibility of attaining in his old age the kind of purified attitude of which the dream of the white and golden tabernacle (Dream Thirty-Four) seemed to speak. In that dream, the tabernacle represented the external, conscious, masculine life, and the inner, grey-silvery material represented the substance of the feminine soul. The dreamer sees himself with his portrait in a room reminiscent of the official rooms of his mother's ancestors. If he is able to distinguish himself from his Anima and represent masculine, spiritual values, he will be accepted, like his ancestors, as a carrier of his nation's culture.

His professional situation is still unsatisfactory, but this dream brings him consolation and the hope that his patience will not be in vain. The sacrifice of the hart—the sacrifice of his ambition—is here compensated by this vision of the future. The sacrifice of his youthful impulsiveness will help him obtain a spiritualized old age. He himself must change; his own being must, as shown by the picture, be spiritualized and elevated.

Dream Sixty-One: The Church of the Magna Mater

First Part: "I'm with a large party on a somewhat tiresome voyage. At first we travel by railroad on a track that frequently requires repairs and causes delays. Then we continue by bus. Again, there are delays because the streets are often torn up and must be repaired. After a railroad crossing, we reach a parking lot from which a beautiful, large, paved road leads into the far distance. This is the last stop. From here the buses can reach their last station without impediments. After the last stop, we will have a fairly

long walk on a level street which should not cause any exceptional hardship. The route of the entire journey—the bus trip and walk—follows a large arc. Our final goal is a well-known pilgrimage church which one can now reach easily on foot. From the last bus stop another path leads through woods and meadows up to the same goal. It is not any longer than the other route, but it is steeper, more arduous and beautiful. I decide to take this footpath and leave the bus. I ask whether anyone wishes to join me. A young man does and we start out. As I look back, I see that two more people are following. They walk more slowly, and I repeatedly admonish them to catch up with us. Thus we are four. To my companion I point out the beauty of this path from which one has a view of the meadows and hills before the Alps and which runs alongside magnificent, dark oak groves. I explain to him that at a certain point we will see the pilgrimage church above us, a view the others will not see. When we reach this point, we notice that the church is surrounded by other buildings in different styles. Besides the Baroque pilgrimage church there are Romanesque structures, towers reminiscent of the church of St. George in Prague, Gothic elements, and, finally, walls with towers and battlements resembling a medieval castle. All these structures are linked by arches, military hallways, and walls. It seems to be a city of God or a temple-city. As we arrive, we look through various archways. We detect colonnades like those in the Cathedral of St. Paul in Rome or the Alhambra in Granada. Inside, everything is in white and gold. The columns are of white alabaster, and the capitals are golden. I just know that I have seen this temple-city once before. I explain to my companion that the castle contains the graves of such knights and emperors as Redbeard, Karl the Great, and Karl V. Frederick II of the Hohenstaufen, however, was not buried here but in Sicily."

Second Part: "I'm boarding a large, modern streetcar. Ahead of it is another, old-fashioned one with an open platform. I jump off the large streetcar and run ahead. I prefer to ride the small, old one. It will reach my goal just as fast. I arrive at my mother's apartment. Though small, the apartment is full of people. The entire family is congregated. All the relatives are here. I sense that the 'second one' is beside me. He is upset that so many relatives have come when there is so little space. I calm him, saying, 'Just leave them alone. Why shouldn't they have come? There will be enough

to eat for everyone even though there isn't too much food.' As I say this, I know that everyone will receive a small portion which will satiate them, just as the bread and fish miraculously fed the multitudes in the Bible. It occurs to me that this time I am the one who calms the other. Our roles have been reversed. When I reach the antechamber, the fourth and smallest room, I find three uniformed Hungarians smoking and conversing. They don't pay much attention to me. They have intelligent, noble faces. I assume that they are officers, though they wear the uniforms of enlisted men. The 'other' asks how they got in and is dissatisfied because they do not seem to belong. I reply that one should just leave them there. They make a good impression and are probably refugees who are happy that they could come."

The evening before this dream, the dreamer had expressed the desire to rediscover the faith of his childhood. However, he realized that he had to find the path to religion alone, through his own experiences and reflections. In spite of his many failed attempts to reach the mystery within the church, he still brings his widened knowledge, after each new step, back to the church. He measures his individual experiences against the church's teachings and incorporates them into its comprehensive doctrinal structure. The dream shows him that his goal is basically that of everyone else, but by following the narrow, tedious path he gains a more magnificent and profound insight into the church than those who reach the same goal by the level road. He walks the narrow path with the "other one" and two additional companions lagging behind. Their sluggishness indicates that they are the two inferior functions, thinking and sensation. Their goal is a well-known church of Saint Mary. Here the mother of God is worshiped as the true *Magna Mater* (Great Mother) of the country, and various tribes and races make pilgrimages to her shrine. The Catholic church, then, is presented in this dream as a transpersonal mother who encompasses populations and epochs within her womb. The pilgrimage church of the dream consists of Romanesque, Gothic and Baroque elements, joined into a medieval castle by battlements, towers, hallways and arches.

These elements express the dichotomy of the church's character—defensive and bellicose outside, monastic and other-worldly inside. The colonnades of alabaster and gold from early

Christian cathedrals and the Alhambra remind one of the contribution of Moslem culture to Christianity. The white columns and golden capitals which support the church symbolize the numerous individuals who supported the church and exemplified its teachings in their behavior. White and gold are characteristic of the conscious, masculine spiritual stance. With these colors, he is to be accepted by his ancestors (Dream Sixty) and within the Christian community.

On top of the castle-like structure in this dream was a Baroque section. It is the high point of stormy movement, jubilation, power and magnificence. The dreamer comments that it resembled the city of God, the heavenly Jerusalem descended upon earth. It is the goal of all human dreams, the linkage of opposites, and an image of all-encompassing wholeness realized in the church. In the womb of this great mother are buried kings who figure importantly in the histories of Western Europe and Christianity: Karl the Great (Charlemagne) who embodied European culture of his time and whom the French as well as the Germans claimed as their emperor; Frederick Redbeard who united Germany and Italy and stretched his sword towards the Near East; and Karl the Fifth in whose realm the sun never set and who, as king of Spain, represents a link with the Alhambra and Moslem art.

One emperor was clearly excluded: Frederick the Second, the nephew of Redbeard. He was a great emperor who reigned over Germany, Italy, Sicily and Jerusalem. However, he was equally fond of Eastern and Western spirituality. His concept of the empire did not include a Christian foundation, and Germany was rather foreign to him. When he showed up at the imperial Diet, he brought along foreign goods, blacks and exotic animals. He was battling the papacy and died excommunicated. The three Christian emperors are an earthly reflection of the trinity that dominates the Christian world. Frederick the Second, however—who, in the opinion of his contemporaries, was much too engaged in the Orient, the exotic, and primitive nature—symbolizes the excluded, devilish aspect which has no place in the church.

The dream makes the dreamer aware of the church's openness, its ability to harmonize a vast spiritual scope. But it also reminds him of the limits of this openness. It is a grandiose dream, a peak from which one can only descend.

This descent takes the dreamer from the majesty and splendor of

the church and its emperors to the narrow, small apartment of his distinguished but poor mother. He experienced in the church the reunion of the great representatives of nations. Here he finds in his mother's apartment the reunion of his family. All are present, all have a place, and each one receives a small portion of the food which proves as sufficient as the bread and fish in the biblical feeding of the five thousand.

At this point he notices that his "other" becomes critical, while he assumes a positive, affirmative, conciliatory role, the attitude of a well-adjusted consciousness. He distinguishes himself clearly from his shadow. The former positive traits of the shadow can now be assumed by the conscious ego. In his mother's apartment, there is room for all the relatives. All are invited to a shared meal, a "small communion." All, even the small, uninteresting persons among them, are welcome. This last statement indicates a fading of the psychological inflation caused by the unconscious contents. Now the dreamer accepts, not only his shadow-aspect, but the inadequate parts of his being as well. This is important. Both one's own darkness, personified in the shadow, and middle-class narrowness must be accepted. Only that which one forgives in oneself can one tolerate in others. Insight into one's own shortcomings leads to tolerance for the weaknesses of others. Space is created within the dreamer's soul for all that is embodied in his relatives and all that his ancestors have bequeathed upon him. By using the positive, masculine attitude anticipated in the dream of the ancestral picture with the satin dress (Dream Sixty), he is able to distinguish himself from the shadow. Because he has now a more reliable consciousness and a firmer ego, he can, at the same time, accept his unpleasant, petty aspects without succumbing to them.

Three Hungarian refugees with intelligent, noble faces have found shelter in the fourth, smallest room. In the cathedral in which the three great emperors were laid to rest, the *fourth* one was excluded. His mother's domicile offers space to the three refugees in a *fourth* room. We may assume that they represent the fourth, dark side. The collective darkness, or shadow-side of our collective unconscious, cannot be totally accepted. That would be a catastrophe. However, from an excluded *minority,* a few are accepted who embody to an unusual degree the characteristics and values of the other side. The three Hungarian officers, as if coming from the land behind the wooden partition and the other side of

the river, are probably an evolved version of the horrid wart-men of Dream Thirty-Eight. Now the threesome is being harbored in the fourth room, the dreamer's personal realm. If we are right in assuming that the three Hungarians evolved from the wart-men, then we may say that the natural human being who developed from the instinctual soul has found access to his mother's home.

This is true even though his mother endeavored to give him an overly rigid, Catholic upbringing. Her critical attitude condemned whatever was at odds with her convictions. Her son was quite attached to her, but he could be around her only for brief periods. She had changed but little during the last few years, but the dreamer's attitude towards her had changed a great deal. Earlier, he dreamed he had visited her, and she had placed a serpent around his neck. The dream made him shudder, but he reminded himself of all that he had learned from his dreams. The serpent represented her instinctual nature which she was unwittingly projecting upon her son. Thanks to this insight, he was able to tolerate her with understanding and empathy during his next visit. His different attitude has led to a change of the image of the mother within him. The feminine-maternal sides of his soul have become more open-hearted, broader and kindly.

At one time the Hungarians, as Magyars, belonged to the North Eurasian horsemen.[244] In admitting these three Hungarians, the dreamer accepts the representatives of a population that has achieved a synthesis of Asiatic and Western culture. The three Hungarians still carry in their blood the Asiatic characteristics that formerly sent the dreamer into a state of panic. What slumbered deep within him as a nomadic-rapacious and gruesome disposition and what, as long as he was not aware of it, appeared to him as a projection upon Asians have now changed and become capable of assimilation. The Hungarian officers, whose noble air the dreamer stresses, seem exceptionally courageous and disciplined. By suffering and self-discipline, they have grown a long way from the wart-men.[245]

Dream Sixty-Two: Betrothal

"My little sister is betrothed to the sultan."

The Hungarian language is related to that of the Turks. The dreamer, having admitted the Hungarian officers to his mother's house, again expands his contacts with the East. One of the daughters from this house is to be married to a sultan and live in an Eastern country. In past centuries the Chinese offered noble, young Chinese women in marriage to the Mongol rulers of adjacent lands.[246] Through these marriages, they were able to appease the wild nomads.

The dreamer's little sister is to be engaged to the sultan. As his closest relative, she approximates his essence. She is an aspect of his rejuvenated Anima which is to be wedded to the sultan. The archetype of the royal wedding, then, is operative here. We may assume that this royal wedding will take place in Turkey, a distant country to the dreamer. It is beyond his native country, beyond his consciousness. In the dream of the riding lesson (Dream Forty-Nine), three imperial couples appeared. In the following dream, these couples were supplemented by an animal couple. Later a flying hart, symbolizing masculine instinctual drive, fell into a large river, returning to the unconscious.

In this dream a *new* masculine, royal being, the sultan, emerges from the unconscious. He is a central figure. Because his bride is not of royal origin, she is subordinate to him. The sultan symbolizes the dreamer's *Self* which gradually, beginning from the unconscious, assumes leadership. Through the betrothal, the Anima is to return from her projection onto the outward world to her proper place, the unconscious. She is to become the dreamer's intermediary to the unconscious and its center, the sultan. As long as the Anima is projected upon nature or upon a woman, a man remains dependent. Part of his soul is outside. By reclaiming the Anima, he becomes free and independent. He gains his Anima, and in the sultan he finds a new center of gravity. The sister-Anima is elevated through her marriage to the sultan. She simultaneously becomes queen as well as one of the many ladies of the harem. Her dual position embodies the goddess and represents the individual

life. She is goddess and yet only one of the goddess's thousand aspects.

This dream is strangely laconic. One single sentence remains in the dreamer's memory. Background events barely reach consciousness. The next dream occurred a few weeks later.

Dream Sixty-Three: End of the World

First Part: "I enter a cathedral through a side portal. People are crowding each other inside and outside. They are standing on the steps of the portal in the antechamber. I stand there too. I look around. I see many Catholic fathers from my school. They greet me by nodding. They are standing outside in simple robes and do not officiate as priests. They allow me to go forward to the highest step. I look inside. The archbishop celebrates the mass. The altar should have been to my right in the main nave, but a wall stands in its place. The office consists in the archbishop writing on the wall what he wants to preach. Then he is carried outside, like the pope, on a sort of *sedia gestatoria*. However, it is not high on the crowd's shoulders but much lower, as in a sedan-chair. Before I can get close enough to talk to him, he is already outside, being carried through the crowd."

The dreamer comments: "At one time the sinners who had not received absolution in confession had to remain in these antechambers until they did obtain absolution. I always place myself in the antechambers during a service, as I think of myself as a publican, not a Pharisee. In this particular context, the fathers represent my former teachers, not priests. The dream illustrates my early development. There is no altar, only a wall, an obstacle. The pastoral letters, the revelations, the dogmas are written on it. These words are law. The spiritual leader who writes these words allows no contact or opportunity for questions. The crowd, however, seems to be satisfied. They kneel down as he is carried away. His rank is indicated by the sedan-chair."

Second Part: "From this cathedral I proceed towards a mountain. I reach a village where a festive celebration is taking place.

Students in old costumes with colorful caps and ribbons (some even dressed like Bajazzos in colorful silk dresses) roam through the streets. I wear a simple, ordinary suit. I recognize many former friends from my student days. I call to them, but they do not respond. They don't recognize me. I think that I, too, should wear a student cap. Then they would recognize me."

Dreamer's commentary: "My early development continues. My inner potential leads me from high school to the university. It also leads me from a relative sense of individuality, fostered by my teachers who recognize and greet me, to a collective experience of the student body where I am not recognized as an individual but through badges and color."

Third Part: "I leave this small town and reach a mountain road. Here I see a winding road descend into the valley. Military vehicles with soldiers drive on it. I think of joining them. I hope I know one of them. Maybe we'll go into war. I run downhill and reach a company of foot soldiers. I go to the front of the group where an officer is marching. I walk beside him. He looks at me and says, 'Remain here in front. This is your proper place. You undoubtedly outrank me. We are marching into battle.' While marching we sing, but the song is appropriate to dancing, not marching. I am annoyed, and when we pass through a town with numerous people (similarly as before with the archbishop) I lose my troops in the crowd. When the march and the music do not fit, everything falls apart."

Comments by the dreamer: "After my studies and a brief period of employment, I joined the service where I descended further into a collective situation. I attained a high position, but the military was not my proper ambience. My feelings and my actions no longer coincided, and everything fell apart."

Fourth Part: "I'm climbing a mountain path. I see high mountain peaks and valleys with rivers that glitter in the sun like winding ribbons. I rejoice. Then I see behind me rocky peaks like sheet lightning. The air trembles. I see flashes and feel distant shocks. Are cannons firing in the distance or bombs exploding? Suddenly I realize that it is much worse. It may be an atomic explosion. No, it

is even worse. It is the beginning of the end of the world. Horrified, I tell this to the 'second one' beside me. He does not want to believe it, but I'm more and more convinced. The flames in the sky become brighter and brighter. The air trembles. Everything shakes. I suddenly see flames spurt out in the mountains. The peaks tumble upon each other and bury the rivers and valleys below. I recall the passage in Revelations which describes mountains tumbling upon each other. Blue flames spit everywhere from the mountain. They come closer and closer. I turn around to flee. It is useless. No one can escape. Where can I turn? What can I do? In a few minutes I will burn and die. I want to repent my sins, make peace with God, and prepare myself for death. Where can I do this? At that instant, I see the kind of tiny chapel one often finds in the open fields. I run towards it, but when I get there I see that it is nothing more than one column with a picture and a cross above it. I cannot enter for shelter, not even for the few minutes before the catastrophe reaches me. I run on. I see a slightly larger chapel. I know that it is dedicated to the Virgin Mary. Inside its cool walls I will be safe for a few minutes. I will be able to pray and collect myself. Then I make a decision that has become possible only as a result of my development. I think, 'No, I shall not seek a refuge for praying and repenting. In these last minutes, I must *do* something. I must somehow be of help, rather than selfishly think of my own salvation and wait for the end.' I renounce my temporary security and salvation and run on towards the valley, the depths of the erupting inferno. I do so voluntarily. I want to help, to be useful to the very end. I pass an arched court with green arbors and vines (similar to the court of the monastery where, instead of entering the throne hall, I looked for a room of my own). I see a woman. She is my wife. Another feminine being, possibly my daughter, is there along with a boy, who may be my son or myself. I approach my wife who apparently does not understand that a catastrophe is approaching. I embrace her protectively and hide her head against my chest so that she will not see the horror. I could confess and tell her of all my failings, but it seems unimportant. What counts is to spare her and to be with her in death. A wonderful calm comes over me. I'm entirely free of fear. I look forward to death. I don't flee it, because I have overcome it within myself."

The dreamer comments: "I don't know what the end of the

world signifies. The fear in the dream was enormous. The decision to renounce my own safety and to stop being concerned with my own salvation was an act of courage. It was quite similar when the Russians arrived. . . .

Especially interesting is the development in my relation to the church. The early part of the dream with the archbishop is followed by the search for salvation in the first country chapel. This chapel, however, is but a rustic pillar with a picture, almost like the posts erected for Pan in the country-side of ancient Greece. I cannot go *inside,* because there is no inside. The chapel of the Virgin Mary, on the other hand, is a simple structure. It has no pictures, but its dedication to Mary gives it importance. It would offer shelter. Its small size contrasts with the ostentatious cathedral in the earlier part of the dream. For me, size is unimportant. I prefer the Mary chapel with its protective, naked walls. It is limited to the most simple and essential. It reminds me of the simple and concrete theme of the speech about Mary (Dream Forty-Eight): Mary as woman and working person.

At this point, I make the decision to renounce salvation. Finally I reach the woman, my wife, whose health has been my constant concern and whom I have tried to protect from wrongs and insults. The woman may also represent the Anima and the fourth member of the quartet. The message of the dream's finale seems to be: 'One's inner development is crucial even when facing the end of the world. One must eventually be in harmony with the Anima and unite the four figures. If one can achieve that, life is fulfilled. Death is insignificant because it is no longer an interruption of the journey. Inner development is the ultimate task. After its completion, the great peace follows.' I felt as if all heaviness had fallen from me. Inside I experienced a blissful calm. It was completion. As a whole, the dream shows the inner journey of a mortal human being."

There is little to add to the dreamer's comments on the first three phases of the dream. His explanation of the "end of the world," however, is insufficient. It is hard not to desist from interpreting dreams with such powerful, numerous emotions. Who knows what future destinies they anticipate? The inner images are so overwhelming and the accompanying emotions so strong that such a dream is first taken as a presentiment of external events (espe-

cially as we have good reason to fear a fiery end of the world caused by atomic explosions). However, once we gain some distance from the dream, we may find an inner, collective and individual meaning. The dreamer can discover analogous motifs in mythology and religious history. One must keep in mind that such an impressive, archetypal dream does not address the dreamer alone. The dream portrays something essential to the transition, reorientation and continuation of our entire culture. The dreamer is thus a carrier of historical developments. He has not chosen this path arbitrarily. After World War II, he had reached a point at which his education, his willingness and his consciousness could no longer help him. He therefore had to listen to his dreams and follow his inner images. Whoever looks within himself encounters the collective unconscious and touches the very course of historical development.

Jung states: "The fantasy of a world holocaust, the catastrophic end of the world, is the projection of the fundamental, original picture of the great, complete change."[247]

In *Odin and Germanic Faith in Destiny*, Martin Ninck describes the Ragnarok, the Germanic twilight of the gods:

> Fate unfolds in unbroken sequence. Battle follows upon battle. Contrasts become more extreme. The most beloved god succumbs. A brief armistice follows the shackling of Loki, but there are increasingly ominous signs. Discontent grows among the giants and human beings. The brood of Loki (the fire) grows alarmingly, frees itself, and storms with the Thurses into the last battle, the destiny of the gods, as the Edda calls it. Even the highest gods are fated to fall and perish. Everything old founders, but out of the womb of destiny a new, more beautiful world arises.[248]

And later: "In the woods of Hoddmimir two human beings hide from the blaze."[249] "Thus there is no end," states Ninck, "no last judgment, no stiffening in the grasp of a motionless eternity. Ragnarok represents the birth-pangs of a world-bearing pregnancy. It is a return, a renewal of the world."[250] This dream seems to anticipate a world holocaust, but it, too, brings renewal along with destruction. It anticipates a peace which the dreamer compares with Nirvana, a fully detached state of eternal happiness.

In the dream, the world ends, as it did in the Ragnarok, in fire.

Flames spurt everywhere from the mountains and ground. We already encountered the fire hidden within the earth in Haggard's *She*. [251] In Haggard's book, the pillar of fire is divine energy which preserves the earth and makes it fertile, a spiritual fire which inspires creative deeds. This magic fire burns all inessential attributes in order to free the pure *being,* the essence, and elevate nature to eternal life and heavenly beauty. This same fire is also the judgment which transforms the haughty She into dust and ashes so that she may reappear in a transfigured shape. Simon Magus speaks of the purifying and spiritualizing force of fire. In the Old Testament, fire is the wrath, the light, the creative and destructive power of God. In Christendom it is the suffering of hell and purgatory as well as the flame of the Holy Spirit. In alchemy, fire is at once the prime matter and driving force of the opus (process). In the earth-fire, the alchemist sees the divine love of God. In the earth-fire, She encounters both creative godhead and substance for matrimonial union, the blending and refounding of the opposing principles: sun and moon, spirit and soul.

The catastrophic end of the world, then, is—like the Ragnarok—a transformation of the gods, the divine powers in the world, and the human beings. An aged world dissolves in the fire of the Creator, so that its quintessence may emerge heightened and transfigured. The erupting flames express those spiritual energies from which the earth and all its creatures originated. They express the spirit that sustains the world and to which, according to Simon Magus, the world is being returned, "as if into a barn." According to Heraclitus, the cosmos continually transforms itself into this fire. In the Apocalypse of John and Henoch, this same fire is purification as well as punishment and annihilation. Even here it is the being of the godhead. In a moment of heightened experience, the dreamer is able to see the energies or the spirit underlying all life. He who had been no match for the low spirit of the brandy is now able, as a psychic-spiritual being, to cope with the panic of the physical person. In the course of the eruption of such cosmic emotions, the human being is in danger of perishing as natural being. He may lose consciousness and reason. Alchemy, however, asserts that through fire, and by means of many fires, the quintessence of gold can be extracted from the prime matter of unconscious life, and human beings can be made to glow as the "stone."

According to the dreamer, this dream is similar to the experience of life passing before a dying person's eyes. The first three parts of the dream can be clearly correlated with three phases of his life: childhood, studies, and years of travel. The fourth part, the great peril and decision, may be a final test. It follows the previous steps and encompasses the development of the dreamer after his wartime experiences. Once more, in heart-rending symbolical images, he lives through a summation of the previous path, in order to be able to give his own conscious, decisive answer.

After leaving the broad military road, the dreamer climbs up a narrow footpath used by mountaineers and shepherds. A rarely frequented path, it offers a wonderful view of high mountain peaks, wide valleys and a winding river. From this elevated path, he can survey his environment and the flow of his life (the ribbon of the river sparkling in the sun). From here he observes new peaks, new spiritual heights. The solitary path does not lead to conformity nor external success, but to himself. One must walk this narrow path alone. At first the sky is sunny and clear. Then distant sheet-lightning announces the storm which assumes frightful proportions. At first the path of internal development seemed pleasant and easy, no more difficult than a hike in the mountains, but then inner danger and shock announce themselves in the storm and in the approaching noise of war.

In Dream Forty the dreamer experienced an atomic explosion. "Nuclear changes" had to occur within the soul in order for the split-off fourth element to be integrated. Once more he sees the dangers he incurred and to which he is inwardly exposed. He had always been driven by an inner fire, a zealous spirit eager for change and transformation. He had always sought in the church refuge from the passions slumbering in his soul. The church protects the human being from the soul's abysses. Even this time he could have fled into the chapel to seek Mary's protection, but he sees the fire's inevitable approach. Sooner or later, it will reach him and everyone else.

Now, when he cannot escape annihilation, he sees clearly that, rather than protect and purify himself, he must act. Thus he no longer runs in order to save himself, but in order to seek those closest to him. He finds his wife and children. When his care and loving concern are turned towards his wife, transformation occurs. Instead of being driven, hunted, and tormented, he is ful-

filled. Along his long path of development, he has tried to cope with the dark, dangerous and burning side of his instinctual nature. But now, in the extreme peril, he escapes from anxiety into love. He comments that his wife was simultaneously his inner Anima and that his son was also himself. Those closest to him thus represent the inner figures which complete his four-fold wholeness. The four figures are, as in fairy tales, in two couples, indicating the equalization between masculine and feminine tendencies. In this moment of fulfillment, the contrast between inside and outside is suspended by the coincidence of the inner figures with external reality. Eros who sought fulfillment in a distant country returns home to the family.

Had the dreamer fled to the chapel, he would have found once more protection from himself and from radical changes. Love would have remained for him, as for most men, a religious matter, a concern of Mary, the saints, the priests and women. He would have remained committed to the logos and action. Feeling would have remained unconsciously identified with nature, country and church. However, over a number of years, the dreamer—broadening his understanding of religious contents and the veneration of the mother of God—became aware of the possibility of realizing, in his own life, the aims of religion. The long sought-for transformation has finally occurred in an unexpected way. The fire turns devouring greed and inferior spirit into warmth of heart and light of understanding.

In the dream, the transformation occurs as a result of a single, courageous decision. In actual life many smaller decisions will have to follow, but because reorientation has occurred once, it will be easier for consciousness to follow up on it.

I shall mention five additional, brief dreams, some to show that such an experience of transformation does not automatically set everything straight, others to show the foundation for a new beginning.

Dream Sixty-Four: Arrogance

"A fat and conceited fellow attacks me with arrogant insults. I respond with even greater arrogance. He becomes increasingly angry. I goad him further. Finally, he jumps up, grabs a towel or

napkin, and tries to strangle me from behind. A woman beside me screams in terror and he desists."

The fat, conceited fellow is in many legends the hero's shadow-companion. He is a lazy pleasure-seeker whose indolence is disturbed and overtaxed by the hero and his journey. He is the body-person who arrogantly fights the demands of the ego and Self. This arrogance comes from the overtaxed body, from the shadow whose natural needs have not been adequately heeded. Heightened self-control and increased consideration of the outer world would further endanger him. What the dreamer needs is consideration for and indulgence of the weaker one within himself.[252] Respect for the weakness of one's shadow will deflate its arrogance. The Anima saves the dreamer; she does not side with the shadow.

Dream Sixty-Five: Baggage

"We arrived at our destination in an enormous truck. Soldiers were loading and unloading baggage from the oversized vehicle. I had to continue my journey by train. I didn't have far to go. My baggage was light. I was surprised that I had only a knapsack and a handbag. The knapsack had a carrying frame. It was far too large and hindered me in walking because my heels hit its steel pipes. At the lower end of the frame was a round section of human bone, a bundle, and a tuft of dried plants, among them mimosas. I cannot remove these appendages by hand, and I try to rub them off against the ground. The bone and the bundle come off easily, but the dried plants are hard to get rid of. It takes a long time before they are stripped off."

The dreamer's baggage has become light. He carries only a few things. The frame of his knapsack, however, is still too large. He can easily free himself of the attached bones which represent the thoughts of death that still bother him occasionally. On bottles containing poison, crossed bones symbolize death. The second appendage is not defined. The mimosas and his mimosa-like irritability are harder to get rid of. These two difficulties seem to be linked to the oversized frame he continues to carry. Being an

extroverted-intuitive person, he recognizes after this dream that he must restrict his outward "frame" even more in order to become free and flexible.

Dream Sixty-Six: *The Giantess and Her Child*

"In the midst of a crowd I'm sitting in a fine armchair. I discover an acquaintance who was unable to get a seat. I ask him, 'Where is your wife?' I would have given her my seat. He comes closer as he did not understand me. As he approaches, a woman, a well-proportioned and extremely beautiful giantess, is in his stead. She talks to a two- or three-year-old child who is also exceptionally beautiful. The child sits on a cupboard in order to be level with the woman's eyes. I repeatedly draw the attention of a woman sitting in front of me to the giantess's beauty and the child's charm."

The dreamer characterizes his acquaintance as a decent and fair comrade-in-arms who never let his people down. In place of this positive person, the extremely beautiful, gigantic woman and the lovely child appear. The Anima presents herself as a superhuman, semi-divine figure. Her transformation through the fire has elevated and embellished her. The dreamer is related to his family, and she is related to the inner child. The inner union of opposites is to become reality in her child. The child's loveliness is the fruit of the combination of red and white. In the tale of Snow White, the queen wishes for a child as black as ebony, as white as snow and as red as blood. In other words, she wishes for a child who combines the steps of the alchemical process: black, white, and red.

Dream Sixty-Seven: *The Oversized Farmer*

"On the edge of a freshly plowed and harrowed field with good, black soil stands a healthy, good-looking, and oversized farmer. As I look at him, I think that more men like him are needed to till the field. In that instant my wish is granted, and several oversized men appear on the field. I realize that there are too many now. The first one could have managed the field alone."

The farmer belongs to the same race of giants as the woman in the preceding dream. He is an archetypal man. One is sufficient; more would be superfluous. He is a superman, but not because he feels superior or takes himself too seriously. His large size is not expressed in ambition but in the tilling and tending of an earthly field, that is, in the fulfillment of the simplest duties of life. Significantly, the dreamer no longer identifies with inner figures but conceives of them as the larger ones within himself. Equally important, someone knows how to till the field in this dream. The seed is no longer left to the hazards of nature as it was in the dream of the field on the mountain slope (Dream Thirty-Nine). The sower of the field is not the ego but one who is larger than the ego and who tends to the simple work of this world so that the field of life will not remain unused. One worker can till the entire field. Individual responsibility is required, not spectacular achievement. In an alchemistic treatise titled "Secrets of the Nature of the Large and of the Small Farmer," the farmer himself is a symbol of the alchemical process.[253] He is aware of the union of the white and red lily.

Dream Sixty-Eight: The Oversized Couple

"From the stony bank of a wild river, an oversized, beautiful, blond man and woman [the farmer had had dark hair] board two small boats made of bark. Instead of using paddles, they give themselves up to the current. Full of joy and happiness, they shoot down the river through whirlpools and rapids. They stand, jump, and even squat, but they maintain their balance and master the wildest currents."

The oversized, beautiful couple are reminiscent of the two human beings who, after the fall of the Nordic gods, became the parents of a new human race. From the fire of the world holocaust arises a new generation who surpass their predecessors in size, self-assurance, force and beauty. The couple succeeds the old gods and heroes. They symbolize the reality of spirit and soul in the life of the ordinary human being and the encounter between superhuman and human nature. The two happily balance themselves as they ride on the light boats through the river's whirlpools. They are

unencumbered, and the boats have neither paddle nor rudder. They give themselves up to destiny and necessity. They let themselves be carried by the river of life. The stony bank and whirlpools, representing life's difficulties, test their strength and skill. In previous unrecorded dreams, the dreamer was able to abandon his boat just before reaching the rapids where he would have been shipwrecked and drowned. However, after this dream he is able to cope with approaching difficulties and to pass the tests. He no longer needs to be afraid of problems that had seemed insurmountable. The dream's optimism gives him courage.

In conclusion we add a last dream that deals with the dreamer's religious concerns.

Dream Sixty-Nine: The Chapel in the Vatican

"During a trip, I lodged inside the Vatican. Before my departure, I began looking for my baggage. Through a hallway I reached a fairly large room, resembling a chapel, where a woman knelt, praying. In front, near an altar, a bright light was burning. The woman faced the light. The entire room was filled with magnificent, white marble statues of Greek and Roman gods which were turned with their backs towards the entrance. I did not find it disturbing that pagan gods were placed in a Christian room of worship."

The dreamer has recognized ancient gods in the forces of nature. Now this last dream reveals a synthesis of the pagan sense of nature and the Christian spirit. The Anima's worship includes both Christianity's spiritual revelation and an experience of the powers within the natural soul. The dreamer had experienced those powers as both dangerous and helpful. Now he knows that he must respect and accept them. If he tries to avoid them, they will avenge themselves through illnesses and psychological failure. However, once he has become aware of himself and his requirements, and once nature and spirit, consciousness and the unconscious, masculinity and femininity, and present and past are integrated, he finds a new inner peace, a deep understanding of Christian virtues, a live piety, and true, warm human concern. By our accepting and including the natural soul, the barbarian within

us is allied with spiritual consciousness, and both are thereby transformed. The poacher became the good-looking, strong farmer who tills his field. The heath-cock became the troll who was transformed into the beautiful, oversized woman with the lovely child. These dream-figures remind one of the ancient gods who were also oversized human beings. Since the beginning—when first vermin, then rats, then whores dressed in red appeared to him menacingly in his dreams—there has been a progressive transformation in the dreamer. With the appearance of these large, luminous figures, a new path into the future has opened up.

Concluding Remarks to the Series of Dreams

We have followed the dreamer on the long, intertwined paths of inner clarification. Through his dreams, we have discussed everything that has affected him: profession, environment, family, ancestors, his own nature, women, the war, his religious education, God. Naturally, many people deal with such problems. They pose questions concerning God and the meaning of life and draw conclusions in accordance with their world views. However, only a few appreciate the importance of consulting their dreams in these endeavors.

The dreamer began his inward path by assessing and clarifying his present difficulties and inadequacies. He then had an intuitive presentiment of a new goal: the search for the royal couple. Insight into his ties to his mother and sister was followed by an experience of his own feminine side. While he explored the light and dark inner figures, he experienced the Anima's ambivalent aspects. Only by differentiating himself from the shadow and the Anima's changing demands and negative moods can a man gain full possession of his masculinity. On the other hand, he reaches the wholeness of his Self only by allowing the Anima to speak and by giving proper consideration to his feelings. True spiritual masculinity develops through conscious questioning of accepted world views.

At first the dreamer felt that his relationship with the Anima should not be mixed with religious questions. He felt the two were different, even opposite topics, but his dreams allowed no such separation. At one time the Anima dressed in dark soul-material

was hidden in the tabernacle. At another time, to the dreamer's distaste, a woman officiated as priestess in the church. The queen was acclaimed as heavenly queen thereafter. Mary was discussed as a simple worker. Another dream reveals the Mother Church as the *Magna Mater,* the great mother of the country and the Christian Anima of the world. Only towards the end did the dreamer recognize the interdependence and interconnectedness between the dreams relating to his religious attitude and those dealing with his exploration of and dialogue with the Anima. The Anima mediates the inner images. What arises from the unconscious is represented by or through her first, and assimilated by male consciousness later.

The dreams go beyond the dreamer's conscious intentions. In fact, they frequently act in contrast to his wishes and will (for example, Dream Twenty-Eight, "The Church Collapses," and Twenty-Eight A, "The Bomb"). They also anticipate insights which he has not consciously attained (for example, Dreams Thirty-Four, "The Tabernacle"; Forty-Eight, "Four Speeches"; and Sixty-Three, "End of the World"). Many pose riddles which are solved only by subsequent dreams (for example, Dreams Thirty-Six, "Brandy"; Thirty-Seven, "The Transition"; and Fifty-Nine, "The Flying Hart"). The dreams lead towards a widening of consciousness (for example, Dreams Eleven, "The Heath-Cock"; Twelve, "The Bathing-Suit"; and Thirty, "The Eagle"). They demand a radical reorientation of consciousness (for example, Dreams Twenty, "The Woman-Commander"; Twenty-Five, "The Runner"; and Fifty-Three, "Imprisonment in the Rocky Cliff"). A few aim at restricting the unconscious (for example, Dreams Eighteen, "The Anima Warns Against the Eleven Crows"; Nineteen, "The White Bull"; and Fifty-Four, "The Taming of the Anima"). They also aim at the differentiation of consciousness and at a genuine Christian attitude which can only be attained through slow, patient growth (for example, Dreams Thirty-Four, "The Tabernacle"; Forty-Six, "The Convent with the Throne Room"; and Sixty-Three, "End of the World"). Finally, they offer the foundation for a new spiritual orientation (for example, Dreams Thirty-Three, "The New Church"; Thirty-Four, "The Tabernacle"; Forty-Seven, "The Round Church"; Sixty-One, "The Church of the *Magna Mater* and the Mother's Home"; and Sixty-Nine, "The Chapel in the Vatican").

The dreams brought about profound discussions of the darkest, as well as the highest and holiest, contents of the soul. Gaining insight and knowledge is an important part of the journey, but realizing this insight in everyday life is more important and difficult. One must continually struggle towards this realization. All too often it is at this point that one fails. Once the symbols of the Self—the circle, the royal couple, or the quaternity—approach, there is a presentiment of an inner consolidation. Such inner wholeness, however, must prove itself in actual life. Only through continued effort can one overcome recurring relapses and deficiencies to actualize this wholeness. Relapses which follow truly important, inspiring dreams are especially disappointing, but Jung's comment may serve as consolation:

> The proficient person will constantly find, either because of unfavorable circumstances, technical errors, or seemingly demonic incidents, that the completion of the process is hindered, and that he, therefore, must begin anew. Whoever attempts to establish his security in the everyday world by following an analogous psychological journey, will have similar experiences. More than once he will find that what he has achieved falls to pieces in the collision with reality. However, he must tirelessly examine the inadequacies in his orientation and the blind spots in his psychological visual field. Just as the philosopher's stone, with its wondrous powers, has never been actually produced, so psychic totality will never be reached empirically. Consciousness is too narrow to ever comprehend the full inventory of the soul. We will always have to begin again. The adept in alchemy always knew that it was ultimately a matter of the "res simplex" [the simple thing]. Human beings today will learn by experience that the process will not prosper without the greatest possible simplicity. The simple, however, is also the most difficult.[254]

The dreamer experiences this simplicity at the end of the dream series in the joyful human couple, the tall woman with the lovely child, and the farmer who tills the field. The series dealing with the Anima, then, finds its natural conclusion in these last dreams.

III. Summary

The first part of this book, "Psychological Interpretations of Rider Haggard's *She*," examines a novel of the late nineteenth century. In the second part, the dreams of a contemporary man were analyzed. Through these analyses, we intended to show that Haggard's book is not a unique, solitary fantasy. In fact, it reflects contemporary inner pictures of the unconscious. Starting out from a few introductory dreams, the series grew until it found a natural closure in the dreams of the end of the world (Dream Sixty-Three) and the oversized human beings (Dreams Sixty-Six through Sixty-Eight). That which Haggard imagined was intuited and inwardly experienced over a period of eight years by a modern, professional man. These inward experiences were elucidated in the psychotherapeutic dialogue. They were then integrated with the dreamer's conscious world view.

We find a number of elements shared by the novel and the dream series. The steps of inner development which they describe are largely the same, even though the two men belonged to different periods, religions, countries, and professions.

Differences in form and details may be attributed to differences in time-scales. Haggard wrote *She* in six weeks. The dreams, on the other hand, were experienced and assimilated over a period of eight years. Haggard's novel portrays in one single sketch the mythology latently present in the unconscious and describes it as a manifold event containing various steps. The dreams, on the other hand, are related to daytime experiences and gradually mix events close to consciousness with archetypal motifs from the deep layers of the collective unconscious. In the course of development, these motifs keep changing.

For a Protestant, the archetypal images tend to signal an eruption from the irrational sphere. The mere experience of those images is a powerful event for him. He is, however, in danger of remaining in a state of admiration—for example, in a romantic glorification of antiquity or in a modern paganism.[255] For a Catholic, pictures and symbols represent a familiar world. Today, however, many Catholics and Protestants live on two levels. Their lives are characterized by natural-scientific thought which remains unharmonized with their religious views. Most grow up without a true religious education. Those who had religious training discard it, as religious and natural-scientific thinking appear incompatible.

When the unconscious soul announces itself in dreams or fantasies, it is advisable to pay attention to them. They bring forth the forgotten, original, religious images. These are contents which are necessary for shaping a full life attaining inner wholeness. They contain the remote past and the future. One must reflect upon their meaning and confront and integrate them with traditional, conscious world views. Our dreamer is quite aware of his religious beliefs. When he is preoccupied with the unconscious, he is eager to compare its contents with the great, religious models. This effort leads to a link between the conscious and the unconscious, the development and differentiation of the contents of the unconscious, and a broadening and deepening of consciousness.

Conflicts exist in *She* between the views of the two Englishmen, Leo and Holly, and the views of She. Haggard remains stuck in the conflict. He is unable to bring his Protestant, Victorian ideal of the gentleman into harmony with the Anima's demands.

Although we have pointed out parallels between the developments described in the novel and the dream series, we must emphasize that the inner process can also evolve differently. Each individual's unconscious follows its own path.

Both in the novel and the dream series, we find that the approach to the Anima can take place only after the death of the old ego and a confrontation with animals, that is, the instincts. *She* begins with the death of Holly's friend, Vincey, who represents Haggard's ego. Similarly, the dreamer's ego symbolically dies in the dream of the airplane-crash (Dream Two). In both cases, youthful mastery of the world has reached a limit. In order to progress further, a radical reorientation is required. One must painfully renounce the primary function. As the poet and the dreamer were intuitive types, they must abandon intuition for a while in favor of such inferior functions as *thinking* and *sensation*. After the renunciation of intuition, several companion-figures who represent the inferior functions are introduced. They are shadow-figures who, however, can intercede helpfully or take on the role of lagging reflection. Holly, the hero's shadow in the novel, is also his reflection and guide. He is later joined by Billali, the old wise man. The dreamer, too, often experiences "another" beside him. The other may be a younger brother; an indefinite, dark companion; a hunting assistant; or an old man who assumes leadership.

As we stated earlier, the approach to the Anima can take place only after one has confronted one's instincts in the form of animals. Leo and Holly hunt the animals which they discover, but we notice that the dreamer, though an eager hunter, gradually manages to refrain from firing his rifle. He gives the animal time for transformation. He is not allowed simply to kill the game. He must listen to it, find a relationship with it, recognize it as part of himself, and humanize it. In the beginning, when the poacher shoots the young hart, he is punished by the dreamer (Dream Thirteen). Only towards the end of his development does the dreamer aim at the heavenly hart because he must now sacrifice his identification with the nature-divinity (Dream Fifty-Nine).

In *She* the Anima announces herself first in the sphinx. The unconscious, feminine nature-soul is contaminated by the animal instincts. Later appears Ustane, a human aspect of the Anima that is still close to nature. Over her stands Ayesha as goddess.

In the dreams, the Anima develops from a heath-cock to a troll; then to an impersonal, female army commander; and, finally, to the heavenly queen. She also appears as the whore-Anima, the opposite of the elegant lady on the upper floor. As sisterly companion, and later as his daughter, the Anima becomes directly related to the dreamer and assists him in his confrontation with the animals. She enables him to grow beyond his blind instinctual ties without needing to kill the animals.

In the novel, first Ustane and then She assists the hero against the savages, the blind affective reactions. Here, defense requires radical means as there were no prior conscious experiences with the instinctual side.

Once the dreamer has found the link with his ancestors and the proper level of emotional relatedness (symbolized by the heart), he

begins to explore the spiritual tradition of the East and, subsequently, his own religion. In the novel, the heroes similarly reach the burial city of Kor (heart), housing previous generations. Here Holly and She have long discussions dealing with spiritual and religious traditions. This broadening of consciousness is a necessary development.

For the dreamer, spiritual discussions are followed by the discovery or reconstitution of spiritual reality. The dream concerning the tabernacle leads the dreamer to a new evaluation of his life. His outward life is likened to the tabernacle and his inner soul-life to the "holiest of holies" within it. Later he obtains from the queen the sapphire ring with the crown of white pearls, the symbol of a purified and spiritualized experience of reality and of love. Through effort and proper devotion, a trans-temporal meaning becomes manifest in one's life.

The white pearls decorating the sapphire ring correspond to the mummy's little foot in *She*. Both ivory whiteness and mummification symbolize the immortal body. The foot itself emphasizes this body's concrete presence. Holly sees in the mummy's foot a portrayal of the eternal life-cycle of the spirit. The body is the temporary residence of the eternally alive spirit. The novel has no symbol which corresponds to the sapphire, the transparent, blue, hard gem. In the novel, new insights are not solidified in everyday life.

Subsequent dreams raise issues concerning *red* and *white*, the alchemical symbols for spirit and soul. The dreamer must now purify, elevate, sacrifice, and transform spirit and soul.

White is dispersed, once more, in the explosion of the white powder (Dream Forty), and red is dispersed in the volcano's eruption (Dream Forty-One). The danger of passionate nature, symbolized by red, manifests itself. The development of white, the soul, takes place in the dream alluding to the sacrifice of Aida, where the Anima is installed as priestess, and later in the humble worship and discussion of various aspects of the heavenly queen. Mary turns into the archetypal image of the human soul. When she is worshiped as simple woman, every woman, as well as every man's humble soul, is elevated through her. The dreamer's mother, too, is a simple woman (Dream Sixty-One, second part). In her modest habitation all the relatives, even the least liked and insignificant ones, as well as three Hungarian delegates from a realm beyond the river, find acceptance. Mary, the queen of all creatures,

never turns away anyone who comes to her. Similarly, the mother-Anima, together with her son's soul, admits the split-off fourth in the fourth room. The differentiation of white leads to a stepwise change of the Anima-image and eventually to the sister's betrothal with the sultan, who represents the yet unconscious Self. The youngest sister, as youthful form of the Anima, becomes here the bridelike soul.

The production of red is far more difficult. One cannot simply accept the traditional spirit. The dreamer must search for the raw material of the spirit, primitive emotionality or impulsivity, which in itself is neither good nor evil. It can easily become immoderate and destructive rather than creative. Before he can uncover and purify the red, the dreamer has to meet the unredeemed crowds, the three wart-men, and, later, Mephistopheles. The dreamer must neither identify with evil, with Mephisto, nor with Faust, who represents what the world commonly regards as good. The riding lesson with the princesses and the transformation into a hart establish the dreamer's connection with his nature. Accepting his impulsive-instinctual side requires an increased sense of responsibility and a more differentiated understanding of the shadow. The dreams demand the submission of the ego to an inner judge. Thus, the chthonian figure of the Egyptian is arrested, and the Anima is tamed. Transformation now affects the dreamer quite personally. The sacrifice of the heavenly hart, symbolizing the offering of the instinctual nature, and scaring away the ugly red and blue bird are also essential to the purification of red. In the end, the dreamer must expose himself to transformation in the fire of the world's end.

In the novel, when She drops her dark cloak, she emerges "like a blessed spirit from the grave, like Venus from the waves, like Galathea from the stone." She is the *white* queen who shines like a light. With her Leo seeks the fire of life that glows in all colors and glitters like lightning. The pillar of fire is the *glowing red spirit* of nature which works within the earth's womb. Leo is to unite himself with this creative spirit, but this union fails because there has been no prior testing and actualization in life.

It is important that Leo does not allow himself to be carried away by the Anima's intoxication with power. The novel ends with She's sacrificial death. Only as a result of the unintentional self-

sacrifice of the Anima does the reverse aspect of the fire, the danger inherent in passionate, creative seizure, become manifest.

The dreamer, on the other hand, endangered by the threatening flames, is able to go beyond his fears and to think of others. He succeeds in confronting the flames with a conscious decision. As a result, he is transformed and capable of experiencing wholeness. He compares the peace that overcomes him with the experience of Nirvana. The quiet which fills him he calls "fulfillment." The wedding to which he had been invited did not take place the first time. Later, it occurred on several different experiential levels. Now, in face of the fire, it is experienced again, when he lovingly and protectively turns towards his wife and, simultaneously, his inner Anima. Ultimate despair suddenly changes into profound, inward peace. By caring for those nearest to him, he accepts his Anima as the capacity for loving relatedness and as inner reality. Since he goes beyond his ego and commits himself wholly, he experiences himself as a whole.

This extreme experience is followed by a descent towards everyday life. The human being is and remains the same in terms of his talents and shortcomings. He cannot escape being the psychological type he is. However, the environment to which he returns is closer to his heart now because he has been linked to the three figures, represented by his wife and children. In addition, he is able to handle external and internal problems with more self-assurance. He finds the *inner* causes of his errors with greater ease. What previously caused him despair is now an occasion to test the wholeness he has experienced.

At the end of the dream series, the Anima is no longer an animal or whore. She is an oversized woman accompanied by a lovely child (Dream Sixty-Six). She has become mother. In his novel *Ayesha,* Haggard also envisions the Anima's motherhood in a picture within a volcanic temple. The last dreams show the Anima as *companion and mother* (Dreams Sixty-Six and Sixty-Eight). The circle is complete. The man's feminine soul was awakened and influenced by the mother. If he is to mature, the son must separate from the mother in order to find his life's companion in his beloved. When his young wife becomes a mother, he is compelled to withdraw once more the projection of his soul image in order to experience his own soul independently of wife and mother. It is a

long journey of exploration aimed at freeing the soul from the unconscious and from projections. He is to transform the Anima's two aspects, goddess and nixie, into a capacity for human relatedness within the concrete world. His own soul is to become capable of relating and mothering.

The arch-image of the soul always retains the rank of goddess. She stays "She-who-is-to-be-obeyed," the superior, benevolent and abysmal mistress soul. Our consciousness experiences and grasps only a small fraction of her unlimited disguises, among them, earth- and death-mother, Anima Mundi, Sophia, and heavenly queen.

In the search for the Anima, both the soul and the masculine aspect are changed. The latter meets the dreamer in the guise of two inner figures who, like Holly and Leo, represent two different functions. One is the farmer patiently tilling the earthly field (Dream Sixty-Seven); the other is the oversized man with the little boat made of bark (Dream Sixty-Eight) who portrays the courageous, independent spirit of enterprise confidently entrusting itself to the stream of life. In these two figures we may recognize transformations of Faust and Mephistopheles. The earthbound farmer uses the instinctual nature and practical knowledge of Mephistopheles. He satisfies his needs with his own strength. The boatman adopts Faust's zeal for research in a way which does not ignore human relationships. We may view the four oversized figures as the fruit of the transformation. They combine superhuman strength, assuredness, and freedom.

In the second volume of the novel *(Ayesha),* an altar picture hangs high above the priestess in the temple. It portrays the winged great mother, Isis, and her child. Similarly, we find in one of the last dreams (Dream Sixty-Six) the exceedingly lovely child who sits, remarkably, on a ledge at the height of the giantess's eyes. In both situations, the child points beyond what has been achieved to an inner unity where the opposites of mother and companion, doing and thinking fuse into the individual oneness of being. That the child is seated at the height of the giantess's eyes may indicate that the center of consciousness is to be at this level.[256] In the novel we also find that the altar image is elevated. Jung points out that, in the end, Faust becomes a "blessed boy" whose "astonished seeing" replaces the previous need to possess.[257] At this point, one might also mention the frequently misunderstood words of Christ in

Matthew (18:3): "Unless you turn around and become as young children, you will by no means enter the kingdom of heaven."

The dream series ends with the inner child who is a promise of the future. Based on a widened consciousness and a sharper sense of responsibility, this child embodies a return to life's spontaneity, to the kind of immediacy that feels obligated both to the unconscious and the superpersonal spirit. This obligation includes the task of delving deeper into the meaning of Christian tradition and God's image. The child represents the beginning of a new inner attitude that must be experienced, affirmed and fought for. While the dreams speak of a live child, the child in the novel appears in an altar picture. In the dreams, the symbol for inner integration is close to life; in the novel, it is an unattained ideal image.

Both in Haggard's *She* and the dream series, the search for the soul is depicted as a human being's confrontation with nature and divine powers. The approach of human consciousness to the great figures of the unconscious leads to the birth of an inner divine child. However, as instrument or carrier of this process, the human being must, more than ever, be conscious of his/her limits. He must strive for the narrow region between the opposites, identifying with neither side. Otherwise, he becomes prey to a subhuman or superhuman state. If he seeks to maintain the human middle between the inner opposites and respects the inner structure, he can mature towards becoming a whole human being. This inner completeness can never be reached fully and permanently during one's lifetime. It remains a goal that must be constantly striven for, but which, at times, can be happily and serenely experienced.

A Note to the Reader

Not only the text of this book but also all quotations from German-language works have been translated into English by Julius Heuscher and David Scott May. The reader is being referred, not to C. G. Jung's English-language *Collected Works,* but rather to the text of his German writings, for the most part collected in *Gesamtausgabe,* ed. Marianne Niehaus-Jung, 16 vols. (Olten, Switzerland: Walter, 1971). For the sake of brevity, references to this opus are abbreviated as follows: Jung, *CW* volume number, inclusive paragraph numbers.

Otherwise in the endnotes, if a title is given first in German, then with an English translation in parentheses, an English edition of that work may not be available. In those cases where we could locate an English edition, we have supplied that bibliographical information following the German.

The poem by Andrew Lang printed below was omitted in error from the text of this book. It should have appeared on page 31.

Spring Publications

SHE!

To H.R.H.
Not in the waste beyond the swamp and sand,
The fever-haunted forest and lagoon,
Mysterious Kor, thy fanes forsaken stand,
With lonely towers beneath a lonely moon.
Not there does Ayesha linger—rune by rune
Spelling the scriptures of a people banned,
The world is disenchanted! Oversoon
Shall Europe send her spies through all the land!

Nay, not in Kor, but in whatever spot,
In fields, or towns, or by the insatiate sea,
Hearts brood o'er buried loves and unforgot,
Or wreck themselves on some Divine decree,
Or would o'erleap the limits of their lot—
There—in the tombs and deathless—dwelleth SHE!

Notes

1. "Soul-images, Anima and Animus are, respectively, the complementary aspects of the feminine nature in the unconscious of the man and of the masculine nature in the unconscious of the woman. We meet her countersexual personifications of the unconscious in the shape of a semi-bestial or semi-divine woman in the man, and in the shape of analogous masculine figures in the woman. Just as men and women have masculine as well as feminine genes, so they also have masculine as well as feminine traits. Of these, however, one portion is not lived consciously. Within the unconscious experience of man the Anima portrays through her personal aspect unconscious feelings, emotions, moods and inclinations, and through her archetypal aspect she represents the integrated mother-woman-image. Within the unconscious experience of the woman, the personal aspect of the Animus portrays affects, enthusiasms and opinions of the man, while the archetypal aspect represents mankind's multilayered condensation of father-man-images. When they are lifted to the conscious level, these contents and images give up some of their autonomy and thereby become mediators between the deeper levels of the unconscious and consciousness. The Anima becomes the inspiring woman—for example, Dante's Beatrice—the Animus becomes a 'logos spermaticos,' a creative word, who uncovers new spiritual dimensions of time." Kurt V. Sury, *Wörterbuch der Psychologie* (Vocabulary of Psychology), 2d ed. (Basel/Stuttgart: Benno Schwabe, 1958), 358.

2. Jung felt constrained to make a conceptual distinction between *soul* and *psyche*. By *psyche* he means "the totality of all psychological processes, whether conscious or unconscious. . . ." By soul, on the other hand, he means "a specific, delineated matrix of function which is characterized best as 'personality.'" "As far as the character of the soul is concerned, one can say that . . . the general thesis is valid to the extent that the soul is all in all *complementary* to the external character. The 'unconscious' soul tends to contain all those universal qualities which are lacking in the conscious orientation." Jung, *CW* 6, §§877, 884.

3. Jung, *CW* 9, ii, §41.

4. See also Esther Harding, "She: A Portrait of the Anima," in *Spring 1947*: 59–93.

5. Jung, *CW* 15, §§51–53.

6. Intuition or the ability to surmise is, according to Jung, one of the four

basic functions: thinking, feeling, sensation, and intuition. During one's youth it is the most easily developed function that is commonly used, whereby arises, for example, the "intuitive functional type." Introversion designates an attitude which tends to orient itself primarily in relation to inner psychic processes, in contrast to the extroverted attitude which is interested principally in external events. Cf. Jung, CW 6, §834.

7. This presentation of H. R. Haggard's life is based upon his autobiography written in 1912, *The Days of My Life,* 2 vols. (London: Longmans, Green and Co., Ltd., 1926), as well as on the biography, *The Cloak That I Left* (London: Hodder and Stoughton, 1951), which was published by his daughter Lilias Rider Haggard.

8. L. R. Haggard, *The Cloak,* 24.

9. H. R. Haggard, *Days of My Life,* I: 17. Once, when the youngest of the brothers wished to travel to Egypt, the father invited him for leave-taking to his club in Pall Mall. Then he took leave from him at the door. As the son was walking away, he suddenly heard the father call loudly, "Arthur, Arthur." To avoid drawing excessive attention from the bystanders, the son started to walk faster. Now the father called him even more loudly. Arthur began to run and the people became startled. One exclaimed, "Stop the thief!" But Arthur kept running, followed by the crowd and a policeman until the guard at Marlborough House stopped him. Finally he gave up and allowed the crowd to accompany him back to the Oxford and Cambridge Club. At a distance he still heard his father yell, "Don't forget to greet mother!" The father then disappeared laughingly into his club, and Arthur proceeded to the railroad station, from whence he departed, via Bradenham, to Egypt.

10. An unconscious tie of son or daughter to the mother. Sury, *Wörterbuch der Psychologie.*

11. Jung, CW 9, i, §§161 ff.

12. Jung, CW 6, §726. See also above, n. 6.

13. Myers, *Human Personality* (London: Longmans, 1906), I: 7.

14. Gurney, Podmore and Myers, *Phantasms of the Living.*

15. L. R. Haggard, *The Cloak,* 268.

16. Bernhard Fehr, *Englische Literaturgeschichte des 19. & 20. Jahrhunderts* (History of English Literature of the 19th and 20th Centuries) (Leipzig: Tauchnitz, 1934), 314.

17. See also Jung, CW 11, §619.

18. This had come about in the following way: the English declared Cetewayo, a Zulu chieftain, to be king. This proclamation created difficulties, however, since Cetewayo did not wish to be appointed by England. Eventually a way was found to save the situation. The Zulu chieftains announced in a large meeting that the spirit of Chakas, the great barbaric, bloody Zulu king, had entered Sompseu (which was the African name of Shepstone), whereupon he was entitled to perform the coronation of Cetewayo. As a result of this, Shepstone gained innocently the reputation of being possessed, which stood in strange contrast to his benevolent, responsible, and prudent personality. Throughout the period of Shepstone's administration there was hardly one black rebellion to speak of. H. R. Haggard, *Days of My Life,* I: 70–71.

19. *Days of My Life,* I: 104: "I thank my father Sompseu for this message. I am glad that he has sent it, because the Dutch have tired me out and I intend to fight them once, and once only, and to drive them over the Vaal. Kabana [name of messenger] you see my impis [armies] are gathered. It was to fight the Dutch; I called them together; now I will send them back to their homes."

20. L. R. Haggard, *The Cloak,* 218.

21. The first relay (on the journey to one's self) leads to the experience of the shadow, which symbolizes our "other side," our "dark brother" who invisibly belongs inseparably to our wholeness. Jolande Jacobi, *Die Psychologie von C. G. Jung* (1959), 165; English edition: *The Psychology of C. G. Jung,* trans. R. Manheim (New Haven: Yale University Press, 1959).

22. By the term "Anima" Jung understands the feminine soul of the man. See discussion of Rider's mother-complex, pp. 5–7 above, and Jung, CW 7, §§297 ff.

23. *Jess* is one of Haggard's most likeable books. It takes place in the beginning of the Boer war, on the English side; yet it was well-liked even by the Boers and was found even in their trenches.

24. H. R. Haggard, *Jess* (1887), I: 265–66.

25. Ibid., 272.

26. Jung, CW 9, ii, §20.

27. H. R. Haggard, *Jess,* I: 886: "But it was a lie, and they both knew it was a lie."

28. H. R. Haggard, *Days of My Life,* 292.

29. For example, Winston Churchill.

30. H. R. Haggard, *Days of My Life,* II: 96.

31. Ibid., 103.

32. H. R. Haggard, *Allan and the Ice-Gods: A Tale of Beginnings,* ed. R. and D. Menville (Tauchnitz: Reginald Ayer Co., 1976), 188.

33. L. R. Haggard, *The Cloak,* 277–78.

34. H. R. Haggard, *Days of My Life,* I: 245–46.

35. Pronounced: E'scha.

36. In Rider's early youth there lived in the wall-closet of his room a rag doll with unusually frightening features: shoe buttons for eyes, black wool for hair, and a spooky smile on the painted face. As a child, Rider viewed the doll as a fetish and was terribly scared of it. L. R. Haggard, *The Cloak,* 28.

37. H. R. Haggard, *Jess,* I: 265.

38. By primary function, Jung means the one of the four functions (thinking, feeling, intuition, and sensation) which is most developed and relied upon most often, usually to the exclusion of the other three.

39. The ferryman of the dead in the underworld of antiquity.

40. Helmuth Jacobsohn, "Das Gegensatzproblem im Altaegyptischen Mythos" ("The Problem of Oppositions in the Myths of Ancient Egypt") in *Studien zur analytischen Psychologie C. G. Jungs* (Studies Concerning the Analytic Psychology of C. G. Jung) (Zürich, 1955), II: 192.

41. Ibid., 190: "Wherever difficult or dangerous situations occurred for the gods or for the human beings, Thoth was at hand. Because of this he also was in the deepest sense the Psychopompos. Thus he helped in the resurrection of Osiris during the drama of the Egyptian Gods, and he helped the Ba-like Osiris NN in

his ascent to Heaven."

42. Jung, *CW* 8, §§131 ff. Of the four functions (sensation, thinking, feeling, and intuition), the least developed and "inferior" one remains most closely linked with the unconscious. If later in life this inferior function is given increasing attention, it succeeds in establishing a relationship between unconscious contents and consciousness. Jung, therefore, named it the transcendent function, not in a theological but in a psychological sense, because it is capable of catching and integrating contents that are beyond consciousness, that otherwise are barely perceived motions of the unconscious.

43. By "quest" is meant the journey as a mystical search. Such "quests" are a recurrent concept in the medieval epics.

44. Jung, *CW* 9, §281.

45. Larousse, *Mythologie Générale,* 18.

46. Jung, *CW* 5, §566: "At Siegfried's birth Sieglinde dies, as anticipated. The foster mother, however, is not a woman, but a cripple-like dwarf, belonging to the gender that renounces all love (cf. Grimm, Myth. I, p. 314). This dwarf is exemplified by Mime or Mimir, a colossal being of great wisdom, an earlier Nature-god of the Ages.... Just as Wotan goes to a wise woman for advice, so Odhin goes to Mimir's fountain, where wisdom and prudent council are kept.... Mimir's fountain points unequivocally to the mother-image. In Mimir and his fountain, mother and embryo are fused. At the same time, in the guise of mother, Mimir is the source of wisdom and art. Just the way Bes, the dwarf and educator, is an extension of the mother-goddess, so Mimir is an extension of the maternal spring.... They are mythological Animus figures. The Egyptian god of the Netherworld, the crippled shadow of Osiris, who celebrates a sad resurrection in Harpocrates, is the educator of Horus, who must avenge his father's death."

47. Just as the man's Anima embodies his eros, his ability to relate, so does a woman's Animus (or the mother's Animus) represent her logos, her spiritual and intellectual abilities.

48. Jung, *CW* 16, §421, n. 19.

49. Jung, *CW* 5, §265; and K. Kerényi, *Die Mythologie der Griechen* (Zürich, 1951), 56; English edition: *The Gods of the Greeks,* trans. Norman Cameron (London: Thames and Hudson, 1951).

50. H. Jacobsohn, "Die dogmatische Stellung des Königs in der Theologie der alten Aegypter" ("The Dogmatic Position of the King in the Theology of Ancient Egypt"), in *Aegyptische Forschungen,* Heft 8 (Glueckstadt und Hamburg, 1939).

51. Ibid., 51.

52. H. Jacobsohn, "Das Gegensatzproblem," II: 176. "Originally the Ka is the Mana power that flows from the creator-god Ptah or Atum or Horus, through which the god disperses himself in the world and the living creatures: the power that acts upon and within the world. In the 5th Dynasty the Ka became the *Creator Spiritus,* the spirit of the Sungod grown conscious of his creativeness and fatherliness, the spirit in whom the son, the god-man, was conscious of being one with the father. It became the spirit by means of which the father was creative in the world and in human beings through his son. The last manifestation, the final stage of the creativeness of the Ka, was the god Osiris (the 'Ka of Horus'), the god who, for the time being, is completely attached to the world and its materiality."

53. Margarete Riemschneider, *Augengott und Heilige Hochzeit* (Eye-God and Holy Marriage) (Leipzig: Koehler, 1953), 230.

54. Margret Ostrowski, "The Anima in the Prometheus Books of Carl Spitteler," lecture given in the Psychology Club, Zürich, 1957.

55. Jung, *CW* 16, §421.

56. Kerényi, *Die Mythologie,* 224.

57. Ibid., 265.

58. S. Hurwitz, *Die Gestalt des Sterbenden Messias* (The Figure of the Dying Messiah) (Zürich, 1958), 211–12.

59. Riemschneider, *Augengott,* 1 ff.

60. Alfred Hildebrandt, *Lieder des Rgveda* (Songs of the Rgveda) (Goettingen, 1913), I, 118: 5—"May the virgin, the daughter of the sun be pleased, as she joins you in your chariot, oh Asvins. . . ."

61. According to Jung, the first approach to the collective unconscious during an analysis frequently manifests itself in dreams of water. See also Part II, Dream Five, of this book.

62. See Jung, *CW* 12, §31, for a discussion of quaternity as wholeness.

63. Erich Neumann, *Die Grosse Mutter* (Zürich, 1956), 212; English edition: *The Great Mother,* trans. R. Manheim (Princeton: Princeton University Press, 1964).

64. M.-L. von Franz, "Die Passio Perpetuae," in C. G. Jung, *Aion* (Zürich, 1951), 467 ff.; published in English as *The Passion of Perpetua,* trans. Elizabeth Welsh (Dallas: Spring Publications, 1980).

65. Jung, *CW* 14, ii, §383.

66. Jung, *CW* 9, ii, §14.

67. *Jess* had been sitting beside a bush with reddish blossoms when she became aware of her love. And legend has it that the coffin with Osiris, drifting down the Nile River, was stopped by a tamarisk, which also carries reddish flowers.

68. Jung, *CW* 12, §518.

69. Jung, *CW* 12, §240: Illustration III of the figurine of Lambspringk of the *Musaeum Hermeticum* (Frankfort, 1625).

70. Riemschneider, *Augengott,* 224, 283.

71. Jung, *CW* 5, §415.

72. Kaigh, *Witchcraft and Magic of Africa* (London, 1947), 13.

73. Hercules overcame both serpent *and* lion!

74. Laurens van der Post, *Das dunkle Auge Afrikas* (Berlin, 1957), 50; English edition: *The Dark Eye of Africa* (London: Hogarth Press, 1955).

75. In Jung's conception, the Self is the goal of the process of individuation, of the subjective development. The Self embraces the entirety of the human being, consciousness and the unconscious, both personal and collective data. This is in contrast to the ego which forms the center of consciousness. As such, the archetype of the Self transcends consciousness. It is not an intellectual concept but rather an irrational concept. It manifests itself in various symbols of wholeness. For example, it is in circular drawings which enclose contrasting tendencies of the personality, in the rose, in the lotus blossom, or as we find in Master Eckhart, in the small circular castle within the soul. See also Jung, *CW* 12, §247.

76. Kerényi, *Die Mythologie,* 84.

77. Inasmuch as we focus in this book upon the Anima, that is, on the unconscious, emotional side of the man, we must leave undone the description of the Animus and the opinionatedness with which the wife may torment the husband. The account of guilt in marital difficulties is fairly evenly divided between the sexes. Esther Harding writes about the woman's Animus in *Der Weg der Frau,* 4th ed. (Zürich); English edition: *The Way of All Women* (New York: Harper & Row, 1975).

78. In various sites of Africa, relics of earlier Mediterranean cultures can be found. In *Das dunkle Auge Afrikas,* 47–48, van der Post states, "The bushmen in the Calahari desert still live like in the beginning of our civilization. Visiting there recently, I had the opportunity to observe them in their natural, innocent, communal life. The man still performs his ancient love-ritual with the bow of Cupid which up to then had been for me no more than a picture on an old Greek vase. At the foot of the large, high mesa, where the sleeping sickness is endemic, I saw black people with beautiful bodies. They unexpectedly appeared and approached me joyfully with garlands of wild flowers around their necks. They played on flutes that resembled those of the god Pan. I had also known them from the pictures of old Greek vases."

79. Neumann, *Die Grosse Mutter,* 54.

80. Jung, *CW* 13, §170.

81. Jung, *CW* 9, ii, §334.

82. Ibid., §344.

83. Jung, *CW* 5, §438.

84. Mandalas are circular drawings made for cultural purposes to represent the wholeness that is the seat and temple of the deity. They are found predominantly in India and in Tibet. See Jung, *CW* 12, §§122 ff.

85. *Handwörterbuch des Islam,* 29.

86. Ibid.

87. Margaret Smith, *Rabi'a the Mystic* (Cambridge, 1928), 120.

88. Ibid., 121.

89. Erwin Rouselle, *Eranos Jahrbuch*—1933, 170: "The spinning woman sets in motion. . . ."

90. Pierre Benoit, *L'Atlantide* (Paris: A. Michel, 1919), 98–99.

91. Ibid., 109.

92. Edmund O. Lippmann, *Entstehung und Ausbreitung der Alchemie* (Origin and Dissemination of Alchemy) (Berlin: Springer, 1919), 5 and 34.

93. *Gilgamesch* (Insel Buecherei), no. 203, p. 25: "You shall have to hear of all your shameful actions. I shall settle with you: Year after year you caused bitter suffering to Tammuz, the youthful lover, the god of spring. You fell in love with a colorfully dressed shepherd-boy; you broke his wing. . . ." Thus Gilgamesh settles with Ishtar in regard to her lovers' fates.

94. Benoit, *L'Atlantide,* 313.

95. Ibid., 167–68.

96. Jung, *CW* 5, §83.

97. M.-L. von Franz, lecture concerning St. Exupéry's *The Little Prince,* held before the Psychology Club, Zürich.

98. Arthur Avalon, pseud., *Die Schlangenkraft* (Berlin: Wilmersdorf, 1961),
207; English edition: *The Serpent Power* (New York: Dover, 1974).

99. In this respect he is different from Saint-Avit, the hero in Benoit's novel.

100. These are the same words as used in *Jess*.

101. Caminada, *Die Verzauberten Taeler, Kulte und Braeuche im alten Rae-
tien* (The Bewitched Valleys, Cults and Customs in Old Romansh Areas) (Olten,
Switzerland, 1961), 75 ff., and Frazer, *Der goldene Zweig* (Leipzig, 1928), 933
ff.; English edition: *The Golden Bough* (New York: St. Martin's Press, 1980).

102. Riemschneider, *Augengott,* 223 ff.

103. Neumann, *Die Grosse Mutter,* 255.

104. M. Eliade, *Schamanismus und archaische Ekstasetechnik* (Zürich,
1957), 103 ff. and 152; English edition: *Shamanism: Archaic Techniques of
Ecstasy,* trans. Willard R. Trask (Princeton: Princeton University Press, 1964).

105. Gen. 6: 2 f.

106. Jung, *CW* 6, §810: "I distinguish, therefore, between Ego and Self, inasmuch as the Ego is only the subject of my consciousness, whereas the Self is the
subject of my entire psyche, including its unconscious part. Thus the Self would
be viewed as an ideal magnitude that contains the Ego within itself. In unconscious fantasies the Self tends to manifest itself as a superordinate or ideal personality such as, for example, Faust in Goethe, or Zarathustra in Nietzsche. Yet
for the sake of the ideal, the archaic traits of the Self are occasionally presented as
separate from the 'higher' Self in Goethe's *Faust*. . . ."

107. Plutarch, *De Iside et Osiride,* quoted from Neumann, *Die Grosse Mutter,*
211: "I'm everything that was, that is, and that shall be, and there never was a
person who lifted my veil." Neumann says of her: "She keeps the key of the
fertility-goddesses, the key to the doors of the womb and the netherworld, to
death and rebirth."

108. Eliade, *Schamanismus,* 445 ff.

109. Ibid., 448–49.

110. Ibid., 195 ff.

111. Jung, *CW* 14, i, §§149 ff.

112. Jung, *CW* 13, §273.

113. Jung, *CW* 5, §659.

114. Ibid., §528.

115. K.H. De Jong, *Das Antike Mysterienwesen* (The Ancient Mysteries)
(Leiden: Brill, 1909), 22; quoted by Jung in *CW* 5, §528.

116. Wilhelm Nestle, *Die Vorsokratiker* (The Presocratic Thinkers) (Jena:
E. Diederichs, 1929), 120.

117. Ibid.: "The fire is the treasury of all things perceived physically or
spiritually, which Simon Magus calls the hidden and the visible things. . . .
Whatever part of the world is preserved, is thus divine; what is corporeal is consumed in the world-fire. Yet inasmuch as the fire is the force of god, the burning
of the world means also the world's complete dissolution in the godhead. Already
in the Orphic mysteries we find this purifying and deifying force of fire: 'Each
night Demeter holds Baubo's child that has been entrusted to her into the fire, in
order to burn off the mortal part of its being and to make it divine.'"

118. Riessler, *Altjuedisches Schrifttum: Henochbuch, aegyptisch* (Ancient

Hebrew Texts: Book of Enoch), 18: 11 ff.

119. Dante, *The Divine Comedy,* Purgatory, 27: 10 ff.

120. "Introitus Apert.," in *Mus. Herm.* (1678), 654, cited by Jung, CW 13, §§256, 257.

121. "Gloria Mundi," in *Mus. Herm.,* 246, cited by Jung, CW 12, §446.

122. For example, in the symbols of Lambspringk (*Mus. Herm., 372*)—cited by Jung, CW 12, §446.

123. "Aquarium Sapientium," in *Mus. Herm.,* cited by Jung, CW 13, §§256, 257.

124. Jung, CW 14, i, §42: "Of the three essences."

125. Kees, *Des Götterglaube im Alten Aegypten* (The Faith of Ancient Egypt) (Leipzig, 1941), 95 ff.

126. Ibid., 97.

127. Ibid., 129.

128. Ibid., 98.

129. Eliade, *Schamanismus,* 251 ff.

130. Ibid., 260.

131. Neumann, *Die Grosse Mutter,* 268, 270.

132. Ibid., 210.

133. Ibid., 234.

134. Hegemonius, *Acta Archelai VIII* (Leipzig: Beeson, 1906), 11. This citation was kindly given to me by Prof. Jung.

135. Quispel, "Zeit und Geschichte im Antiken Christentum" (Time and History in Early Christianity), in *Eranos Jahrbuch*—1951, 122; as well as Eliade, *The Myth of the Eternal Return,* trans. W. R. Trask (Princeton: Princeton University Press, 1954).

136. Kerényi suspects that the proclamation in Eleusis contained the news that the goddess of Death had borne a child inside the fire, as a guarantee of rebirth after death. *Die Mysterien von Eleusis* (Zürich, 1962), 99; in English, see: *Eleusis: Archetypal Image of Mother and Daughter,* trans. Ralph Manheim, Bollingen Series 65/4 (New York and London, 1967).

137. L. R. Haggard, *The Cloak,* 129.

138. Jung, CW 16, §504.

139. Jung, CW 11, §351.

140. Jung–Kerényi, *Einführung in das Wesen der Mythologie* (Zürich, 1951), 199; English edition: *Essays on a Science of Mythology,* trans. R. F. C. Hull, Bollingen Series 22 (Princeton: Princeton University Press, 1969).

141. H. R. Haggard, *She and Allan* (Tauchnitz), 255.

142. Ibid., 254.

143. Plato, *Das Gastmahl* (The Symposium), trans. Kurt Hildebrandt (Leipzig, 1934), 129 ff.

144. H. R. Haggard, *Wisdom's Daughter* (Tauchnitz), 267.

145. Jung, CW 16, §494, illustr. 9 of Rosarium.

146. The primary function is the one of the four (sensation, thinking, feeling, and intuition) which is most easily developed and through which adjustment to life is accomplished most easily.

147. The "shadow" is "the inferior personality"; it is the sum of all those per-

sonal and collective psychological dispositions which are not being lived on account of their irreconcilability with the consciously lived way of life; thus they group themselves in the unconscious as a relatively autonomous, partial personality with contrary tendencies. "The dreamer and the figure of the shadow that appears in dreams are of the same sex. As a fragment of the personal unconscious the shadow belongs to the Ego; as the archetype of the antagonist it belongs to the collective unconscious." Sury, *Wörterbuch der Psychologie.*

148. Individuation—becoming a Self; becoming whole; realizing one's own being.

149. Jung, *CW* 6, §§681 ff.

150. *The Egyptian Book of the Dead,* trans. Wallis Budge (London, 1928), 4, n. 2, concerning Khepera: "He is an aspect of the rising sun and has his place in the boat of the sun-god. He is the god of matter in transition from inanimateness to life, as well as of the dead body in the instant in which a spiritual, glorified body emerges from it. His symbol is the beetle."

151. Jung, *Bericht über das Seminar von Prof. Hauer* (Report about Prof. Hauer's Seminar) (Zürich: Seminardruck, 1932), 120.

152. Jung, *CW* 14, ii, §§1 ff.

153. Andreae Johann Valentin, *Chymische Hochzeit Christiani Rosencreutz* (Berlin, 1922), 2; English edition: *The Hermetick Romance: or, The Chymical Wedding,* written in High Dutch by Christian Rosencreutz, trans. E. Foxcroft (London: A. Sowle, 1960).

154. See Part I of this book: "Psychological Interpretation of Rider Haggard's *She.*"

155. Andreae, *Chymische Hochzeit.*

156. Jung, *CW* 12, §§332 ff.

157. Andreae, *Chymische Hochzeit, 2.*

158. Jung, *CW* 16, §461.

159. Martin Ninck, *Wodan und Germanischer Schicksalsglaube* (Odin and Germanic Faith in Destiny) (Jena: E. Diederichs, 1935), 257 ff.

160. Emma Jung, "Die Anima als Naturwesen," in *Studien zur analytischen Psychologie C. G. Jungs* (Zürich, 1955), II: 78–79; in English: "The Anima as an Elemental Being," trans. Hildegard Nagel, in *Animus and Anima* (Dallas: Spring Publications, 1957/1985).

161. Eric Graf Oxenstierna, *Die Goldhoerner von Gallehus* (The Golden Horns of Gallehus) (1956), 155.

162. Jung, *CW* 14, i, §§181, 182.

163. Ninck, *Wodan,* 282–83.

164. Ibid., 34 ff. "Berserk" originally meant "bear-skinned."

165. The contents of the collective unconscious are in themselves morally indifferent (as is nature itself). It is, however, imperative that a human being consciously distinguish between the positive and negative, healing and dangerous aspects of these contents in order to prevent the irruption of the collective shadow.

166. Jung, *CW* 18, ii, §§1692 ff.

167. Jung, *CW* 9, ii, §§43 ff.

168. See also Part I of this book, concerning the crater as mandala.

169. Jung, *CW* 12, §13, and *CW* 9, i, §693 and *CW* 9, ii, §59, concerning the foursomeness and rotation of the mandala.
170. Ninck, *Wodan*, 37.
171. Ibid., 174.
172. Basil Ivan Rakoczi, *The Painted Caravan* (S'Gravenhage, 1954), 47.
173. Linda Fierz-David, *Der Liebestraum des Poliphilo* (Zürich, 1946), 77; English edition: *The Dream of Poliphilo*, trans. Mary Hottinger, Bollingen Series 25 (New York: Bollingen Foundation/Pantheon, 1950).
174. Goethe, *Faust*, Part I.
175. See Part I of this book: "Psychological Interpretation of Rider Haggard's *She*."
176. Gilles Quispel, *Gnosis als Weltreligion* (Gnosis as World-Religion) (Zürich, 1951), 61–62. B. Leisegang, too, points out in his *Gnosis* that Simon Magus saw in Helen of Troy the incarnation of the divine Ennoia (2d ed., 66). Ennoia means "constancy of consciousness, representation, thought, concept, and reflection." K. Kerényi told me that Helen was venerated as a goddess in Sparta.
177. Jung, *CW* 18, ii, §§1692 ff.
178. Jung, *CW* 5, §354.
179. H. Jacobsohn, "Die dogmatische Stellung," 19.
180. In Switzerland the immense "bull of Uri" is a silvery-white male calf raised exclusively on cow milk for nine years. It had to be led daily to a certain place by a pure virgin. K. Gisler, *Geschichtliches, Sagen und Legenden aus Uri* (Historical Facts, Sagas and Legends from Uri) (Altdorf: Buchdruckerei Altdorf, 1911), 88.
181. H. Jacobsohn, "Die dogmatische Stellung," 62.
182. Communication from Mary Elliot.
183. The "Asian commander" has the same role as She in the second volume of *Ayesha*, where She attempts to spread her rule from Central Asia to China and the entire world. See Part I of this book, 110–12.
184. See Part I of this book. There we find Billali as the executor of She's orders.
185. Avalon, *Die Schlangenkraft*, verses 28–29, and picture 6, pp. 233–38. "Chakra" means wheel.
186. Jung, *Seminar von Prof. Hauer*, 133–34.
187. Jung, *CW* 9, i, §449 and *CW* 16, §425.
188. Ninck, *Wodan*, 11.
189. Jung, *CW* 13, §350.
190. Herrigel, *Zen in der Kunst des Bogenschiessens* (Munich: Planegg, 1953); English edition: *Zen and the Art of Archery* (New York: Random House, 1971).
191. In this connection, see *Die Philosophie des I-Ging*, trans. Richard Wilhelm (Dusseldorf, 1960); English edition: *The I Ching, or Book of Changes* (London: Routledge and Kegan Paul, 1950).
192. Edgar Hennecke, "Hirt des Hermas," in *Neutestamentliche Apokryphen* (1904), 235 ff.; also published in *New Testament Apocrypha* (Philadelphia: Westminster Press, 1966).
193. See also Dream Eighteen of the eleven crows.
194. Jung, *CW* 12, illustr. 4.

195. Jung, *CW* 13, §420.
196. Ibid., §355.
197. Ibid., §403, n. 158.
198. Mary Elliot kindly drew my attention to this nursery rhyme:

> I had a little nut tree and nothing would it bear
> But a silver apple and a golden pear.
> The Queen of Spain's daughter came to visit me.
> All on account of my little nut tree.

199. In the alchemical garden one finds not only Mercury, representing the earth, and the sun- and moon-tree, but also the other planets, Saturn, Mars, Jupiter, and Venus. The gardener's strong brother, who recognizes the necessity to dig, seems to correspond to the "gardener Saturn." In the blackness of depression, the latter conveys insight into the inadequacy of the current condition. It seems justified to assume Mars and Jupiter to be the other two male figures, and Venus to be the fourth, feminine, helpful person. See Jung, *CW* 13, §355.
200. According to the dictionary, *tabernaculum* is the Latin word for "tent."
201. Jung, *CW* 13, §459.
202. Ibid., §321.
203. See Jung, *CW* 14, ii, §419, on the *"coelum"* or "air-colored liquid."
204. Jung, *Seminar von Prof. Hauer,* 133.
205. Jung, *CW* 16, §§516 and 517.
206. See Jung, *CW* 14, ii, §362.
207. In the following, we refer to Jung, *CW* 11, §§309 ff. and 381 ff.
208. Ibid., §384.
209. Jung, *CW* 11, §§269–72.
210. In *She,* the old wise man, Noot, has been dead for two thousand years. The conflict between Leo, Holly, and She fails because this leader-figure is lacking. Haggard was compelled to repeat this symbolical story in numerous variations because of this lack. Only in his last novel, *Queen of the Dawn* (published in the last year of his life), does the old wise man re-emerge as a positive figure and as teacher of the Anima.
211. Robert Graves, *The White Goddess* (New York, 1948), 77.
212. Jung, Kerényi and Radin, *Der Gottliche Schelm* (The Divine Rogue) (Zürich: Rhein-Verlag, 1954), 191; Jung, *CW* 9, i, §§465–66.
213. Jung, *CW* 18, ii, §§1692 ff.
214. Jung, *CW* 13, §268.
215. See part I of this book: "Psychological Interpretation of Rider Haggard's *She.*"
216. Andreae, *Chymische Hochzeit,* 64.
217. For the significance of "the fourth" see Jung, *CW* 11, §§250–52.
218. In Negro spirituals we find an expression of this piety of black people.
219. Jung, *CW* 9, ii, §342.
220. Briffault, *The Mothers,* 3 : 184 ff., cited in Esther Harding, *Frauen-Mysterien* (Zürich, 1949), 85–87; English edition: *Women's Mysteries* (New York: Harper & Row, 1976).

221. Ernesto Buonaiuti, *Maria in der Christlichen Ueberlieferung* (Mary in the Christian Tradition) (Zürich, 1938), 396–97.

222. A lasting identification with an animal would indicate a danger. In this dream, however, the hart transforms back to a human being.

223. See Jung, *CW* 9, i, §449.

224. Andreae, *Chymische Hochzeit, 59*; Jung, *CW* 14, i, §31; and von Franz, "Die Passio Perpetuae," 463 ff.

225. In *Ephesians* 4 : 1–2, Paul states: "I, therefore, the prisoner in [the] Lord entreat you to walk worthily of the calling with which you were called, with complete lowliness of mind and mildness, with long-suffering. . . ."

226. Cited from Ninck, *Wodan,* 299.

227. Von Franz, *Die Visionen des Niklaus von Flue* (The Visions of Nicholas from Flue) (Zürich, 1959), 41 ff.; reprinted by Daimon Verlag (Zürich).

228. Jung, *CW* 5, §§659 ff.

229. Such a fate befell Hölderlin and Novalis. The former was driven early into permanent insanity; the latter died in his twenties.

230. In German, red horses are called "foxes."

231. *The Complete Grimm's Fairy Tales* (New York: Pantheon Books, 1972), 244.

232. For example, Pu Sung-Ling, *Gaukler, Daemonen und Fuechse* (Jugglers, Demons and Foxes) (Basel, 1955).

233. *Grimm's Fairy Tales,* 272.

234. See also Jung, *CW* 9, i, §§422 ff., dealing with the tale "The Princess on the Tree."

235. Ninck, in *Wodan,* 256, speaks of the bird "griff" as the "clawing wrath."

236. See Part I of this book, 41.

237. "According to C. G. Jung, 'synchronicity' is a meaningful coincidence of an inner and an outer experience which cannot be attributed to a causal relationship. This phenomenon exists apart from causality and seems to rest on an archetypal basis." See Sury, *Wörterbuch,* and Jung, *CW* 8, §§849–50.

238. Oxenstierna, *Die Goldhoerner,* 155.

239. Waldemar Fenn, *Grafica Prehistorica* (Mahon, 1950), 166, fig. 153.

240. Ibid., fig. 23, rock painting of the cave of Arce (Cadiz).

241. Graves, *The White Goddess,* 261.

242. Jung, *CW* 9, ii, §44: "I wish to mention that the Ego approaches the Self more and more as it assimilates meaningful contents of the unconscious. This approach will invariably create an inflation of the Ego, unless one is able to discriminate between the Ego and the unconscious figures. Such a discrimination, however, is successful only if one is able to gain reasonable, human limits to the Ego and accord a certain amount of autonomy and reality to the figures of the unconscious, especially the Self, the Anima, the Animus and the Shadow."

243. Jung, "Der Geist der Psychologie," in *Eranos Jahrbuch*—1946, 485, and *CW* 8, §§835–36 on synchronicity.

244. Michael de Ferdinandy, *Historia Mundi,* V: 208.

245. Von Franz, *Niklaus von Flue,* 59. Reference to an analogous visionary experience of St. Nicholas from Flue in which three noble men of pagan origin visit the saint, furthering in him the development of a new, comprehensive per-

sonality.

246. Mabel Smith Waln, *Im Lande der schnellen Pferde* (In the Land of the Fast Horses) (Wiesbaden, 1958).

247. Jung, *CW* 5, §681.

248. Ninck, *Wodan,* 190–91.

249. Ibid., 217.

250. Ibid., 312.

251. In connection with the following remarks, see Part I of this book about the pillar of fire, 98–99.

252. We already mentioned this need to limit one's consideration of the outer world in our discussion of the transition dream (Dream Thirty-Seven). See also Jung, *CW* 13, §§433–34.

253. Jung has kindly directed my attention to this treatise: "Geheimnis der Natur des grossen und des kleinen Bauers," in *Gresshoff nach Ferguson,* ed. Walch (1731).

254. Jung, *CW* 14, ii, §§413–14.

255. As was the case during the Hitler period.

256. Avalon, *Die Schlangenkraft,* 240, referring to tantra yoga.

257. Jung, *CW* 18, ii, §§1692 ff. and *CW* 9, i, §268.

Recent and New Titles from Spring

PAGAN MEDITATIONS
Ginette Paris

An appreciation of three Greek Goddesses as values of importance to our twentieth-century collective life: Aphrodite as civilized sexuality and beauty; Artemis as solitude, ecological significance, and a perspective on abortion; and Hestia as warm hearth, security, and stability. This contribution to *imaginative* feminism addresses both the meditative interior of each person and the community of culture. (204 pp., ISBN 0–88214–330–1)

HERMES: *Guide of Souls*
Karl Kerényi

The famous mythographer, classicist, and friend of Jung here presents a beautiful, authoritative study of the great God whom the Greeks revered as Guide of Souls. Chapters on Hermes and Night, Hermes and Eros, Hermes and the Goddesses illuminate the complex role of Hermes in classical mythology, while also providing an archetypal background for the guiding of souls in psychotherapy. (104 pp., ISBN 0–88214–207–0)

ANIMA: *An Anatomy of a Personified Notion*
James Hillman

Anima and Eros, Anima and Feeling, Anima and Feminine, Mediatrix of the Unknown—ten succinct chapters, accompanied by relevant quotations from Jung (on left-hand pages facing Hillman's essay), which clarify the moods, persons, and definitions of the most subtle and elusive aspect of psychology and of life. (188 pp., ISBN 0–88214–316–6)

"In spite of the stimulating complexity of this analysis, this book captures and retains the fascinating and living quality of the anima."—*Choice*

A CELTIC QUEST
Sexuality and Soul in Individuation
John Layard

This classic Welsh tale of heroic youth in search of soul finds a master equal to its riddles in John Layard, Oxford anthropologist and Jungian analyst. The quest proceeds as a boar hunt, encountering giants and dwarfs, bitch-dogs, helpful ants, the Witch Hag, until the soul is won. Brilliant appendices, together with scholarly apparatus and a full index, have established this volume as the standard interpretative psychological text of Celtic legend. (264 pp., ISBN 0–88214–110–4)

COMMENTARY ON PLATO'S SYMPOSIUM ON LOVE
Marsilio Ficino, trans. Sears Jayne

Marsilio Ficino, the head of the Platonic Academy in Renaissance Florence and the first ever to translate the complete works of Plato, also wrote this Latin essay on love. Popular in European court-circles for almost two hundred years, this book influenced painters such as Botticelli and Michelangelo, and writers such as Spenser and Castiglione. Jayne's English translation, based on Marcel's edition, includes an introduction. (213 pp., ISBN 0–88214–601–7)

"Jayne's translation is eminently readable, copiously annotated, and contains a bibliography of particular value."—*Choice*

Spring Publications • P.O. Box 222069 • Dallas, TX 75222

that stone of the Temple was removed, and faithless men transformed passion and emotion, reason and humour, into thrones
from which to preside as lawgivers. The temple was slowly
reduced to fragments and ruins—and around it we heard the
lament and the tears of the prophets, of the children of the
desolate city. But the sacred stones of Charlemagne reached
far away lands of the earth. Even now the construction of a
greater temple has probably begun, and the foundation has
been laid by invisible workers, who have nothing but scorn
and laughter for those who try to build the Tower of Babylon
once more, instead of their own new Temple of the World
Jerusalem. The scorn from above answers the tumult of Babel,
a tumult which will die down as others did before it. On high
no struggle rages between diversity and unity, between quality
and equality. The voice of prayer alone is heard there from the
altar of the Temple:

*Et in personis proprietas, et in essentia unitas, et in maiestate
adoretur aequalitas.*

DATE DUE